The Ultimate Aquarium

The Ultimate Aquarium

A Definitive Guide
to Identifying and Keeping
Freshwater and
Marine Fishes

MARY BAILEY & GINA SANDFORD

LORENZ BOOKS

This edition published by Lorenz Books
27 West 20th Street, New York, NY 10011

LORENZ BOOKS are available for bulk purchase for sales promotion
and for premium use. For details, write or call the sales director,
Lorenz Books, 27 West 20th Street, New York, NY 10011;
(800) 354-9657

Lorenz Books is an imprint of
Anness Publishing Inc.

ISBN 1-85967-081-4

Publisher: Joanna Lorenz
Editorial Manager: Helen Sudell
Designer: Elizabeth Ayer
Special Photography: John Freeman
Illustrations: Kate Simunek

Printed and bound in Hong Kong

© Anness Publishing Limited 1995
Updated © 1998
1 3 5 7 9 10 8 6 4 2

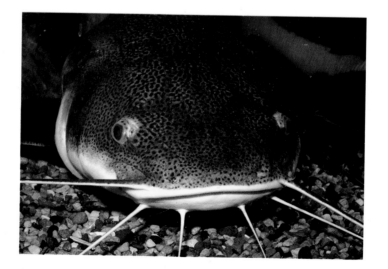

Half-title page: Astronotus ocellatus (oscar)
Title page: Poecilia reticulata (guppy)
Above: Phractocephalus hemioliopterus (redtailed catfish)
Opposite, from top: Botia macracantha (clown loach), *Amphiprion rubrocinctus* (Fijian clown),
Microgeophagus ramirezi (ram cichlid)

Contents

Introduction ~ 6

Getting Started ~ 8

Water Management ~ 16

Foods and Feeding ~ 36

Equipment ~ 44

Decor – the hardware ~ 50

Decor – plants ~ 64

Setting Up ~ 76

Buying and Adding the Fishes ~ 102

Keeping them Healthy ~ 108

Breeding ~ 118

The Fish Groups ~ 126

Cichlids ~ 128

Catfishes ~ 141

Cypriniformes ~ 155

Cyprinodonts ~ 167

Characins ~ 179

Anabantids ~ 190

Miscellaneous Freshwater Fishes ~ 200

Brackish Water Fishes ~ 218

Marines ~ 228

Glossary ~ 251

Bibliography ~ 252

Acknowledgements ~ 253

Index ~ 254

Introduction

You have decided to become a fishkeeper, or you are at least thinking about it. You may have been impressed by an aquarium you have seen recently, or perhaps you are looking for an interesting spare-time activity. You may not realize it, but you are standing at a crossroads! Ahead of you lies not just a new hobby, but, provided you take the right path, a lifetime of enjoyment and a host of new friends. The other roads, however, lead to disillusionment and disaster, and yet another "aquarium for sale" advertisement in the local paper.

This book aims to point you in the right direction, and to ensure that you stay on the straight and narrow thereafter. Our unique hands-on approach tells you not only what to do, but also what to avoid. Between us we have more years of fishkeeping experience than we care to remember, during which, like all aquarists, we have learnt from our mistakes; and, as "aquatic agony aunts", we have come across most of the other likely (and unlikely!) pitfalls and problems. We hope to help you avoid them. You may find us sometimes blunter than other authors, but that is because there must be no misunderstandings where lives are at stake.

The key to success is always to know what you are doing *before* you start doing it. That may sound obvious, but it is astonishing how many people think fishkeeping is just a matter of filling an aquarium with water and adding fishes. Everyone knows that water can be hard or soft, so why assume all fishes will thrive in what comes out of a particular tap? And hardness is just one of the parameters to be considered. From the fishes' viewpoint it is irrelevant that you are only a beginner – if you don't get it right then they will be at best stressed, at worst dead. The moment you acquire a fish you become responsible for its welfare, hence our golden rule: no matter how expert you become, *always do your homework first*. We cannot hope to tell you everything you will ever need to know, nor can we guarantee success – that still depends on you – but we will guide you through the basic principles of aquarium management.

We will discuss the role the aquarist can – and should – play in conservation, a topic which nowadays is increasingly important in our hobby. New species help to stimulate continued interest and fresh blood is needed to strengthen captive breeding lines, but over-exploitation of wild stock must be avoided. It is essential that every aquarist shows a responsible attitude, taking the best possible care of his or her fishes, and making every attempt to breed them.

As your experience increases, you will realize that your new hobby can, if you choose, involve far more than a living-room ornament or casual pastime. You may become a botanist, entomologist, geologist, handyman – the list is almost endless. No matter in which directions your interests lead you, we hope this book will be your guiding light.

Right: **Take as much care when buying your plants as when purchasing your fishes, and avoid specimens that have dead and dying foliage.**

Getting Started

It is easy to decide that owning an aquarium would be a nice idea, but it can be difficult to know just where and how to start. We have already introduced you to the concept of "homework", and in the first instance this means making sure you know exactly what is involved before you acquire any equipment, let alone fishes. You are already on the right track in that you are reading this book before making any purchases, and we would urge you to finish it before going any further, as you will then be in a better position to make various basic decisions – including whether you want to be a fishkeeper after all! If, as we hope you will, you decide to go ahead, you can then re-read this book, using it as a step-by-step guide to planning, setting up, and running your first aquarium.

Having done your preliminary homework, you must ask yourself a number of basic questions: What size aquarium can I accommodate (and afford)? What sort of fishes would I like to keep? Small or large (aquarium size permitting)? Freshwater or marine? Coldwater or tropical? What are their specific requirements and habits? Will they live in my tap water and, if not, am I prepared to go to the trouble and expense of providing the right conditions? Will they get along with each other? Do I want to grow plants? Will my preferred fishes eat them? Life being what it is, you may have to compromise when it comes to your personal inclinations, but *never* do so when it comes to the fishes' welfare. That must *always* come first.

Above: A magnificent coral reef aquarium.
Right: A selection of small community fishes suitable for a well-planted aquarium with soft, acid water:
Microgeophagus ramirezi (ram or butterfly cichlids),
Gymnocorymbus ternetzi (black widows), *Hyphessobrycon pulchripinnis* (lemon tetras) and *Corydoras* (dwarf catfish).

Deciding What Kinds of Fishes To Keep

Although considerations of expense and the space you have available may limit your options, do, if possible, let your preferred choice of fishes dictate factors such as aquarium size rather than *vice versa*, as keeping the species you really want is bound to increase your motivation and enjoyment. Establishing your preferences will require a certain amount of effort in finding out what species are available, making a list of those you find attractive, and applying the above questions to them. You are bound to find that some are incompatible with available space, each other, and your personal concept of a miniature underwater paradise, but the wide choice available should enable you to compile a suitable shortlist without undue trouble.

In deciding what fishes to keep you must consider how many your aquarium can accommodate. This is often calculated in terms of oxygen requirement, based on centimetres of fish (length excluding the tail when full-grown) relative to the surface area of the tank: for freshwater fishes 2.5 cm of fish per 194 cm^2 (1 inch per 30 square inches) of surface (coldwater) or 2.5 cm per 64 cm^2 (1 inch per 10 square inches) (tropical). For marines the formula is 2.5 cm of fish per 18 litres (1 inch per 4 gallons) for the first 6 months, then 2.5 cm per 9 litres (1 inch per 2 gallons). For some fishes, however, population density may be governed by territorial requirements, and fewer fishes can be kept than is suggested by the above formulae.

Fish Compatibility

The compatibility (or otherwise) of fish species must always be taken into consideration before they are mixed. First of all, environmental requirements must be similar. Mercifully, few people try to mix marine and freshwater species, but many attempt (unsuccessfully) to keep brackish water fishes in freshwater aquaria. Even more fail to realize the varying degrees of hardness and acidity/alkalinity occurring in different freshwater biotopes, and that fishes from these different water chemistries do best if given natural conditions in captivity. Temperature requirements should also be similar. Some fishes come from fast-flowing streams, others from still pools, and the needs of both cannot be satisfied in one aquarium. Some prefer rocky habitats, others jungles of plants, yet others open space; some require bright light, some require dim. All these points must be considered when evaluating their environmental compatibility.

Carassius auratus (the goldfish) is a coldwater fish which can be kept in an aquarium or pond, but should never be confined to a bowl or other small container.

Monodactylus argenteus (the mono) requires a good-sized brackish water tropical aquarium.

Corydoras catfishes, by contrast, will not tolerate salt.

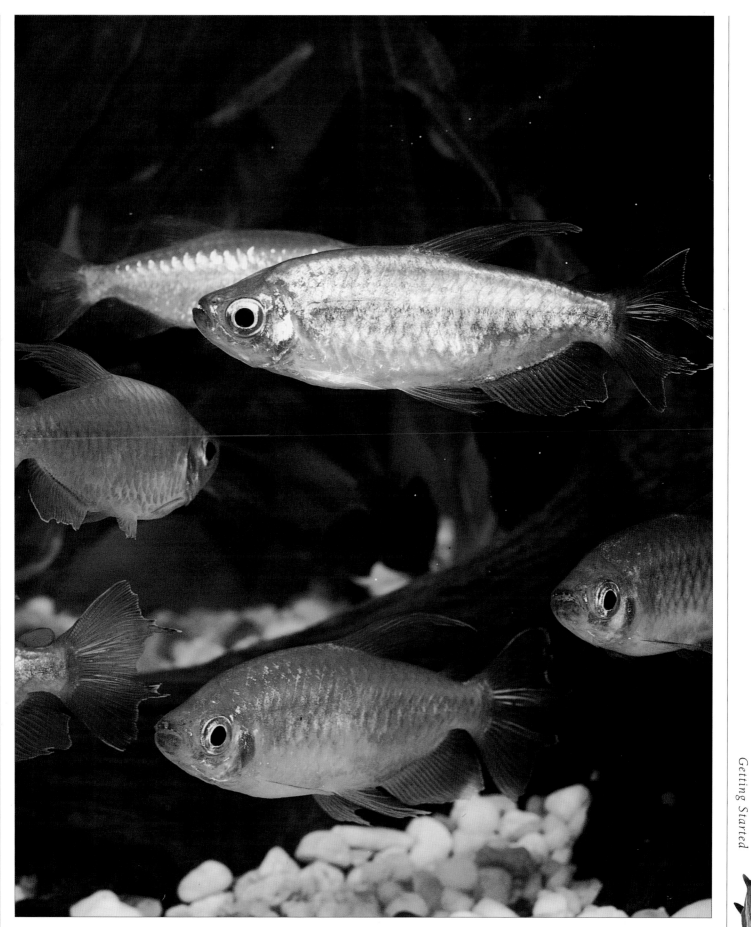

When selecting fishes, avoid poorly coloured specimens such as these *Phenacogrammus interruptus* (Congo tetras) as this is often the first signs of stress due to poor or wrong water conditioning.

There are several interesting North American cold water fishes available such as this *Phoxinus erythrogaster*.

Lake Malawi mouthbrooding cichlids such as this *Melanochromis chipokae* require very specific conditions.

Pterois volitans (the lion or dragon fish) is a lurking predator of the coral reef, and may eat small tankmates.

Thorichthys meeki (the firemouth) is often sold as a community fish, but is quite unsuitable. It grows to 10 cm (4 in), is territorial, and may eat smaller tankmates.

Size and Temperament

Size and temperament are just as important. Although not all species feed exclusively on other fishes, it is natural for larger fishes to eat smaller ones. So, except where dealing only with strict vegetarians, always ensure the smallest fish is too big to fit into the largest mouth – and that, allowing for future growth, it will remain so. Some fishes are territorial, occupying an area which usually represents either their private larder or their intended nursery (feeding and breeding territory respectively). They are usually aggressive towards conspecifics (members of their own species) in particular, and frequently towards other species as well. They can sometimes be kept with other fishes if the latter are evenly matched (in size and temperament), but they may need their own tank.

Think about feeding. Do you really want to keep fishes with varying specialized dietary needs, requiring you to serve a variety of foods at each meal? Will the slow and steady eaters get any food at all if you include a number of fast-swimming greedy species? Will that harmless but large and boisterous fish you like the look of frighten the life out of smaller, shyer tankmates? These are all questions that must be answered.

Never make any assumptions on the basis of apparently successful and uneventful cohabitation in a dealer's tank; the fishes' behaviour may be affected by relative crowding, lack of decor, and by their age (often fishes offered for sale are sub-adult). Give them space, something to fight over, and a few months' growth, and the story may be quite different!

Making Your Selection

In making your selection, don't let your reading stop at this volume. There is a considerable amount of aquarium literature available, ranging from assorted magazines to a host of specialized books on specific groups of fishes. You do not have to buy them – simply ask your local library to obtain them for you. You can also visit public aquaria and aquatic retailers to see some of the fishes in the flesh.

Don't succumb to your understandable impatience to get up and running – this preliminary research should be regarded as all part of the fun. Patience is an essential quality to cultivate if you want to succeed, so the sooner you practise it the better! We cannot over-emphasize the importance of getting everything right first time. There is no

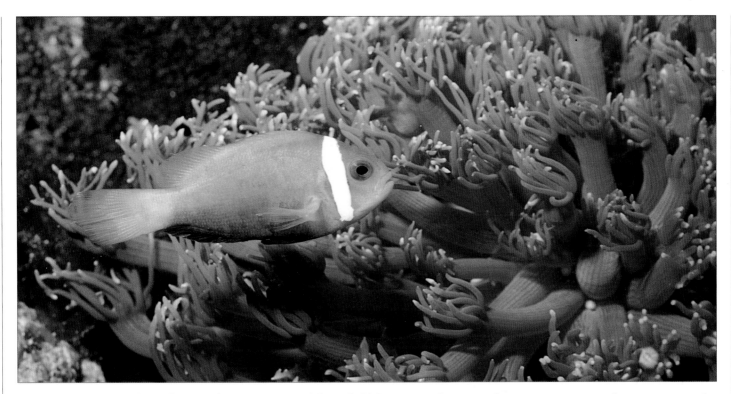

Anemone fishes, such as this *Amphiprion* species (clownfish) live in symbiosis with sea anemones on their native coral reefs. A suitable anemone must, therefore, be provided for the clownfish in captivity.

point in setting up your tank and then finding it won't do for the fishes you want to keep; that will mean settling for second best or starting again from scratch. Get it wrong and you risk causing suffering to your fishes, not to mention wasting your time and money; what should have been a source of immense enjoyment for many years could turn into a nightmare.

Far too many aquarists set about the task in completely the opposite fashion, setting up an aquarium and populating it with whatever their local pet shop has to offer that month. Only later do they realize what they are missing when they see a fish they really like, often totally unsuitable for their aquarium. The sensible few go home and find out about their dream fish – *before* buying it. The majority, regrettably, take it home without doing any homework, usually discovering their error the hard way – upsetting for the aquarist, but catastrophic for the fishes.

Be assured, we do not exaggerate. Every year we receive numerous letters from aquarists asking us if the fishes they have bought will live together harmoniously, or, all too often, why their chosen combination has proved disastrous. Others set up an aquarium and then ask if it is suitable for the fishes they fancy. While we have no desire to put ourselves out of a job, we would prefer it if people would find out first!

The Fishkeeping Network

Apart from books, there is another invaluable source of information available to you – the accumulated knowledge of other aquarists, both professional (dealers) and other amateurs like yourself. Fishkeeping is a friendly hobby, and you will find that most enthusiasts are more than willing to help. If it was seeing a friend's aquarium that stimulated your interest in the first place, don't be afraid to go back to him or her and pick his or her brains. He or she may know other aquarists who will be only too happy to let you see their set-ups

Killifishes are beautiful but usually shortlived; their native pools dry up in summer, and only their eggs survive until the rains come.

Above: *Poecilia reticulata* (the guppy) is a very popular and easy-to-maintain livebearer. Numerous varieties are available, but although they are all very easy to breed, carefully planned line-breeding is needed to produce quality stock.

Below: A well-planted freshwater aquarium is a miniature underwater garden, and an ornament to any home.

Above left: Botia macracantha (the clown loach) is often kept singly, but actually prefers the company of its own kind. It grows rather larger than many aquarists realize.

and answer your questions. Consider joining your local aquarists' club – you will be made welcome even though you don't yet have any fishes of your own. Such clubs exist in most large towns and cities, although it is not always easy to obtain a contact address. Local aquarium shops may be able to help; if not, most countries have a national federation of fishkeeping clubs which can supply details, and whose contact address can usually be found in fishkeeping magazines.

Even if you are not by nature the sociable type, there are many advantages, apart from shared knowledge, to belonging to a club. If you have fishkeeping friends then you have people you can call upon in all sorts of otherwise difficult situations – getting a large tank home and into place; looking after your fishes while you are on holiday; helping out if some vital item of equipment fails at 3 am on Sunday morning. There is the possibility of spare equipment and home-bred fishes at bargain prices, and perhaps the loan of extra reading material.

The Aquatic Dealer

It will also be to your immense advantage to find a good aquatic dealer and make a friend of him. You will need guidance when it comes to buying equipment, because the quantity and variety available nowadays is confusing even to the expert, and positively daunting to the beginner. He will be able to advise what is best suited to your particular circumstances, and what brands are most reliable. A good dealer is also a mine of information on fishes and fishkeeping. You may not buy all your fishes from him (he may not have what you want – though if you are a good customer he may get it for you), but you should reward his investment of time and patience in you, his customer, by always going to him for "dry goods". He may not be right on your doorstep, but his help will more than recompense you for any expenditure in time and travel.

So, how do you find a suitable dealer? Firstly, ask other aquarists for a recommendation. Failing that, the most important difference between a good dealer and a bad one is one of attitude. Both have a living to make, but money is the chief motivation of the bad dealer. He will rarely be prepared to spend time talking. Don't expect him to net out a particular fish from a batch of 20 – it will be too much trouble. He will grumble if you insist on a pair, even if the species is easily sexed. He will allow you to buy any combination of equipment and fishes without question.

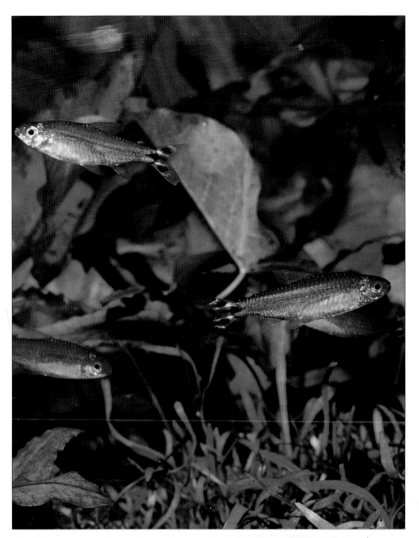

Small tetras such as those pictured above should never be housed with *Astronotus ocellatus* (oscars), although unscrupulous dealers may sell both together as suitable for the general community tank.

The honest dealer, by contrast, will try to deter you from any folly, and perhaps even refuse to sell – he values his reputation and integrity more than the proverbial quick buck. If he can't answer your questions, he will get a book out. Ask for two fishes, and he will catch you a pair if they are sexable. He will be patient and will take time to talk, even if you are a stranger who may never darken his doors again – and he will probably recognize you when you do go back.

If in doubt, try going along with an outrageous shopping list of totally incompatible fishes (we suggest, for example, the oscar cichlid and the neon tetra), and let it be known that you have just (yesterday) set up a 60-cm (24-inch) tank and intend introducing both to it immediately. The bad dealer won't bat an eyelid and will get out his nets and polythene bags. The good one will politely, but firmly, read you the riot act.

Water Management

Water is an essential constituent of all life forms; to fishes, however, it is environmental as well as metabolic – the medium in which they live, just as we live in air. Like us, fishes pass water through their excretory and alimentary tracts; but they also "breathe" it, using their gills (and sometimes other organs) to extract essential oxygen and discharge carbon dioxide. There is also an exchange of metabolic and environmental water by osmosis.

We become uncomfortable or ill if we drink polluted water, or if the air we breathe doesn't suit our individual preferences (usually what we are used to) or the general requirements of our species – it may be too hot, cold, still, windy, dry, or humid for our liking, too low in oxygen, or polluted with smoke or toxic gases. Air, however, has a fairly uniform chemical composition throughout the world, so someone from one part of our planet can survive in any other, though he or she may find the local climate unpleasant.

Water, by contrast, is highly variable in its chemistry: it can be fresh, brackish, or saline; hard or soft; acid or alkaline; rich or poor in oxygen; pure or polluted. Unlike us, fishes are restricted in their distribution – we can go anywhere there is air, but not all bodies of water are accessible to all fishes, for reasons of geography (for example a sea fish cannot enter a land-locked lake) and environmental unsuitability. The latter is usually the end-product of the former – geological activity isolates a body of

Above: Different species of *Tetraodon* (puffers) can be found in fresh, brackish, and marine waters.
Right: Correct water chemistry and A1 water quality are absolutely essential when dealing with sensitive coral fishes and invertebrates.

Gouramis such as *Trichogaster trichopterus* (three spot gourami) come from muddy, oxygen-depleted waters, and have an accessory respiratory organ (the labyrinth) which enables them to breathe atmospheric air. They will not, however, be inconvenienced by the water clarity and ample oxygen levels required by other community fishes.

water and its fauna; subsequently there is gradual modification of water parameters (chemistry, temperature, quality) paralleled by adaptation of the fishes to the changing conditions. Their systems, thus specialized, are then often unable to cope with any subsequent change. They may suffer discomfort or poor health, or even die, if the water in which they find themselves – which they "drink" and "breathe" and which interacts with their body fluids – does not meet their specific requirements – especially if the change is abrupt.

We must therefore never assume that water is a uniform element, or that any fish will live happily in what comes out of the tap. The aquarist must be a "water technician", providing the correct environment in terms of chemistry, temperature, oxygen content, movement, and freedom from pollution ("water quality"). There are instruments and test kits for monitoring aquarium water, and a huge variety of equipment for adjusting its chemistry, quality, and other factors, so there is no excuse for hit-and-miss water management.

Water Chemistry

This is the term used by aquarists to describe the combined salinity, hardness, and acidity/alkalinity (pH) of water. For a fish to survive its metabolism must be in tune with these aspects of its environment, and successful adaptation to significant alterations normally requires changes to be gradual, allowing time for metabolic adjustment. Sudden change can be fatal if a fish's organs cannot cope with the altered environment ("chemical shock"). While some fishes can be adapted to "unnatural" water chemistry, this may prove detrimental in the long term; and the difference between certain environments, for example salt and fresh water, are too great to overcome.

There are two sensible ways of approaching this question of water chemistry: you can either keep fishes suited to the water you can provide from the tap, or modify your local water to meet the needs of more demanding species. Modification of water chemistry can be expensive and time-consuming, with the possibility of error, so we suggest that beginners take the former course. We do not recommend the third option of attempting to modify the fishes!

Your dealer should be able to tell you which species are "hardy", and which will not live long in your tap water. Even so, check whether the hardy types are actually found in water similar to yours in the wild – if not you may still need to modify it for breeding. Some species occur naturally in several

In nature *Dimidiochromis compressiceps* (the Malawian eyebiter) feeds on the fry of other species and is reputed to eat the eyes of adults. In captivity it is rather timid, and does not behave "antisocially" if well fed. It should, however, be kept only with other Malawi cichlids, and like them requires moderately hard, alkaline, well-oxygenated, water.

different bodies of water sometimes offering quite diverse environments. Without specific data on origin the best approach is to create average conditions for the species, modifying these slowly if the fish appears unhappy.

Sudden increases in hardness or dramatic alterations in pH are the changes most likely to have dire effects; even natural water chemistry may prove harmful if the fishes' systems have adjusted to different conditions. Local shops usually use tap water (except for marines and some delicate freshwater species – do check in each case), so it may be best to do likewise initially and gradually adjust water chemistry after introducing the fishes. Later on you may wish to buy additional fishes, possibly accustomed to different conditions to those now prevailing in your aquarium. In such cases set up a temporary tank with conditions suited to the new arrivals, then adjust water chemistry gradually to match your main aquarium.

You may be told that chemical shock can be minimized by mixing small amounts of aquarium water with that in the bag prior to releasing fishes. That is rubbish – the necessary metabolic adjustment takes days or weeks, not minutes.

Let us now look at the various aspects of water chemistry in more detail:

Overpage: Microgeophagus ramirezi (the ram or butterfly cichlid) requires soft, acid water to thrive. The other fishes seen here come from the same type of biotope, but are "hardier".

Chemicals which can be used to alter water chemistry. Marine salt (*bottom left*) for increasing salinity; Sodium bicarbonate (*top left*) for increasing pH; proprietary pH adjusters come in tablet (*top right*) or powder (*bottom right*) form.

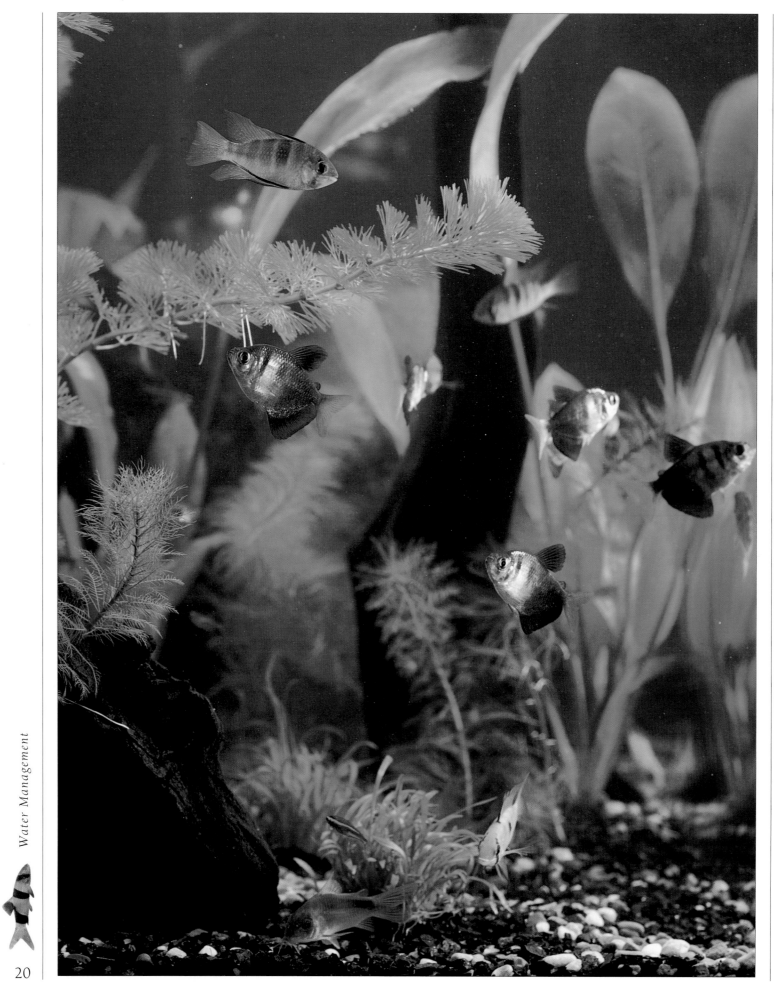

Salinity

This is the measure of common salt (sodium chloride, NaCl) content, and is normally applied only to salt and brackish water (fresh water, by definition, does not contain measurable quantities of NaCl). It is measured using a hydrometer. Nowadays, because of coastal pollution, water for the marine or brackish aquarium is normally "created" (rather than collected), using tap water and special "marine salts" containing not only sodium chloride but also desirable trace elements. Instructions are normally provided, but the salinity of the mix should always be checked. (It is important to remember never to use "domestic" salt, which may contain additives toxic to fishes.)

Most killifishes (this is *Nothobranchius furzeri*) require soft, acid water...

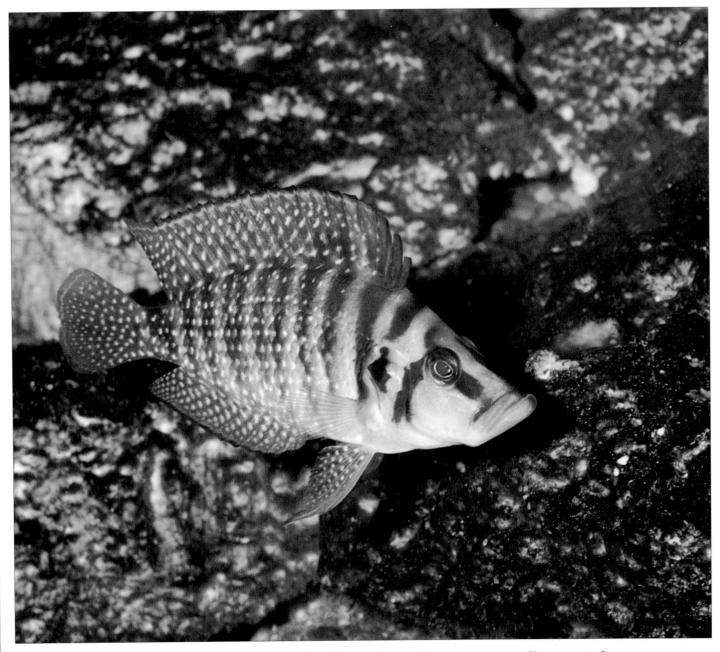

...while the cichlids of lakes Malawi and Tanganyika, like marines, require very pure, well-oxygenated, alkaline water – but no salt.

Hardness

Hardness is the measure of dissolved mineral salts (mainly chlorides, bicarbonates, carbonates, and sulphates of calcium, sodium, magnesium, and potassium); the harder the water the more salts it contains. It is generally expressed in terms of calcium carbonate ($CaCO_3$) content, measured in degrees (dH) or parts per million (ppm) using a special test kit. Care is needed with regard to "degrees of hardness", the definition of which varies from country to country and test kit to test kit, depending on origin.

Water becomes hard by dissolving soluble salts from the rocks or soil over or through which it flows. Some rocks, for example slate, granite, and gneiss, contain little or no soluble material and have a negligible effect, while others, notably limestones, are quite the opposite. Rocks and other "hard" decor in the aquarium may affect water chemistry: corals and shells are largely calcium carbonate, and gravel often contains fragments of limestone or shell. Hardness-free decor is a pre-requisite of the soft-water aquarium.

It is easy to harden soft water with lime-rich decor or the special salt mixes (*not* marine salt) available for simulating conditions in east African lakes, and, as luck would have it, fishes from hard water seem not to suffer any ill-effects from softer-than-natural conditions (but see pH, below). Unfortunately the reverse does not apply: reducing hardness is troublesome, and soft-water fishes often fail to thrive in hard conditions.

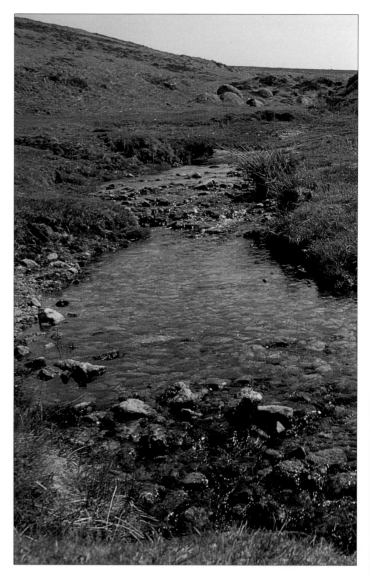

Some waters, such as this high moorland stream, are acidified by the peat bogs across which they flow.

Using a Test Kit

1 Add the reagent – which can be a tablet, as here, or a liquid from a bottle – to a measured sample of water in the vial supplied.

2 Replace the cap on the vial and vigorously shake the reagent/water for a few seconds to mix properly.

3 Once the time required for the necessary reaction has elapsed, compare the colour of the sample with the colour on the chart provided.

Softening Water

There are various methods of softening water:

1 By boiling, which removes some, but not all, of the dissolved salts.

2 By dilution with rain water. This is the cheapest method, the only outlay being suitable containers, made of non-toxic material, for collecting and storing water. Roofs, gutters, and downpipes must be as clean as possible, and avoid cemented roofs as cement is powdered limestone. Water collected close to, or downwind of, industrial areas may be polluted. Collect only during prolonged downpours, and wait a few minutes while dust and any other rubbish is washed away. It is advisable to strain the water through filter floss straight away to remove any stray detritus. Rain water may carry the risk of pollution, but so may tap water (see below).

3 By dilution with artificially softened water. This may be: a) distilled; b) softened using an ion-exchange resin (use only resins sold for aquarium use). This may affect pH, and, as it exchanges calcium ions for (usually) sodium ions, the result may be soft but still mineral-rich (and unsuitable for fishes from mineral-poor waters); c) processed by a reverse osmosis unit, available from aquatic retailers (but expensive). This removes all minerals but is wasteful – some 45.5 litres (10 gallons) of tap water are needed to produce 4.5 litres (1 gallon) of mineral-free water.

The collected or treated water can be used "neat" to create very soft conditions. Distilled and reverse-osmosis water should *never* be used "neat"; not, as often stated, because they contain no minerals, but because both processes remove free oxygen so there is nothing to "breathe". Aerate thoroughly before use to rectify this problem.

You may come across the following additional terms: "Temporary hardness" is that which can be removed by boiling, while "permanent hardness" is that which cannot. "Carbonate hardness" (KH) is that contributed by (bi)carbonates, but not other salts such as sulphates and chlorides. "General hardness" (GH) includes all dissolved salts, and is sometimes referred to as "total hardness" or "total dissolved salts" (TDS). Scientists often measure mineral content in terms not of hardness but of electrical conductivity, the units employed being micro-siemens (μS).

Sphaerichthys osphronemoides (the chocolate gourami) requires specific water conditions, unlike most other popular anabantids.

pH

The pH scale is used to indicate the acidity or alkalinity of a substance; it runs from 0 to 14, 0 being the extreme of acidity, 14 that of alkalinity, and 7 neutral. Most fishes come from waters with a pH between 5.5 and 9.0, although there are outliers at either end of the scale. It is vital to remember that the scale is logarithmic – each step up or down from neutral is 10 times the previous one: pH 4 is 10 times more acid than pH 5, and 100 times more acid than pH 6. Apparently small variations can thus have dramatic effects on fishes. Luckily the scale is the universally accepted method of measuring acidity/alkalinity, so there is no problem with different units as with hardness. Special test kits are available and affluent aquarists may wish to buy electronic pH meters.

The pH of water is affected by substances dissolved in it. The salts which harden water usually also render it alkaline; soft water, by contrast, is often slightly acid, because rain reacts with atmospheric carbon dioxide to form dilute carbonic acid. Decaying organic material, such as is found in peat bogs and forests, acidifies water flowing through such areas.

There is little point in trying to acidify aquarium water which is being constantly buffered back to neutral or alkaline by dissolved salts derived from tap water or the decor. First minimize hardness, otherwise you are wasting your time. Soft water is easily acidified using peat filtration (see below). Loose peat will "migrate" and is best placed in a nylon bag (a stocking will do), and the whole rinsed to remove tiny particles. Peat is fairly quickly "exhausted" and needs renewing at intervals established by monitoring pH.

Water can be made alkaline by using calciferous decor or by filtering over coral, crushed shell, or limestone chips. Such material should always be included in systems for fishes which cannot tolerate acid conditions, to act as a buffer against the acidifying effects of metabolic byproducts.

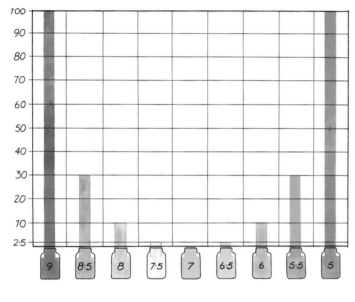

pH Scale chart

Using Peat as a Filter Medium

1 Peat needs to be contained in a fine-meshed bag in order to prevent it escaping from the filter. A section of nylon stocking is ideal for the purpose.

2 Push the peat into the nylon stocking, packing down tightly. Once the bag is filled tie a knot in the open end.

3 Rinse under the tap or in a bucket of water to remove any particles. The bag of peat can then be used in a box filter, or in most types of canister filter.

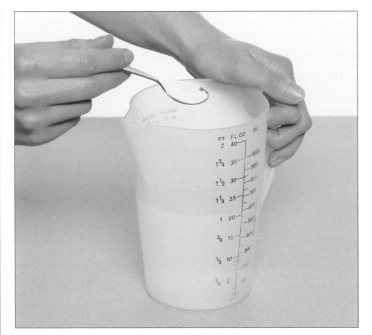

Above: Always dissolve bicarbonate of soda in a little water before use. The solution can be mixed with the new water for the aquarium and an accurate test result achieved. Adding the "bicarb" dry risks incorrect test results if some remains undissolved at the time of the test.

These methods are gradual in effect; to avoid "pH shock" when you change part of the aquarium water you may need to adjust the pH of the "new" water rapidly before use (though in practice partial water changes with neutral water rarely have any ill-effect). If you use a proprietary "pH adjuster" follow the instructions to the letter – failure to do so may prove fatal for the fishes. We prefer to prepare new water in advance (leaving it to stand over peat or calciferous material), or to use bicarbonate of soda ($NaHCO_3$) to raise pH, or peat extract (made by boiling peat) to lower it. Dosage must be established initially by adding small amounts to the new water and measuring the pH. Always treat the water *before* adding it to the aquarium.

Water chemistry is in fact far more complex than we have intimated, because mineral composition (the salts contributing to the hardness) varies considerably from area to area. There is, however, rarely any need to simulate the exact formulation, as fishes are able to extract the amount of each vital element they actually require.

In nature the volume of water relative to fish populations, together with the action of plants in removing wastes, ensures adequate water quality.

Water Quality

Water quality is equally as important as chemistry. Most of the complexities of the latter can be avoided by keeping fishes suited to local water, but providing and maintaining good water quality is a continuing process. This falls into two parts: ensuring no harmful chemicals enter the aquarium from outside; and dealing with waste products produced by its occupants. Many fishes come from virtually unpolluted water and are highly sensitive to any contaminants. Some are more tolerant, but it is nevertheless unwise to provide less than optimal water quality in captivity – the sheer volume of natural waters acts as a safety net, whereas any problem can rapidly escalate in the restricted capacity of the aquarium.

All equipment and decor must be non-toxic – where possible use items intended specifically for aquarium use. "Non-aquatic" plastics should ideally be "food quality"; avoid coloured types, especially those with a nasty taste. Metals may corrode (especially in salt water), producing toxic salts, so use only those metal items designed for aquarium use (for example aluminium hoods) and always check suitability for marine aquaria. Rocks should not (unintentionally) affect the water, but beware of coloured crystals which may be poisonous. Garden items (such as flowerpots and stones) may be contaminated with pesticides or fertilizers. Wood (for example hoods) may leach tannins, or worse, preservatives, unless coated with polyurethane varnish. Insecticide aerosols, spray polishes, paint fumes, and other domestic chemicals can poison fishes. A definitive list is impossible, so always be on your guard.

As if this were not enough, the water from your tap may contain invisible nasty surprises. Water that has stood in metal pipes may be tainted with

Although *Carassius auratus* (the goldfish) is a cold water fish, some fancy varieties are prone to fin-rot if exposed to very low temperatures.

metallic oxide. This contamination is normally slight but can accumulate in the aquarium, so run the tap for a while before using any water. Never use water from a copper hot-water cylinder.

Water companies are required to provide water "of potable quality". This does not always equate with aquarium quality, as chemical treatments and pollution levels deemed harmless to humans can be lethal to fishes. The commonest additive is chlorine gas, highly toxic to fishes but easily dealt with: if water is left to stand for 24 hours the gas will disperse into the air. The process can be speeded up by aeration, and if chlorine content is low (the gas can't be smelt), it is often sufficient to run the tap hard into a bucket. Some water companies now use an alternative, far more toxic, purification agent, chloramine, which does not disperse naturally. Water conditioners are available (from your local dealer) to neutralize this chemical, as well as chlorine. Ask your water company if they use chloramine or intend to do so, and ask to be warned whenever they intend to flush the mains to eliminate aquatic invertebrates, as the DDT used is toxic to fishes. Be friendly and polite – their only obligation is to provide drinkable water. Help with your fishes is voluntary.

Tap water may contain nitrates and phosphates (the result of agricultural fertilizers leaching into rivers and aquifers, or of incomplete "purification" during recycling), especially when water levels are low and pollutant concentrations correspondingly high; fortunate the aquarist whose tap water originates from a moorland reservoir or other uncontaminated source. Nitrate test kits are available from dealers. Nitrates should be removed from water intended for the aquarium reverse osmosis, or a special filter connected to the tap.

The Nitrogen Cycle

However good your initial water quality, it will deteriorate when fishes are introduced. Fishes excrete wastes, plants lose leaves, and inevitably there will be particles of food uneaten. In both nature and the aquarium such detritus is broken down by bacteria during a series of processes termed the nitrogen cycle. The first stage in this cycle is highly toxic ammonia (and its compounds), excreted by fishes and produced by the decomposition of organic matter; this is rapidly converted to nitrites (still dangerously toxic), which are in turn processed into nitrates. These are relatively harmless, though sudden or long-term exposure to high concentrations can be harmful.

Although the nitrogen cycle will operate in any mature aquarium, fish population density is generally higher than in a comparable volume of water in nature, so the system is unbalanced; a tank may look clean but have high levels of ammonia or nitrite. Action is necessary to redress the balance and avoid such problems. The process normally used is filtration, during which the aquarium water is passed through one or more materials (filter media) to remove wastes. There are three main types of filtration – mechanical, chemical, and biological – and aquarium systems are usually a combination of at least two of these.

Nitrogen Cycle in the Aquarium

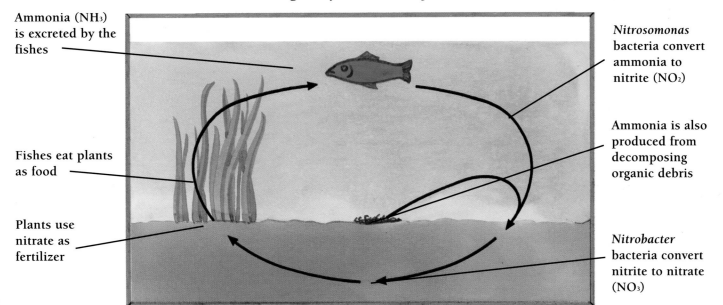

Ammonia (NH_3) is excreted by the fishes

Fishes eat plants as food

Plants use nitrate as fertilizer

Nitrosomonas bacteria convert ammonia to nitrite (NO_2)

Ammonia is also produced from decomposing organic debris

Nitrobacter bacteria convert nitrite to nitrate (NO_3)

Types of Filtration

Mechanical Filtration: During mechanical filtration solids are trapped by the filter; they are, however, still part of the aquarium system until the medium is replaced or cleaned, just as dust swept under the carpet is still in the house! The commonest media used are filter floss, plastic foam, and gravel/sand.

Chemical Filtration: This process uses media which alter the chemical composition of the water, for example the alteration of pH using peat or lime-rich material, reduction of hardness by ion-exchange resins, and removal of metabolic products by activated carbon or zeolite (which remove carbon dioxide and ammonia respectively). Chemical media also trap solids mechanically.

Biological Filtration: Biological filtration involves enhancing natural populations of the bacteria which operate the nitrogen cycle by providing the conditions they require – surfaces to colonize, supplies of wastes to process, and, for those which convert nitrites to nitrates, a constant supply of oxygen. The filter medium offers living space, and the flow of water through the filter ensures a constant supply of wastes and oxygen. Biological filtration takes place in any mechanical or chemical filter which has been left undisturbed long enough to develop a bacterial population, and the media used in biological filters also have a mechanical (and sometimes chemical) effect. As well as those already mentioned there are plastic, ceramic, and glass media, all of which maximize the surface area available for colonization. Efficient biological filtration is the key to maintaining water quality on a day-to-day basis.

The nitrogen cycle must be considered when planning and maintaining a filtration system, as whether you want biological filtration or not you are going to get it! It takes about two weeks for the nitrogen cycle to become properly functional in a new system (aquarium and filter(s)); fishes cannot be introduced until after this maturation period because of ammonia/nitrate toxicity. If the established nitrogen cycle is subsequently interrupted there will again be a risk of toxicity. This commonly happens when "dirty" filters are cleaned because they are considered to be unhygienic and life-threatening; in fact most of the "dirt" in a mature filter is the inert (and harmless) residue left by bacterial processing. Removing it does nothing to improve hygiene, but the accompanying elimination of the established bacterial population can wreak havoc. It is, however, sometimes necessary to clean filters if clogging by inert matter is impeding flow, or if chemical media are exhausted. Only part (50 per cent maximum) of the filter contents should be cleaned or replaced; this will leave an adequate residual bacterial population, but feeding should nevertheless be reduced for a few days to lighten the load on the biological system while it regenerates to full strength.

FILTER MEDIA

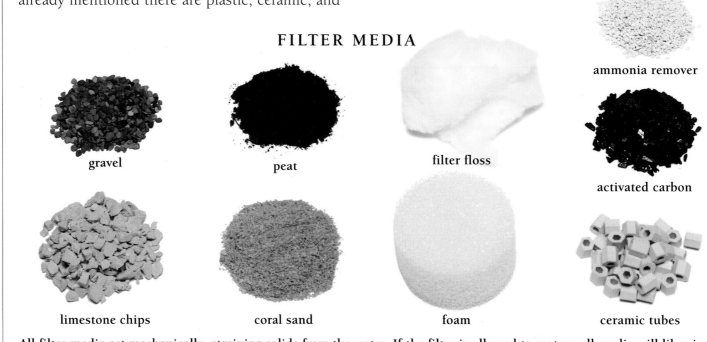

gravel   peat   filter floss   ammonia remover

limestone chips   coral sand   foam   activated carbon   ceramic tubes

All filter media act mechanically, straining solids from the water. If the filter is allowed to mature all media will likewise be colonized by beneficial bacteria. Some, for example the hexagonal ceramic tubes shown here, are specifically designed to optimize bacterial activity. Some chemical media (for example carbon and ammonia remover (zeolite)), remove certain toxins, while others (for example peat, limestone chips, coral sand), are used to adjust hardness and/or pH.

Types of Filter

Canister Filters: These are self-contained units with a container (the filter chamber) for media and an electric pump to circulate water. They may be external, with inlet and outlet pipes from and to the aquarium, or internal, with slits to allow water into the filter and an outlet from the pump. They combine mechanical and biological filtration, with chemical optional. Special external filters using diatomaceous earth optimize water clarity by mechanically removing particles but are expensive to run and need frequent maintenance as they clog rapidly.

tank

filter

Canister filter

Canister filters are mechanical and biological, sometimes chemical, in operation. Water is siphoned out of the aquarium into the filter canister, then pumped up through the filter media and back to the aquarium, in this case via a spray bar.

Undergravel (UG) Filters: UG filters consist of a plastic plate positioned between the aquarium bottom and the substrate, with one or more uplift pipes. Water is drawn down through the substrate and returned via the uplift(s). UG filters can be powered by: a) the airlift principle (rising bubbles of air draw water with them), an airline being inserted in the uplift tube; b) powerheads, electric pumps which fit on to the uplift tubes; or c) an external canister filter with its inlet tube inserted in the uplift. The substrate, which should be 5-7.5 cm (2-3 inches) deep for maximum effectiveness, acts as the filter medium, and its action is both mechanical and biological, sometimes chemical. The advantages of undergravel filtration are that the "inlet" is the entire aquarium bottom so wastes cannot escape processing, and the large amount of

filter medium available for bacterial colonization. The main disadvantage is that when the system eventually becomes clogged cleaning involves a major upheaval.

A reverse-flow UG system minimizes this problem by using an external canister filter as a mechanical pre-filter, the outlet being attached to the UG uplift so that water is pumped up through the substrate. This unfortunately also negates the advantage of UG – the system inlet is now that of the pre-filter, which is also probably the main site of bacterial activity! Reverse-flow systems create no surface turbulence and this may result in oxygen depletion unless the aquarium is aerated independently of the filtration system.

Undergravel Flows

In conventional flow UG (*top*) water is drawn <u>down</u> through the filter bed (substrate) and <u>up</u> the uplift pipe (by airlift or powerhead). In reverse flow (*bottom*) a canister filter pumps water <u>down</u> the uplift and <u>up</u> through the substrate.

Trickle Filters: These consist of one or more trays with perforated bottoms, part-filled with filter media, stacked above the aquarium, and used in conjunction with an external canister filter, whose return is sprayed on to the (top) tray and trickles back into the tank via the perforations. The water is thus exposed to air, optimizing its oxygen uptake and hence bacterial activity. A further advantage is that its capacity (the volume of media) can be increased by means of additional trays without the need to increase turnover (water flow rate). Trickle filters may alternatively be situated beneath the aquarium, with the water being siphoned into the filter and pumped back.

External Box Filter

Water is siphoned out of the aquarium, descends through the filter media, and is returned via an airlift.

Trickle Filter

Trickle filters are usually sited on top of the aquarium and fed by the return from a canister filter (spray bar). Water and filter media are exposed to atmospheric oxygen, making for excellent biological efficiency.

Box Filters: Box filters may be internal or external and are driven by the airlift principle. They have, however, largely been superseded by more complex systems, but the internal type is still useful for small tanks, tanks with minimal loading, and supplementary chemical filtration.

Internal Box Filter

The airlift principle is used to draw water down through the filter and up the return pipe.

Sponge Filter

Sponge filters are ideal for small aquaria.

vent

froth collects in
removable cup

air from
air pump

water
returns to
tank

air from
ionizer

air
flow

diffuser

reaction
tube

Protein Skimmer

Protein skimmers work only in salt water and are
essential for marine aquaria.

air from
air pump

Sponge Filters: A sponge filter consists of a perforated plastic tube fitted with a cylindrical sponge. Air is passed through the tube, drawing water through the sponge. These filters act mechanically and biologically; they are best suited to aquaria with low filtration needs.

Protein Skimmers: Protein skimmers, essential in the marine aquarium, utilize a process known as "air stripping". Proteins and other organics adhere to air bubbles, forming a foam which rises to the top of the unit to be collected in a removable container which is emptied at least once a day. They do not work in fresh water.

Optimizing Water Quality

The amount and type of filtration required depends on the nature of the individual aquarium. Biological efficiency is a function of bacterial population size, in turn dependent on available colonizable area (filter capacity) and oxygen supply – not, as many aquarists assume, purely on turnover rate. In choosing a filtration system take into consideration tank size, probable metabolic loading (number, sizes, and feeding habits of the fishes relative to water volume), and water movement requirements (of the fishes), in order to decide what filter type, capacity, and turnover rate suit your specific circumstances. Expert advice (for example from your dealer) can be invaluable. Filter efficiency can be monitored using the kits available for measuring ammonia, nitrites, and nitrates.

Although biological filtration will deal with ammonia and nitrites, it will not eliminate nitrates, and without additional action a gradual build-up of these is inevitable, even if some are utilized by plants. Although nitrates are relatively harmless, long-term exposure to high concentrations may shorten lifespan and reduce resistance to disease. Sudden exposure to high nitrate levels is often fatal for example if new fishes, unaccustomed to high levels, are introduced. Far too often the retailer is blamed for selling poor-quality fishes!

The most effective way of reducing nitrates (you cannot eliminate them altogether in a functioning system) is to replace part of the aquarium water regularly; how much and how often depends on the individual tank, but 20 per cent weekly is a good starting point. Monitoring with a test kit will indicate whether the routine needs to be modified. It is inadvisable to change more than a third of the water at a time, and replacement water should be

1 Internal box filters are often used as additional chemical filters, filled with peat, zeolite, carbon, or another chemical medium. Filled with filter floss, however, they are perfectly suited to small aquaria. Fit the uplift section into the box and pack the medium round it.

2 The filter wool should be firmly packed down into the filter. Then fit the top and attach the airline to the air supply tube. The filter is now ready to be installed in the aquarium.

detoxified (if necessary) and be of the correct chemistry and temperature. Although chemical media are available for removing nitrates, fresh water is preferable because it has the added benefit of stimulating fishes and replenishing minerals exhausted by them. Just topping up to replace water lost by evaporation does not constitute a partial water change, because any chemicals (whether organic – for example nitrates – or inorganic) are left behind during evaporation and so remain in the water.

Other Aspects of Water Management

Fishes have evolved to function at particular temperature ranges just as they have adapted to local water chemistries. In nature, variation within a species' acceptable range is normally gradual; sudden changes (as inflicted by careless aquarists) may be harmful, with a rapid drop in temperature more serious than a rise. There are species-dependent upper and lower limits above and below which metabolic failure (and death) are probable, but most species will continue to function (at least for a while) at temperatures slightly outside their optimal range. They may be sluggish if the temperature is abnormally low (never skimp on heating), and suffer respiratory distress if it is higher than normal: increased temperature results in increased metabolic rate and hence oxygen requirement, but there is a concomitant decrease in the oxygen content of the water – so the gills need to work harder on both counts. Oxygen requirements themselves vary from species to species, yet again as a function of the natural habitat. The more turbulent the water the more rapidly it can absorb oxygen from the atmosphere and the greater its oxygen content is likely to be. The reasons for this are two-fold: first, oxygen is absorbed only at the interface between air and water (its surface), which increases in area when in motion; second, water movement speeds up circulation of the oxygen, which, in completely still water, would spread from the surface only very slowly, by diffusion.

Large bodies of water (seas, large lakes) are subject to massive water movements (tides and storms) which result in high oxygen concentrations; not surprisingly the resident fishes have adapted to these levels, and, if deprived of them,

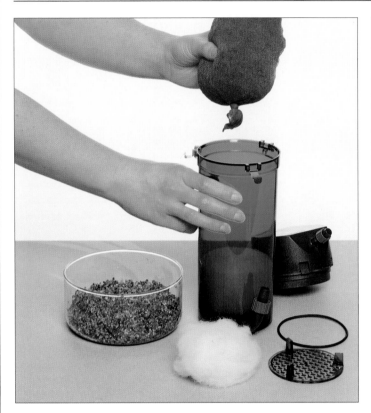

1 Remove the top of the filter and any internal top grid (bottom right of picture) designed to keep the media in the filter canister. Instal the desired media – here a peat-filled stocking, gravel, and a topping of filter floss.

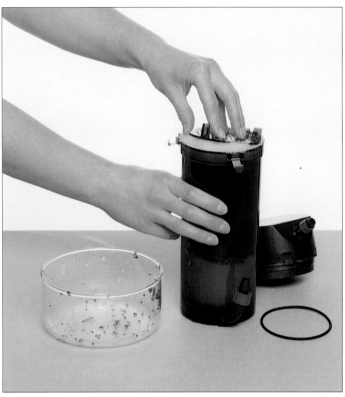

2 If using a filter with internal media containers, each can be filled with a different medium. Fit the internal top grid (if any) on top of the media.

3 Fit the rubber sealing ring to the lid, position the latter, and do up the retaining clips.

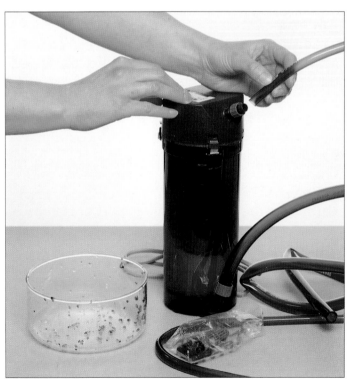

4 Attach the inlet and outlet pipes; it is easier to fill a new filter before fitting these pipes, but when the filter is subsequently cleaned they are normally left attached.

Left: **Symphysodon aequifasciata** (the discus) comes from still waters and does not appreciate strong currents.

Opposite above: Very large lakes are highly oxygenated through surface movement, and even have surf zones where waves break on rocky shores, as here in Lake Malawi.

Opposite below: **Labeotropheus fuelleborni** is a characteristic cichlid of the Lake Malawi surf zone.

may die by gradual suffocation. Some species from fast-flowing rivers may be similarly affected. At the other end of the scale there are bodies of water which contain very little oxygen, yet fishes nevertheless survive there, often because they have evolved the ability to supplement their air supply directly from the atmosphere.

It is vital to ensure suitable oxygen levels in the aquarium, using artificial aeration if necessary. The return from the filter may supply the necessary turbulence, or an airpump and aeration device (an airstone or other diffuser) can be used. Most of the uptake of oxygen results not from the rising stream of bubbles but from the turbulence created as these break the surface. Filtration and aeration also serve to circulate oxygen around the aquarium. Do, however, beware of creating unnecessary turbulence in tanks housing fishes from still waters (generally with low oxygen content) as their bodies and finnage are usually adapted to conditions in their natural habitat, and they may find it hard work to swim in a miniature jacuzzi; the resulting long-term stress may prove harmful.

To conclude this chapter, a few additional do's and don'ts. Always follow manufacturers' instructions when using chemicals, test kits, and equipment. Never guess quantities when adding chemicals - measure accurately and test the result every time. Don't however, take test results as gospel if they don't make sense (for example a zero nitrate reading) – test kits often have a shelf life, and occasionally defective batches occur. If a test result differs dramatically from what appears reasonable, test again, with another kit if necessary. Finally, do always remember the immense importance of providing water which is correct in every respect, and if in doubt, always imitate nature.

Hardness Table				
1 English or Clark degree of hardness				= 14.3 ppm
1 French	"	"	"	= 10.0 ppm
1 American	"	"	"	= 17.1 ppm
1 German	"	"	"	= 17.9 ppm

(Note: English, French, and American degrees of hardness are a measure of calcium carbonate (CaCO₃), while the German is of calcium oxide (CaO).)

Foods and Feeding

As a beginner you may be tempted to buy only proprietary dried foods, of which there are types to suit almost every variety of fish. Huge amounts of time and money have been expended in ensuring that they provide all necessary dietary elements, and, of course, are palatable. They are incredibly convenient for the aquarist *but* . . . how would you like to live your entire life on convenience foods, or even chocolate bars? You need only feed flake and live foods simultaneously to see how much fishes appreciate the "wriggle factor".

First, of course, you must consider the requirements of individual species. In their natural habitats fishes consume a variety of items – other fishes, aquatic and terrestrial invertebrates, vegetation, and so on. Some are opportunistic feeders, eating anything remotely suitable that comes along, and have a generalized digestive system to match.

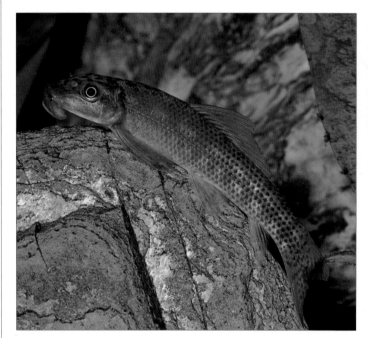

Above: Gyrinocheilus aymonieri (the sucking loach or Chinese algae eater), as the name suggests, feeds largely on algae growing on rocks and branches.

Right: Not all fishes feed from the surface in nature. Although most, like these barbs, will nevertheless learn to take floating dried foods in captivity, not all are physically capable of surface feeding. Such special requirements must always be considered.

Others are highly specialized, consuming only specific items (obligatory feeding), and have evolved intestinal tracts suited to digesting only the correct diet. Thus a piscivore (fish-eater) has a short digestive tract as its high-protein food is quickly and easily digested. A herbivore, by contrast, needs a much longer intestine to handle the large quantities of relatively indigestible food it needs to consume. Feeding either of these the other's food is akin to asking a cat to eat grass or a horse meat! In practice, a piscivore will refuse vegetable material, but some species which are normally herbivorous may gorge themselves on meaty foods, sometimes suffering short-term digestive troubles and long-term problems of obesity and fatty degeneration of the tissues, these in turn resulting in sterility and shortened lifespan.

Don't forget that fishes usually follow their natural instincts where food is concerned, perhaps eating items you hadn't intended as food – usually plants and smaller fishes, though ornamental snails and even bogwood may be attacked. Bottom-sifters can totally disrupt a decorated aquarium. Never

Top: Toxotes jaculator (the archer fish) is a highly specialized predator which feeds on insects that it "shoots" down from above the surface with a jet of water.

Bottom: Some fishes, like this *Corydoras adolphoi* catfish, are bottom-sifters. They require a fine, siftable substrate and small particles of sinking food.

Top: **Although live *Tubifex* worms are enjoyed by many fishes, their use carries a high risk of introducing disease; frozen or freeze-dried *Tubifex* are preferable.**

Bottom: **Paratheraps synspilum is a large herbivore which requires vegetable material in its diet, and may supplement this with aquarium plants if not fed properly.**

blame the fishes for behaving as Nature intended – it is your fault for not doing your homework.

Feeding strategies – where, when, and how fishes feed – are also important. Some feed at the surface, some in mid-water, others on or in the substrate. Many learn new habits in captivity – but some don't, especially if mouth position dictates feeding posture. Bottom-feeders may starve if offered floating food, or if all the food is eaten before any reaches the bottom; surface feeders, by contrast, may go hungry when sinking foods are given. Nocturnal feeders need to be fed after "lights out".

Food size is equally important. It should be small enough to be ingested and large enough to be worth the effort, but it does not end there. Don't expect a large lurking predator to chase around after small fry – it requires a single large prey item suited to its large mouth and hunting habits. A pursuit predator, by contrast, is often designed to capture smaller prey. Then again, a large mouth may denote a plankton feeder requiring small particles. More homework!

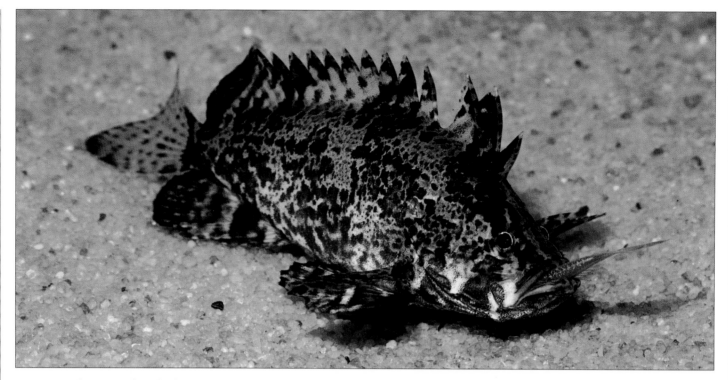

Notestes robustus, a brackish-water predator, polishing off a live fish. If you find the sight distasteful, obligatory piscivores are not for you.

You must consider whether your sensibilities will allow you to keep species that will eat only live prey, particularly live fishes. Don't try to convince yourself they will learn otherwise when they get hungry; if thousands of years of evolution have conditioned a fish to react only to live prey, it simply won't recognize anything else as food. It may perhaps learn eventually that anything you put into the tank is food, but then again it may not. It will certainly need live prey initially. So *never* buy a fish unless you can reconcile your conscience to feeding it what it needs.

While what to feed is largely a case of homework, how much is another matter, to be learned only by observing your particular mix of fishes. "As much as is eaten in five minutes" is an oft-quoted formula – all very well, but how much is that the first time you do it? The trick is to keep giving small amounts until interest wanes; and always siphon off uneaten food after every meal unless you have scavengers who will clear it up, in which case you must use your own judgement as to how much to leave.

How often should you feed? Well, that depends. If you have a piscivore which in nature eats one fish half its own size every other day, feed it that often. Fishes which feed continuously benefit from several small meals per day. Juveniles grow faster if fed more, and seasonal breeders need more to bring them into spawning condition. On the other hand, coldwater fishes kept in outdoor ponds shouldn't be fed at all during the colder months when they are inactive. Most aquarists overfeed, if only because feeding evokes a response from their pets. Perpetually bloated bellies, however, (except in gravid females) are as much a sign of ill-treatment as hollow ones.

The following are some of the different types of foods that can be used:

Dried Foods

There is no denying that dried foods such as flakes and pellets can, used sensibly, be a useful basis for the diet of many aquarium fishes, ensuring all the necessary proteins, vitamins, trace elements, and so on. There is an enormous choice available, and initially the best course is to buy the type which your fishes have been fed previously. Be aware of the dangers – apart from boredom – of using dried foods alone: unlike live foods they contain no coarse roughage, and fishes fed only on dried foods (especially by over-generous owners) often suffer digestive troubles and/or constipation, which can easily be fatal. Dried foods swell when thoroughly moistened, with potentially disastrous consequences if, as sometimes happens with greedy individuals, this takes place in the stomach. Avoid this by feeding sparingly when appropriate.

DRIED FOODS

Dried foods come in many varieties with different
shapes, colours, and sizes: this is just a tiny selection of
the different pellets and flakes available.

Koi pellets

Floating food hoops

Wheatgerm sticks

Spirulina flakes

Floating red pellets

Carnivore flake

Plant diet

Floating green pellets

Basic tropical flake

Goldfish food

Pond Foods

Most fishes relish anything that can be found swimming or crawling around in a pond (though for reasons of conservation do not feed them frogs, toads, newts, or their tadpoles). The most commonly used pond foods are *Daphnia* (water fleas) and bloodworm (midge larvae), both available commercially. Others – for example *Bosmina*, *Cyclops*, mosquito larvae, and, for larger fishes, water boatmen – you will normally have to catch for yourself. Some aquarists prefer not to use such foods for fear of introducing diseases and/or parasites, but this is highly unlikely, as ponds containing fishes (the source of diseases and parasites) tend not to have populations of live foods worth collecting! Do beware of predators such as dragonfly larvae and *Dytiscus marginalis* (the great diving beetle), which will eat small fishes and damage larger ones. Pond foods can be an essential element in conditioning breeding stock, and contain beneficial amounts of roughage. Many are now available frozen or freeze-dried (fishes appear to prefer the former).

Pond foods are much enjoyed by most fishes, and are excellent conditioning foods. *Daphnia* (water fleas) (*below*) are common in duck ponds, as are mosquito larvae (*bottom*), which can also be found in smaller bodies of water such as cattle troughs.

Other Live Foods

Earthworms, enjoyed by many fishes, can be fed whole or chopped to suit mouth size. Woodlice (collected) and crickets (bought) are suitable for larger mouths.

Whiteworms and grindal worms are small worms cultured in boxes of loamy soil. Starter kits can be obtained from dealers or by mail order. But feed only in small quantities as they can be fattening and constipating.

Tubifex are small red worms which live in mud (often around sewage outfalls) and are available from dealers. Always wash them before use. Although fishes enjoy them, you use them at your own risk, as their habitat makes them likely carriers of disease. Frozen or freeze-dried *Tubifex* are considered safe.

Before feeding to fishes, earthworms should be rinsed under the tap, or in a bucket of water, to remove any soil particles.

Culturing Whiteworms

1 Whiteworms can be cultured in a wooden or plastic box – large plastic food containers are ideal. Lay moist bread for the worms on the surface of the culture and cover with a piece of glass or perspex.

2 Keep the culture in darkness, but punch holes in the lid to allow for ventilation.

Foods and Feeding

42

Artemia (brine shrimp) nauplii can be hatched from eggs for feeding fry; adults can be purchased for larger fishes. They should be rinsed in fresh water before use, to remove salt residues.

Live fishes used as foods are usually surplus fry, deformed or damaged (*never* diseased) specimens, or cheap, readily available aquarium fishes (often livebearers and goldfish). There is always a chance of introducing disease, so this diet should be used only where essential; never use wild native fishes.

Hatching Artemia (*brine shrimp*)

Brine shrimp are usually hatched in clear, preferably glass, containers (such as large bottles) filled with salt solution, which should be made up according to the instructions accompanying the eggs. (In the absence of any instructions, use 25 g (1 oz) of marine or cooking salt per litre (2 pints) of water.)

The containers should be stood in a warm place 18-24 °C (65-75 °F) and strongly aerated so that the eggs do not settle (if they "clog" on the bottom, the hatch rate will be greatly reduced).

When the eggs hatch, usually after 2-3 days, the nauplii (baby shrimps) can be harvested. Turn the aeration off and stand a light next to the container so that an area halfway up one side is brightly lit. The shrimps will be attracted to the light and can be siphoned off (using airline tube) relatively free of unhatched eggs and empty shells, which tend to sink to the bottom or float on the surface. Strain the shrimps through a fine net (to avoid adding salt to the aquarium).

Always remember to turn the aeration system back on.

Cultures will remain active for only a few days, so 3 should be started at 2 day intervals to ensure a succession of shrimps. Each can then be restarted from scratch on its 7th day, for as long as required.

Frozen and Freeze-dried Foods

These are available from most dealers, and represent a safe and convenient way of feeding pond and other natural foods. Frozen foods are, however, expensive and have a high water content, while freeze-dried ones are not always enjoyed, at least not at first.

Frozen and freeze-dried foods

Frozen (*left*) and freeze dried (*right*) foods are a safe and convenient way of feeding "live" foods. Frozen foods come in bubble-packed blocks or in plastic envelopes; small organisms such as *Tubifex* and bloodworm are usually freeze-dried in cubes (*top right*), while larger ones, such as river shrimp, are processed singly (*bottom right*).

Human Foods

A number of excellent foods can be "borrowed" from the kitchen – ox heart, liver, prawns and shrimps, mussels and other shellfish, cooked chicken, raw and cooked fish, and cod roe for carnivores; cucumber, courgette, peas, lettuce, and spinach for herbivores. Beware of feeding too much mammalian protein, which can cause digestive upsets and fatty degeneration of the tissues.

A selection of human foods suitable for various fishes. As long as additives are avoided, the only real limitation is your imagination.

Last, but not least, always regard feeding time as an opportunity to observe your fishes: to make sure they are all present and healthy, and that they are all getting their share.

Equipment

Preliminary visits to local retailers will probably leave you aghast at the sheer quantity and variety of equipment available – and its cost! Let us re-assure you that you don't need to buy every available gadget and gizmo – no amount of expenditure on hi-tech equipment can buy success. Instead, supplement basic equipment with effort and observation. If you have doubts, remember that committed aquarists with multiple tanks could never afford all those gadgets for every one, yet they have healthy fishes and more fry than they know what to do with.

We have listed the items you need to get started, but the variety of different types available means you must make your own decisions about which kind to buy. Don't be afraid to ask your dealer for his opinion, or your hobbyist friends what they use, what they think of its reliability and convenience, and what they have to suggest by way of DIY.

The Tank

Obviously the first requirement is a tank. These are no longer made by fixing glass into an iron frame; instead sheets of glass are stuck together with silicon sealant, a by-product of the American space programme. This has made possible some interesting tank shapes, though they are not all as practical

Above: *Betta splendens* (Siamese fighting fishes) can be kept in small tanks as they can breathe atmospheric air. They should, however, have sufficient swimming space.

Right: Some fishes may jump during the dash to feed at the surface, and a hood and cover glasses are essential to keep them in.

Check that the tank has bracing bars along the top edge of the long sides. Tanks more than 40 cm (15 inches) wide will normally have bracing along the short sides as well, and those more than 1 metre (36 inches) long a central glass "strap" from front to back.

as the traditional rectangular box in terms of surface area and accommodating equipment. Acrylic tanks are also available, but scratch easily. There are branded glass tanks which usually have a trim concealing some of the joins, but your dealer may make his own (or have a local supplier) at a far lower price. You must decide whether the plastic trim is worth the extra! Always check that tanks are made from new glass of a thickness appropriate to their size, and that the upper edges have reinforcing bars and, for tanks of 100 cm (3 ft) or more in length, a cross-bar to prevent water pressure bowing the long sides. *Never* use this to lift the tank – always lift from beneath.

Tank Sizes

Metric tank sizes differ from imperial tanks i.e. the metric tanks are not the exact equivalent size of the imperial tank. The table below lists both metric and imperial standard tank sizes. These sizes have been quoted throughout this book.

Metric	Imperial
50 x 25 x 25 (cm)	18 x 10 x 10 (inches)
50 x 30 x 30	18 x 12 x 12
60 x 30 x 30	24 x 12 x 12
100 x 40 x 40	36 x 15 x 15
120 x 40 x 40	48 x 15 x 15
150 x 50 x 50	60 x 18 x 18
180 x 60 x 60	72 x 24 x 24

The Stand

Next you need something on which to stand your aquarium; this must be flat and level, and capable of carrying the load involved. The most expensive unit is the purpose-built cabinet, which usually includes an aquarium and has a cupboard underneath for equipment and storage. Alternatively, there are welded metal stands, or you can make your own from bolted angle or treated timber, but seek expert advice. You may have a suitable solid surface in your home. Unless you are using a purpose-built cabinet you will need to buy a piece of exterior-grade plywood the size of the tank bottom and at least 15 mm ($^5/_8$ inch) thick; and between this and the tank it is essential to have a 13 mm ($^1/_2$ inch) thick (minimum) sheet of expanded polystyrene. These can be obtained from a hardware store, and are needed respectively to distribute the load and cushion the tank against any unevenness.

The Hood

The next essential is something to keep the fishes in the tank, minimize water loss by evaporation, and exclude intruders (furry pets, children, and dirt). The most basic option is to obtain from a glass merchant one or more pieces of glass (cover glasses) cut so as to fit on the glass struts inside the tank. A proper hood, however, offers more protection against intruders, keeps wiring tidy, and accommodates lighting. Hoods can be purchased or made, but in the latter case remember that the materials and construction must be such that there is no danger of contamination. Those used for marine aquaria must be resistant to salt corrosion.

A hydrometer is essential if you intend keeping marines.

Heating

Unless you intend keeping coldwater fishes you will need equipment to maintain your tank at the right temperature. There are a number of options, and you must choose the one which best suits your needs. The most commonly used type is the combined immersion (internal) heater/thermostat; one problem with these, however, is that the thermostat usually lasts far longer than the heater element, so you may find yourself throwing away 50 per cent of your outlay unnecessarily at regular intervals. Separate thermostats, both internal and external, are also available, as are internal heaters and heating mats which go under the tank; remember, however, that if the latter type goes wrong you will be faced with either breaking down the tank to replace it, or using an internal heater instead.

Most thermostats are mechanical, operated by a conventional bimetallic strip opening and closing a set of electric contacts; the external type has to contact the tank side in order to sense the water temperature through the glass. Unfortunately these are sometimes affected by room temperature if this fluctuates significantly. Nowadays some external "stats" are electronic, with a sensor in the tank, but these are much more expensive and not necessarily more reliable. External stats are easier to adjust than internal ones – but beware of unauthorized adjustments by children!

The wattage of heating required depends on tank volume and ambient room temperature. Bear in mind that what suffices in summer may not be adequate at 3 am on a winter's night when the central heating is off. We suggest 50 watts per 30 litres (7 gallons) of aquarium water as a useful starting point, but try to err on the generous side rather

Filters range from the very basic (and cheap) internal box filter to highly sophisticated motorized units.

than risk chilling. The wattage of a heater makes little difference to its price, and a high wattage will heat the tank more quickly than a low one, costing the same but avoiding undue wear-and-tear on the heater(s).

Ideally, spread your eggs between two baskets and your wattage between two heater/stats: then if you don't notice that one heater element has failed, there will still be some heating; and if a thermostat jams on (more common than off) there is less chance of overheating.

Filtration and Aeration

Unless you are planning a heavily planted, low-population tank you will need a filter, and, for the marine aquarium, a protein skimmer. We have already discussed the various types on pages 29-31. Remember that filter volume and turnover rate should relate to aquarium volume, size and

A selection of heating equipment.

When selecting an air pump discuss your likely air requirement with your dealer before choosing a model of suitable capacity. Remember it is better to have too much rather than too little air. You will also need airline, a non-return valve for each pump outlet, and possibly some of the other accessories shown here.

number of fishes (and their appetites), and their preferences regarding water movement. If your tank is reasonably large it is worth considering having two small- or medium-sized filters instead of a single large one: their separate inlets can be better positioned to maximize waste intake; they can be cleaned out alternately to avoid loss of biological filtration; and if one breaks down there is still the other . . .

Don't forget to buy a supply of suitable filter media. Although there are various hi-tech types available (at a price), we suggest you use inexpensive media such as floss or foam in the first instance; alternatively aquarium gravel (coral sand for marine aquaria) makes an excellent medium (not just for UG filters).

Even if you do not expect to need additional aeration, and your filtration is power- rather than air-driven, we suggest you give consideration to the purchase of an airpump and some airline, if not at this stage, as soon as your pocket has recovered from the initial outlay. You may need it to operate a box filter or provide an air supply in a quarantine or hospital tank, to aerate brine shrimp hatcheries, to drive off chlorine from tap water, and for a thousand and one other uses.

Lighting

Although fishes generally look their best in natural light, it is difficult to arrange enough of this in the house to provide the average 12 hours per day needed by fishes and plants, and for a large part of the year it is not available in the evening - which may be the only time you are at home to enjoy your aquarium. Consequently you will require artificial lighting even if your tank receives some natural light. The most commonly used type is one or more fluorescent tubes inside the hood, controlled by a special choke unit. Use only chokes specifically designed for aquarium use – the ordinary domestic types lack certain safety features needed where water is involved. Chokes are designed to operate one or two tubes of the same wattage; unfortunately a 15 watt choke won't operate a 40 watt tube, so you must consider the likely amount of lighting required in advance. Tubes come in standard lengths/wattages, normal practice being to use a tube rather shorter than the aquarium, for example 60 cm (24 inches) tube (20 watts) for an 80 or 100 cm (30 or 36 inch) tank, and a 100 cm (36 inch) tube (30 watts) for a 110 or 120 cm (42 or 48 inch) tank. In tanks up to 40 cm (15 inches) wide and deep this will generally be sufficient for reasonable plant growth if a white light is used, and perfectly adequate for viewing the fishes. If you want to grow plants in deeper tanks, then give consideration to having two or more tubes to increase the amount of light penetrating to the bottom. Bear in mind, however, that this also increases the light in the upper layers, possibly to the discomfort of fishes from shady forest waters – if the lighting is too bright they may retaliate by hiding, although this can be overcome with a few floating plants. Marine aquaria are usually more brightly lit, this being necessary to encourage the unicellular algae needed as food by some invertebrates.

Special damp-resistant control units and tube leads are used for aquarium fluorescent lights; a variety of special tubes, which produce light in different areas of the spectrum, is available from good aquatic dealers, but ordinary domestic tubes can also be used.

Recent years have seen the development of spotlights for aquarium use, and these can provide a very attractive light and shade effect, allowing light to be concentrated where needed without over-illuminating the entire aquarium. Unfortunately they cannot be accommodated inside the standard aquarium hood, and also work rather better without cover glasses. Use only spotlights designed for aquarium use.

Tubes and spotlights come in a variety of types producing light in different areas of the spectrum. Those near the blue end favour plant growth, but don't necessarily optimize fish colours. Lights with a high ultra-violet output can be harmful to human eyesight and should be screened from direct view. Ask your dealer to show you different tubes in action and then decide on the basis of your personal needs and preferences.

Ancillary Equipment

You will need a variety of testing equipment. First a thermometer for monitoring temperature; two types are available – stick-on external liquid crystal displays, and conventional alcohol or mercury thermometers which are fixed to the inside of the glass with a sucker. Both are frequently of dubious accuracy; the glass type can be calibrated by taking your temperature (37°C, 98.6°F) and noting the degree of inaccuracy. You will also need test kits – ammonia, nitrite, nitrate, pH, and hardness – and, for marines, a hydrometer for measuring salinity.

Don't forget any items needed to adjust your tap water chemistry and quality, as previously discussed; salt for marines; peat for lowering pH; coral sand as an alkaline buffer; something to remove nitrates; and, for creating soft water in a

Remember that all equipment for the marine aquarium must be non-metallic.

hard-water district, a reverse-osmosis unit, an ion-exchange softener, or a water butt for rainwater.

Finally, various bits and pieces: two nets of appropriate size, in case you need to catch a fish; a siphon/gravel cleaner; at least one plastic bucket; and, if you need to store water, one or more plastic bins. Use only plastic items designed for aquarium use or human foods (home brewing bins are ideal): white or clear plastic is usually safe.

New or Secondhand?

On adding up the cost of these basics you may be tempted to consider secondhand equipment, but be aware of the potential problems: used equipment may carry disease; tanks may be scratched, electrical equipment defunct, near the end of its lifespan, or unsafe – and you have no guarantees or other comeback. Ideally see equipment working before buying. "Complete set-ups" at knockdown prices can be tempting, but usually include fishes – do you really want someone else's choice, and are you capable of moving an aquarium and reinstalling its occupants in a matter of hours? If you must buy secondhand it is better to do so from your dealer, who may sometimes have suitable equipment, with, because he values your custom, some sort of guarantee.

There are various test kits available on the market for testing the quality of your water, and they are all quick and simple to use.

Decor – the hardware

Aquarium decor is not just a matter of creating a beautiful underwater landscape to please the onlooker: it also provides shelter and shade for the fishes, as well as a means of hiding unsightly equipment. It can be roughly divided into three sections: background, substrate, and interior decor proper. In this chapter we deal with the "hardware", while the "software" – that is to say, plants – is covered in the next chapter.

The prime consideration when choosing decor must be the requirements of the fishes. It should not be harmful (causing unintentional alteration of water chemistry, or worse, poisoning by unsuitable materials), and it must satisfy their psychological needs; there is no point in providing plants for fishes from rocky biotopes, or vice versa.

Above: When constructing your imitation reef, whether from coral, tufa, or other rocks, remember to leave plenty of holes and crevices as refuges for small fishes.

Right: Hardware can mean rocks or bogwood in a planted tank, but to many aquarists it conjures up something more dramatic, such as this Rift Valley cichlid aquarium.

Background

Remember that fishes of suitable size for aquaria are often several stages down the food chain, so their natural preference is not for wide open spaces but for the proximity of shelter, often at the edge of their biotope. You must, of course, provide them with shelter that they can actually utilize (caves, plants), but it is also important to offer them the security afforded by a background representing the edge of the river, lake, or pool – generally a bank with exposed tree roots, a rock face, or perhaps a reed bed. The marine equivalent is a rock face or coral reef.

Few aquarists give sufficient, if any, consideration (other than aesthetic) to the essential matter of background, and we have considerable misgivings about freestanding tanks that lack even the basic reassurance of a wall behind. It is in the aquarist's own interests to provide security at the back of the tank (and perhaps the ends as well), for if fishes feel secure they will parade confidently around the tank. Otherwise they may be nervous and hide much of the time; deprive them of hiding-places to prevent this and they will respond by cowering in corners.

Backgrounds can be external or internal, though in the latter case they must, of course, also be non-toxic and not have any adverse effects on water chemistry. Internal backgrounds prevent any mirror effect from the glass, an important factor when it comes to photographing your fishes – many a photo has been ruined by reflections in the back glass. Roofing slates (real, not synthetic) can be stood and/or glued against the back glass, or slivers of rock can be stuck to it using silicon sealant. Cork tiles (the plain type, without backing) can represent an earth bank in rainforest biotopes. Coral gravel can be used to simulate the side of the reef. For those with the time and inclination, styrofoam can be sculpted, or fibreglass moulded, to appropriate shapes, then painted in natural colours (non-toxic). Obviously the background should be appropriate to the natural habitat of the intended occupants, and the rest of the decor should be an extension of it.

This type of background can also be used externally, or there are a number of simpler alternatives. The outside of the glass can be painted a plain colour; dark blue or green is often used for marine tanks ("the sea"), black or dark brown ("earth" or "rock") for freshwater. Even though a plain background of this sort is not entirely natural, it provides a solid and unobtrusive backdrop to the rest of the underwater scene. Light colours, by contrast, may dominate; they can hardly be said to simulate the security of the riverbank, and, while perhaps initially attractive to the human eye, the novelty soon wears off. Bear in mind that once paint has been applied it may be difficult to remove if you change your mind.

An alternative is to glue coloured paper or plastic sheeting (the above suggestions on colours apply equally here) to the outside of the glass. Although paper is cheaper, it is vulnerable to damp, and difficult to keep in place without the liberal use of glue – just as difficult to remove as paint, and visible through the glass. Plastic can be secured by spots of glue along top and bottom edges, where it won't show. Most dealers stock rolls of background, for sale in appropriate lengths. These are waterproof, but, like paper, flexible and thus difficult to keep in place. They depict underwater scenery, and in our view are horribly artificial when combined with the real thing. They are, however, much better than no background at all. There is no real restriction on what you use externally, provided you remember that it should offer security and be either unobtrusive or a match for the rest of the decor. Stained chipboard or plain dark carpet are two further possibilities.

Above: **A selection of background materials.** *Clockwise from bottom left:* **slate, styrofoam, cork tiles, freshwater and marine "background on a roll".**

Right: **Cichlids can be prevented from digging by using a pebble substrate, though it is unkind to thus inhibit their natural behaviour. Some cichlids may improvise bizarre spawning "pits" as these mouthbrooders have done with an empty shell.**

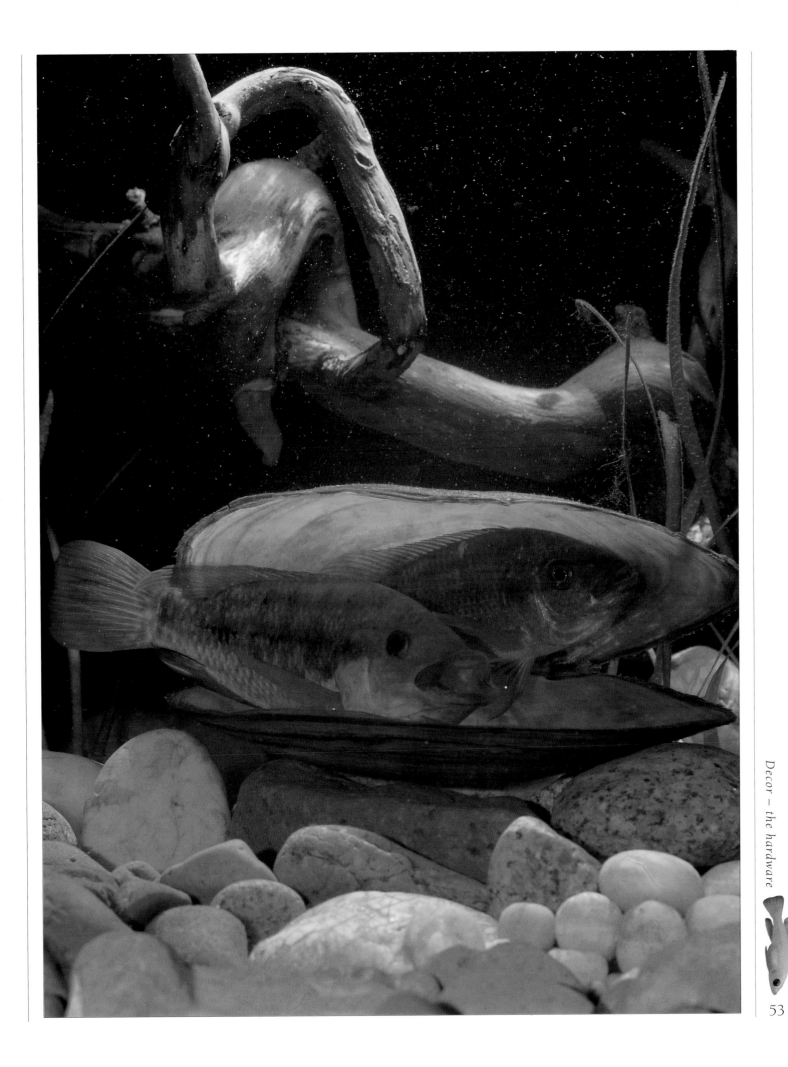

Substrate

A substrate is essential, not just because the aquarium looks unfinished without it, but because fishes do not live over bare glass in nature, and prefer a natural base to their world. It provides an anchoring medium for plants and other decor, and, even if UG filters are not used, a home for essential nitrogen cycle bacteria.

In freshwater aquaria the substrate is usually gravel or sand, while for marines coral sand (or coral gravel) is the norm, providing not only a natural setting (most tropical aquarium marines are coral fishes), but also an ever-present pH buffer. Unfortunately this buffering capacity has led to the use of coral sand for freshwater fishes from alkaline waters, and, by extension, occasionally for other freshwater species, regardless of their requirements. Although small amounts can be mixed with gravel as a pH buffer where appropriate, coral sand should otherwise be regarded as unsuitable for freshwater aquaria; its light colour leads to glare, resulting in timid and poorly coloured fishes, and its use can also produce outbreaks of scratching, apparently gill irritation caused by tiny particles suspended in the water.

Opposite: **Small coral fishes such as this *Pomacentrus coeruleus* (electric blue damsel) find refuge from predators in crannies in the coral reef. Similar hiding places are appreciated in captivity.**

Below: **Some Lake Tanganyika cichlids live in shells, and it is cruel to keep them without this type of shelter.**

Some killifishes, such as these *Aphyosemion sjoestedti* (blue gularis), require a substrate of loose peat to spawn in.

SUBSTRATE MATERIALS

Freshwater

Various different types of gravel are available for the freshwater aquarium. *Top*: black gravel is ideal for fishes from shady habitats. *Above left*: "ordinary" aquarium gravel. *Above right*: ungraded granite gravel – this is "hardness free" and thus suitable for soft-water set-ups. The varied grain size creates a more natural effect than with graded types.

Marine

Coral sand (*top*), and limestone chips (*above*) are suitable substrates for the marine aquarium. The latter can also be used in hard freshwater set-ups, but the use of coral sand for such aquaria is not recommended.

Gravel, like water, is of variable composition. It comes in various grain sizes and varying degrees of sharpness, not to mention different colours. Much aquarium gravel contains calciferous material which will increase hardness and pH, so for soft acid water aquaria you must track down some "hardness-free" sand or gravel. Remember that in shady forest streams the bottom is often covered with leaf litter, so fishes from such waters may prefer a darker substrate. Some fishes dig as part of their feeding or breeding procedure, and will have problems if the grains are too large for their mouths. Those which sift substrate through their gills when feeding may be harmed by large or sharp-edged grains. Fine sand clogs easily, and is not ideal for UG filtration. All these factors must be considered before making a final decision.

If you are using UG filtration a substrate 6.5–7.5 cm (2½–3 inches) thick is needed; otherwise about 4–5 cm (1½–2 inches) is sufficient. A 25 kg (56 lb) bag of gravel will provide roughly a 2.5 cm (1 inch) layer in a 100x40 cm (36x15 inch) tank. Some fishes are avid diggers, and this has led to the invention of the "gravel tidy", buried in the substrate to limit excavation. Remember it is unkind to prevent instinctive behaviour, and position any tidy so that some digging is possible. Gravel tidies can also cause problems with planting and with "bedding" rocks in place, so consider carefully whether you really need one.

Acanthophthalmus sp. (the Kuhli loach, *bottom left*) likes to burrow in the substrate, which should be of fine sand. The only problem for the aquarist, however, is that it may make them impossible to catch.

Interior decor

Here again all materials must be non-toxic, must not have any adverse effect on water chemistry, and be appropriate to the natural requirements of the fishes. For marines the usual materials are rocks and dead corals, and, for those prepared to satisfy its stringent requirements, "living rock" (live corals, molluscs, crustaceans and so on). The rock sold for use with marines is tufa, a highly porous, and thus lightweight, limestone which can be piled up into impressive structures. There is, however, no reason why other types of rock shouldn't be used provided they don't adversely affect water chemistry and contain no veins of metals or other toxic contaminants.

Right: Concern about damage to coral reefs has led to the manufacture of artificial corals for aquarium use. Once they have developed a coating of algae they look quite natural.

58 Bogwood provides shelter, resting places and nutrient for some fishes such as *Panaque nigrolineatus* (royal plec).

A selection of rocks suitable for aquarium use

Clockwise from right: Slate, sandstone, red granite, limestone, mica schist, banded gneiss. Limestone is suitable only for hard and salt water set-ups. Water-worn rocks, such as the red granite shown here, give a more natural effect.

The same applies to rocks for freshwater tanks. Tufa is popular for fishes from rocky habitats, but should be used (as should any calciferous rock) only for hard-water biotopes. A point not often realized is that it is too rough for use as a spawning substrate by many species which lay their eggs on a rock surface. Other rocks which may be suitable are granites, schists, slates, sandstones, gneisses, and many more. Rock is sold by weight and is not cheap, so you may be tempted to collect your own – but don't do so unless you are able to identify different types of rocks and spot any contaminants in them. Smooth water-worn pieces look more natural than jagged lumps.

Many cichlids, such as *Amphilophus citrinellus* (Midas cichlid), dig as part of their breeding behaviour. This behaviour can be prevented by covering the tank bottom with rocks and pebbles, but may in turn prevent successful breeding.

Rocky Shoreline (as for many East African lake set-ups)

1 Bed the foundation rocks firmly on the filter plate or tank bottom. Use large pieces whose weight will add to the stability of the structure.

2 Conceal flowerpots in bottom storey caves to help avoid substrate infilling from behind, deter unauthorized excavation, and provide an increased sense of security for the occupants.

3 Add the rest of the substrate, carefully infilling around the foundations with your fingertips, so that they are completely secure and safe.

4 Position the "roofing" slabs. Large pieces are often easier to fit securely and create a more stable structure.

5 Check that each superimposed rock fits tightly on the foundations. If necessary, experiment with different pieces until a good fit is obtained.

6 Continue to build up the rockwork, again checking the stability of each new piece, until the desired effect is achieved.

7 Bogwood is lighter than rock and useful for adding extra height (i.e. if you wanted to conceal any equipment) without overloading the structure.

8 Bogwood should be suitably "weathered" or varnished for alkaline water set-ups. The odd piece of "driftwood" is quite likely to occur in natural rocky settings.

Although this completed rocky decor looks bleak at this stage, the rocks will develop a coating of algae over time and thus a more mellow appearance.

The blind cave characin is the blind, albino, cave-dwelling form of a normally sighted species, *Astyanax mexicanus*.

Many catfishes, like cichlids, appreciate a cave for shelter. This is *Malapterurus electricus* (the electric catfish).

The amount of rock to be used will depend on the biotope you are trying to replicate, and may range from scattered stones on the floor of a forest stream to large and complex rockpiles representing an area of rapids or rocky lake shore. Stones can be used to support raised terraces of substrate material. Never position rocks on top of the substrate – always bed them in it so they cannot be undermined, either by substrate slippage or fish excavations. Always make sure rocky structures are solidly constructed so they cannot collapse, crushing fishes or crashing through the glass; consider sticking them together with silicon sealant for added security and stability.

Some fishes require caves as shelter and/or spawning areas, and these can, of course, be made from rocks. A popular alternative is to use clay flowerpots or drainpipes (which may, however, increase hardness and pH), or food-grade plastic pipe, which can be concealed under rocks or among plants. Always use new pots and pipes – old ones from the garden may be contaminated with pesticides or fertilizers. Resist the temptation to use shells as caves except for fishes which use them as shelter in nature – and then only in hard-water biotopes, as they contain calcium carbonate and will increase hardness and pH. Avoid ornate marine shells in freshwater aquaria as they look horribly out of place. The same goes for corals, which also increase hardness and pH.

Flowerpots and drainpipes make excellent "instant caves". It does not matter if they are broken!

Rainforest biotope simulations benefit from the use of bogwood, coconut shells, and cork bark. All of these will tend to leach tannins into the water, acidifying it and turning it brown; even in acid-water aquaria this can be too much of a good thing, so new materials of this kind should be "aged" by soaking, or leaving them outside to weather. Coconut shells should be free of fibre and nut residues. These wooden items can be varnished for use in alkaline conditions, but check that none of your fishes has a taste for nibbling wood, as varnish is toxic if consumed. Wooden items have a disconcerting tendency to float until thoroughly waterlogged, and may need to be wedged into place with stones.

The materials discussed above are natural ones, but there are also a variety of "artefacts" available. These range from excellent simulations of wood, virtually indistinguishable from the real thing, to plastic mermaids and shipwrecks, which can hardly be said to benefit the fish or help provide a natural underwater scene! For those lacking green fingers, or who want greenery able to survive the attentions of herbivorous fishes, there are plastic versions of most popular aquarium plants. Again these range from the remarkably realistic to the unmitigatedly

Stream Bed with Cork Bark Logs and Plastic Plants

1 Cork bark can be used to conceal equipment such as a UG filter uplift. It can be prevented from floating by wedging the bottom end in the substrate and the top under the tank's bracing bars.

2 Rocks can be used to prevent sideways slippage. As always they should be firmly bedded on the bottom, and large enough for the intended purpose.

3 A second piece of cork bark acts as an imitation log on the river bed. This time it must be weighted with slate attached to its underside, or with stones concealed inside.

4 Provided the water is added carefully, plastic plants can be added at the dry stage of setting up. As with living plants, groups of a single species often create a more natural effect.

5 The finished decor. Note there are spaces within the rocks and the cork bark, such as the "hollow log" for the fishes to use as hiding places. Algae will eventually grow on the rocks, wood and the plastic plants. While this may look realistic on the wood and rocks it should be removed from the plants by taking them out and scrubbing them.

Cork bark (*right*) and bogwood (*centre*) require careful preparation before use. Artificial wood (*left*) can be extremely realistic, needs no treatment, and has the added advantage that, unlike real wood, it doesn't float!

awful; fishes don't appear to be aesthetically affected, so the choice is up to you.

Never forget that in choosing and arranging your decor you must always keep the fishes' requirements – water chemistry, shelter, swimming space, and so on – in mind, and be prepared to forego any ideas which may please your eye but cause them physical or psychological discomfort. Your aim should be to provide them with a replica of their natural environment in which they will feel at home. They will reward you by looking their best.

Julidochromis (this is *J. regani* 'Kipili') are obligatory rock-dwellers which rarely stray more than a few centimetres from rocks.

Uaru will nibble at bogwood, which should therefore n e v e r be varnished for use in their aquarium.

PLASTIC PLANTS

Ceratopteris thalictroides
(Indian fern)

Ludwigia

Vallisneria

Ambulia

Some plastic plants – for example those at the top – are more realistic than the other examples below them. Greater realism can sometimes be achieved by positioning two plants together to create the effect of a single, larger, more vigorous plant.

Decor – plants

There is a great variety of plants offered for sale as aquatic plants. They fall into three categories: a) true aquatic plants, b) marginal plants and c) terrestrial plants, and it is important that you understand the difference between the three types. It is also wise to find out about the water conditions the plants like because, just as with your fishes, there are those that prefer hard, soft, acid, alkaline, or brackish water. Some will tolerate a wide range of conditions but there are others that have very specific requirements if they are to thrive, so it's homework time again.

True Aquatic Plants
These spend all their time submerged in water; so to remove them from it is to condemn them to death. They are usually sold as cuttings, and *Cabomba* is a prime example.

Marginal Plants
Marginals spend only part of the year submerged; during the dry season they grow out of water and most flower and seed at this time of year. The majority of our aquarium plants are from this group. Marginals may be sold as rooted plants, for example *Echinodorus* and *Cryptocoryne*, or they may be cuttings such as *Hygrophila*.

Above: Marginal plants, and those which are submerged for only part of the year in nature, are best grown in the paludarium rather than the aquarium.

Opposite: *Trichogaster trichopterus* (three-spot gourami) with a dwarf tropical water lily.

Decor – plants

In the "Dutch aquarium" plants, rather than fishes, are the most important feature of the display.

Terrestrial Plants

As their name suggests, these grow out of water, and can survive without being submerged at all. Although they can live for up to three or four months underwater, they are not recommended for aquarium use. Indeed some of them, for example *Dieffenbachia* (dumb cane), have poisonous sap but are nevertheless still offered as aquarium plants.

Caulerpa (*bottom of picture*), a kind of algae, is the only plant available for marine aquaria. Sea anemones (*top of picture*) are, of course, animals, not plants.

Purchasing

We need to treat aquarium plants with as much respect as fishes. Some are tropical, and therefore need to be kept warm. It is important not to chill them when bringing them home or by planting them in cold water because, just as a tropical houseplant will shed its leaves when chilled or, worse, curl up and die, so will your aquatic plants. Avoid buying tropical plants from cold tanks (feel the glass) or from trays of cold water (dabble fingers). Some plants, for example *Vallisneria*, get "transparent" patches in the leaves if they've been chilled. So long as they are kept damp and warm, they need not be submerged in water to carry them home. The plants you purchase may be cuttings, which are just lengths of stem with leaves and a growing tip but no roots, or they may be individual rooted plants.

Before going to buy your plants you need to plan, on paper, the layout for the aquarium and the plants you think will be suitable for each area. Just as importantly, pick the plants that you like because it is you that has to live with the finished aquarium. Check up on the size they grow to and the colours and textures of the leaves, and try to combine the groups of plants so that they complement each other. Murphy's Law states that when you go to your dealer he won't have all the plants you've chosen, but that really doesn't matter because you can leave a gap and add the others at a later date, building the plant stocks as carefully as you build the fish stocks because, just as too much fish waste can cause a strain on a new filtration system, so can too many dead leaves.

Having bought your plants and got them home, the fun begins. Lay the plants out in shallow trays of warm water so that you can easily see what you have – roasting tins are ideal for this. Check the length of cuttings and, if they are too long, trim them to the right length before planting. Cut the stems with scissors rather than pinching them with your fingers so that you avoid bruising – any tissue damage leaves the plant open to disease.

Planting
The substrate used for plants must allow the free passage of their roots and free movement of water. A fine gravel or coarse sand is ideal.

Whatever plants you have chosen the planting methods will be basically the same. Treat them as you would a garden plant – after all, your aquarium is to be a miniature underwater garden. Just as you would never plant two rose bushes in the same hole and expect them both to grow to their full potential, so aquatic plants should never be planted in bunches. Space the plants so that light can penetrate to the substrate and thus the lower leaves are less likely to turn yellow and die back. The distance between the plants should be the span of their leaves, and to achieve the effect of a wall of plants when viewed from the front, place the plants in staggered rows.

Not all plants need to be planted; some float and others require attachment to rocks or wood. *Microsorium pteropus* (Java fern) may be tied on to wood or rock with fishing line and eventually its roots will anchor it in place. *Vesicularia dubayana* (Java moss) is often left free until it finds its own anchorage point. Once established it grows prolifically and needs frequent trimming back.

In general, tall plants should be sited at the rear of the aquarium and smaller ones at the front.

Cuttings

The main plants sold as cuttings are *Cabomba*, *Myriophyllum*, *Synnema*, *Rotala*, *Elodea*, and *Hygrophila*. Of these, the fine-leaved *Cabomba* is probably one of the most popular aquarium plants for beginners, though it is also one of the hardest to succeed with. Its bushy, ferny appearance makes it ideal for hiding filter pipes and heaters, but this all too often means that it is in the most turbulent areas of water. Its fronds are delicate and easily damaged, so it is best used in a quiet area of the aquarium. The many *Hygrophila* species are far better suited to hiding pipes, as their leaves and stems are more robust and able to cope with the flow of water. So, once again, it's a case of doing your homework and checking on exactly what your plants need to succeed. If they are not growing well in one area of the tank don't be afraid to move them, but bear in mind that they will often take several months to settle – so don't expect instant rapid growth.

These plants feed mainly through their leaves, using their fine roots just to anchor them in the substrate; indeed, many will grow equally well if left floating free in the water and are thus often used as a spawning medium and hiding place for the subsequent fry.

Sometimes the cuttings offered for sale are taken at a time when the plant is growing above water. The stems are hard and woody, sometimes with hairs on them, the leaves are quite tough, and, when you hold them at their base, they stand upright (those that have been grown underwater flop down as they need water to support them upright). These woody cuttings can be planted in the same way as others but be aware that all the leaves will die off and you will be left with just bare

Plants such as *Cabomba* can be propagated by cutting off the top section and planting it. The rooted bottom section can be left *in situ* or replanted.

stems. Be patient. Shoots should appear from the leaf joints and as they grow you will notice that their stems are soft and their leaves may be a totally different shape and colour from the emersed leaves of the original cuttings. When they are long enough, cut off the shoots and plant as you would any other cutting – it is this underwater growth that you now need to propagate, planting each cutting individually and spacing the young plants so that light can reach the bottom leaves. What you have done is re-create the rainy season when the floods come and submerge the plants, thus encouraging them to grow in their submerged form.

***Microsorium pteropus* (Java fern) is a very hardy plant which will withstand low light levels and attacks by herbivores, and can be grown on the hard decor if digging is likely to be a problem.**

Rooted Plants

Rooted plants require a little more effort. Depending on the size of your aquarium, choose them with care. Some of the *Echinodorus* species (Amazon swordplants) can grow large – right out of the water in fact – but there are some which are manageable, notably *E. paniculatus*, which makes a nice specimen plant for the average-sized aquarium, and *E. tenellus*, (the pygmy chain sword), an ideal plant for the foreground as it will quickly carpet the substrate.

Cryptocoryne species are other favourites. Although they are slow growers and take time to establish themselves, once settled they will grow into attractive clumps of plants which will eventually need thinning out to maintain their vigour. Again, choose your plants with care as they come in many sizes and leaf colours.

Echinodorus species (sword plants) are popular aquarium plants from South America. They require good light to thrive. In nature they have an emerse period during which they reproduce by flowering.

Basket-grown Plants

These days many plants are offered as basket-grown specimens. These have been cultivated in nurseries, usually by mist propagation, whereby they are grown in very humid conditions. You have two choices as to how you plant these in your aquarium: you can either sink the complete basket in the substrate, in which case the plant roots will grow out through the holes in the basket into the gravel, or you can remove the plant from the basket. Personally we prefer to remove the plant and gently tease away the fibreglass growing medium from the roots. This is a time-consuming, painstaking job as you must try not to damage the roots. When buying *Cryptocoryne* plants you may find that what was purchased as one plant often turns out actually to be four or five smaller plants potted up as one. By planting them individually in the aquarium each will eventually grow into a good plant. One point of interest, and one of the main reasons for originally deciding to remove the plants from their growing medium, is that the fibreglass material is irritating to the fingers – what then might it do to bottom-dwelling fishes that rubbed against it? Some plants are grown in a papier-mâché-type medium: its drawback is that bits of it float around in the aquarium if fishes dig about in the basket. Another reason for removal of the baskets is that no matter how hard you try to conceal them, eventually they appear above the surface of the substrate, either excavated by fishes or because the sand/gravel has been moved by the flow of water in the tank.

Some pots actually contain several plants which should be planted separately. The *Cryptocoryne beckettii*, shown to the right, in fact consisted of the four smaller specimens seen below.

Some plants are sold in plastic pots, often containing rooting media which are "suspect" for use with fishes. If plants are to be grown in pots – for example to prevent disturbance by bottom-sifting fishes – they should be re-potted using gravel or sand, or compost topped with gravel, as the medium.

Below: This aquarium, with healthy plants of varying shapes and sizes – taken into account when designing the lay-out – is a pleasure to behold, as well as an ideal home for small, non-destructive fishes such as these tetras.

Bulbs and Corms

There are also various bulbs and corms that can be planted in the aquarium. Of these, *Aponogeton* and *Nymphaea* species are the best known. *Aponogeton* plants grow well, producing long, attractive leaves, and will even flower in the aquarium. If conditions are right, they may set seed which will eventually grow into new plants.

Nymphaea species are tropical water lilies and their one aim in life is to throw up lily pads and flower. This is fine if that is what you bought them for, but in your community aquarium such a lily would cover the whole of the tank surface, cutting out light to all your other plants. When these lilies start into growth, they produce a rosette of soft, pink to red underwater leaves which are very attractive. To maintain this lush underwater growth it is necessary to pinch out any leaf that heads for the surface. By doing this you will maintain the basal rosette but will never get any flowers: the choice is yours!

Above: Some plants, such as this *Anubias* species, have attractive coloured stems complementing the green of their foliage.

Below: Some dwarf tropical water lilies (*Nymphaea* species) are suitable for the aquarium, though they may shade/crowd out less vigorous plants. A large air-space above the water's surface is required for them to flower, and the blossoms are best viewed in an unhooded tank.

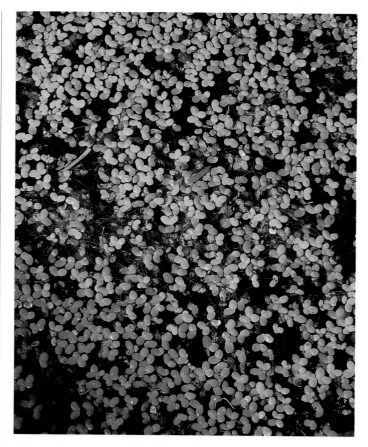

Floating Plants

Floating plants are rarely used in community aquaria as they reduce the light reaching other plants, but, like Java moss, they are very useful as spawning sites and hiding places in breeding tanks. Those most commonly used are *Pistia stratiotes* (water lettuce), *Ceratopteris thalictroides* (Indian fern), and *Riccia*.

There is, however, one floating plant to avoid: *Lemna* (duckweed), which will quickly multiply to cover the water's surface, cutting out the light to other plants. It also clogs filters!

A few fishes will eat it, but prevention is the best course. Check all plants for duckweed before you put them in the aquarium, to avoid introducing even a single piece. If you do get an infestation then net out every offending piece, and avoid transferring this pest to other tanks on your nets.

Feeding

All the rooted plants, including *Aponogetons* and lilies, need feeding with pellets of proprietary fertilizer or clay to promote healthy growth, but don't overdo it: one or two pellets per plant every month or so, poked into the gravel within the root run, is fine. If you keep rabbits or guinea pigs, their droppings are an excellent fertilizer, and come ready pelleted! Dry and store in a tin, for use as above.

Above: Lemna minor (duckweed) is a pest to be avoided at all costs...

Below: ...although it can be useful for deterring hatchet fishes such as *Carnegiella strigata* from jumping out of the water.

Although large cichlids (and some other fishes) are inimical to plants, most dwarf species are well-suited to, and require, a well-planted aquarium. This is *Microgeophagus ramirezi* (the ram or butterfly cichlid).

Lighting

Tropical plants require tropical lighting. In an ideal world they would get 12 hours of light and 12 of darkness, but as most people like to observe their fishes late into the evening the lights are usually on for longer than this. What many do require is more intense lighting than we would normally give them – the use of three 40w strip lights over a 120 x 50 cm (48 x 18 inch) aquarium works well. Use time switches so that they come on in sequence, ideally building up to a peak of intense light lasting for eight hours, and then go off in sequence, over a total lighting period of 12 hours. Lighting for plants must be compatible with the fishes' preferences; plants will reduce light by providing shade.

Some plants require more light than others – for example, some of the *Cryptocoryne* species require shady conditions, whereas water lilies require intense light if they are to maintain their pink or red colour. In this case plant the "Crypts" where they receive shade from a broad-leaved plant, and the lily in the open. It's just like gardening – if a plant needs shade you position it beneath a larger, broad-leaved plant.

Propagation

It is possible to propagate your plants. Some multiply readily, especially those, such as *Vallisneria* and many of the *Cryptocoryne* species, which throw out runners that root into the substrate, forming new plants. Other plants will grow from seed. Probably the easiest method for the beginner, however, is taking cuttings – you can venture into the more difficult realms of aquatic plant cultivation once you've gained some confidence in your ability to grow the easier types.

If your original cuttings are growing well and getting too tall, remove them and cut them to size, replacing the shortened top sections in the aquarium. The lower part of the stem can be planted in another tank and allowed to grow. Shoots that appear from the leaf joints can be nipped off when large enough and planted in the main tank.

Some of the *Rotala* and *Bacopa* species can be layered. Pin down the stem with a hairpin and within a few weeks shoots which can be used as new cuttings will appear from the leaf joints.

Other plants produce adventitious growths – small plantlets grow on the leaves. When these are large enough, they fall from the parent plant or can be removed and used as new plants. *Microsorium pteropus* (Java fern) and *Ceratopteris thalictroides* (Indian fern) use this method of reproduction.

Propagating *Microsorium pteropus* (Java fern)

1 Java fern produces long woody stems with clinging roots which attach the plant to suitable surfaces on rocks, roots, and branches. Groups of leaves grow all along the stem, which can be severed...

2 ....to produce two or more separate plants. These extra plants can then be planted in the substrate, ensuring that the crown remains clear of the gravel.

3 It is, however, better to grow this plant on rocks or bogwood. Secure each plant with thread or a rubber band, which is removed once the roots have established a grip.

4 In addition damaged leaves, or those which have become detached, will produce adventitious plantlets (*left*), and by the time the parent leaf has rotted away these are usually large enough to survive independently. Sometimes a leaf will produce only one or two plantlets (*right*) which thus grow more quickly and may be ready for planting while the parent leaf remains.

5 Secure the plantlets to a suitable surface as before. Alternatively the parent leaf, complete with plantlets, can be sited so that the plantlets can attach themselves naturally.

Algae

In the freshwater aquarium algae are considered a nuisance. No tank is ever completely free from them but they can be kept under control. When an aquarium is first set up with fresh water and new plants, it takes time for the latter to adapt to their new conditions, put out roots, and start to grow. Algae adapt far more quickly and an algal bloom occurs as they feed on the nutrients in the fresh water. At this stage the reaction of most people is to change the water and start again, but this will only aggravate matters as the new water will once again feed the algae.

As the higher plants begin to grow they feed on the nutrients and eventually outgrow the algae – you never get rid of all of it, but most of us think that a little bit of algae gives the aquarium a lived-in feel and some fishes certainly benefit from browsing on it. Various products are available to kill algae but they can be more trouble than they are worth. Unless all the dead algae are removed, they put a strain on the filtration system. It is far better to allow Nature to take its course and the tank to progress through the natural cycles. Achieving a fully planted aquarium with healthy fishes and plants takes time – months, in fact.

In the marine aquarium algae are of two types: unwanted and wanted. Beneficial algae, for example *Caulerpa* species, are grown to decorate the aquarium, while the unwanted algae are not really algae at all, nor are they bacteria, but belong to a class of their own, the Cynophycea. Commonly referred to as "blue-green algae" or "slime algae", they are often found when the water quality has deteriorated (even in freshwater tanks) as they are quick to utilize light and carbon dioxide to multiply, producing oxygen which can be seen as bubbles within the slime. During the maturation period, brown diatomaceous algae and hair algae may also be present but as conditions improve these algae should decrease. Attention to water quality is essential to prevent these unwanted algae from ruining your aquarium.

The beneficial algae may be purchased from your dealer. Buy as large a piece as you can afford as they can be difficult to establish. They attach themselves to rocks with a holdfast and "leaves" grow out from the runners. You should check on the fishes you intend to keep before purchasing the *Caulerpa,* in case they feed on algae.

As with the freshwater aquarium, successfully establishing these plants takes time and patience.

Vallisneria species propagate naturally by runners, and will eventually carpet the substrate. Young plants can be removed – ideally not until they are 7.5 cm (3 inches) or more high – without uprooting the parent plant, and replanted elsewhere. *Vallisneria* should always be planted with their crowns just above the substrate; if the crown is buried the plant will not thrive.

In sunlight, plants and algae (freshwater and marine) will produce visible bubbles of oxygen.

Pistia stratiotes (water lettuce) is an attractive floating plant best suited to open-topped aquaria or indoor pools.

Setting Up

Setting up your aquarium is not, we must warn, a five-minute job. Indeed, when we hear horror stories of tanks and fishes bought on the same day, we cannot help but wonder how it was done, unless the approach to the job was the same as that to fish-keeping in general – slap-dash!

Your exact plan of action will depend on the type of set-up you have chosen, the type of equipment, and other variables. We will take you through all the steps involved, but you may wish to alter the sequence to suit your own requirements. In any case, we strongly suggest that you make your own personal list of jobs to be done and keep it by you during the actual setting up. As things may get a little damp, it may prove sensible to protect it with a plastic bag or clear film.

Siting the Aquarium

Whatever your set-up and equipment, there are some preliminary considerations and preparations which apply in every case. First, before you even buy your aquarium, you must decide where you are going to put it – not just where it will fit, but the safety and accessibility aspects of its siting. Otherwise it may have a greater impact than intended on your household!

*Above: **Periophthalmus** (mudskippers) require a special aquarium with shallow water and exposed rocks or sand onto which they can climb.*

Right: The aim is to design your aquarium as a pleasing underwater picture.

Whatever base you are using for your aquarium must be able to carry the not inconsiderable weight you are planning to put on it. So must the floor beneath! Calculate the volume of your proposed aquarium (internal length x width x height) and use the table of weights and measures at the back of the book to calculate the weight of water involved. This may come as quite a shock – and there is the weight of the tank itself, the stand, and the hood to be considered as well. Equipment supplied specifically for supporting aquaria should have been designed with this consideration in mind; if you are building your own or using a built-in feature in your home, you should seek professional advice from a builder, carpenter, or engineer.

A professionally laid concrete floor should be capable of taking any load you are likely to put on it; the same is not, however, true of wooden floors. These are supported by load-bearing timbers (joists) which run at right-angles to the floorboards and can be located without taking up the floor by looking for the rows of nails where the flooring is nailed down. Heavy loads must be positioned *across* the joists so that the load is spread over several, rather than just one or two. The legs of the stand should be positioned above rather than between joists, as the load will be concentrated at just those four locations. If the stand cannot be positioned as indicated, then stand it on 5 x 10 cm (2 x 4 inch) timbers laid across the joists. You must also consider whether the flooring system can take the planned load at all. If in doubt, on either count, seek professional advice.

One further point, often forgotten until the tank is installed (when it is too late!), is the importance of checking that the proposed site is level – not just side-to-side but also front-to-back. Major irregularities must be compensated for, as otherwise the tank may be unstable; minor ones can be ignored, as long as you don't mind a sloping water surface bearing witness to the actual slope of the floor. Never use small wedges of wood directly under the stand legs as these may split or slip, with disastrous consequences. Instead use pads of exterior-grade plywood of appropriate thicknesses, and at least 10 cm (4 in) square, under the feet of the stand or cabinet. These can also be used to protect floor-coverings from the "stiletto heel effect". Do not use packing pieces if you are using cross-joist supporting timbers; instead plane the latter to size.

Consider whether the proposed location of the aquarium will be safe, for both the aquatic and the other occupants of the household. You do not want to be forever bumping into the aquarium, so there should be no protruding corners near walkways – an alcove is the ideal site. You also do not want accidents to livestock, or broken glass, water, and

Domestic furniture is rarely capable of supporting the weight of any but the smallest aquaria. This chest of drawers is visibly sagging.

fishes all over the carpet, so it should be out of the reach of unsupervized small children and boisterous pets, and of movable furniture such as chairs. If there is no electric wall socket close by, the mains lead must be fixed (with cable clips) to the edge of the floor or the skirting board, never left trailing where it could be tripped over, played with, or chewed. Likewise, make sure no other temptations – such as tins of food, external thermostats and filters, and so on – are left accessible to small fingers, and paws.

On the other hand, the tank should be accessible for viewing and maintenance. Think about the water supply. One of us once maintained 10 aquaria in a bedroom a considerable distance from the kitchen and bathroom taps downstairs, and with the benefit of hindsight, would not do so again! There will also be waste water to be disposed of. Spillages are inevitable when water is carried around – so, given a choice of rooms, perhaps the one with the old carpet would be better.

Preparing for Installation

Think about any help you are going to need when setting up. Unless you are confident about your electrical ability, consider asking a professional electrician to advise on the wiring; you do not want to lose your fishes – or worse, burn the house down – by getting it wrong. Alternatively, seek assistance from an experienced aquarist. Although we do not recommend that beginners do their own electrical wiring, it is important to learn how to

from an experienced person, so that you can, for example, wire in a new heater yourself later on.

All but the smallest tanks and stands are best moved by two people, so you will probably need an assistant in the early stages. You may need to organize special transport for a large aquarium, or arrange to have it delivered. Think about the help you *don't* need – arrange for the rest of the family, and pets, to be well out of the way during the proceedings. You will not want any smaller members of the household under your feet, and you may not wish a non-aquatic partner to see what gets spilt on the carpet. Apropos of which, put down plastic sheeting, or at least newspaper, before you start – there is bound to be some mess, so make it easy to clear up, and avoid permanent damage.

As you should have realized by now, there is a lot of planning to be done in advance. Likewise some of the work can be carried out before the actual installation of the aquarium; this will give you more leeway if something doesn't go quite as planned. Make sure you have all the equipment you will require – not just for the aquarium itself, but any necessary tools and accessories. A selection of tools and equipment, including screwdrivers, pliers, scissors, a sharp knife, plugs, cable clips, a spirit level (carpenter's level), insulation tape, and adhesive tape may come in handy. Do not, however, buy your plants in advance; they will not benefit from a period in a bucket somewhere, without proper light and, in the case of tropical plants, probably at the wrong temperature.

Making Decor Items

1 Composite decor items need to be prepared in advance so that the glue has time to dry. Terraces can be made by sticking rocks together. Apply silicon sealant to one rock...

2 ...and press the next firmly into place, securing with tape or rubber bands if necessary. Allow each join to dry before adding further sections.

3 Similarly bogwood – and cork bark – can be siliconed to pieces of slate which are subsequently buried in the substrate to prevent the wood from floating away.

USEFUL TOOLS

Tools and other
items needed for
setting up an
aquarium

Spirit level
(carpenter's level)

Scissors

Insulation
tape

Adhesive tape

Screwdrivers

Pliers

Cable clips

Screws

Craft knife

Remember that paints and glues take time to dry. So, if you are painting the back of your aquarium, or sticking something to it to provide a background, you will need to do so at least 24 hours before you can do anything else. (Unless, that is, you are using paper, or "underwater-scene-on-a-roll", which is best applied after the tank is in position, to avoid tearing.) The same applies to siliconing rocks together to form caves or terraces, and varnishing bogwood.

You can wash your gravel (or other substrate) as long as you have somewhere clean to store it afterwards; otherwise you will have to do this rather time-consuming chore on setting-up day, putting each freshly washed batch in the tank as it is ready. Do not skimp on substrate-washing; newly purchased material is often remarkably dirty, and you do not know what that dirt contains – it could be harmful. You must wash your substrate until the water runs clear. This can be done in a plastic

Washing Gravel

Gravel can be washed under the tap in a colander (*left*) or by stirring it vigorously with a spoon in a bucket of water (*right*). The latter method usually involves several changes of water before the gravel is finally clean enough to use, but it is nevertheless normally less wasteful.

colander (bought for the purpose, to avoid detergent residues – and because it will be fit for nothing but gravel-washing after you have finished) under the tap; or by quarter-filling a bucket with gravel and putting it under running water, stirring the gravel with, for example, a wooden spoon. Again the equipment should be specifically for fish-keeping, and not for anything else.

Make sure any other "hard" decor, for example rocks and flowerpots, is scrupulously clean; give everything a good scrub in hot, but *never* soapy, water – soap could leave poisonous residues. Even if you have nowhere clean to store these materials you can get the worst of the job done, and then a quick rinse under the tap will suffice on the day. Take this opportunity to give all rocks a final once-over to make sure there are no suspicious-looking metallic deposits or coloured crystals in them, and discard any you are unsure about.

As previously explained, all-glass aquaria require a baseboard topped with a layer of expanded polystyrene. This too should be prepared in advance. There can be problems persuading the three layers (wood, styrofoam, and glass) to align, and you may wish to avoid problems of this sort by attaching the styrofoam to the baseboard. *Never* use nails or tacks of any kind as these will act as tiny pivots and shatter the bottom glass; instead, use pieces of Blu-tac or double-sided adhesive tape, or a few spots of a suitable glue – that is, one which will not "melt" the polystyrene.

All rocks, flower-pots, bogwood, and other "dirty" items of decor must be scrubbed thoroughly before being positioned in the aquarium. A hard scrubbing or nail brush and plenty of water is all you will need.

Below: The coldwater aquarium can be just as attractive as its tropical counterpart, and a pleasing backdrop to its occupants, in this case lionhead goldfishes.

If you are collecting the aquarium yourself it is a good idea to take along the pre-assembled base-board to protect the bottom of the tank in transit. You should also make sure the tank cannot move around in the car, and protect the glass from knocks and scratching (blankets are useful!). Always lift tanks from beneath, never by the top rails or bracing-bar(s) which are likely to break or come off if subjected to strains of this sort.

Before the tank arrives, however, make sure you have uncluttered access to the house and the "site", and that you have plenty of room in which to work. It will be helpful to have two pieces of timber (say 5 x 5 cm (2 x 2 inches) x tank width) on which to rest the tank (and baseboard) while you install the stand, so that you can easily get your hands underneath to pick it up when the time comes to put it in place. You may wish to add the background at this stage.

Setting Up

When it comes to the actual setting up, obviously the first step is to locate the stand or cabinet (if used) in place. It must be stood squarely on the centre of any supporting pads or timbers; make a final check that it is level (in both directions) using a spirit level (carpenter's level), and that it does not rock (any slight unevenness, however, will be taken out by the load once the tank is filled). Make sure you have left enough space between stand and wall(s) to allow easy access, because you will at some stage need to put your hand into the gap when servicing or replacing equipment.

If you are using a heating mat, then carefully slide the aquarium off the baseboard until you can get your hands underneath to lift it, and put it to one side (on wooden bars, as already described); position the heating mat(s), normally with the cable(s) to the rear, and replace the tank on top.

Preparing and Installing the Tank

1 Cut a piece of styrofoam the size of the tank base. The easiest method is to use the tank as your template.

2 Place the tank on the styro-foam on the baseboard; you will probably need to have the board cut to size professionally when you buy it.

3 The styrofoam and board can be concealed with tape, or you may prefer a more elaborate method such as a mitred wooden frame for the entire front glass.

4 Once the aquarium has been sited on the stand or other base, make a final check that it is level in both directions.

5 Internal backgrounds such as cork tiles must be stuck in place well in advance so the glue can dry before the tank is filled. Apply silicon sealant to the glass and press the tiles into place.

Do not be afraid to use plenty of rockwork if designing a Rift Valley cichlid aquarium.

The entire assembly can now be carefully lifted into place on top of the stand (or other base). You should now install your background if you have not already done so.

Next position the undergravel filter plates (if used) *and* uplifts and start adding the washed substrate. If the UG plates don't cover the entire tank floor then hold them down while adding the first few bucketfuls, as otherwise they may slide around and pieces of substrate may get between them and the glass, spoiling the seal.

How much substrate material you add at this stage will depend on your plans for the decor, and whether or not you are using a gravel tidy. You may, for example, wish to bed rockwork down to the bottom of the tank (or the UG plates), and this is sometimes easier, especially with large rocks, if you put in just enough substrate to locate them initially; the rest is added once all your "foundations" and/or terrace supports are in place. You may decide to bend the gravel tidy under these foundations (not easy), or to cut holes in it to accommodate them (but you cannot then alter the decor if you don't like it!). We regard gravel tidies as more of a nuisance than they are worth; excessive digging is better remedied by burying pebbles or small

pieces of slate in the substrate as and when (and where) needed. Alternatively, nylon net curtain (bought for the purpose) is much more flexible than standard gravel tidies.

Large heavy aquaria require large solid bases.

1 Assemble the undergravel filter plate and airlift (if applicable), position in the aquarium, and add a 2.5 cm (1 inch) layer of substrate in which the decor can be bedded.

2 Any rocks – such as this pre-built terrace – should be bedded firmly on the filter plate or tank bottom. Flat-bottomed pieces of rock will be more stable.

3 Add the rest of the substrate material, filling in behind terraces to produce a tiered substrate effect. The surface should be slightly proud of the top of the rocks.

4 Check one more time that the rockwork is stable, and smooth out the surface of the substrate with your hand. The substrate will settle further once water is added.

5 Small light flowerpots do not need to be bedded on the tank bottom (large heavy ones do!), but are simply pushed into the surface of the substrate, making sure the entrance is clear.

6 Flowerpots are not normally found on forest stream beds, so achieve a more realistic effect by hiding them under natural materials. The slate attached to the bogwood (to stop it floating) is carefully worked into the substrate next to the "cave". This bogwood will also help conceal the heater, which will be positioned on the back glass.

7 Complete the hard decor with a piece of artificial wood, which will later be used to conceal the heater cable.

Hard Decor

The installation of the hard decor is one of the most enjoyable parts of setting up, and can equally be one of the most frustrating and irritating experiences, especially if you are using a lot of it. Even if you have drawn up a plan beforehand the materials may refuse to cooperate, or worse, the result may not be quite what you envisaged. Be prepared to fiddle around until you have created a scene you will be happy to live with for some time; the fishes may not appreciate your rearranging their home once they are in it.

Important points to remember are:

1 All rockwork must be securely positioned – rockslides are disastrous and must be avoided at all costs. Foundations of rocky edifices, whether a simple cave or complex pile, should have a reasonably flat underside and be securely bedded right down to the bottom, with plenty of surrounding substrate to retain them laterally. It should be impossible for digging fishes to undermine them; do not, however, worry if substrate is removed along one or two sides, as their weight, the remaining substrate, and any upper layers will keep them in place. Flowerpots are not strong enough to support large heavy rocks, and should be placed in, rather than forming part of the structure of, rocky caves. Ceramic drainpipes, however, are generally made of sterner stuff.

Heaters and heater/stats are normally held in place by special heater holders, which are attached by suckers to the back or end glasses. They can be installed either before or after the aquarium is filled. Multiple heaters should be evenly distributed to assist even heating. Remember that heat rises, so avoid positioning heater/stats vertically or they may switch off prematurely.

2 Superimposed rockwork should fit securely on to the foundations without rocking. Large pieces will be more secure than small ones, as their weight helps to hold them in place. Never lean superimposed rockwork against the glass, or rely on the glass to keep it in place. Beware of any edifice which could be knocked over – if there is any subsidence it will topple, perhaps injuring fishes, or worse, avalanching through the aquarium glass. These dangers can, of course, be avoided by siliconing rocks together, but if this is done in advance the final effect may not be quite what you had in mind, and if done *in situ* you will need to wait a few hours for the silicon to dry before proceeding further.

3 Until waterlogged (which will take several weeks) bogwood and cork bark will float, and (unless pre-waterlogged by soaking) must be wedged down with rocks. If this is not appropriate they can be anchored to heavy objects with cotton or nylon fishing line; this can be hidden by other decor, and removed later by snipping and pulling. Another method is to silicon a piece of slate to the underside and bury this in the substrate, whose weight will keep the wood in place.

Bogwood and plants make a pleasing backdrop to this *Helostoma temmincki* (kissing gourami).

A soft water community of Amazonian fishes.

4 When building terraces remember that substrate material, even with minimum current, will tend to the horizontal and will not take long to flatten out if you slope it. If you want to have different levels you must resort to terracing, using stones to support the upper layers. Even so, material such as gravel will tend to slip between these stones so that you eventually end up with a flat substrate with a wall sticking out of it! It is thus best to design your terraces in advance and silicon the stones of your retaining walls together.

5 Remember to leave spaces for heaters, filters, and other equipment, which will ideally be concealed behind the decor. We do not, however, recommend actually positioning these prior to arranging the hard decor, because of the danger of accidental knocks. Hot water rises, so, even with circulation by means of the filtration, it is best to position heaters just above the substrate to ensure a reasonably even temperature at all levels. Combined heater/thermostats should be positioned horizontally (or at no more than 45° to the horizontal) to avoid the thermostat reacting to rising heat and switching off prematurely. Heaters should not be placed where they may contact (and melt) plastic items, nor too close to plants.

Although you should design your "hardware" so as to accomodate any planting you have in mind, you obviously cannot add the plants until the aquarium has been filled with water, and, for tropical aquaria, warmed up to operating temperature. Plastic plants are, of course, another matter.

Adding Water

You are now ready to add water if you choose; this can then start warming up to room temperature (which will mean less wear and tear on heaters than expecting them to heat the tank from cold) and developing a population of beneficial bacteria. Meanwhile you can be organizing the electrics – perhaps postponing this until the next day if the work so far has taken longer than scheduled. Alternatively you may prefer to install all your equipment before filling the tank – this does have the advantage that there is no risk of getting electrical equipment wet. You do not need to "age" your water – it will be some time before you are ready for the fishes – before filling the tank, but you should treat it, if necessary, to remove nitrates, chloramine, and other pollutants, and soften it if required. You may also need to adjust the pH at this stage.

If you simply tip buckets of water into the aquarium you will disrupt the substrate where the cascade impacts; this can be avoided by placing a plate or bowl (well rinsed to remove every trace of detergent) on the substrate and pouring on to it. Alternatively, if you can manage to pour one-handed, use your spare hand to divert the stream just below the surface.

Place a plate on an open area of substrate, and carefully pour water on to this to avoid disturbing the substrate.

Electrical Wiring

We cannot over-emphasize the need for care when it comes to the electrical wiring, as water and electricity can be a lethal combination – hence the need for professional help. Under no circumstances should you attempt to wire anything yourself – call in a fully-qualified electrician. Once you are up-and-running you should always disconnect the electricity supply before working on the tank as even if the wiring is correct there may still be danger from a cracked heater or other equipment malfunction. In the U.S., make sure to use only "UL approved" devices, and ground all metal surfaces with green wire; especially the fluorescent lamp.

Although it is possible to buy "cable tidies" which wire all the necessary equipment into a single lead to the mains, we prefer not to have all our electrical systems – heating, lighting, and filtration – dependent on a single fuse in the plug at the wall socket. If this fuse blows then everything will go off; fishes might survive a chilling by itself, but chilling plus loss of filtration will be very stressful.

In addition, using a single fuse to protect several electrical circuits is bad practice and potentially dangerous – fuses should *always* be of a suitable rating for the device in question. For these reasons, instead of a cable tidy we recommend a rubber 4-gang multiple socket and individual, correctly fused (protected by circuit breaker), plugs for heating, lighting and filtration circuits. In the U.S. use a multistrip outlet which comes with one circuit breaker that protects the total current. The multiple socket should come ready-fitted with a fuse representing its maximum safe loading, to protect it against overload by the user; the total amperage of devices plugged into the socket must not exceed this rating. The plug connecting the multiple socket to the mains supply should be fitted with a fuse of the same rating. You should also fit a Residual Current Device (RCD) (Ground Fault Interrupter (GFI)) to protect yourself from electrical accident; if you switch off during maintenance, of course, you will be safe anyway, but you should take this extra precaution, to protect your family in case any interference does occur.

The multiple socket (in the U.S. multistrip outlet) approach is also more versatile: cable tidies and multiple sockets can both be screwed on to the outside of the hood (never the inside, as condensation is likely to cause electrical short-circuits), or sited in the cupboard underneath cabinet aquaria. With a multiple socket or multistrip outlet you can also unplug each separate item if it requires attention – for example you can unplug the filter and take it to the sink to clean it, leaving the heaters and lighting running.

A significant number of aquaria suffer terminal disasters as the result of someone unplugging the mains lead; the intention is usually temporary disconnection (for example while vacuuming), but it is all too easy to forget to plug the aquarium back in. A wise precaution against this is to place an explanatory label:"Aquarium – do not touch!" by the mains switch.

Adequate lighting is an important factor in maintaining healthy plants in the aquarium.

Installing Equipment

If you have opted for the multiple socket or multi-strip outlet approach the order in which you connect and install your electrical equipment is irrelevant; with a cable tidy, however, things are rather different, because there can be problems moving and repositioning all the equipment once it has been joined together. We suggest the following sequences. Do not attempt to wire the equipment yourself, ask a qualified electrician to do it.

Multiple socket

Wire up equipment and install.
Attach multiple socket or multistrip outlet (with mains lead fitted) to hood.
Fit hood to tank.
Plug in equipment.

Cable tidy

Connect any separate heaters and thermostats.
Install equipment.
Fit cable tidy to hood and wire in mains lead.
Fit hood to tank.
Wire equipment to cable tidy.

The cable tidy/multiple socket should not be plugged into the mains supply at this stage!

Hoods normally come complete with apertures (usually at the back) through which to pass various leads, as it is not a good idea to trap these between the hood and the tank glass – the resulting crimping can damage the cable. One disadvantage of using plugs is that they won't always go through the holes provided – and, of course, if you pass the cable through and then fit the plug, you are left

Xiphophorus (swordtails) are essentially hardwater fishes.

with your equipment irrevocably attached to the hood, just as with a cable tidy. This problem can be solved by cutting slots, of a width to take the cables concerned comfortably, in the bottom rear edge of the hood. If the hood is made of wood the cut surfaces should be sealed with varnish or silicon sealant. Keep the slots as small as possible – large holes may let fishes and water vapour out, and dirt in.

The installation procedure for individual items of equipment is as follows (but always read the manufacturer's instructions carefully as well).

1 Heating

If you have opted for combined heater/thermostats, simply wire the leads into the cable tidy or fit plugs if using a multiple socket (multistrip outlet). If you are using "separates", the heater (or heaters) is connected to the thermostat "power out" cable, while the "power in" cable of the thermostat is wired to the mains (cable tidy or plug). Silicon sealant can be used to good effect to waterproof and insulate the join between heater and "'stat". Even so, make sure the join is never immersed in the tank; ideally pass the cables on either side out through the hood and tape the join to the back of the latter, out of harm's way.

Position internal heaters and thermostats, fixing them in place on the glass with the heater holders which normally accompany them (but can be bought separately). Bi-metallic strip external thermostats are fitted at one end of the aquarium using a specially designed wire clip which fits over the rim. Electronic thermostats are usually attached in a convenient position on the hood, with the sensor fed through one of the wiring apertures into the aquarium. **External thermostats should never be put inside the aquarium**, and due care should be taken to avoid splashing them during tank maintenance.

2 Lighting

The control equipment (choke and starter) for a fluorescent tube is nowadays a single unit with a built-in on/off switch and special leads, with damp-proof (but not waterproof) "cap connectors", to fit the tube. Two clips to hold the tube are usually supplied. The tube itself has to be purchased separately. Start by screwing or bolting the clips to the required positions inside the hood; they should be located 7.5–10 cm (3–4 inches) from the ends of the tube when this is fitted – the next step. Screw the control unit to the outside of the hood, or fit it in the compartment provided (if any) and feed the tube leads through the holes provided (or purpose-cut) in the hood. Fit the cap connectors so that the pins on the ends of the tube are secure in the corresponding slots inside the connector. Wire the controller mains lead to the cable tidy or plug.

Spotlights, whether wall- or ceiling-mounted, come ready-assembled and need only to be screwed to the appropriate surface and connected to the electricity. You may wish to do this by plugging directly into a wall socket, given that the equipment is otherwise completely separate from the aquarium. The descending cable should be clipped to the wall, and, if desired, a wall-mounted on/off switch fitted.

The lighting in this aquarium perfectly displays the iridescent emerald green of the killifish, *Aphyosemion oeseri*.

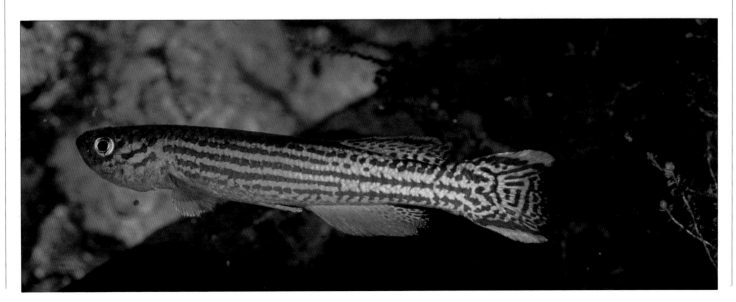

3 Filters

If the filter is one which has to be filled with one or more media, do this, following the manufacturer's instructions. Air-driven filters (including UG) need simply to be attached to the airpump via the airline (see (4) below). If using an external power filter, run the inlet pipe through the hood, using the suckers provided to fix it in place on the tank side; next hold the outlet pipe below tank level and suck on it until you hear or see water filling the filter chamber. The outlet pipe can then be located in the same way as the inlet; but if you are also using a trickle filter, position the tray(s), attach the spray bar to the power filter outlet, and fix in position above the (top) tray. Internal power filters are normally secured with suckers. Powerheads push-fit on to UG uplift pipes. Run any electrical leads through the hood (for internal equipment), and wire into the cable tidy or to a plug.

A Lake Tanganyika community. Similarly grand rockwork is required for some Lake Malawi cichlids.

Setting Up

An airstone can be fitted in the under gravel uplift tube (*above left*) to create a more efficient airlift – but one requiring more air pressure from the pump.

Airlines can be fitted to filters either before or after filling the aquarium, but until the air supply is connected the free end(s) should be secured above water level, or fitted with non-return valves, to prevent accidental siphoning.

An undergravel filter airlift in action (*above*).

Fitting a Powerhead

Powerheads can be fitted to UG filters already installed in the aquarium, but the top bracing bars of the tank may make this difficult. If this is likely to be a problem the equipment can be assembled beforehand and is then easily manoeuvred into place. Uplift pipes usually need to be shortened to accommodate powerheads, and can easily be cut using a small hacksaw.

Fitting an Internal Power Filter

Internal power filters are normally positioned, using the suckers provided, in one or both of the rear corners, with their outlets directed along the length of the aquarium. To restrict turbulence, however, the outlet can be directed towards the back or end glass.

Fitting a Sponge Filter

Sponge filters are best suited to small tanks, and are attached to the rear or end glass using the suckers provided. For optimum effect they should be positioned just above the substrate and angled as shown. The airline is easier to fit before rather than after installation.

Fitting a Box Filter

Box filters are normally located in a rear corner. If installed before the aquarium is filled they are likely to float when water is added; this can be avoided by pre-filling them with some of the water intended for the aquarium: those filled with light-weight media (eg. floss) will benefit from a layer of substrate material above or below the media.

Fitting an External Canister Filter

The inlet and outlet tubes are normally positioned at opposite ends of the aquarium to optimize water circulation and thus debris intake. The inlet – with strainer to exclude gravel, plants, and fishes – is attached to the glass using rubber suckers, with its opening close to the substrate. The outlet can be attached in the same way; or to a spray bar above the water's surface or over a trickle filter; or inserted in an undergravel filter uplift to power reverse-flow UG filtration.

Air Pump

The air pump should be protected from "back-siphoning" by a non-return valve (*right*) sited close to the pump outlet. The air supply can then be split between multiple devices using "gang valves" (*front centre*) which also regulate the amount of air to each device, in this case a wooden diffuser (*front left*) and internal box filter.

Starting a Filter

1 Powerful filters are sometimes started only after the plants have started to root, to avoid them being displaced by the current. External canister filters are started by the siphon principle, using a siphon starter attached to the outlet (as shown here), or by sucking on the outlet pipe. It is a sensible precaution to do this over a bucket.

2 Once the filter has filled with water, lower the end of the tube (still over the bucket!) below tank level so that the tube fills with water and all air is expelled. A thumb over the end of the pipe will keep air out and water in while the outlet is placed in the aquarium, thus reducing the likelihood of "airlocks" when the power is switched on.

4 Air pump

This should simply be connected to the cable tidy or a plug. Fit any necessary airlines to equipment (for example, UG filters, airstones) and pass out through the holes or slots in the hood. If more than one airline is to be used on a single-outlet pump then the supply must be split using special valves obtainable from your dealer. These fit together to form the size of set required; each set must have an end valve. There is a danger of the individual valves separating in use, and it is a wise precaution to secure them together with insulation tape round the entire set. They can be located inside or outside the hood; the latter usually makes adjustment easier, but this is not necessarily a good thing if you have children.

Air pumps are generally hung from the back of the hood or stood in the cupboard of a cabinet set-up. If an air pump fails for any reason (including powercuts) water may "back-siphon" along the airline, and empty part (or even all) of the aquarium water on to the floor, ruining the pump electrics in the process. Always protect against this by fitting a non-return valve in the airline close to the pump. Alternatively, the pump may be located well above water level, but it has to be said that an air pump on the living room wall is a poor substitute for a Rembrandt!

Having installed all your equipment, store the instructions, guarantees, and shop receipts in a safe place for future reference.

Starting the System

It remains to fix your thermometer in place and, if you have not already done so, to fill the aquarium with water as described above. Connect the mains lead to the electric supply and check that each device is working. Thermostat indicator lights should, with the tank full of cold water, indicate that the 'stat is on; if the heaters are working you should be able to see a slight current of rising water above each, or you can switch off the electricity after they have been on for a few minutes and feel each heater to see if it is warm. If the fluorescent tube fails to light up, try flipping the switch on the control unit!

External power filters sometimes have difficulty dispelling any air trapped inside. Switching off and on again a few times, and/or tipping them gently from side to side, normally does the trick. If not you will need to switch off and suck on the outlet

Installing the Thermometer
Internal thermometers (*left*) are best positioned after the aquarium has been filled, to avoid movement and possible damage as the water is added. External liquid crystal display (LCD) thermometers (*right*) can be fitted at any point in the setting up. Take care to get their positioning right, as they will not readily stick a second time, and often cease to function if moved at a later date.

pipe again. Make sure external filters are not leaking, and that trickle filters are emptying properly.

The air supply to the various devices may need adjusting using the valves; if you have a single air-driven item and too much air then, if the pump doesn't have a regulator, fit a double valve in the airline and use the spare to bleed off excess air. This is preferable to the alternative of clamping the airline, which increases back-pressure between clamp and pump and may shorten the life of the pump diaphragm. Over the next few days you may have to tinker with the air supply until it is in perfect balance – it is part of Murphy's Law that air supply initially alters spontaneously without any intervention by the aquarist!

You will probably have to alter the setting on your thermostat(s) at least once before the temperature stabilizes at the desired level. Some 'stats have temperature scales on their adjustment dials, but in our experience these do not always bear much relation to the temperature actually achieved! Expect the 'stat to have a range of 1–1.5°C (2–3°F) between switching on and off; more than that and we would be inclined to take it back to the shop and change it.

Planting

When working temperature has been reached you can buy and add your plants. Once these are installed you should start lighting the aquarium for at least 12 hours each day, and it is a good idea to get into a proper lighting routine so that it becomes habit before the fishes arrive. You should always allow a period of external light (daylight or room light) both before switching the tank light on

and after turning it off at night. Sudden changes from "night" to "day" are highly stressful (causing shock), and while "day" to "night" isn't quite so dire, many species will be stressed if forced to spend the night in the open because they had no warning of its approach. If you are likely to be away at "dawn" or "dusk" it is worth having a time switch to operate the tank light and a room lamp on another timer, which is set to come on and go off twice daily at times appropriate to simulate dawn and dusk.

The Maturation Process

You will need to allow about 10–14 days between filling the tank and adding fishes, during which the filtration system will develop the population of bacteria necessary for biological filtration (filter maturation period). At some stage during this period a very high nitrite level will occur; when nitrites have reduced to zero after this peak it will then be safe to begin introducing fishes to the aquarium. It is essential that you ensure the peak has been passed (it might take longer than 14 days) – so monitor nitrite levels every day during this maturation period.

If you fail to take this precaution and add fishes as soon as working temperature has been reached, you will almost certainly experience a phenomenon known by aquarists as "New Tank Syndrome", which is the technical term for the production of fish corpses by means of ammonia and nitrite toxicity. You do not, however, need to monitor ammonia levels as these peak before nitrites, which are thus the critical factor in establishing whether or not the tank is mature.

The bacteria will need something to feed on as they develop, otherwise the minimal numbers present in the water won't increase. There are various ways of achieving this. A small piece of raw meat can be dropped into the aquarium and left to decay, or a pinch of flake can be dropped in daily.

It is now possible to buy special additives which speed up the maturation process - but always monitor nitrite levels rather than relying on time estimates on the container. An alternative solution is to obtain a couple of handfuls of substrate from a mature (and disease-free) tank which can be sprinkled on your substrate to act as a bacterial starter culture.

If you have to clean out your tank at some time in the future, it is worth noting that "used" substrate material, if rinsed clean in cold water, retains a good population of bacteria and tank maturation will be appreciably quicker than it was with new substrate the first time around. Likewise an active filter can be transferred to a new tank, in which case maturation takes very little time at all. Even so, it is always advisable to monitor those nitrites in any newly set-up tank.

Planting

1 Tall plants such as these *Echinodorus* (Amazon swords) are normally sited towards the back of the aquarium, and can be used to help conceal cables and pipes. If possible allow them enough room to spread their leaves in all directions.

2 Small plants can be sited nearer the front, and again used to camouflage unnatural items such as flowerpots. Always check with your dealer that the plant you like is truly aquatic and will flourish under water.

3 It is often more effective to plant groups of a single small species – here *Cryptocoryne beckettii* – close together, instead of a mixture. Do not overplant – in a few month's time what may seem initially sparse should burgeon into an underwater garden.

Finishing touches

1 Once all the decor and equipment is installed fit the condensation tray (or cover glass(es))...

2 ...and finally the hood. It is also advisable to cover the aquarium during any pauses in the setting up, to exclude dust as well as intruders such as insects, pets and children.

3 The water will be slightly cloudy initially; this will normally clear after a day or two, certainly before it has matured sufficiently for fishes to be introduced.

Marine and Brackish-Water Set-Ups

The first thing to consider is the size of your aquarium. It is far easier to maintain a large body of marine water in good condition than a small volume. The minimum recommended size for a marine tank is 100 x 50 x 50 cm (36 x 18 x 18 inches) - if you can accommodate something larger so much the better.

The techniques for setting up marine or brackish water aquaria are exactly the same as for a freshwater tank. The main difference is that you are dealing with water which has had salt added to it

Left: **A mature marine aquarium, with coral fishes, "living rock", and** *Caulerpa*, **is a stunning spectacle.**

Below: **Although relatively few brackish water fishes are available, they are diverse enough to present an interesting and attractive picture.**

and is therefore more corrosive, so you need to avoid using any metallic objects in the aquarium. The breakdown of metals in water can poison your fishes, so extra care is needed when setting up your aquarium.

Ensure that buckets, colanders, spoons, and so on used in preparing water, washing substrate, or whatever, are plastic. If you are using external thermostats, stick them to the aquarium glass – do not hang them over the side of the tank by the wire hanger provided. Likewise heater/thermostat clips –even the clips used to hold fluorescent tubes in the hood – should be non-metallic.

The Water

For the majority of us, the practicalities of collecting our own clean seawater are impossible, as we may live too far from the sea or the seawater may be polluted. Manufacturers can now supply salt to create artificial seawater with the correct balance of minerals for fishes, so that all that needs to be done is to mix the salt with tap water according to the manufacturer's directions until the correct specific gravity is achieved.

multiplied by the number of bucketfuls. Put the required amount of salt (in accordance with the manufacturer's instructions) in a plastic bucket.

2 Mix the salt with water so that it is at least partially dissolved before adding to the aquarium. During partial water changes – as opposed to initial filling – the salt should be completely dissolved so that the correct aquarium salinity is achieved virtually immediately.

1 Calculate the amount of water required – as the decor occupies part of the aquarium volume, and accuracy is essential, the easiest way is to fill the aquarium using a bucket of known volume which is then

3 Check the aquarium salinity with a hydrometer after initial filling and then after every partial water change and evaporation top-up.

Specific gravity (SG) is measured using a hydrometer and is a scale showing the total amount of dissolved salts in the water. This can also be measured in grams per litre but in the hobby is usually expressed in terms of SG. The SG varies with the water temperature, for example, a salinity of 17.2 gm per litre gives an SG reading of 1.020 at 15°C (50°F) and 1.017 at 25°C (77°F). The range we require for marines is 1.021 to 1.024 at a temperature of between 24° and 25°C (75° and 77°F).

For brackish-water fishes the SG can vary considerably as these fishes may be found in anything from virtually fresh to almost totally marine waters. Most are estuarine species, so the salinity they experience can vary from hour to hour as the tide comes in and goes out. In the aquarium, it has been found that mixing salt to half the strength recommended for marines works very well for brackish-water species.

When evaporation occurs, it is pure water that is lost; the salts remain in the aquarium, so do

not top up the aquarium with more salt water or you will increase the SG. At times of high evaporation, that is midsummer, top up the aquarium with fresh water. If you are carrying out a partial water change and refilling with fresh salt water, ensure that you check the SG. A well-fitting cover glass will reduce the amount of water lost through evaporation.

It is very important to check the nitrite and ammonia levels during the maturation period and ensure that your filtration system is beginning to function efficiently. The length of the maturation period will vary from aquarium to aquarium and there is no really successful way of speeding it up to any great degree, so just be patient and let nature take its course – slow and steady is far better than fast and dangerous! The use of a protein skimmer in the system is beneficial as this helps to reduce the amount of toxic waste at an early stage; indeed, many marine aquarists would not consider a set-up complete without a protein skimmer.

Lighting

The amount of lighting required depends on what you intend to keep in the marine aquarium. For the purposes of this book, we will be dealing only with fishes, so the amount of light required is simply what is sufficient to see them by. If you are considering marine invertebrates the lighting becomes a whole new ball game and you will need to do your homework in other, more specialized publications. For the majority of aquaria, a combination of two fluorescent tubes will be adequate, say a daylight and an actinic blue. "Gro-lux" may enhance the colour of the fishes, but red light is absorbed first by seawater so it will not illuminate your aquarium as well as the actinic blue, which will penetrate the water furthest.

Decor for Marine Aquaria

The best substrate for a marine aquarium is coral sand. However, this is expensive and many people like to use a coarser substrate of crushed tufa as a base and overlay it with coral sand. In order to avoid the sand disappearing between the larger pieces of rock, place a gravel tidy over the first layer of substrate before adding the coral sand.

Tufa rock can form the basis of your "reef". It is a very crumbly rock and cannot be glued together, so be sure to seat the pieces well. Fishes dig, and if they undermine your structure this can have dire results such as cracked tanks, flooded living rooms, and a great deal of explaining to be done to the non-fishy members of the household! So seat the rocks securely on the bottom, and build carefully

Below: "Living rock" may include a fascinating variety of organisms such as this tubeworm, but also unwelcome invaders such as small crabs. Marine invertebrates are even more delicate than coral fishes.

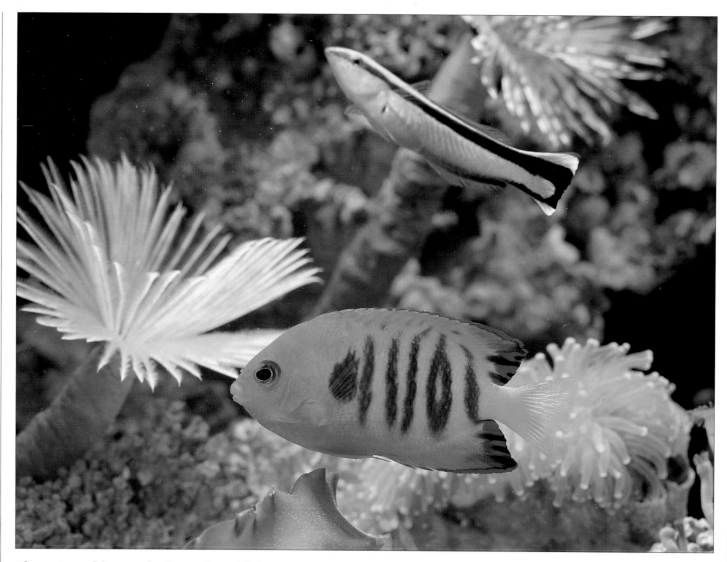

The variety of form and colour of coral fishes is almost endless. Here we see *Centropyge loriculus* (flame dwarf angel) (*bottom*), with corals, fan-worms, and *Labroides dimidiatus* (cleaner wrasse) (*top*).

using large pieces that interlock well rather than a lot of smaller, easily dislodged pieces.

An alternative to tufa rock is lava rock, which is darker in colour and of a different texture. Depending on the type of fishes you are keeping, you may also like to add clusters of giant barnacle shells to provide hiding places for smaller species. If you use other shells, ensure that the fishes cannot become trapped in them. Dead corals are available but the ethics of using them is down to the individual. Some have been obtained by destroying a reef, killing the coral and bleaching it clean for use in the aquarium, while others are collected by hand so that only prime specimens are used. A far more environmentally friendly substitute is artificial coral. Once this has a growth of algae on it, it blends in quite nicely.

Whatever final design you use, ensure that there is a free flow of water around the aquarium. The rocks will be hiding the heater/thermostat but you still need to be able to get at this should it fail without having to demolish the decor. It is also essential that water flows over the heater so that it does not overheat and burn out.

Your "reef" can be enhanced by the addition of some pieces of "living rock" but make sure that you have high enough lighting levels to maintain it. Living rock is now being cultured artificially in an effort to conserve natural reefs.

Decor for Brackish Aquaria
Rocks, plants and wood may be employed as decor for the brackish-water aquarium, but check that the plants are salt-tolerant before using them. Brackish-water aquaria normally have the appearance of a freshwater biotope, with all the possible variations that may entail; the main difference between fresh- and brackish-water aquaria is that the water has salt added and it is therefore necessary to take care to avoid metal fittings in the system.

1 The background should be appropriate to the planned occupants; coral reef "background on a roll" is available.

2 Install the undergravel filter plate(s) and uplift(s) if this type of filtration has been chosen.

3 Add a thin layer of substrate material (coral sand is used in this set-up).

4 Bed the foundation rocks (tufa is used here) firmly into the substrate so they rest on the filter plate (or bottom of the tank). Use large stable pieces of rock to create a solid basis for the imitation reef.

5 Add the remainder of the substrate, filling in between the foundation rocks. Roughly level the surface of the substrate by smoothing it out with your hand.

6 Build up the "reef", ensuring each piece of rock seats securely on the layer beneath. The importance of stable rockwork cannot be over-emphasized even when working with tufa.

7 Add corals and any other decorative items, again ensuring these are securely positioned.

8 The finished decor. Once algae have grown on the rocks and corals the "reef" will look far more natural than it does at this stage.

Buying and Adding the Fishes

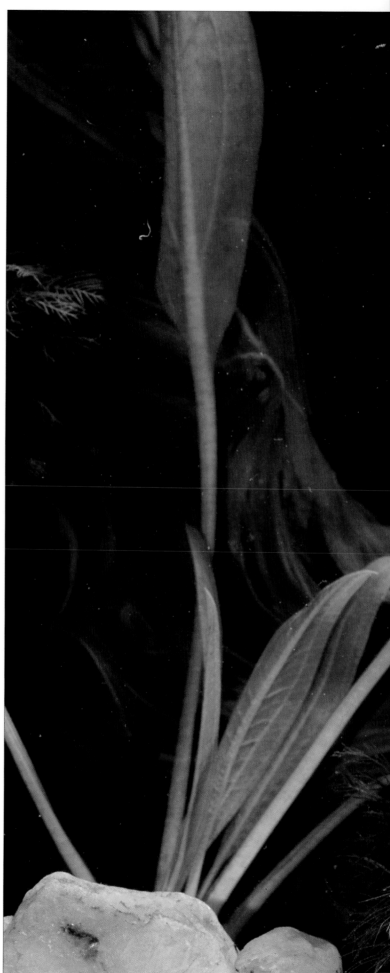

While your tank matures put the final touches to your shopping list of fishes, perhaps visiting local shops to check what is available – and resisting any temptation to buy! You can, if you wish, reserve fishes, but expect to have to leave a deposit or even pay in full. It is, however, worth reserving only unusual species not generally available; remember too that come "the day" you may be left with the poorer-quality specimens no one else wanted.

You should already have calculated the number of fishes your aquarium can accommodate; you must now decide whether to introduce them all at once, or in stages (remember the filter will have to adjust to the increased loading). If you intend buying juveniles you will be imposing only a fraction of the planned eventual load, and can add them all at once. It may, however, be sensible to introduce adults in two or three batches with a few days between. It is usual to introduce marines a single fish at a time.

Before we discuss buying and introducing fishes, a few words on stress. Being caught, bagged, transported, and released into a strange environment is a highly stressful experience for a fish.

Above: Puffer fishes are found in fresh, brackish, and sea water so make sure you get the right type for your aquarium. This is *Tetraodon palembangensis*, a freshwater species.

Right: Poecilia species (sailfin molly). The raised dorsal fin of the displaying male has been damaged and regenerated at the front. This fish would never win prizes, but will not pass on its defect to its offspring.

When buying a fish, ask the dealer to trap it between net and front glass, then make a final check that it is a good quality, healthy specimen. This is a standard procedure so do not be afraid to insist.

Bags should be "cornered" for small fishes, to prevent them being trapped and injured. Right to left: bag with welded corners, corners tied with rubber bands, corner being taped "square".

Stress can kill, so minimize the upset. Avoid buying fishes which have just arrived at the retailer's as they need time to recover from that last upheaval.

Pick a quiet time for your shopping, when the dealer can give you his or her undivided attention. When buying fishes you are perfectly entitled to choose specific individuals, although in practice if there is little difference between most of a particular batch it is more appropriate to reject instead of select, simply refusing any which are deformed or undersized. Ask the dealer to hold each fish in the net against the tank front while you give it a final once-over. Never buy from a tank containing diseased or dead fishes – the rest may be dead in a few days. Be particularly selective if buying breeding stock: you want only the best, as poor quality parents usually produce poor quality fry which you won't be able to sell.

Left: Fishes should be transported in darkness to keep them inactive and to avoid stress. Brown paper bags are commonly used for this purpose.

Below: An insulated container – this is a styrofoam "fish box" – is useful for maintaining the correct temperature during transportation.

The dealer will pack your fishes in polythene bags, usually putting these in brown paper bags or a carrier so the fishes won't be frightened by what is going on around them. Fishes more than 7.5 cm (3 inches) long, and adults of territorial species (for example cichlids), should always be bagged singly to avoid murders in transit. If the dealer won't comply, shop elsewhere! Ideally take along suitably sized lidded buckets for very large specimens.

If you will be travelling some distance ask the dealer to "double-bag" (in case of leaks) and to fill the air space in the bags with oxygen. For long journeys, or in very hot or cold weather, take along an insulated container – a "cool box", a cardboard box lined with styrofoam, or a proper fish box borrowed from a friend. If you are buying a lot of

Buying and Adding the Fishes

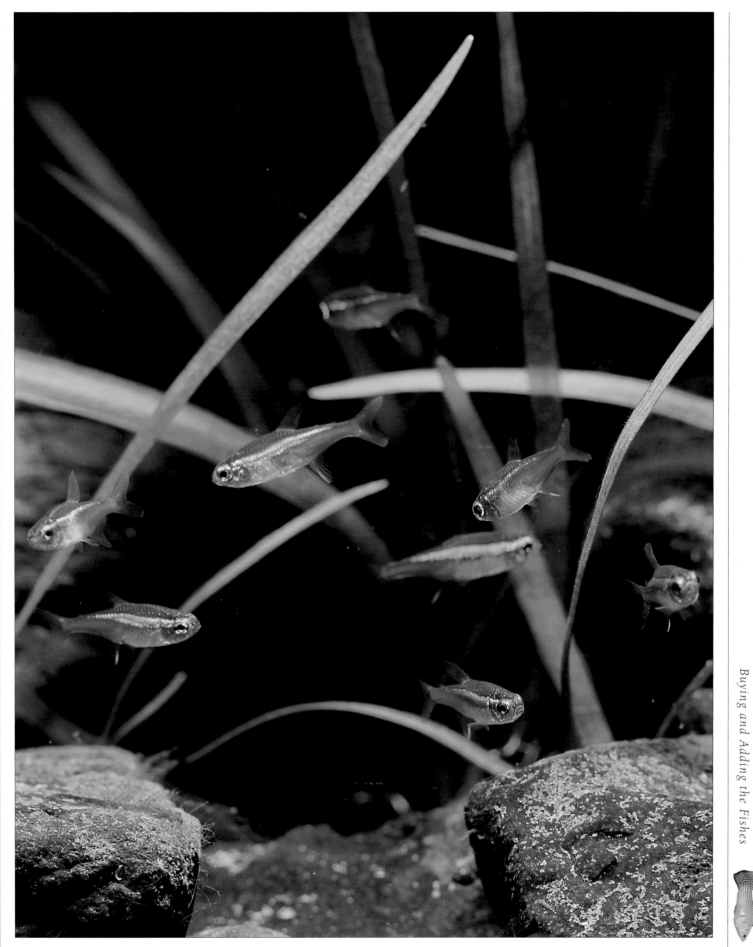

Paracheirodon innesi (neons) should be kept in a shoal – but don't expect them to all face the same way.

fishes most dealers will supply a box if asked. Head for home straight away, and resist the temptation to keep checking the fishes in transit – every time you let light in you will be causing stress.

On arriving home, remembering the need to avoid undue stress, keep handling to a minimum: take out each bag in turn, undo it, and float it in the tank to let the temperatures equalize. Secure the top by trapping it with the hood or clipping it to the tank edge with a clothes peg, otherwise it may sink and release the fishes prematurely. Repeat this process for the other bags. Equalization normally takes only minutes; check with a thermometer, and once the temperatures are within a degree or so of each other the fishes can be released. The longer a fish is floated, exposed and with nowhere to hide, the greater the stress, especially when the tank is already occupied by inquisitive fishes. Submerge the top of the bag, ensure it is wide open, then gently tip the fishes out. Always check they are all free!

Although you will be eager to watch your new pets, they will be frightened and confused, so turn the tank light off; the room light (or daylight) will suffice for them to settle in. Next morning turn the room light on about 30 minutes before the tank light, and make this part of your normal routine. Never the other way round; sudden changes from "night" to "day" (and *vice versa*) are extremely stressful. Resist the temptation to feed your fishes for the first 24 hours; let them recover from their upheaval, then feed lightly, gradually increasing daily rations to maximum, so that the filter can take up the additional loading.

Subsequent Additions

If, after a few months, you want to add another fish or two (only if this doesn't mean overcrowding), you won't want to risk introducing disease, so it is worth investing in a quarantine tank. This must be large enough for its temporary inmate(s) and set up and matured as for a permanent aquarium, except that decor can be rudimentary, just enough to provide shelter. The water chemistry should be what the newcomer has been used to; adjust it (if necessary) to match your aquarium during the quarantine period (normally two to three weeks). This period will also allow the new fish(es) to recover from transit and adapt to your routine before meeting future tankmates.

Introducing New Fishes to the Aquarium

1 Undo the bag and float it in the aquarium to let the temperatures equalize. Secure the bag (for example with a clothes peg) so that it cannot sink and release the fishes prematurely.

2 When the temperatures are approximately equal (within a degree), submerge the neck of the bag, holding it wide open with one hand, and gently tip the fishes out.

Above: This quarantine tank contains just the basics for the physical and psychological well-being of its occupant(s): heater/'stat and (UG) filter, and decor which provides shelter but leaves the fish(es) visible for observation.

Always check nitrate levels (and remedy if necessary) before introducing new fishes to an established aquarium; your fishes will have adjusted gradually to any slow increase in nitrate, but a newcomer may suffer toxic shock if suddenly exposed to a high level. Many mystery deaths in new fishes are probably due to this.

Finally, sooner or later you will visit a retailer's and fall for a fish about which you know nothing. The temptation to buy it will be overwhelming, but you must resist – our golden rule about doing your homework first never ceases to apply!

Below: Some fishes are attractive and charming as small juveniles, and are often mistakenly purchased for community aquaria. Unless you do your homework you may end up with a "monster" like this *Astronotus ocellatus* (oscar).

Keeping them Healthy

General Maintenance

Maintenance is largely a matter of continuing to apply the principles learned when setting up your aquarium, thus ensuring continued optimal living conditions for your fishes. What is needed, and how often, depends on the individual aquarium and its occupants, and must be determined by you, the aquarist; the routine suggested below is suitable for the average general community.

Daily: Check temperature, health of fishes, and that equipment is working.

Weekly: Make a 25 per cent water change, siphoning any accumulated debris from the substrate surface. Remove dead vegetation. Check nitrite level.

Monthly: Clean filter(s); "hoover" gravel if necessary. Check nitrate level.

Remember to adjust the chemistry and temperature of "new" water to match tank conditions, and to eliminate any nasties such as chlorine. Filter and substrate maintenance disrupts bacterial populations, so reduce feeding for a couple of days before and after monthly maintenance sessions.

For routine maintenance you will need a bucket and a piece of tubing for siphoning off water from the aquarium. Optional extras are a gravel cleaner (*bottom right*) and siphon starter (*centre*), though many aquarists start their siphon simply by sucking the tube.

Right: Bottom-sifting *Corydoras* catfishes may suffer damage to their delicate barbels if kept over a coarse substrate.

Siphon off the required amount of water, using the siphon to remove any "mulm" (accumulated debris) and other detritus. Take care not to siphon off fishes or plants! If the tank is sited near a window or outside door, it is quicker, with less risk of spillages, to siphon on to the garden using a long tube, instead of into a bucket.

The substrate can be "hoovered" periodically with a gravel cleaner, taking care not to uproot plants. Avoid excessive hoovering, however, especially where under-gravel filtration is used, as it disrupts populations of beneficial bacteria living on and in the substrate.

When refilling, pour the new water into the palm of your hand to avoid disturbing the substrate and decor. Alternatively stand the bucket on the hood and siphon the new water into the tank.

Obviously, action is required if any check reveals a problem. Counter high nitrite with twice-daily 25 per cent water changes until the level returns to zero; identify and eliminate the cause(s) – for example over-feeding or inadequate or interrupted filtration. An increase in nitrates suggests a need for larger (maximum 30 per cent) or more frequent water changes, or adjustments to the tank population or feeding regime.

The importance of regular observation of the fishes cannot be over-emphasized; abnormal behaviour – loss of appetite, clamped fins, increased respiration, scratching or shimmying – is usually the first warning of an environmental problem or outbreak of disease. Prompt action may make all the difference.

Diagnosis and Treatment of Illness

There are three main points to remember about illness in the aquarium:

1 At least 95 per cent of illnesses are environmental rather than pathogenic (caused by an outside organism). Moreover many pathogenic diseases remain dormant unless the fish is weakened by environmental factors.
2 There is no point in medicating a fish unless you know exactly what is wrong.
3 Prevention is better than cure.

Point **1** is a bitter pill to swallow when you have tried to provide optimal conditions; many aquarists find it impossible to accept, and continue to kill their fishes while laying the blame elsewhere. A small closed ecosystem is, however, extremely vulnerable to imbalance or overload, even in experienced hands, so always suspect environmental causes (unless pathogenic disease is obvious); even if water quality checks out OK an extra water change does no harm, and often effects a cure.

Point **2** may sound obvious, but many aquarists panic when a fish falls ill, administering a succession of patent remedies in the hope of hitting the right one. The resulting chemical brew is more likely to poison the entire aquarium. Remember that fishes, like us, suffer organ failure, so a single corpse is a reason for concern, but not alarm. If more fishes become ill, and you cannot identify the cause, seek help from other more experienced aquarists or your vet, who should be able to arrange post-mortem diagnosis. Few vets routinely offer this service, so discuss the possibility before the need arises.

1 Unplug the filter from the mains, carefully remove it from the tank, and take off its top. Lift out the dirty media. This can be a messy job, and is best performed over the sink or bath – or outdoors if weather permits.

2 Remove the media from any refillable internal containers. Part (no more than 50%) of the used media can be discarded if desired. The remainder should be re-used to maintain continuity of bacterial action.

3 Rinse the remaining media (in this instance, filter floss) in a bucket of tank-temperature water (ideally tank water) to remove the worst of the dirt. Thoroughly rinse out the filter canister and any internal containers.

4 Refill the internal containers with recycled and replacement media.

5 Replace the containers in the filter canister.

6 Replace the top and secure. The filter is now ready to be re-installed in the aquarium.

Keeping them Healthy

Once a specific disease is diagnosed you can normally obtain the appropriate medication from a dealer, or, in the case of prescription drugs, the vet. Always follow any instructions to the letter, not only using the correct dosage, but completing the full course of treatment; otherwise you may destroy active pathogens, but not those waiting to hatch. Avoid medicating healthy fishes by treating non-infectious patients in a hospital tank (your quarantine tank in another guise) or by "spot treatment" (for example for fungus), after which the fish is returned to the community.

Remember that some medications – for example copper-based treatments – are toxic to some fishes.

Some may harm plants, marine invertebrates, and beneficial bacteria in your filter, and should, where possible, be used only in the hospital tank.

Prevention (point 3) includes correct setting-up, suitable maintenance, quarantine of all new arrivals, and constant observation of your fishes. But beware of "transferred hypochondria", a serious malady which affects all aquarists at some stage, leading them to imagine their fishes are suffering every ailment in the book. Not wishing to encourage this, we will cover only a few of the commonest problems here:

Symphysodon species (discus) are particularly prone to Hexamitiasis (hole-in-head disease).

Constipation

Symptoms: reduced appetite; minimal or no faeces; the fish may have a slightly swollen abdomen and/or rest on the bottom of the tank.
Cause: incorrect diet or over-feeding.
Treatment: half a level teaspoon of magnesium sulphate (Epsom salts) per 4.5 litres (1 gallon). If the fish recovers, improve the diet.

Dropsy/"Malawi Bloat"

Symptoms: swollen body, especially the abdomen, due to build-up of fluid in the tissues.
Cause: environmental, or organ failure. "Malawi bloat", which affects East African mouthbrooding cichlids, is caused by excessive salt (sodium chloride) levels, high nitrates, or unsuitable diet.
Treatment: none; remedying the cause occasionally effects a cure.

Fin-rot

Symptoms: fin membranes disintegrate and the rays become inflamed.
Cause: bacterial, triggered by poor water quality or injury to the fins.
Treatment: remedy the cause; spot treatment with gentian violet.

Fungus

Symptoms: white fluffy growths on body/fins.
Cause: fungus attacks areas where the protective mucus coating is damaged by injury, parasites, or environment.
Treatment: remedy the cause; spot treatment with gentian violet, or use an aquarium fungicide for major outbreaks.

Gill Parasites

Symptoms: scratching, laboured respiration (both, however, normally symptoms of environmental problems); in severe infestations heightened colour, glazed eyes, and loss of motor control as oxygen shortage affects the brain.
Cause: usually flukes (*Dactylogyrus*).
Treatment: "Sterazin", from aquatic dealers.

Hole-in-Head

Symptoms: white stringy faeces; sometimes enlarged, pus-filled sensory pores on the head. Affects mainly cichlids.
Cause: *Hexamita*, an internal parasite normally harmful only when the fish is weakened by other factors (age, stress, environment).

This *Colisa sota* (honey gourami), seen here in a "hospital tank", is distended through dropsy.

A *Xiphophorus* species (platy) with a patch of fungus on its head, probably following an injury.

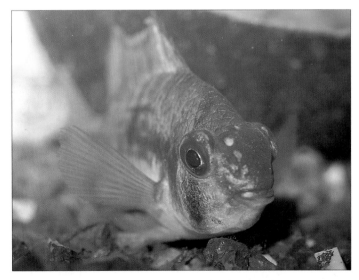

This *Microgeophagus altispinosa* is suffering from Hexamitiasis (hole-in-head disease).

A *Gasterosteus aculeatus* (3-spined stickleback), its belly distended with a tapeworm. Internal parasite infestations are not usually so obvious.

Exophthalmus (pop-eye) is usually triggered by poor water quality.

Treatment: metronidazole ("Flagyl") or di-metronidazole (prescription drugs); 50 mg per 4.5 litres (1 gallon) mixed with water before use; repeat after three days.

Intestinal Parasites
Symptoms: emaciation despite good appetite; worms sometimes protrude from the vent.
Cause: various species of intestinal worms.
Treatment: a suitable anthelminthic (from the vet) administered in food.

Large Skin Parasites
Symptoms: scratching; individual parasites are visible on skin.
Cause: fish lice (*Argulus*) are round and almost transparent, lying flat against the skin; anchor worms (*Lernaea*) are worm-like, attached at one end; leeches are also roughly worm-like but attached at both ends. All are more common in ponds than in aquaria.
Treatment: remove with tweezers, and apply antiseptic to the site. For serious pond infestations treat with 1.125 – 1.8 mg per 4.5 litre (1 gallon) of Metriphonate (an insecticide).

Life Cycle of the Fish Louse

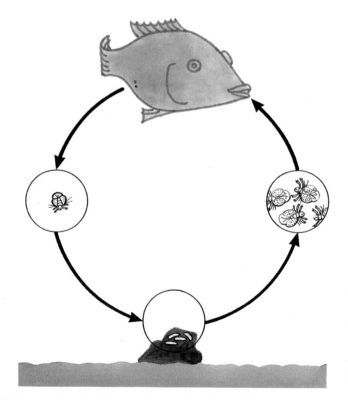

Adult Argulus (fish lice) cling to the skin of fishes. Mature females leave the host and lay their egg capsules on any hard surface; the young hatch after 4 or more weeks. When mature they seek out a host fish. Treatment of the water is effective against adults and juveniles.

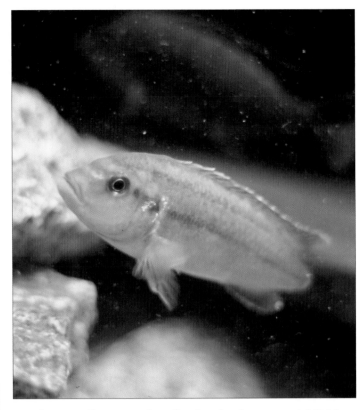

Fin damage (for example, after battles between cichlids) often leads to infection with bacterial fin-rot. Severe cases can result in death or permanent deformity.

Pop-Eye (Exophthalmus)
Symptoms: the eye protrudes from its socket, which is inflamed.
Cause: usually environmental, rarely parasitic (which is incurable).
Treatment: correct water quality/chemistry. Recovery may take several days.

Skin Slime Disease
Symptoms: scratching/shimmying; a fine grey coating on body/fins.
Cause: parasites of the genera *Costia*, *Cyclochaeta*, and/or *Chilodonella*; these generally attack only when the body mucus has been affected by poor environment.
Treatment: use a proprietary remedy; correct water quality/chemistry.

Swim Bladder Disease
Symptoms: loss of balance, swimming upside-down or on on side.
Cause: a) swim bladder bruised during handling, fighting, or breeding; b) bacterial infection, usually associated with poor water quality.

Life Cycle of the Anchor Worm

Life Cycle of the Fish Leech

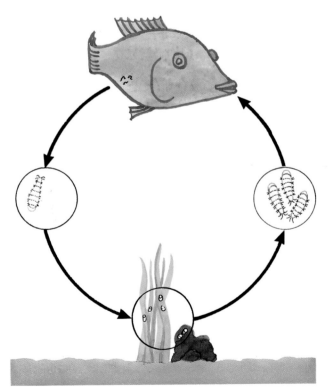

Females anchored to the host's skin release eggs into the water. Juveniles seek out a host and moult before attaining maturity. Males die after mating, leaving the females to renew the cycle. Adults can be removed manually from the host, while juveniles can be elimated by treatment of the water.

Adult leeches suck their hosts' blood, but detach themselves to lay eggs in oval cocoons on rocks/plants. The young leeches need to find a suitable host to survive. Control is by removal of adult leeches from the fish, and of decor which may harbour eggs.

Treatment: transfer fish to shallow water; for b) improve water quality and treat the fish with a broad-spectrum antibiotic. If there is no improvement after a week, consider euthanasia.

Velvet
Symptoms: a golden velvety coat on body/fins; scratching, increased respiration.
Cause: the parasite *Oodinium*.
Treatment: use a proprietary remedy.

White Spot
Symptoms: tiny white spots on body/fins; initially few, increasing dramatically after a few days.
Cause: the parasite *Ichthyopthirius*.
Treatment: use a proprietary remedy.

Finally, we suggest you do not keep a medicine chest. Buy medicines only when you need them, as you will then be less likely to panic dose unnecessarily or incorrectly.

"White spot" or "Ich" is caused by the parasite ***Ichthyophthirius multifiliis***, and is probably the most common disease of aquarium fishes.

Life Cycle of White Spot

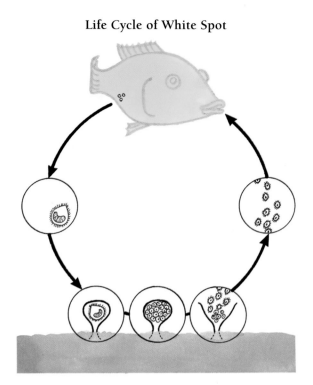

The single-celled parasites lodge under the skin of the host, breaking free when mature and encysting on the bottom. Each cyst attaches to the substrate while cell division produces more than 1,000 new, infective, parasites within. The cyst ruptures, releasing these to seek out a host. Only this infective stage can be treated effectively.

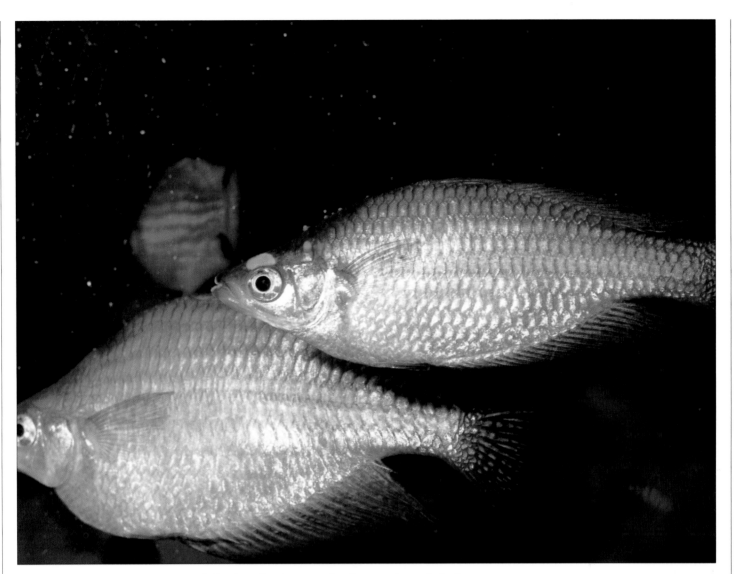

Melanotaenia species (rainbow fishes) with a bacterial infection (*Myxobolus*).

Other Crises

Euthanasia

Sooner or later you will need to destroy a fish which can no longer function properly as a result of illness or old age. The quickest and most humane method is to sever the spinal cord by cutting down hard just behind the head using a sharp knife. If you can't face the task, consult your vet.

Equipment Failure

Keep spares of items which go wrong commonly and suddenly, for example heater, air pump diaphragm. In the event of major failures – tank breakage, filter breakdown – at unsociable hours, seek help from the fishkeeping friends you should have made (including your dealer).

Power Cuts

Notify the electricity company of the loss of supply and get an estimate of duration. Keep tanks warm with blankets/quilts; plastic lemonade bottles, filled from the hot water tank, can be used as heaters. Use a battery-operated air pump or improvise aeration, for example hourly short sessions with a bicycle pump. Filter bacteria may be affected, so reduce/stop feeding and monitor ammonia/nitrite for a few days.

Going on Holiday

Properly maintained set-ups need no special preparation. Ask someone to check the fishes daily – ideally an aquarist, but if not leave the phone number of a "trouble-shooter" in case of any problems with the fishes or equipment. Most fishes will survive a fortnight without food and probably be healthier for it, but if you must have them fed, never leave a container of food – other people are invariably over-generous – but instead provide individually wrapped daily rations.

Breeding

Many aquarists soon develop a yearning for the patter of tiny fins, perhaps because a species breeds unprompted in its community tank, perhaps because of an interest in conservation. Indeed anyone maintaining a rare or endangered species should feel duty bound to try to breed it in order to reduce depletion of wild stocks. Legislation is currently being discussed which may forbid the importation of many (perhaps all) fishes from the wild, so the continued presence of many species in our aquaria may depend on captive breeding. You too may have an important role to play, rather than just breeding fishes for interest and amusement.

Unfortunately far too much breeding is unplanned and/or ill-considered, resulting in inferior stock. Many species which have been captive-bred for generations are now mere shadows of their splendid wild ancestors. They are also often unhealthy as lack of selection has reduced inherited vigour. A comparison of today's stock with photographs taken of the same species 20 or 30 years ago can be horrifying.

Breeding top-quality fishes depends on three factors: selection of parent stock; avoiding indiscriminate inbreeding; and rigorous culling of inferior offspring. Fishes intended for breeding should be vigorous, of good size and colour, with no inherited flaws in form and finnage – *never* the little chap you felt sorry for because he was the smallest, or the one with the funny twisted tail. Ideally they

Above: **Deformed fishes should never be used for breeding, and deformed fry culled at an early stage.**

Right: **A pair of *Hemichromis guttatus* (jewel cichlids) spawning.**

should be unrelated, although line-breeding (the planned mating of related individuals with a particular objective, usually the breeding of "fancy" strains of fishes, for example guppies) is acceptable. Rear only the best of the brood, even if there is a ready market – always cull deformed and undersized specimens (runts). The normal practice is to feed rejects to other fishes but if you are too soft-hearted, an aquarist friend will probably have a hungry predator.

Right: An *Oreochromis mossambicus* (Mozambique mouth-brooder) female taking her babies into her mouth to protect them from danger.

Below: Male anabantids such as *Betta splendens* (Siamese fighter) build bubblenests for the eggs, which they, rather than the females, subsequently guard.

A male *Barbus tetrazona* (tiger barb) (*right*) courting a female.

Most fishes do not actively care for their eggs, relying on sheer numbers to ensure the survival of a few – but in the restricted space of an aquarium all tend to become caviar for tankmates. Some species produce live young – which likewise usually become snacks. Some fishes, however, notably cichlids, actively care for both eggs and fry, their attendant territoriality often being to the detriment of anything sharing their aquarium. The courtship of some types can be equally traumatic for tankmates. For these reasons any serious attempt at breeding will usually require intervention by the aquarist, and frequently separate quarters for the breeding individuals.

The Breeding Tank

Natural requirements for water chemistry and habitat may have been compromised in the community tank, but the breeding tank should provide optimal conditions for its occupants, because without the correct water chemistry eggs often fail to hatch. Some species are seasonal breeders, requiring one or more triggers to stimulate spawning – in effect a simulation of what happens in Nature: the rains come (frequent water changes), food supply and quality improves (lots of live food), and then it gets hotter (raise temperature). Species from cool and temperate zones may also be triggered by longer day length (increased light intensity and duration). Some fishes require a particular spawning substrate (the surface on which, or material in which, eggs are laid). These special conditions are best created in a separate breeding tank, which must, however, in other respects conform to normal criteria for setting up and maturing aquaria for the species concerned.

The key to successful breeding is PATIENCE. Do not expect your fishes to breed the moment they are installed in their desirable residence – a change of environment is often the fishy equivalent of a cold shower! If nothing happens after a few weeks resist the temptation to fiddle with the environment (triggers apart); the fishes will probably have only just settled down enough to consider breeding, and your interference will set them back to square one.

Rearing

Mating and post-mating procedure varies for different types of fishes but there are general principles for fry rearing, whatever the species. First, fry are more delicate than their parents. They tend to be more susceptible to poisoning by nitrogen cycle by-products, so particular attention must be paid to water quality. Filtration turnover must, however, be gentle, as otherwise fry may be sucked in; small air-operated sponge filters are ideal. Zeolite, a material which absorbs ammonia, can be useful – a small amount scattered on the bottom of the tank, or suspended in a nylon bag (made from a stocking), will compensate for any hiccup in the filtration. Small fluctuations in temperature and water chemistry can have dire effects, so water changes, which should be small and frequent, require extra care.

Avoid moving tiny fry if possible – this often causes losses and/or a check in growth. Never use a siphon to move fry; this will cause physical damage. Instead use a meat baster or small soup ladle (extremely useful items when rearing fry) to transfer tiny fry; and for larger ones a small fine-meshed net designed for the purpose and available from your local dealer.

Above: A male *Gasterosteus aculeatus* (3-spined stickleback) with a week-old baby.

Below: Pterophyllum scalare (angelfish) with eggs on a leaf.

Types of Breeding Tanks

The illustrations below show some of the different techniques that the fishkeeper can adopt to help his or her fishes to breed in a safe and efficient manner.

1 Some fishes, for example small barbs, commonly eat their eggs. Reduce the level of water in the tank and place a layer or two of marbles along the tank bottom. The reduced water level means a shorter time that the eggs are in danger while they fall to the bottom of the tank, and the marbles act as a highly efficient fish-proof egg trap. Once spawning is over, remove all the eggs.

2 Another way of saving eggs is to drape a piece of finely meshed netting in the water. The fishes are placed above the netting, and when they spawn the eggs fall through it to safety. This method is suitable for small fishes such as danios.

3 A dense section of plants is required for breeding tetras. The fishes make spawning runs through the plants; their eggs are adhesive and remain trapped in the plants, safely hidden from other predators, to hatch.

4 Rainbowfishes can be successfully bred by the use of artificial mops. These are placed just inside the tank and provide a safe environment for the female fish to lay her eggs. It is then a simple job to collect up the eggs and hatch them in separate shallow dishes. Spawning mops are also used for breeding some killifishes (egg-laying cyprinodonts).

5 A useful device for breeding livebearers is a breeding trap which can be placed in the main aquarium. The holes in the netted trap allow the fry to swim to safety. It is advisable to allow the female to rest for a few days after giving birth before being released into the main aquarium.

Feeding Fry

Fish eggs, if viable, hatch after one or more days, but the larvae obtain nourishment from their yolk-sacs for several more days thereafter. They cannot swim at this stage and normally lie on the bottom or remain attached to the spawning substrate. When all the yolk has been absorbed they become free-swimming fry and start to look for food. Although they will find some natural foods (micro-organisms, algae) if the tank has been set up for some time, they usually need supplementary feeding immediately.

The type of food offered initially depends on the size of the fry; the tiniest will need infusorians: microscopic aquatic organisms which can be cultured by putting a lettuce leaf in a jam-jar, adding boiling water, and leaving the jar on a sunny window-ledge. When the water goes cloudy it is ready for use, and a portion can be drawn off with the meat baster and squirted into the shoal of fry. If the culture fails, there is a commercial substitute called "Liquifry" available.

The next size up of food, suitable for many newly free-swimming fry, is the freshly-hatched nauplii of the brine shrimp (*Artemia salina*), whose eggs (available from retailers) are hatched in salt water in lemonade bottles or large sweet jars.

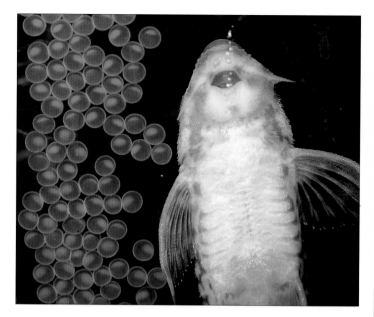

Loricaria species (whiptail catfish) with eggs.

The salt concentration depends on the geographical origin of the shrimps, so buy a brand with instructions. Start a culture two to three days before the fry are due to become free-swimming; once active, this will last for two to three days, so three, started at two-day intervals (and replenished on their sixth day), should suffice. Brine shrimp should always be rinsed in fresh water before feeding, to remove excess salt.

Below left: Male livebearers such as guppies and swordtails have a modified anal fin, the gonopodium, to permit internal fertilization of the females. *Below right*: Female *Xiphophorus* (swordtail) giving birth.

Breeding

Breeding coral fishes presents almost insuperable problems, though some success has been achieved with damsel and clown fishes. Feeding the fry remains a major hurdle to be overcome.

Another excellent fry food is microworm, cultured in plastic tubs of cold porage (or similar); the worms proliferate rapidly and crawl up the sides of the container away from the culture medium, and are harvested on a fingertip which is then rinsed in the tank. Starter cultures, with instructions, are often advertised in the aquatic press; thereafter a spoonful of established culture can be used to start others – after about 10 days the aroma tends to become unpleasant.

As fry increase in size they can take increasingly larger items – tiny pond foods such as *Cyclops, Bosmina,* and small *Daphnia*; cod roe; crumbled flake; and small particles of other foods. You will need to raise the young fishes to at least 2.5 cm (1 inch) long before they can be sold; good water quality and ample space are just as essential to growth as diet, so raise only as many as you can sensibly cope with, and regularly cull substandard individuals. The wise breeder canvasses potential customers (friends, dealers) early on (perhaps even before breeding a species at all) to find out how many fry it is worth raising; even if you could sell the entire brood, remember it is preferable to raise a small number of top-quality fry rather than a large number of poor ones.

The Fish Groups

There are a great many fishes for the novice aquarist to choose from, in fact, so many that he or she can often become confused as to the best ones to choose. One glance around a retail aquatic store will reveal large and small fishes, colourful and plain fishes, herbivores and carnivores – somewhere are the right ones for you.

No single volume can include all the many thousands of fishes suitable for aquarium or pond. Most authors cover a selection of those commonly available, but we have adopted a different approach, discussing the main families of freshwater aquarium fishes, and within them groups with similar requirements and behaviour. We have also included a selection of "oddballs", together with brackish water and marine fishes suitable for the aquarium.

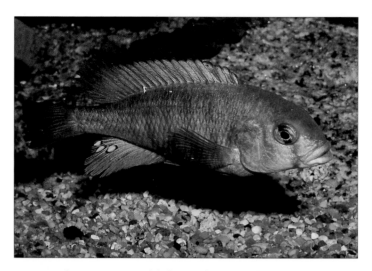

Many Lake Victoria cichlids, such as *Haplochromis sauvagei* (*above*), are threatened with extinction in the wild.

Some aquarists like to try to re-create a biotope in their aquarium. Here we see a hard water, rocky Lake Malawi habitat.

Others prefer the peaceful serenity of an underwater garden such as this soft and acid water Amazonian aquarium.

In the pages that follow, each major group of freshwater fishes is looked at with the emphasis on how to succeed in keeping them rather than a dictionary of fish names. Names are nevertheless important, so for each fish discussed we have given the scientific (Latin) name and, if there are any, the popular names used in English-language aquarium literature. A word of warning here: popular names are not always universal, and are sometimes used for more than one species, whereas scientific names always refer to the same single species wherever you are in the world. To avoid confusion, always use the Latin name even if it seems complicated and often unpronounceable. We have given current scientific names, but you may find that not all retailers, books, and magazines are quite as up-to-date as we are! So, in cases of recent taxonomic change, we will tell you the old name as well.

We suggest that you read through each chapter, taking various things into account. If you have a large amount of time to devote to your new hobby, once you have got your tank established and are feeling confident in what you are doing, you might like to try breeding some of the killifishes. Picking eggs off mops at regular intervals, rearing live foods and dealing with batches of fry in small containers takes time and dedication. But if time is at a premium, you may prefer a set up that requires the minimum amount of maintenance; for example a furnished aquarium with shoals of characins and a few catfishes or loaches. Apart from daily feeding

Rasbora reticulata (reticulated *Rasbora*) is a favourite fish for the mature aquarium.

and a glance to see that everything is working, maintenance can be carried out in a couple of hours or so on Saturday afternoon. You will also need to look at the finances because taking on the responsibility of a large, predatory fish can be expensive with regard to food alone, never mind the price of its aquarium, filtration system, etc.

Be sure you are happy with your choice of fishes. It doesn't matter if the neighbours don't like them, or your brother, mother, uncle, cousin or whoever thinks they are ugly. If you like them that's fine because it is far easier and more rewarding to care for an animal you like than one you don't. We hope you will succeed with your hobby and, above all, enjoy it.

Note: the degrees of hardness used in the following chapters are English.

Cichlids

Cichlids (family Cichlidae) originate primarily in tropical America and Africa, with a few species in the Middle East and Asia. They are mainly freshwater fishes, though a few species require or tolerate brackish conditions. Size – adult Standard Length (SL) – ranges from 2 cm to 91 cm (3/4 in to 36 in) with a similar diversity in form, diet, and behaviour. Some species are very colourful and are thus attractive aquarium occupants. Many aquarists are, however, attracted by their interesting behaviour, character, and apparent intelligence; large specimens in particular can become genuine pets.

Cichlids can be divided into a number of more or less discrete groups, based largely on geographical distribution, but also habitat, size, diet, and behaviour. Before discussing the major groups, however, we must present an overview of "cichlid psychology" – how they behave, and, more important, why. A thorough understanding of this is essential to their successful maintenance.

Who's watching who? Cichlids, especially large ones, show considerable interest in the world outside their tank, and can become real pets. This is a female *Nandopsis dovii*, one of the largest species and a real character.

Cichlid Behaviour and Its Management

All cichlids practise brood care, guarding both eggs and young. This ensures a high survival rate, so clutch size is small compared to that in egg-scattering fishes, which rely on sheer numbers of eggs for genetic survival.

Cichlids have two brood-care strategies: substrate brooding and mouthbrooding. In the former, (normally) adhesive eggs are laid on a "spawning substrate", for example a stone, plant, or piece of wood; then guarded against predators, kept clean by regular "mouthing", and fanned with the pectoral fins to ensure a constant supply of oxygenated water. Both parents may share these duties, or one (usually the female) may concentrate on tending the eggs while the other guards the breeding territory. When the larvae hatch they are often placed in a pre-dug nursery pit, and sometimes moved at regular intervals to new pits. Once free-swimming, the fry may be escorted around in search of food, or allowed to forage, independently but under supervision, in the breeding territory. Brood care usually

Teleogramma brichardi is a cave-spawning rapids cichlid from the Zaïre (Congo) River. The large eggs are opaque even when fertile, and are tended by the female alone. The fry are correspondingly large.

Cichlids are noted for their brood care: *Pelvicachromis pulcher* (the krib) is easy to keep, easy to sex, and easy to breed, and can be kept in the general community. This is a female guarding fry.

This cichlid is one of the smallest, *Lamprologus ocellatus*, a tiny Lake Tanganyika shell-dweller. This is a male: females are even smaller.

continues until the parents are ready to spawn again (which may be from 10 days to several months, depending on the species).

This strategy is often known as "substrate spawning", and is further divided into "open brooding" and "cave brooding", according to the location of the spawning substrate. It requires a strong pair bond which may last for a single spawning episode, a breeding season, or life. In some species a male may bond with several females ("harem polygyny"), each holding her own breeding territory within his "super territory".

Mouthbrooding, by contrast, protects the eggs and young in the mouth of one or both parents until they are old enough or large enough to stand a good chance of survival alone. Mouthing and fanning are replaced by the drawing of clean, oxygenated water through the mouth by gill action. This, coupled with a reduction in or cessation of food intake, imposes a considerable physical strain on the parent(s).

The majority of mouthbrooders belong to one of the two main lineages of African cichlids, the haplochromines, in which eggs and fry are incubated by the female alone (maternal mouthbrooding). Upon release, normally after about three weeks, the fry are often abandoned. Males do not bond with females, but hold spawning territories, often centred on laboriously constructed "nests", from which they display to potential temporary partners. Frequently males hold adjacent territories and compete for females ("arena breeding"). The non-adhesive eggs are laid in the nest. Sometimes they are fertilized

A pair of *Tropheus duboisi* "yellow band" spawning. The female (*left*) is nuzzling the vent area of the male, ingesting milt to fertilize the eggs already in her mouth.

A brooding female *Haplochromis pyrrhocephalus,* one of the Lake Victoria "haps". Note the characteristic distended (with fry) throat and "pursed" lips.

A *Labeotropheus fuelleborni* (orange morph) releasing her fry.

before collection by the female, but in many species males have ocelli, the colour and size of eggs ("eggspots"), on the anal fin, and in trying to collect these the female ingests sperm, released from the nearby vent, to fertilize the real eggs that are already in her mouth.

In tilapiines, the other African lineage, brooding may be maternal, paternal, or biparental, the last usually involving a pair bond and shared territory, as in substrate brooding. Brood care may continue after release, with fry returning to the mouth or being guarded like substrate-brooder young. Some species have eggspots, while others have evolved different egg dummies such as "genital tassels" and egg-like tips to the pelvic fins. Many tilapiines are, however, substrate-brooders, and where mouthbrooding has evolved it often appears less advanced than in the haplochromines.

Mouthbrooding has also arisen, quite independently, in some American cichlids but is far less common.

Breeding may be seasonal or continuous. The former is the norm in bodies of water affected dramatically by climatic change, and is often triggered by the onset of the rains and a concomitant increase in food supply and available territory (flooded areas). Piscivorous species may spawn later when their food supply is augmented by fry of other fishes! Some species raise more than one brood during a breeding season, often with the same partner. The pair bond commonly dissolves at the end of the breeding season, with a new partner being selected next time.

Continuous breeding is normally found where changes in the climate have less effect, for example in large lakes. Overpopulation is prevented by cyclical fluctuation in food supply and breeding success; when the food supply is good females produce large clutches, but the resulting population explosion depletes the food supply and reduces breeding success until the food supply recovers. In captivity constant abundant food may lead to unnaturally frequent and/or large clutches and excessive physical drain on the female, with gill strain a serious danger in mouthbrooders.

Courtship may be stormy. A pair of *Nandopsis octofasciatus* (Jack Dempseys) mouthfighting.

Most cichlids can be induced to breed in captivity (some need little persuasion), but it must be understood that in some species there is a downside to their breeding behaviour. This has given the entire family an often undeserved reputation for being difficult, destructive, aggressive, and so on. The worst problems can be avoided by understanding the reasons for their actions and taking their behavioural (as well as physical) needs into account.

Digging is a natural and instinctive part of cichlid behaviour, and attempts to curb it, for example by having no substrate, are cruel. "Aquascaping", sometimes with uprooting of plants, is often a necessary preliminary to breeding – the construction of nursery pits or nests. Large cichlids may try to remove intrusive decor and equipment by brute force – and worse still, succeed! In general, the larger the species, the greater the extent, and likelihood, of disruption.

Plants can be protected by planting in pots, or between rocks and/or pebbles; or omitted. Equipment can be fixed in place, and heavy, immovable, decor used. The environment should be tailored to natural behaviour – you will never achieve the reverse!

A fish which needs to hold a private territory to attract a mate (mouthbrooders) or raise a family (substrate brooders) will quite justifiably regard tankmates as competitors, intruders, or potential fry-predators, and do its best to eliminate such threats. Even if the aquarist is aware of the need for an exclusive territory, he rarely comprehends the amount of space required by substrate brooders. Although some small species are content, in nature as well as captivity, with an area 30–40 cm (12–15 in) in diameter, many others occupy an area the size of a good-sized room in the wild, and while they are obliging enough to make do with

Substrate spawners such as *Amphilophus citrinellus* often dig nursery pits.

Mouthbrooders dig too, some building huge crater nests.

a 120 x 40 cm (48 x 15 in) aquarium, they draw the line at sharing it. So, although many species can be included in general or cichlid communities, it must be accepted that some need their own aquarium.

Sometimes the hostility of the

Cichlids

territorial male extends to the female. In nature a female can simply swim away from a male when she does not wish to breed. To stay is to indicate interest. In the aquarium she cannot swim away, the male assumes she wants to breed, and when she rejects his courtship he attacks her like any intruder – but she has nowhere to go, and may be killed. So, unless the tank is rather longer than natural territorial diameter, care must be exercised with sexually mature adults; the problem can often be solved by using a clear divider to separate them until the female responds to the male's display.

Where aggression between the sexes is likely, or absence of sexual dimorphism makes sexing impossible, it is best to grow on six to eight juveniles together and let them pair naturally. This makes for greater compatibility. "Spare" fishes can be rehomed.

Even with a compatible and bonded pair, perhaps with eggs or fry, the male may suddenly turn on the female if they are alone in the aquarium. His prime instinct is to defend his territory and family against intruders, but if there are no actual enemies to repel, this may be turned upon the only suitably sized fish available – the female. This can be avoided by placing the tank adjacent to one containing fishes large enough to pose a threat, or by partitioning off part of the breeding tank with a clear divider to accommodate a "target fish". Target fishes must, however, always have adequate living space, and never be exposed to actual aggressive contact.

The novice cichlid breeder is often devastated when hitherto attentive parents suddenly eat

Occasionally even *Apistogrammas* have to be "contained" with a divider.

their young. In the wild fry gradually wander further and further afield until eventually they become independent. Often there is not room for this to happen in the aquarium; the parents tolerate the youngsters until either the latter grow large enough to represent competition, or the urge to breed again renders them a potential threat to the intended brood. Fry must be removed before this stage if they are to be grown on.

With arena-breeding mouthbrooders, where territory is not needed for fry-guarding, territoriality can be turned on itself by crowding, so no male can claim a significant area except when his motivation peaks in the presence of a "ripe" female. Often these fishes cannot be kept alone in single pairs as the male then harasses the female to death in his attempts to persuade her to spawn; again her presence implies willingness. In the crowded mouthbrooder community, however, males have plenty of distractions and females can "hide" among the other fishes. Such an aquarium is a hive of activity, and it is generally best to move brooding females to individual small brooding tanks until fry release.

Territoriality is usually greatest

towards conspecifics, as they are the chief competitors for suitable habitat, mates, and breeding space. Next come other cichlids, especially those of similar size and appearance – often members of the same genus. Non-cichlids are often a threat only to the brood, but not to the chance to breed, and are ignored if they keep their distance.

Care must be exercised in introducing new fishes to any tank in which a cichlid holds territory; again conspecifics and similar species are most likely to fare badly. "New" fishes include former residents which have been absent for a period – for example while brooding. They will have become strangers and have lost their position in the tank hierarchy.

By now you must be wondering if cichlids are worth the hassle, but this doubt will evaporate the first time you see a pair with young, or watch a mouthbrooder release her fry. Many a confirmed fish-hating partner has softened at the sight! Moreover many species *can* be kept and bred without problem in a general community. We trust, however, it is quite clear that you must always research behaviour as well as environmental requirements before making any purchase.

GROUPS OF CICHLIDS

Central American Cichlids

This group comprises several genera closely related to the South American genus *Cichlasoma*, and assigned to it until recently. The earlier name, and also *Heros*, is still commonly used. Their distribution encompasses lakes, rivers, and streams in not only Central America but also the southern United States and some Caribbean islands. The water in these regions is normally hard and alkaline (pH 7.5–8.0), and still or with a slow to moderate flow. The maintenance/breeding temperature is 24–27°C (75–80°F).

All are monogamous, seasonal substrate brooders, with a fairly large territorial requirement – a diameter roughly 5 to 10 times adult male length. Many are highly competitive, and only the smallest species are suitable for a Central American community, and then only in a large (120 cm/48 in) tank. NONE IS SUITABLE FOR THE GENERAL COMMUNITY. They should never be mixed with their Amazonian cousins, whose temperament and water requirements are completely different, though some can be housed with some cichlids from hard water areas of north-west South America. Digging is often frequent and extensive.

Males are usually larger than females and have longer finnage; one sex may be more colourful than the other. Ideally pairs should be given their own quarters, at least for breeding, with 80 cm (30 in) the minimum tank length for the smallest species. The males of some large species may represent a serious danger to the females.

Archocentrus nigrofasciatus, the ever popular "convict cichlid", is small but highly territorial, probably because of heavy competition for breeding sites in the wild.

Copora nicaraguensis is relatively peaceful, and aspects of its breeding behaviour are unique among Central Americans. Shown here is a female.

Thorichthys pasionis, like its better known cousin *Th. meeki* (the firemouth), has "eye-spots" on its gillcovers, which, when the latter are flared, make it look like a much larger fish.

A *Paratheraps fenestratus* female. This attractive herbivore is not yet as widely available as the popular *P. synspilum* (Quetzal cichlid).

Archocentrus, *Neetroplus*, and *Herotilapia* (7.5–18 cm/3–7 in) are omnivorous cave brooders, feeding on invertebrates and some vegetable matter. Apart from *Herotilapia* and *Archocentrus centrarchus,* they tend to be very belligerent for their size. *Thorichthys* (10–15 cm/4–6 in) breed in caves or other sheltered sites (for example, between rocks, or beneath overhangs) and are insectivores.

Chuco, *Copora*, *Paraneetroplus*, *Tomocichla*, and *Theraps* (13–30 cm/5–12 in) are also cave brooders, but occur in faster-flowing water than other Central Americans. They require a rocky habitat. *Paraneetroplus* are herbivorous and the others largely insectivorous. *Copora nicaraguensis* is unusual for a substrate spawner in that its eggs are nonadhesive, laid in a pit, and taken into the mouth for cleaning.

Herichthys, *Paratheraps*, and *Vieja* (20–35 cm/8–14 in) are herbivorous open brooders, generally with little sexual dimorphism. Although peaceful in relation to their size, they require spacious (minimum 120 x 50 cm/48 x 18 in) private breeding quarters.

Amphilophus (20–30 cm/8–12 in) are bottom-sifting omnivores. Some of these open brooders are extremely intolerant of conspecifics or similar-looking congenerics, and males may be a serious threat to females.

Nandopsis and *Petenia* (15–75 cm/6–30 in), the "guapotes", are open-brooding predators with piscivorous tendencies. They are solitary except when breeding, and are therefore intolerant of other fishes. Bonded pairs, however, are often highly tolerant of each other, and will unite to exterminate any competition.

Medium/large South American Cichlids

Most of these are found in the Amazon and Paraguay river systems, as well as rivers in the Guianas, with water chemistry generally soft, and pH ranging from extremely acid (pH<5.0) to slightly alkaline. Soft slightly acid water is a good starting point. Although several species have been acclimated to hard water, the correct conditions are normally required for breeding. Maintenance temperature is 26–27°C (78–80°F).

In these regions cichlids are not the dominant predators and are rarely found in open water (where they would be easy prey for other fishes, birds, and reptiles); instead they occupy the margins of permanent bodies of water – lakes, rivers, and streams – where they can shelter among overhanging vegetation, roots, and fallen trees. Some are found beneath floating islands of plant debris. Most prefer still or slow-moving water, and do not appreciate bright lighting.

When the rains come the surrounding forest is flooded to a depth of many metres, offering an immense area of additional feeding and breeding territory. In consequence most species breed seasonally and may require a series of triggers (large water changes, increased food supply, and raised temperature) to induce breeding in captivity. During the dry season a comparative shortage of habitat means that many live in shoals, so territoriality is usually a problem only during breeding, and is then not excessive, as in the absence of any need to fight for breeding territory competitiveness has remained minimal. Sexual dimorphism is unusual, and females of

Aequidens sp. cf. *rivulatus* (the green terror) comes from north-west South America, where the water is harder and more alkaline than in the Amazon system. Its temperament is more like that of Central American cichlids.

many species will often "pair" in captivity in the absence of a male. Digging and bottom sifting are common (except in *Symphysodon*, *Pterophyllum*, and *Mesonauta*), and plants may be disturbed.

A number of species originate in the harder, more alkaline waters of north-western South America, where there is no significant inundation and breeding territory is often at a premium. Species from this region are sometimes more territorial; these are the only South American cichlids suitable for mixing with Central Americans, and then only with caution.

Cichlasoma, *Aequidens*, *Bujurquina*, and *Krobia* (the "acaras") are small to medium-sized (10–18 cm/4–7 in) omnivores. *Bujurquina* are primitive biparental mouthbrooders, the rest are substrate spawners, sometimes utilizing a cave. Some *Aequidens* come from the north-west and may be aggressive.

Geophagus, *Satanoperca*, *Gymnogeophagus*, *Biotodoma*, *Acarichthys*, *Guianacara*, and *Retroculus*, (the geophagines or "eartheaters") (10–30 cm/4–12 in) are a highly variable group with breeding strategies ranging

from substrate spawning through biparental mouthbrooding to advanced arena-breeding maternal mouthbrooding. They are found throughout tropical South America. Most are bottom sifters and require a fine substrate. *Retroculus* inhabit fast-flowing water. Because of the diversity of the group, it will be necessary to research specific requirements.

Heros ("severums"), *Hypselecara* (chocolate cichlids), *Mesonauta* (festive cichlids), *Hoplarchus* (parrot cichlids, not to be confused with "blood red parrots" which are probably of hybrid origin), and *Uaru* (triangle cichlids), are medium to large (18–45 cm/7–18 in), rather peaceful Amazonian cichlids, often

An unidentified member of the *Geophagus surinamensis* complex. This group was for a long time thought to be a single species with both substrate spawning and mouthbrooding populations, but is now known to include several species.

Uaru amphiacanthoides fry, like those of *Symphysodon* (discus), feed on parental body mucus, but in this species the behaviour is not obligatory. *Uaru* fry eat anything, in quantity, and rapidly become "little bellies with fins". Adults are "gentle giants".

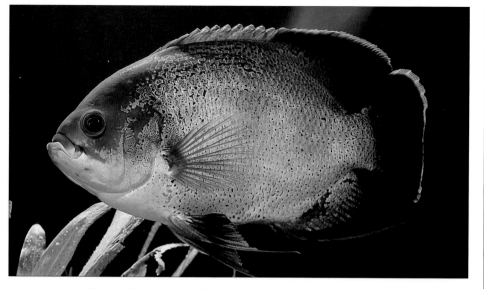

Astronotus ocellatus (the oscar), often purchased by beginners ignorant of its habits and eventual size, is a common cause of "multiple tank syndrome".

even when breeding provided the tank is large (over 180 cm/72 in). *Heros* and *Mesonauta* are often sold as general community fishes, but their ultimate size (20–30 cm/8–12 in and 18–20 cm/7–8 in respectively) will mean a rethink later on. *Heros* are partially vegetarian, and *Uaru* will denude a planted aquarium overnight, as well as digging enthusiastically (they are, however, great characters!). The others are omnivorous. All are open-brooding substrate spawners; *Mesonauta* spawn on the underside of floating vegetation/debris in the wild, and, uniquely, lead their fry from below rather than above. All but *Uaru* were formerly included in the genus *Cichlasoma*.

Astronotus ocellatus (oscars) are large (up to 38 cm/15 in), destructive, territorial, Amazonian open brooders, and are extremely popular because of their character. They are best kept singly or as pairs in a single-species tank in which everything but the gravel has been rendered immovable. (Minimum tank size 100 x 40 cm/36 x 15 in for a single fish, 120 x 40 cm/48 x 15 in for a pair.) They are totally unsexable (and females will

"pair") so a group of fry should be grown on to obtain a pair. They are prone to become habituated to individual foods unless the diet is varied, and to serious digestive upsets if fed an unsuitable diet (for example large amounts of pellets). They are naturally piscivores, but also relish insects and earthworms.

Pterophyllum (angels) are probably the most popular cichlids, and common members of the general community. They are leaf-spawning substrate spawners, peaceful, easy to keep, and non-destructive. They may, however, eat very small tankmates. They originate from the Amazon system, as do their close relatives *Symphysodon* (discus or pompadours), and both are commonly found sympatrically. Nevertheless a remarkable mythos has evolved regarding discus, implying that they are difficult fishes, something which is given the lie by their thriving in general communities when placed there by the aquarist ignorant of their "special requirements". In this one case we suggest you avoid homework in the first instance, and if you want to keep

discus, simply provide a well-planted Amazonian aquarium, smallish peaceful tankmates, and a varied diet including pond foods. Discus fry initially feed exclusively on parental body mucus and cannot be raised away from their parents.

Crenicichla (pike cichlids) is a highly variable genus, which is increasing in popularity now that aquarists are realizing that piscivorous does not necessarily mean aggressive (though some species are). Size ranges from 7.5 to 60 cm (3 to 24 in), and habitat from rapids to slow-moving forest streams and still lakes. All are predators, most lurking under a root or overhang until prey passes. Juveniles and small species eat invertebrates as well as fishes, but the aquarist must be prepared to feed live fishes to wild adults, at least initially. All are sexually dimorphic substrate spawners. THEY MUST NEVER BE INCLUDED IN THE GENERAL COMMUNITY or with other fishes less than two-thirds their own size (including each other!); they are best avoided by beginners, and, given their diversity, must be individually researched.

South American Dwarfs

These are small cichlids (up to 10 cm/4 in) from still or slow-moving streams and pools in rainforests and savannahs east of the Andes; their range, and consequently general biotope conditions, coincides to a large extent with that of the larger species covered above. All are seasonal substrate brooders; most are strongly sexually dimorphic in size, coloration, and finnage, with the male the larger, showier fish. All are vulnerable to predation on account of their size, and are nervous in captivity unless plenty of cover – plants, caves, bogwood – is provided and lighting is moderate. The use of "dither fishes" – shoals of small characins which help instil confidence that no predator is in the vicinity – is recommended.

Soft, slightly acid (pH 6.5) water is suitable for maintenance of all species, though some may require greater acidity for breeding. A few species have become acclimated to hard alkaline water, but high pH is best avoided. Water quality should be excellent and the temperature 25–28°C (77–82°F). A fine substrate should be used to permit the minimal digging essential to breeding in some species. All species feed on invertebrates and relish pond foods when maintained in captivity.

Apistogramma, *Apistogrammoides*, *Taeniacara*, and *Nannacara* are cave brooders, the first of these often practising harem polygyny. *Microgeophagus* (*Papiliochromis*), *Crenicara*, *Dicrossus*, *Laetacara*, and *Cleithracara* (keyhole cichlids) are open brooders, utilizing plant leaves or stones, always in a sheltered spot. Single *mated* pairs can be kept in 60 cm

(24 in) or 50 cm (18 in) aquaria. A "dwarf community" is possible, but as territorial requirements (38–50 cm/15–20 in diameter per pair, 25–30 cm/10–12 in per female in *Apistogramma* harems) would restrict its population to a small number of small fishes, these peaceful non-destructive cichlids can instead be housed in the general community. Males are often very competitive so one per species per tank is a good rule. Fry of some species are tiny and may need infusorians as their first food.

Apistogramma nijsseni, (the panda dwarf cichlid), is like most "Apistos", strongly sexually dimorphic. The male is much larger and blue. The jet black pelvic fins of maternal *Apistogrammas* are used to signal to the fry.

Each "wife" in an *Apistogramma* harem occupies a small (30cm/12 in diameter) breeding territory, centred on a cave, in the male's "super-territory". Here two female *A. cacatuoides* dispute an internal boundary.

Apistogramma caves should have small entrances. The male is not allowed to enter, and uses his tail to fan sperm in – a low ceiling will ensure the eggs are "in range". After spawning, the female walls herself in until the fry are free-swimming.

The rainforests and savannahs of South America are vast, and *Apistogrammas* tiny and secretive, so many species probably remain to be discovered. *A. norberti* (this is a male) is a recent discovery.

Nannacara anomala is a rather neglected dwarf which breeds successfully in hard alkaline water. The colourless juveniles seen in dealers' tanks blossom into attractive orange females (*above*) and turquoise males.

East African Lake Cichlids

The water of the East African lakes is generally hard and alkaline, although actual conditions vary from lake to lake. Lake Victoria is only moderately hard with a neutral to slightly alkaline pH; water clarity is poor and quality unexceptional. Lake Malawi is moderately hard (8–10 dH) and alkaline (pH 7.5–8); Lake Tanganyika is harder (15–20 dH) and more alkaline (pH 8–8.5). The waters of these last two vast "inland seas" are extremely clear and pure, and surface turnover by waves produces a very high oxygen content. In captivity a temperature of 26–27°C (78–80°F) is appropriate.

All three lakes contain a number of biotopes, the chief being rocky shoreline, sandy shoreline with *Vallisneria* beds, muddy river estuaries, and open water. Pelagic species from the last of these are generally predatory, and not normally maintained in aquaria. Those from muddy bottoms are given a sandy substrate in the aquarium for reasons of cleanliness.

Generally speaking, it is not good practice to mix cichlids from different lakes unless one's knowledge and experience are such as to permit sensible temperament matching. Each lake contains a number of discrete groups of cichlids with morphological and behavioural similarities, plus numerous "individualists". Care must likewise be exercised in mixing such groups.

Virtually all Lake Malawi and Lake Victoria cichlids are maternal mouthbrooding haplochromines, while Lake Tanganyika cichlids are thought to be of tilapiine ancestry, and include both substrate spawners and mouthbrooders of various types.

Breeding may be continuous or seasonal, depending on diet. For reasons of space we can cover only the main groups here.

The best-known group of Lake Malawi cichlids is the Mbuna, which are found in close association with areas of rocky shoreline, from which they rarely stray. The genera normally kept are *Pseudotropheus, Labeotropheus, Melanochromis, Labidochromis, Petrotilapia, Iodotropheus,* and *Cynotilapia* (7.5–18 cm/3–7 in). They are highly competitive and should be kept in a large (absolute minimum 1 m/36 in) densely populated community with huge quantities of rockwork. Filtration and water-changing must be correspondingly efficient.

The natural diet consists largely of algae and the aquatic invertebrates living in it, plankton from the water column, and, in some species, more bizarre items such as the fins and scales of other cichlids. Diet and water chemistry/quality require careful attention to avoid the condition known as "Malawi bloat".

Breeding is spontaneous, the only major problem being premature death of females at the hands of over-attentive males; this can largely be avoided if the set-up is as stipulated and two or more females per male are provided. Brooding females are best removed to a brooding tank soon after spawning.

Aulonocara (peacocks) (9–11 cm/ 3½–4½ in) live on the periphery of rocky areas and over open sand. Males are highly coloured, but females are drab olive. They have enlarged sensory pores on the head which enable them to detect invertebrates in the substrate by a form of sonar; they capture the prey by diving into the sand. Their aquarium should

Labidochromis caeruleus is one of the most peaceful of the Mbuna. It feeds on invertebrates which it picks from the algae coating the rocks, as shown here. The minimal black in the fins indicates that this is a female.

Pseudotropheus zebra occurs in several colour forms (morphs), some of which may prove to be separate species, and some of which are partially sex-linked. Most individuals of the white (W) morph are female, but this is a male.

Aulonocara sp. (sunshine peacock) from Maleri Island, Lake Malawi. This species lives at the interface between rocks and sand, using the former for shelter and the latter for hunting invertebrates.

Cyrtocara moorii (blue dolphin) is a popular "Malawi hap".

The blotched pattern of *Nimbochromis livingstonii* simulates a decaying fish corpse. This predator lies on its side on the sand, playing dead until prey approaches.

Julidochromis transcriptus is one of the smaller "Julies"; like other members of its genus it can (and does) swim both upside down and backwards, always with its belly towards the nearby rock surface.

Altolamprologus can be shy until they have settled in, which may take months rather than days. The male *A. compressiceps* (*above*) is very much larger than the female, and the same is true for other members of the genus.

Shown here is a *Neolamprologus buescheri* male guarding his fry, which have been brought out of the parental cave to forage.

contain some rockwork and a substrate of fine sand. They are inoffensive cichlids whose females are rarely at any risk from males, and should not be housed with the far more boisterous Mbuna who will intimidate them. It is also unwise to mix peacocks of similar appearance as you will be unable to identify the different females, and the males also seem to have difficulty – hybrids are not uncommon. Suitable tankmates are *Lethrinops*, which sift the substrate for food, and members of the Utaka group.

The latter consists of species of the genus *Copadichromis* (10–18 cm/4–7 in), like many other Malawi cichlids formerly included in the genera *Haplochromis* and *Cyrtocara*, both names being still commonly used. (*Haplochromis* is now properly restricted to Victorian cichlids, and *Cyrtocara* to a single Malawian, *C. moorii*.) Utaka are relatively peaceful zooplankton feeders and are found over sandy substrates.

Other popular haplochromines include *Cyrtocara moorii* (20 cm/8 in), a rather peaceful invertebrate-feeder, commonly known as the blue dolphin; *Dimidiochromis compressiceps* (20 cm/8 in), a remarkable compressed cichlid which lurks in *Vallisneria* beds and preys mainly on small fishes and insects, although it is said to eat the eyes of other fishes (hence the common name of "eye-biter". It rarely shows this tendency in captivity where rations are normally good, and is in fact a rather timid fish); and *Nimbochromis* (18–25 cm/7–10 in), cichlids with a blotched or spotted pattern which feed on small fishes and insects, and can be

rather aggressive on occasion. These "haps" all require a large and fairly open set-up with some rockwork.

Lake Tanganyika offers a similar variety of biotopes, but here the chief occupants of the rocky zones are small (4–15 cm/1$\frac{1}{2}$–6 in) cave-spawning substrate brooders of the lamprologine genera *Lamprologus*, *Lepidiolamprologus*, *Neolamprologus*, *Altolamprologus*, *Chalinochromis*, *Julidochromis*, and *Telmatochromis*. They are mainly invertebrate feeders which require a rocky set-up similar to that for Mbuna, but this should not consist entirely of tufa, which is too rough to provide a suitable spawning substrate. Territorial requirements are generally fairly small, but must be respected; for example, a 120 cm (48 in) aquarium will house only three or four pairs of 5–7.5 cm (2–3 in) fishes. Separate rock piles help to delimit territories. Alternatively, pairs can be given a tank of their own (60–100 cm/24–36 in, depending on size). One cannot generalize regarding the temperament and habits of these fishes as one can with Mbuna, so any potential purchase must be individually researched. It is, however, unwise to house more than one pair of any species in a single tank, or to house them with look-alike congeners.

Digging is normally minimal. Many species are what are termed "trickle spawners" producing frequent small broods. The fry from previous spawnings are allowed to remain in the breeding territory until they reach "competitive size" (usually just over 2.5 cm/1 in), and guard their younger siblings, often without parental assistance.

In the wild *Lamprologus signatus* lives and breeds in tunnels which it excavates in areas of muddy lake bottoms. Luckily, it seems to be just as content to use shells instead in the aquarium. This is a male; females lack stripes and are deeper-bodied.

Tanganicodus irsacae, a goby cichlid (*below*), with a pair of *Ophthalmotilapia ventralis* (featherfins) (*above*). "Gobies" are good fishes for the Tanganyikan community, but featherfin males rarely show their glorious colours under such circumstances.

Cyphotilapia frontosa (and its mouth) is far too large for the community of small rock-dwellers. Brooding females should be isolated – not because of harassment by the male, but because he will eat the fry.

Shell dwellers are small lamprologines (chiefly *Lamprologus* and *Neolamprologus*) which use the empty shells of *Neothauma* snails as shelter and breeding caves, and must always be provided with suitable shells (for example those of edible snails, obtainable from delicatessens). They are invertebrate/zooplankton feeders. Territorial requirements are normally small, and a pair (or small group for colonial species) can be accommodated in a 60 cm (24 in) tank or as a non-competing addition to the rock-dweller aquarium. Different species have different habits and should always be researched.

Cyprichromis and *Paracyprichromis* (7.5–10 cm/3–4 in) are peaceful plankton-feeding maternal mouthbrooders which live and spawn in open water near rocks. A small shoal is ideal for tenanting the otherwise empty upper regions of the rock- or shell-dweller tank.

Eretmodus, *Spathodus*, and *Tanganicodus* (goby cichlids) are small (7.5–10 cm/3–4 in), biparental mouthbrooders which inhabit the surf zone where waves break on rocky shores. They can be scrappy among themselves, but a pair can be kept in the rock-dweller tank

instead of (not as well as) one of the substrate-spawning species.

Ophthalmotilapia, *Cyathopharynx*, and *Cunningtonia* (featherfins) are medium-size (15–20 cm/6–8 in) maternal mouthbrooders, in which males have egg dummies on the tips of their much elongated pelvic fins. They feed on small particles of anything and inhabit the margins of rocky zones where they build crater nests of sand, sometimes on rocks. They are best kept as a single-species group consisting of a large male, one or more smaller males, and five or more females, in a large (minimum 150 cm/60 in) aquarium.

Tropheus and *Petrochromis* are maternal mouthbrooders and the Tanganyikan analogues of Mbuna, with similar habits and requirements. It is best not to keep them with the substrate-spawners, except in small numbers in very large tanks, as their boisterous activity can intimidate. *Cyphotilapia frontosa*, another rock-dwelling mouthbrooder, grows rather larger (25 cm/10 in) than most aquarists realize, and, although peaceful for its size, eats smaller fishes (for example small rock dwellers) given the opportunity.

Many Lake Victoria cichlid

species have become extinct following the introduction of the predatory *Lates niloticus* (Nile perch), and many of the survivors are endangered. Only a few species are available to aquarists; some imported for the aquarium trade are undescribed and often lack biotope data, though surplus stock from captive breeding programmes (for example in zoos) is generally better documented. Most of the available species are *Haplochromis*, with *Astatoreochromis* also represented.

The aquarist lucky enough to obtain these cichlids has a responsibility to try to breed them, and there is some liaison between hobbyists and scientific institutions to this end. Each species must be researched where possible, otherwise maintenance and breeding are a matter of careful trial and error. Because water clarity in Lake Victoria tends to be poor, these cichlids can be very timid when exposed to aquarium conditions (clear water, bright lighting); this can sometimes be remedied by keeping them in single-species groups so that competition between males counters shyness. This may, however, be impossible with highly territorial species.

West African Cichlids

Dwarf species of the genera *Pelvicachromis*, *Nanochromis*, *Parananochromis*, *Limbochromis*, (all cave brooders), *Anomalochromis* (open brooder), and *Thysochromis* (cave or open) are the West African forest analogues of South American dwarfs, and require similar living conditions (and can share a tank), although in the wild *Nanochromis* is found in rocky habitats. Strong sexual dimorphism is again the norm, with females generally the smaller and more colourful, and often responsible for initiating courtship. Like their transatlantic cousins they are excellent community fishes, although they require slightly more territory per pair. Single pairs can be kept alone in 60 or 80 cm (24 or 30 in) tanks, except in the case of *Nanochromis*, where males are rather aggressive towards females except when breeding, so that two or three females per male and a 1 m (36 in) tank per group is desirable.

Chromidotilapia are sexually dimorphic pair-bonding mouth-brooders, with either or both parents incubating depending on species. Although they can grow to 15 cm (6 in) they are rather shy and peaceful and excellent community fishes despite their size. They require the same conditions as dwarfs.

Steatocranus, *Lamprologus* (not to be confused with Lake Tanganyika species), and *Teleogramma* (rapids cichlids) are small cichlids (7.5–15 cm/3–6 in) found in rapids in the Zaïre (Congo) River and its tributaries. Their swim-bladders have atrophied, and the resulting lack of buoyancy enables them to rest in back-eddies and behind rocks instead of being swept away by

Pelvicachromis taeniatus "Nigeria" is one of several known geographical populations (possibly distinct species). Like its close relative *P. pulcher*, this species is strongly sexually dimorphic: shown here is a male.

A male *Nanochromis nudiceps*, a recently imported species. A very similar, but quite obviously different, species, *N. parilus*, has been available for some years under this name. Females of both species are much deeper-bodied, and, when ripe with eggs, look as if they have swallowed a glass marble.

Teleogramma brichardi is easily sexed by the broad white upper edge to the female's tail. At breeding time her bands disappear and her belly becomes a beautiful salmon-red. Despite its bottom-dwelling habits, this species is an accomplished jumper and requires an aquarium with a tight-ftting cover.

the fast-flowing water. Because of the nature of the habitat, little is known of natural behaviour; stomach contents indicate a diet of aquatic invertebrates. All are cave-brooding substrate spawners. Water should be fairly soft and slightly acid to neutral, with a temperature of 26–27°C (78–80°F). A high oxygen content is desirable, but not strong currents – remember these fishes prefer the calm spots in the torrent. Although wild individuals may be territorial towards

conspecifics, and males hostile towards females, this aggression seems to abate naturally once they have become used to each other. If necessary, use a clear divider during their first months in captivity. Tank-bred specimens are more amenable to company from the outset. Several species, notably *S. casuarius*, have proved suitable for the general community. They do not harm plants, rarely dig, are peaceful towards non-cichlids, and breed readily even in hard alkaline water.

Other African Cichlids

Hemichromis (jewel cichlids) are monomorphic open-brooding substrate spawners, highly territorial, and with piscivorous tendencies. In the wild they occur in a variety of biotopes from western forests to Egyptian oases, and do well in fairly neutral water in captivity. A single pair per tank (minimum 1 m/36 in, well-planted) is the rule, and even then they may fight.

The "tilapias" consist of four genera: *Tilapia, Oreochromis, Sarotherodon,* and *Danakilia* (the last not yet imported). They are found throughout Africa and into the Middle East, occurring in various water chemistries, including brackish, and are noted for their tolerance regarding water chemistry and quality. They are medium to large fishes (20–35 cm/8–14 in) with strongly herbivorous habits and prodigious digging abilities, and a tendency to precocious breeding and the production of huge broods. Thus, while they are ideal for fish farming for food, they have limited popularity in the aquarium.

Tilapia are substrate brooders; large males of some species can be extremely belligerent, including towards females. *Oreochromis* are arena-brooding maternal mouthbrooders. Males, however, represent no threat to females and they are normally kept in pairs. *Sarotherodon* are mouthbrooders which pair and hold a breeding territory, and depending on species either or both parents may brood.

Fluviatile haplochromines include *Astatotilapia burtoni, Pseudocrenilabrus multicolor* (Egyptian mouthbrooder) and *P. philander*, which are the only three species widely available. All

Hemichromis guttatus (the jewel cichlid) has diminished in popularity since the advent of equally colourful and less troublesome species. Like other *Hemichromis* it is a solitary predator by nature, and thus not a community species, although often sold as such.

Sarotherodon melanotheron is a recently imported mouthbrooding "tilapia". The fish in the background is an unidentified substrate-spawning *Tilapia* species.

are maternal mouthbrooders, fairly peaceful, and undemanding regarding diet, water chemistry and quality, providing a low pH (<6.5) is avoided. *Pseudocrenilabrus* can be kept in a general community – they will chase each other but not other fishes. *A. burtoni* can be kept with similar-sized lacustrine haplochromines (but not Mbuna).

Madagascar cichlids are medium to large, and most closely related to *Tilapia*. All five genera – *Paratilapia, Paretroplus, Oxylapia, Ptychochromis,* and *Ptychochromoides* – are endemic to Madagascar and all are substrate spawners. All are endangered in the wild, but fortunately interest in the aquarium hobby has led to the collection of stock for captive breeding, and at least one species is now available in the aquarium trade. It must be stressed that anyone lucky enough to obtain any of these cichlids has a responsibility to provide optimal conditions and make every effort to breed them. They come from a variety of biotopes so research into specific requirements is essential.

Note: Members of the Asian cichlid genus *Etroplus* (chromides) are dealt with in the chapter on brackish water fishes.

Catfishes

Panaque nigrolineatus (royal plec) is a clumsy swimmer. It has three rows of bone plates either side of its body which make the body fairly inflexible and therefore swimming difficult.

Catfishes are arguably the most diverse of all fishes, in body form, lifestyle, size, and distribution. There are over 2000 different species, principally from tropical freshwaters, but also from temperate climes and marine waters. Indeed, catfishes are to be found in every continent and ocean with the exception of the poles. With such diversity, only generalizations can be given in this brief introduction, but this same variety can also be the catalyst for a deeper interest on the part of the aquarist in this group of fishes.

Often catfishes are seen as quirky or a little unusual, more often than not due to their strange body shape, and are frequently accused of being poorly coloured. Mother Nature did not design her catfishes as ostentatious commercial items. They were designed to survive, and in that she was successful.

Most catfishes are benthic, that is, they are found principally at the bottom of the water column. Here the water flow is at its slowest (the fastest currents are usually at the water's surface) but turbulence is greater. This is due to the drag of the water over the substrate, compounded by sunken debris such as fallen trees and rocks. While this environment may seem a little inhospitable, it does offer a variety of foods, and fewer predators are to be found.

In these murky turbulent waters the catfish has to protect itself from environmental factors. Scales would easily be dislodged as a fish is buffeted against debris, leading to infection and possible death, therefore no catfishes have scales. Instead, they are covered either in thick skin with a copious covering of mucus, or with bony plates.

Catfishes invariably have stout pectoral and dorsal fin spines. In many species these fin spines can be locked. A characteristic that provides several advantages: it offers stability as the catfish rests its pectoral fins on the substrate; locked spines enable the catfish to wedge itself into a crevice or hollow; and with the fin spines fully erect it presents a predator with a bigger and more protected prey. The spines can also spell problems for an unwary aquarist, creating a hazard both to a net, as they become entangled, and to a handler's hands. Do not underestimate the sharpness of many catfish spines. Not only can the tip be sharp, but the edges are often serrated, compounding any wound inflicted.

The mechanisms used to lock these spines are ingenious, highly engineered structures. The dorsal spine has a small locking bone just in front of its base. Once the spine is erect and this locking pin is in place, only voluntary action by the catfish will unlock it. The pectoral spines on many species are even more complex, with the fin spine articulating on a ball joint which is so close fitting that by twisting the spine the ball seizes in its surrounding socket.

Those species whose bodies are covered in bony plates do not have the flexibility of movement required to permit prolonged swimming. Their actions when seen in the aquarium seem ungainly and laboured. This is most apparent in many of the South American loricariid catfishes, for example *Farlowella* sp. (twig catfishes, aptly named for their resemblance to twigs). These herbivores spend most of their time grazing on algae, and their body form allows them to blend into their natural forest creek biotope, away from the eyes of lurking predators.

The pungent fin spines of *Astrodoras asterifrons* (star-gazing dorad) act as a deterrent to predators.

Catfishes in the Aquarium

All catfishes have barbels: whisker-like filaments surrounding the mouth. It is this feature, resembling feline whiskers, that has given the Siluriformes the common name of catfishes. There are great variations in the form and number of barbels, dependent on species. Most species have two to four pairs of barbels, usually filamentous, but sometimes fringed with smaller branches as in the African *Synodontis nigriventris* (upside-down catfish), or built into large sucker-like lips.

Irrespective of their form, the barbels are highly sensitive taste organs, used in the search for food. Because some species sift the substrate, careful selection of gravel or sand must be considered, otherwise these delicate organs may become abraded or cut. Fine sand, as used in filtration plants in swimming pools, is ideal as it does not affect the water chemistry. Do not, under

Sorubim lima (shovel-nose catfish) uses its long, sensitive barbels to detect prey. The maxillary barbels are used to triangulate on its target, usually a live fish, before it lunges. This species should be kept with fishes too large for it to eat.

any circumstances, use builders' sand as it has sharp particles and compacts easily.

As a general rule, long barbels, such as those found on *Sorubim lima* (shovel-nose catfish) are an indication that these species may prey on smaller fishes. A similar assumption can be made regarding catfishes with large mouths. *Chaca bankanensis* (frogmouthed catfish) has very small barbels but an extremely

Although *Chaca* sp. (the frogmouthed catfish) has a placid nature, it is a fish to be wary of as it is a fearsome predator. It can be spotted lurking amongst dense vegetation, patiently waiting for any unsuspecting prey to pass within reach.

wide gape, enough to capture a fish more than half its own size.

With over 2000 species of catfishes from which to choose, there is something for all tastes. Sizes can range from little more than 2 cm (3/4 in) to in excess of 2 metres (6 1/2 feet). While some species are unsuited to the confines of all but the largest public aquarium, there are many that will flourish and breed in the aquarist's tanks.

All species of catfishes, even the few that swim in mid-water, require areas of seclusion where they can retreat to hide or rest. These can be provided by the use of bogwood or water-logged vine roots, as well as rockwork and dense planting. With any heavy aquarium structure, such as rocks, make sure it will not be demolished by the catfish undermining the substrate as it sifts the gravel.

Some early aquatic literature suggested that catfishes were mere scavengers, and so were ideal substitutes for a filter. However, nothing is further from the truth. Although catfishes forage for any food they can find, they do, like all fishes, require proper nourishment. Without this they will languish and die.

Although *Synodontis* sp. are commonly referred to as upside-down catfishes, relatively few species actually swim upside-down. *Synodontis nigriventris* (upside-down catfish), however, is one that does.

Corydoras, Brochis *and* Aspidoras

These small, armoured catfishes are ideal inmates for the community tank, where they will swim in small groups in search of food. *Corydoras*, with over 100 different species from which to choose, are often the first catfishes to be kept. *Dianema longibarbis* (porthole catfish) and *Dianema urostriata* (flagtailed cat) belong to the same family as the *Corydoras*, but grow to 14 cm (5½ in). They are placid fishes, and again are well suited to life in a furnished aquarium. Very similar, though smaller than most *Corydoras*, are the *Aspidoras* with only a dozen or so species. *Brochis*, on the other hand, with three species, are generally larger than *Corydoras*, about twice the size, but like the latter are peaceful. These catfishes are found throughout most regions of tropical South America, and are regularly imported for the aquarium. They have two rows of dermal bone plates on each side of the body, almost completely encasing the fish. Two pairs of short barbels are well suited to sifting the substrate for food; longer, more slender or more complex barbels would be quickly damaged or abraded. These barbels form a funnel into the mouth as

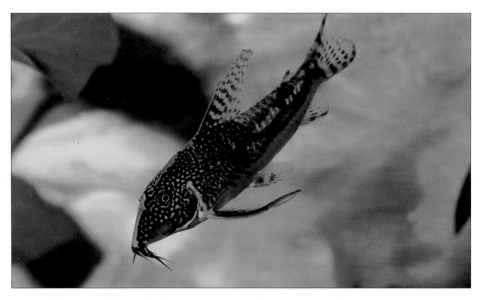

One of the most beautiful species of *Corydoras* is *C. barbatus*. A mature male has more vivid coloration, thickened fin spines, and cheek bristles.

the catfish eats, giving it a taste of what is about to be ingested, and allowing it to identify items to be discarded.

Corydoras and its relatives are often observed dashing to the water surface and back to the bottom of the aquarium. The reason is that this group is able to survive in poorly oxygenated waters by supplementing the dissolved oxygen extracted by the gills with atmospheric air. This is gulped in as the fishes break the surface and stored in the hind gut, which is highly vascularized. Here direct oxygen exchange into the bloodstream is undertaken. *Corydoras* surfacing in this way in the aquarium does not necessarily

mean low levels of dissolved oxygen in the tank: it seems to be a reflex action irrespective of necessity. A good indication of the condition of any of this group is the presence of a body sheen, which is visible on all healthy specimens.

Brochis are larger than *Corydoras*, and distinguished by their longer-based dorsal fin: *Corydoras* have only 6 to 8 dorsal fin rays, whilst *Brochis* have from 10 to 17. The only species of the three to have been bred in small numbers is *Brochis splendens* (emerald catfish), the smallest member of this genus, and the one most often offered for sale.

All these species are best kept

Dianema urostriata (flagtailed catfish) is easily distinguished from its near relative *D. longibarbis* (porthole catfish) by its black- and white-striped caudal fin. It likes a quiet aquarium with plenty of shelter.

Corydoras sterbai (Sterba's *Corydoras*) is a highly desirable and much sought-after fish. If you intend to breed them, you must keep two males and one female.

It is essential to have mature and well-oxygenated water if you wish to maintain *Corydoras* in tiptop condition. Shown here is *Corydoras loxozonus*.

in small groups of four to eight specimens. They benefit from being one of the few catfishes active in the daytime, whereas many other groups are nocturnal. Ideal foods for these catfishes are small aquatic invertebrates such as *Cyclops*, *Tubifex*, and *Daphnia*, supplemented with commercial flake or pelleted foods. Such a diet is recommended for conditioning the fishes for breeding.

Breeding Corydoras

Sexing *Corydoras* is fairly easy. In adult specimens, the female has a fuller, more robust body compared to the more slender male. This is more apparent when viewed from above. Many, though not all, *Corydoras* show dimorphism in the ventral fin shape, with females exhibiting fan-like finnage, and males with spear-shaped ventral fins. The easiest species with which to start a breeding programme is *Corydoras paleatus* (peppered catfish). This species is also the variety most commonly found in a local aquarium dealer's tanks.

In order to breed *Corydoras*, it is recommended that they be removed from the community tank into a small tank away from other species. Whilst *Corydoras* will spawn in the community tank, there is always the probability of the eggs being eaten by other inmates. The breeding tank need be no larger than 10 litres (2½ gallons) capacity, with a fine sandy base, and sparsely decorated with one or two broad-leaved plants. Filtration of some kind is essential. Introduce the *Corydoras* at a ratio of two males to each female. A trio is preferable to six specimens in this size of aquarium.

Often, if in breeding condition, they will require no

Corydoras paleatus (the peppered catfish) is a popular catfish with beginners. If fed correctly, it is also one of the easier *Corydoras* to breed.

Corydoras are shoaling fishes, and as *C. baderi* (shown here) is no exception you should keep several specimens of *Corydoras*, not necessarily, but preferably, of the same species in your tank.

inducement to spawn, but if they seem reluctant, gradually lower the water level of the tank by 30 to 40 per cent over five days. On the sixth day replace what has been removed with fresh water of a marginally lower temperature. This is to imitate the natural environmental conditions of *Corydoras*, who spawn at the onset of the rainy season.

Often the males will excitedly follow the female around the tank as she looks for a suitable spawning site; this is a good indication that spawning is to commence shortly. One of the males will then position himself directly in front of the female in the classic T-formation. The two fishes will shudder while the female releases a small number of eggs which are clasped in her ventral fins (hence her expanded ventral finnage). The male simultaneously releases sperm to fertilize the eggs. The female then places the adhesive eggs onto a

flat surface that has been cleaned prior to spawning. This may be on the plant leaves, or more often than not, on the side of the aquarium. Whatever the anchorage point is, it will be in the upper part of the water column, not on rocks or the substrate.

At this point it is recommended that either the adult fishes or eggs be removed. The eggs can be removed using a razor blade or something similar, taking great care to avoid damaging them, and placed in a plastic sieve of the type available from most aquarium shops. The sieve is then suspended just below the water surface. The water in the sieve is constantly replenished by means of an air-operated sponge filter, in order to ensure that the eggs are always in well-oxygenated water. They hatch within about 48 hours.

After absorbing their yolk sac the young fry can be transferred to a small, unoccupied aquarium, and fed newly hatched *Artemia* (brine shrimp), and as they grow, offered *Daphnia* and crumbled flake foods.

Once you have mastered one of the commoner easy species such as *Corydoras paleatus* (the peppered *Corydoras*) you can move on to one of the more difficult species like *Corydoras panda*. This fish was named on account of its coloration: it looks a lot like a panda, with black eye patches on a light body.

To breed this lovely creature you will need to use a similar set-up to that used for the peppered *Corydoras*, but include a number of artificial mops on the bottom and hanging from the top. More often than not *Corydoras panda* will spawn into one of these, rather than out in the open. It is then an easy job to carefully pull the eggs off the mop and hatch them in the same way as before. This species is not so prolific with only 20 or so eggs produced each spawning, instead of up to 100 for the common species. It also tends to be seasonal in its spawning habits, so no matter how carefully the fishes are conditioned no spawning activity will take place until the correct time of the year – the onset of the rainy season.

Breeding Aspidoras

Aspidoras are generally smaller than *Corydoras*, and although similar, differ from the latter in minor anatomical characteristics of the skull that are not superficially apparent. Aquarium care is similar to that for *Corydoras*.

Once you have successfully bred some of the *Corydoras*, *Aspidoras pauciradiatus* could provide you with another challenge. Use a pair rather than a trio when attempting to spawn them.

Juvenile *Brochis splendens* look so different from the adults that, to the untrained eye, they might be mistaken for *Corydoras* and have often been sold in the trade as sailfin *Corydoras*.

Breeding *Aspidoras* has proven a little more difficult than breeding the commoner species of *Corydoras*, but it is on a par with many of the wild-caught *Corydoras*. The aquarium should be set up with soft water and a mop suspended from a corner of the tank. This should be positioned so that its top is just beneath the water's surface. Additional mops can be positioned on the bottom of the aquarium to provide cover for the adults. It is best not to use a substrate in the breeding tank.

Sexing *Aspidoras* can be achieved in the same way as for *Corydoras*, but the differences in the finnage may be a little more difficult to identify. When selecting potential breeders choose a female which has a nice plump body and a male which is active and showing good coloration. In this case use only a single pair instead of the trio suggested for *Corydoras*. The breeding pair should be placed in the breeding aquarium and conditioned on plenty of live foods.

Aspidoras usually spawn during the early hours of the morning before sunrise, so you are most likely to find the eggs first thing in the morning. They are amber coloured and will most likely be laid in the mop just under the water's surface. The adult pair can now be removed to another aquarium, together with the mops from the bottom of the breeding tank. While the eggs will hatch if left in the mop, they will be more prone to fungus because of the lack of water movement. It is far better to carefully remove the eggs from the mop and spread them out on the aquarium bottom. Using this method virtually 100 per cent of the eggs will hatch.

Brochis splendens (emerald catfish) is an impressive and attractive fish to keep. Healthy specimens will have a greenish sheen over the body and the barbels will show no signs of abrasion.

Brochis britskii (Britski's *Brochis*) is a more recent import and can be hard to acclimatize to aquarium conditions. It is a fish for an experienced aquarist rather than a beginner.

A good spawning will produce in excess of 100 eggs. These hatch on the fourth day and the fry will be free-swimming a day or two after that. The fry will eat newly hatched brine shrimp as a first food, followed by other live and commercial foods. If well fed the babies will reach 3 cm (1¼ in) long in only 10 weeks.

The newborn fry look rather like small tadpoles, because their finnage has not yet developed properly. The dorsal, adipose, anal, and caudal fins are joined together into one long fin, which surrounds the rear half of the body. As they grow this "superfin" splits into four separate parts with the anal fin differentiating first, followed by the dorsal and then the tiny adipose fin.

Loricariids: the Sucker-mouthed Catfishes

The loricariids, from South America, are a most disparate family of catfishes, in both shape and size. All exhibit an underslung sucker mouth and most are herbivorous. The mouth is used to attach themselves to solid objects to avoid being carried away in the current, as they are particularly poor swimmers. The body is encased in body plates that develop from skin folds in the early fry stage, which in later life make swimming a difficult and laborious chore.

Smaller varieties of loricariid make excellent show fishes in the community aquarium. The graceful, slender *Farlowella* (twig catfish) and *Rineloricaria* (whiptailed cats) are particular favourites, and always readily available. *Ancistrus,* too, are fine additions and prosper well in the planted aquarium. Also highly recommended are the *Otocinclus* and *Parotocinclus* catfishes which rarely exceed 3 cm (1¹/₄ in).

The eyes of *Rineloricaria* sp. have adapted to bright conditions. An omega-shaped lobe, which can be raised or lowered at will, reduces the amount of light entering the eye to prevent burning of the delicate retina.

Several small loricariids, such as the *Otocinclus paulinus* shown here, are particularly well suited to the smaller community aquarium. This species likes soft, slightly acid water that is not too warm and has a high oxygen content. The fishes will often be seen resting near the return from a power filter.

Many species of *Hypostomus* can grow to in excess of 30 cm (12 in). Although these peaceful herbivores are too large and cumbersome to be housed in the planted community aquarium, they are ideal catfishes for keeping with larger Central and South American cichlids. Some of the larger *Hypostomus* are known to aestivate (a form of "hibernation") in the absence of water; as their natural water supplies evaporate in the dry season, they burrow into holes in a riverbank, cocooned in damp mud, awaiting the return of the rains.

Intermediate between these two size ranges are *Panaque* and *Sturisoma,* the former being too boisterous for the community tank, and the latter, although growing to around 20 cm (8 in), having the elegance to grace any planted aquarium. *Panaque* can also be a little quarrelsome towards other members of its own species, and even territorial, patrolling what it considers its own area of the tank.

For the larger aquarium, *Hypostomus* sp. (plecs) are popular and often sold as an alternative to *Gyrinocheilus aymonieri* (algae eater). What most people fail to realize, however, is just how quickly a small specimen can outgrow its accommodation.

The prime requisites for keeping *Parotocinclus maculicauda* are a well-matured, furnished aquarium, an efficient filtration system, regular water changes, and plenty of green foods.

Feeding Loricariids

Care for all loricariids, particularly the smaller and intermediate size species, is similar. The majority are herbivorous, and are useful in ridding the tank of green algae. In return for removing the algae they replace it with abundant excreta, which can in turn be beneficial to plant growth. The amount of algae growth in most aquaria will not, however, be enough to supply all their dietary needs, and will require supplementing with commercially produced, vegetable-based flake foods. An alternative, and one much appreciated, is to feed them peas and lettuce.

Frozen garden peas should be first placed in water hot enough to defrost them. Take each individual pea and pinch it between thumb and forefinger so that the two inner halves are separated from the outer skin. The inner parts are used and are quite a delicacy, relished by other species of fishes as well.

Another delicacy for loricariid catfishes is lettuce, particularly the outer leaves, which should first be washed and gently crushed in the hand to break down the cellulose, prior to placing in the aquarium. Plant the leaves in the substrate or weigh them down with a small rock attached with a rubber band, otherwise they will float out of reach of the sucker-mouthed catfishes. Lettuce will also distract the sucker-mouths from broad-leaved plants, which can be damaged by their constant rasping. When feeding lettuce, make sure you are not feeding varieties that have been treated with chemicals. Spinach can also be offered, but we have found that it breaks down fairly rapidly in water, leading to filter blockage and water pollution.

The addition of wood to the aquarium is most beneficial to this group of catfishes. Some species rasp the wood, creating their own hollows into which to retreat, therefore any wood used must be unvarnished to avoid poisoning the fishes. Wood is almost essential if keeping *Farlowella*, *Sturisoma*, and *Rineloricaria*, all of whom spend most of the day resting on it in the mid-water level.

Rineloricaria sp. (whiptails) can be sexed: males have thicker pectoral fin spines. Eggs may be laid on the glass and it is possible to see the fry developing. When the eggs are ready to hatch the parents may mouth them prior to the event.

Of all the loricariids, *Sturisoma panamense* (regal whiptail) is possibly one of the most popular. Their flamboyant finnage and size make them particularly suited to the large, well-planted community aquarium. The fish shown here is a juvenile. As they mature the finnage and coloration improves.

It is not unusual for aquarists to keep and breed *Rineloricaria* sp. (whiptails) without identifying the species.

Breeding Loricariids

A number of the smaller species can be bred in captivity. A good starting point is the *Ancistrus*. The aptly named bristlenosed catfishes can be readily sexed as adults: males have a display of tentacle-like growths on top of and around the snout, hence their common name. Females also have similar but smaller growths confined to the edge of the snout. *Ancistrus* also have interopercular spines on the side of the head, near the base of the pectoral fin spine. These are particularly large in males and are erectile. They are used in territorial disputes between adults.

Adults can be mildly territorial

Ancistrus temminckii (bristlenose) breed with little help from the aquarist, provided you have a pair. The first indication that they have bred will be the emergence of their fry. These 10 day-old fry are quite gregarious.

A brood of young *Ancistrus temminckii* (bristlenose) will strip a large lettuce leaf down to the ribs in half a day, so be sure you have a constant supply of fresh leaves. At three weeks old the fry are beginning to be more independent.

amongst themselves, and the number kept, especially for breeding purposes, should be restricted to one pair. Breeding can be undertaken in the community tank, which is certainly easier than isolating them in specially prepared conditions. They will determine the spawning site, usually a hollow in the base of a piece of bogwood. If the hollow is not the right size it will be enlarged by rasping.

The amber-coloured eggs are attached to the walls of the hollow and guarded by the parents from predation by other fishes. After about three days the fry emerge. Their bright amber yolk sacs make them conspicuous to other fishes, so parental care is continued until the sac disappears and the fry have developed a mottled colour pattern to aid concealment. When they are ten days old the fry will venture into the wider world and the parents relinquish their protection. Often the first sign of any breeding activity is when the ten-day-old fry emerge into the tank.

Lettuce leaves, as described above, make ideal fry food. One lettuce leaf can support about two dozen juveniles for a day.

Rineloricaria and related genera (whiptailed catfishes) are also fairly straightforward to both keep and breed. They have slender bodies and are often found attached to wood, rocks, and broad-leaved plants. The mouth structure and barbels on these catfishes vary from species to species, but essentially they all have large sucker mouths with patches of fine rasping teeth, usually with simple (unbranched) barbels. Some species, such as *Pseudohemiodon laticeps*, a veritable giant of a whiptail, have a delicate array of branched barbels.

Ancistrus temminckii (bristlenose) – the fish above is a male – is often purchased to rid a tank of algae. But when this is depleted feed your bristlenose plenty of vegetable foods or it will eat your plants.

Some loricariids have very ornate barbels such as those seen on this *Pseudohemiodon laticeps*. One of the largest whiptails, they are quite difficult to keep, being very particular about water quality. They need a fine sand substrate so that their delicate barbels are not damaged.

Some whiptail catfishes, such as the male of another giant species, *Loricariichthys*, carry their eggs in a mass attached to their lips.

These last two species are only rarely imported; most of the species available grow to less than 15 cm (6 in) in length, and are well suited to life in the planted aquarium. In many ways their habits, requirements, and breeding are similar to those of *Sturisoma* (regal whiptails) and *Farlowella*. In all cases, clean water with a moderately fast flow is essential and can be provided by a power filter. Feeding is the same as for *Ancistrus*, that is, a principally vegetable diet.

Sex can be determined as males of certain species, particularly *Sturisoma*, but also some species of *Rineloricaria* and *Farlowella*, develop cheek bristles. In several *Rineloricaria* species sex can be determined by studying the pectoral fins: those with fins that incline downward along the back edge are female; while the male's pectoral fin slopes upward.

They select their own mates, often for life. Spawning activity starts with the male cleaning a suitable flat surface. This will often be the aquarium glass, usually at the back of the tank where there is less activity. Once the site is cleaned to the satisfaction of the male he entices the female to it. She lays the adhesive eggs in a mass on the clean breeding site, and the male follows over the eggs in order to fertilize them. Generally it is the male who remains to guard the eggs, but in some species both parents may undertake the task. Infertile eggs, and eggs that accumulate dirt, are constantly removed by a parent to avoid contamination of the healthy eggs. They also fan the eggs with their ventral fins, and this gentle current of water helps wash away debris as well as oxygenating the eggs. When they have hatched, the fry, which look like miniature replicas of their parents, should be fed a vegetable-based diet, especially soft lettuce leaves.

Despite their small size, which makes them well suited to life in the furnished community tank, particularly one well planted, *Otocinclus* and the similar *Parotocinclus* are rarely, if ever, bred in captivity. As with the previous species, moderate water movement, with reasonably high levels of dissolved oxygen, is recommended.

Other species of loricariid to look for are those of the genus *Peckoltia*, of similar shape to *Ancistrus*, except that they lack the bristles on the snout. There are no reports of aquarium

Scientists have reclassified this species, formerly *Peckoltia* (clown plec) as *Panaque maccus*. This territorial species needs space.

spawnings of these, but surely success will come with time. It is mainly a matter of discovering the trigger. Some species of *Peckoltia* exhibit particularly striking colours.

Similar to *Peckoltia* is *Hypancistrus zebra*. Only recently discovered, this catfish is very vivid in its livery of ivory white body with wide black bands. Unfortunately, the law of supply and demand often makes these fishes a little expensive, though usually as demand drops after the initial introduction in the trade, so too does the price.

Many new species of loricariids have been discovered in recent years, so many in fact that ichthyologists (scientists who study fishes) have a back-log of species to name and describe. These newly discovered fishes are given code numbers initially, just as a point of reference. For instance, *Hypancistrus zebra* was at first known simply as L46 before it was given its scientific description – a pretty ignoble name for such an attractive and impressive fish.

If you have a healthy bank balance then this fish is for you. *Hypancistrus zebra* still commands a high price, which is unfortunate as few aquarists can afford to purchase several specimens in order to try and breed them.

The Banjos

Dysichthys (banjo cats) belong to the South American family Aspredinidae. They live in the leaf litter found in shallow forest waters, where their resemblance to dead leaves helps to conceal them. These small fishes (less than 12 cm/4³/4 in) are often available to the aquarist, and are at home in the furnished aquarium, where they burrow into the substrate leaving just their eyes showing. Although rarely active, the sight of a few of them rising from the sandy substrate when food is offered is appealing.

Right: *Dysichthys* sp. (banjos) are inoffensive and reclusive. Mainly active at twilight, they venture out to feed on worms and other small invertebrates.

Below: A substrate with wood and leaf litter allows them to hide and forage.

Feeding Banjos

Feeding is straightforward, as anything is accepted, particularly thoroughly washed *Tubifex* worms. They are not aggressive, and eat only very small fry, and then only if one passes close enough to be eaten without any effort expended in chasing. Only a few, vague reports exist of breeding in captivity. Most of these suggest that a depression is made in the substrate in which the eggs are laid and protected.

Doradids: the Talking Catfishes

Doradids are usually called talking catfishes due to the noise they can make, but they are not the only catfishes to employ noise as a form of communication. Doradids achieve this in two main ways. One method is to stridulate the pectoral fin joint by partially locking it while moving the fin spine. This movement need not be great to make a lot of noise. Another is the so-called "elastic spring mechanism", a muscle that links the anterior of the swim-bladder to the rear of the skull. This muscle is rapidly contracted and relaxed causing the air-filled swim-bladder to resonate. The sounds are used in a variety of ways. They are often heard as the fish is being caught at the dealers, and again as it is transferred to your tank. Noise is also used to locate conspecifics in the vastness of their South American waters. Sound travels further in water than in air.

A particular characteristic of the doradids is the single row of plates down each side, each supporting at least one backward-projecting thorn. These are used for protection, and make handling a little difficult. The use of nets is not recommended as the fish becomes entangled, and the net then has to be carefully cut free. They are best moved by

Amblydoras hancocki (Hancock's talking catfish) is a small, inoffensive dorad. It is quite at home in a community of medium-sized fishes.

hand, but even this is not without problems, the main one being the serrated pectoral spine, which can easily trap unwary fingers between it and the thorned plates on the body – a lesson once learnt, never forgotten. The trick is to grasp the caudal peduncle in one hand while supporting the body with the flattened palm of the other (ensuring stray fingers are well away from the "pinch zone"). This method works well with the larger doradids (some, for instance *Megalodoras irwini*, reach more than 60 cm (24 in)), as well as the smaller species.

There are about 80 different doradids of various sizes, some too big for all but large display aquaria. There are, however, a selection of small doradids suitable for some home aquaria. Few

have been bred in captivity. Possibly the most common species encountered is *Amblydoras hancocki* (Hancock's talking catfish), a relatively small (about 10 cm/4 in) doradid that is peaceful, though it should not be trusted with fry-sized fishes. It is principally an insectivore, with a preference for chironomid larvae (bloodworm) and *Tubifex*, but accepts commercially produced pelleted foods.

They are best kept in small groups of three or four, and spend most of the daytime hours hidden, so provide wood or rockwork, preferably the former, with lots of nooks and crannies in which they can hide. Another good addition to the tank is waterlogged dead beech and oak leaves. With this litter overlying the substrate *Amblydoras* will be

Newly imported specimens of *Platydoras costatus* (humbug catfish) require small, regular feeds to settle them in and build up their strength.

Astrodoras asterifrons (stargazing dorad) is a rare import. This placid, thorny little character adapts well to aquarium life.

Agamyxis pectinifrons is a greedy feeder and it is not unusual for it to gorge itself until it looks as though it has swallowed a golf ball.

seen more often during the day, burrowing under the leaves in search of food.

None of the doradids are active predators, but many grow large and may eat smaller tank-mates. The relatively small *Platydoras costatus* (white-lined dorad) can grow to 15 cm (6 in) and will eat small fishes if given the opportunity. *Agamyxis pectinifrons* (spotted dorad), if allowed to, will gorge itself to such an extent that it appears to have swallowed a golf ball. Both these species are rarely seen during daylight hours. *Megalodoras irwini* and *Pseudodoras niger* are both giants, and are usually expensive, even as juveniles. As they grow large, a correspondingly large aquarium should be planned. *Megalodoras irwini* is often slow-growing, and can be slow to acclimatize. It may not eat for a week or so after being introduced to the tank, but seems none the worst for wear after fasting. Young specimens are reputed to eat snails, but pelleted food is accepted. Beware, *M. irwini* can grow to over 60 cm (24 in), and at this size demands on filtration can be high.

Although it has the potential to grow into a large fish, *Megalodoras irwini* causes few or no problems once it has settled in an aquarium.

Opsodoras stubeli uses its fimbriated barbels to sweep the substrate in search of food. It is especially fond of small worms and crustaceans.

Pseudodoras niger can grow to 70 cm (28 inches) or longer, but even at this size they are "gentle giants". Obviously they are unsuited to the community tank, mainly because of the damage they would wreak on plants as they moved around. Small live-bearers (mollies) have been kept in the same tank as 50 cm (20 in) specimens with impunity. They are best kept in twos or threes rather than in isolation. They will happily accept pelleted foods. Although they take quite a long time to grow, the wait is more than compensated for by their longevity.

Although this fish will grow in excess of 70 cm (28 in), even in an aquarium, *Pseudodoras niger* is really a "gentle giant".

The Glass Catfish

Kryptopterus bicirrhus (Asian glass catfish), is unusual in a number of ways. As its name implies, it is transparent and some internal organs and the skeleton can be seen. It is also one of the few catfishes that is not benthic (bottom-dwelling), remaining in mid-water. The body is compressed, similar to most other pelagic fishes, rather than depressed. They are shoaling catfishes that must be kept in small groups, not individually, otherwise they will not feed. At rest, *Kryptopterus* remain in mid-water at a slight angle, head uppermost, but when swimming the body is horizontal. Water conditions are the key to their viability. The water should be crystal clear, well oxygenated, moderately fast flowing, and not too alkaline. Most planted aquaria are ideal for keeping glass catfishes. Flake foods are acceptable, but should be supplemented with *Daphnia*, *Cyclops*, and/or freshly hatched mosquito larvae.

Kryptopterus bicirrhus (**Asian glass catfish**) **should be kept in small shoals as they often refuse to feed and become reclusive if kept alone.**

Synodontis angelicus (**angelic catfish**) **can be quarrelsome, so keep two of them only if space permits.**

Upside-down Catfishes

Some species of the family Mochokidae are often referred to as "upside-down cats" because they swim inverted. While many of the mochokids can swim in this way, less than half a dozen of the hundred or more species do so regularly. The advantage of swimming inverted is the ability to catch insects on the water surface, as the mouth is on the underside of the head, and one species, *Synodontis nigriventris*, also takes in atmospheric oxygen.

One of the species that stays upside-down on a long-term basis is *Synodontis nigriventris*. One of the smallest members of this family, growing to around 5 cm (2 in), it is peaceful enough for the community tank, but is best kept in small groups. Provide an overhang such as a rocky cavern, or better still a piece of wood with the overhang near the water surface. Here they will rest inverted, and be visible during the day. Most of their feeding activity occurs at dusk. Small surface-dwelling invertebrates such as mosquito larvae and pupae are recommended, though flake food is also accepted. They have not been bred in captivity.

Most of the other mochokids grow larger, to over 20 cm (8 in), and can be too boisterous for most planted community tanks. There are, however, some species worthy of consideration. One of these is *Synodontis angelicus* (angelic catfish). Its distinctive coloration and markings make it a much sought-after species. Rarely do two specimens have similar markings. Some are spotted, others show light, reticulated bands, with all kinds of patterns in between. They can grow up to 20 cm (8 in). An aquarium

Synodontis multipunctatus (**cuckoo catfish**) **lays its eggs near oral-incubating cichlids which then look after them – hence "cuckoo catfish".**

Hemisynodontis membranaceous (**moustache catfish**) **uses its membranous barbels to search for food.**

furnished with rocks providing many hiding places is required. Two adults in a confined tank may indulge in territorial battles, but in the larger aquarium this does not normally happen.

For those who wish to include a catfish in their Tanganyikan or Malawian cichlid collection, a good choice would be *Synodontis multipunctatus* (cuckoo catfish). The common name is derived from their breeding strategy: the eggs are released near oral-incubating cichlids such as *Tropheus duboisi* when they are breeding, and the eggs of both species are picked up and cared for by the cichlid. Even as newly hatched fry, the *Synodontis* are cared for in the mouths of the cichlids. Water conditions need to be similar to those for Tanganyikan/Malawian cichlids (alkaline), and the tank furnished with rockwork. Many *Synodontis*, including this one, are sexable. Males have a short genital papilla near the vent.

Other Catfishes of General Interest

With over 2000 species from which to choose, only a very small selection can be described here. Other species to look out for are *Pimelodus pictus* (angelic pim), often sold as a community aquarium catfish, with a striking silvery body and black markings. This South American naked catfish grows to about 14 cm (5¹/₂ in), and is fairly active during the day. Adult specimens may eat very small fishes, but juveniles are usually harmless. They can, like many catfishes, be extremely

A midwater swimming, shoaling catfish, many people make the mistake of buying only one or two specimens of *Eutropiellus buffei* (African debauwi cat) with the result that they quickly pine away.

difficult to handle owing to their sharply pointed dorsal and pectoral fin spines. If these puncture your skin the mucus of the fish can cause mild blood poisoning, which can be quite painful for an hour or two.

The family Pimelodidae, of which *P. pictus* is an example, includes large carnivorous catfishes such as *Sorubim lima* (shovel-nose), a sleek fish with a flattened snout, wide mouth and long barbels. As an adult can grow to 50 cm (20 in), only juvenile specimens are suited to the domestic aquarium. An even bigger species is *Phractocephalus hemioliopterus* (red-tailed catfish), growing to 1 metre (3 feet). In recent years small (5 cm/2 in) specimens have been offered for sale, a practice that has led to public aquaria being swamped with offers of sub-adults as the fishes outgrow their owners' tanks. To keep any large animal, be it a fish, dog, horse, or whatever, is a commitment that cannot be shirked. Always, no matter what fish you are buying, make yourself familiar with its demands and satisfy them.

For those with an appetite for adventure, how about *Malapterurus electricus* (African electric catfish). Adult specimens, which grow to 40 cm (16 in), can generate a discharge of up to 200 volts. The electricity is developed in a biological battery composed of modified muscle which surrounds the body, from just behind the head to the base of the tail. The fish uses this discharge to stun prey and for defence. Afterwards it takes about 10 to 15 minutes to recharge. It is a sedentary fish, rarely moving from its chosen lair. Needless to say, it is unwise to keep it with other fishes, and special handling is required.

From the above examples it would seem that catfishes need to be avoided, but this is far from the truth. There are many other species that offer grace or curiosity, and are well suited to life in the community aquarium. *Eutropiellus debauwi* (African debauwi cat) is very much at home in this kind of habitat. With an undemanding diet and best kept in shoals, they make excellent additions to the tank.

Although it is a beautifully coloured fish, consider keeping *Phractocephalus hemioliopterus* (red-tailed catfish) only if you can provide it with suitably large accommodation and life-support systems.

Cypriniformes

The Cypriniformes are a large group and include some of the most popular aquarium fishes such as barbs, rasboras, danios, loaches, the freshwater sharks (for want of a better term), and the goldfish. Ichthyologists have classified over 2000 or so species, but this has to be an approximation because they are considered a taxonomic minefield. Cypriniformes are native throughout Africa, Europe, Asia, and the southern part of North America, and have been introduced as sport and/or food fishes throughout the world.

Cypriniformes have a series of bones linking the swim-bladder and the inner ear, which gives them extremely sensitive hearing. This assemblage is known as the Weberian Apparatus, and is also present in the characins (Characiformes) and catfishes (Siluriformes). Cypriniformes may also develop tubercules on their heads and some parts of their bodies. This is especially true for species which live in fast-flowing waters. These tubercules have a hydrodynamic function, reducing the drag effect of water flowing over the body. During the breeding season, mature males of some species also develop tubercules on their heads and these may have a sexual function, perhaps in stimulating the female. Some Cypriniformes also make migratory spawning runs and develop tubercules at this time, so in the case of these fishes either reason may apply, or even a combination of both. Many of the smaller species are ideal for tropical or cold water aquaria. In general, the easiest way of dealing with the Cypriniformes is to divide them into tropical and cold water vareties.

TROPICAL CYPRINIFORMES
Barbs

African and Asian barbs have been exploited by the aquarium trade for many years. Wild stocks of some species such as *Barbus titteya* (cherry barb) from Sri Lanka are very low, but the species is still widely available in the hobby, due to captive breeding. The majority of the small barbs are bred by the thousand in fish farms in the Far East, South Africa, eastern Europe, and Florida. Captive-bred fishes are easier to transport and not as sensitive to changes in water conditions as wild fishes, and so are easier to acclimatize.

Barbs are found in all bodies of water, from streams and rivers to lakes, and are shoaling fishes.

The ever-popular *Barbus titteya* (cherry barb) is now rare in the wild and virtually all aquarium stocks are supplied from fish farms. Males are a deep cherry red when in breeding condition whereas females are red/brown. Males do not bicker with each other so keep a group of both sexes to see them at their best.

Some fishes are bred commercially to enhance certain features as is the case with this *Brachydanio frankei* (leopard danio) which has been selectively bred to elongate its finnage.

Although a large fish, *Cyclocheilichthys apogon* is quite peaceful and may be kept with other, similar-natured fishes in a large community aquarium.

Barbus tetrazona (tiger barb) has a reputation for aggression. Keep a shoal of at least eight to prevent them chivvying tankmates.

When trying to breed *Barbus "odessa"* (Odessa barb) make sure you have a compatible pair: males should be at least 18, females 12, months old.

Keep *Barbus cumingi* (Cuming's barb) in small shoals, because they will react with each other and form a focal point in the aquarium.

Applying this to the aquarium, when purchasing fishes you should get a group of six to ten, more if you have room. A sparsely planted aquarium is ideal as this allows plenty of swimming space in the mid to lower levels. With the exception of *Barbus tetrazona* (tiger barb), most small barbs are compatible with equal-sized fishes in the community aquarium. Tiger barbs are noted for their quarrelsome nature, but even this can be overcome provided they are kept as a shoal of eight or more in a large aquarium, when, as they are so busy chasing each other, they leave the other fishes alone. Only if kept in smaller numbers do they really cause any trouble.

With some of the medium-sized species, keep the aquarium well covered as they may jump, especially if chasing around at feeding time.

For small aquaria (up to 60 cm/24 in) we recommend *B. titteya* (cherry barb), *B. gelius* (golden dwarf barb), *B. cumingi* (Cuming's barb), *B. oligolepis* (checker barb), *B. conchonius* (rosy barb), *B. fasciatus* (striped barb), *B. "odessa"* (Odessa barb), *B. schuberti* (golden barb), and *B. ticto stoliczkae* (Stoliczka's barb) which are all less than 7.5 cm (3 in) when fully grown and will live happily with small tetras, danios, and the smaller livebearers.

If you wish to try something a little more delicate, then perhaps *Barbus barilioides* (blue-barred barb) is for you. Reaching 5 cm (2 in) at most, it is more demanding than most barbs as regards water conditions, requiring mature, soft, slightly acid water but if you can provide this in your community aquarium, and the other inmates are small and very peaceful, it is well worth trying six or seven of these fishes. If kept in lower numbers they are not happy, they cease feeding and hide away.

For larger tanks (up to 1m/ 36in) some favourites are *B. arulius* (arulius barb), *B. everetti* (clown barb), *B. filamentosus* (black-spot or filament barb), and *B. orphoides*. Young specimens of these fishes are more colourful than adults, for example, young *B. filamentosus* are coppery with dark vertical bars, brilliant red on the dorsal and bright red tips to the caudal fin.

Adults are silvery with a pink sheen over the body and a black spot just in front of the caudal peduncle. As some compensation for this, male *B. arulius* and *B. filamentosus* develop extensions to the dorsal fin rays as they mature.

For aquaria longer than a metre (36 in) the choice has to be *Barbus schwanenfeldi* (tinfoil barb). This elegant fish grows to over 30 cm (12 in) long, but, unless you are prepared to give it plenty of space, is really only suited to public aquaria.

Feeding barbs is simplicity itself. They are true omnivores, but, given the choice, they do prefer green foods and may nibble at your plants. They have a pair of barbels at the corner of their mouths which they use to help detect food in the substrate. They do not have teeth in their mouths, but use pharyngeal teeth (situated in their throats) to crush food.

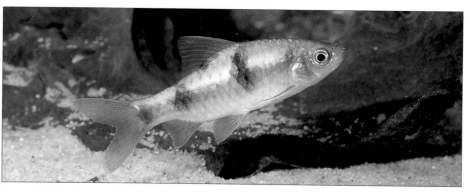

Juvenile *Barbus arulius* (arulius barb) are often overlooked in dealers' tanks as they do not show their true colours and extended fins until later in life.

Breeding Barbs

In some species, for example *B. oligolepis*, telling the sexes apart is easy: in general, the males are more highly coloured and slimmer than females, but in others, for example *B. schwanenfeldi*, it takes one to know one because there are no external sexual characteristics.

Barbs are egg scatterers and are among the easiest fishes to breed. For the novice aquarist *B. conchonius*, *B. oligolepis,* and *B. schuberti* are excellent fishes to try and spawn. Some deposit their eggs over gravel, others shed them through plants. A pair will break from the shoal and shimmy together in mid-water, shedding clouds of eggs and milt, or go through the same procedure among thickets of fine-leaved plants. There is no parental care, the eggs being left to fend for themselves. In the community aquarium such a bounty of food sends the other occupants scurrying about in search of eggs and the parents will even eat their own spawn. Successful breeding can be achieved in a specially prepared breeding aquarium so the eggs can be scattered over marbles, through mesh, or in plants, and the parents removed before they can consume the fry.

You will need plenty of live food and a lot of space to raise the fry, as a single pair of *B. conchonius*, for example, will produce several hundred eggs.

Below top: Barbus oligolepis (checker barb) is one of the best barbs for the community aquarium.

Below bottom: Barbus schuberti (golden barb) is a peaceful fish that will settle in well in a community tank.

For movement in a large aquarium, nothing is more impressive than a shoal of *Barbus schwanenfeldi* (tinfoil barb). They make excellent companions for large, sedentary catfishes.

Purchase young *Barbus filamentosus* (black-spot or filament barb) and grow them on yourself. Feed them on a varied diet of live, frozen, and green foods to get good specimens.

Male *Barbus nigrofasciatus* (ruby barb) are larger and more intensely coloured than females, especially when ready to spawn. Provide them with a well-planted aquarium and incude some floating plants to reduce the light level.

A timid fish, *Barbus eugrammus* (striped barb) likes soft, slightly acid warm water; it can be kept with other peaceful fishes.

Cypriniformes

157

Danios

Danios are very similar to barbs but are much slimmer-bodied. They are Asian fishes and are found in large shoals in fast-flowing waters. In the aquarium they prefer the upper layers of the water and may be seen cruising around all day. Most people buy just a couple, but with only two much of the beauty is lost as the fishes have no others to display to. They are peaceful, ideal community fishes.

They are insectivores and their upturned mouth is ideally suited to taking insects from the water surface. Fortunately for us, they are not fussy about food and will take flake and frozen foods without any hesitation. Bred by the thousand in commercial fish farms, albino and long-finned strains of *Brachydanio rerio* (zebra danio) and *Brachydanio albolineatus* (pearl danio) have been developed. These strains are not quite as hardy as the wild type and require slightly higher temperatures. Both zebra and pearl danios are small fishes, the pearl not exceeding 6 cm (2¼ in) and the zebra 5 cm (2 in).

Danio aequipinnatus (giant danio) is larger, growing up to 10 cm (4 in), and a truly magnificent fish for the larger community aquarium. When they are well fed with plenty of live foods such as mosquito larvae and blood-worm, the blue/green background colour on the body is overlaid with golden yellow spots and bars.

Right: *Brachydanio rerio* var. *frankei* (spotted or leopard danio) was formerly known as *B. frankei* and thought to be a species in its own right but is now considered a variety of *B. rerio*. There is also a long-finned form of this fish.

Brachydanio rerio (zebra danio) needs to be kept in a shoal, with particular attention being paid to water quality if kept for any length of time.

Fed on a variety of small live and frozen foods, *Brachydanio albolineatus* (pearl danio) will display its best colours and may even breed.

Danio aequipinnatus (giant danio), formerly known as *Danio malabaricus*, is an active shoaling fish which requires a spacious aquarium.

Tanichthys albonubes (white cloud mountain minnow) is easy to keep and breed, even in a small aquarium.

Breeding Danios

Danios are prolific and very easy to breed. Males are slimmer and have more intense coloration than females, and often you can separate just a pair to do the job, but, as the male drives the female very hard, some people prefer to shoal spawn them. Set up your breeding aquarium with either marbles over the bottom or some Java moss, so that the fishes can scatter their eggs, but cannot eat them. No parental care is practised. As with the barbs, ensure that you have good supplies of small live foods, starting with infusoria and newly hatched brine shrimp, ready for the fry. Make sure the breeding tank is well covered as the fishes can be so active that they leap from the water.

White Clouds

A small fish that is often kept with danios, and has the same maintenance and feeding requirements, is *Tanichthys albonubes* (white cloud mountain minnow), which is found in streams in the White Cloud Mountains of China. A most accommodating little fish, it can be kept in cool conditions, (as low as 16°C/60°F), and some people keep them outside in pools during the summer. Fishes that have been kept outside have more colour than those kept in aquaria, and this may be due to the abundance of natural foods, from insect larvae to algae.

Tanichthys albonubes breeds in the same way as the danios but ignores its eggs, so, left mostly to their own devices in a well-planted species aquarium or pool, they will multiply rapidly. The white cloud mountain minnow is probably one of the best egg-laying fishes a novice could try.

Rasboras

This group of fishes is one that is, by and large, overlooked by most aquarists, and yet there are a fair number of them in the trade. Inhabiting both still and running water, large shoals can be seen near the surface. They are found in southeast Asia and the Indo-Australian archipelago. In the main they are insectivores, but will take flake foods. Give them a varied diet, especially if you are going to attempt to breed them, and include small live foods or frozen *Daphnia,* and similar-sized items.

Rasboras can be divided into two groups by body shape; those which are long and slim, almost torpedo-shaped, and those which are deeper-bodied. Among the deeper-bodied group of rasboras are some of the best known: *R. heteromorpha* (harlequin), *R. hengeli,* and *R. vaterifloris* (pearly rasbora); while the slim-bodied species include *R. borapetensis* (red-tailed rasbora), *R. pauciperforata* (red-striped rasbora), *R. maculata* (pygmy

rasbora, spotted rasbora), and *R. trilineata* (scissortail).

The majority of the rasboras can be kept in the community aquarium, but a few require a little more attention to water conditions and are really suited only to a species aquarium. One such is the tiny *R. maculata* which grows to 2.5 cm (1 in) at most. These little fishes require soft, acid water and copious amounts of small live foods if you are to maintain them for any length of time, and even more so if you hope to breed them.

Others more particular about water quality, especially when it comes to breeding, are *R. vaterifloris, R. pauciperforata,* and *R. heteromorpha,* which all require soft, acid conditions.

Breeding Rasboras

With the exception of *R. heteromorpha* and *R. hengeli,* pairs make spawning runs through fine-leaved plants until they have produced all their eggs, which stick tightly to the plants. The parents can then be removed. It

takes about 30 hours for the eggs to hatch and the tiny fry hang from the water plants. Only when they are free-swimming should very small foods be offered.

Both *R. heteromorpha* and *R. hengeli* place their eggs on the undersides of broad plant leaves – *Cryptocorynes* are favourites. These eggs also take up to 30 hours to hatch and the fry can then be raised on very fine live foods.

Pair compatibility may be a problem in some species. If your fishes fail to spawn, try giving them different partners. It is worth noting that some pairs will not breed until they have been together for a few days, *R. maculata* being a classic case.

Rasbora hengeli makes an excellent community fish if kept with other small peaceful fishes. To see them at their best feed live foods.

Rasbora vaterifloris (pearly rasbora), from Sri Lanka, requires warm, soft, slightly acid water.

Above: Rasbora heteromorpha (harlequin) have a novel method of spawning: upside down on the underside of leaves.

Right: Provide Rasbora trilineata (scissortail) with plenty of swimming space – and a tight cover, else they may jump out of the tank.

Cypriniformes

159

"Sharks" and Flying Foxes

Both "sharks" and flying foxes are popular in the aquarium hobby. The best known are *Epalzeorhynchus bicolor* (still, incorrectly, known as *Labeo bicolor*) (red-tailed black shark), whose striking coloration – velvety black body and scarlet caudal fin – is all that is needed to sell it; and *Epalzeorhynchus* (formerly *Labeo*) *frenatus* (red-finned shark, ruby shark) which has, as one of its common names suggests, red fins and a dark brown body. The "shark" part of their common name derives from their shape and the manner in which they swim, cruising the aquarium in a shark-like manner, and not from their eating habits! Although popular, they are not ideal community fishes. Both can be quite belligerent and will pick on other fishes, as well as each other, shredding fins and generally bullying them. When fully grown at about 12 cm (4³/₄ in) they can really cause a lot of damage, so keep them only with other fishes large enough to take care of themselves, such as the medium-sized barbs and catfishes. True omnivores, they will eat anything.

Far less trouble, though larger, are *Balantiocheilus melanopterus* (silver or Bala Shark) at 35 cm

Epalzeoryhnchus bicolor (red-tailed black shark) are the villains of the community aquarium. Many aquarists fail to appreciate the damage they can cause.

(14 in), *Labeobarbus festivus* (diamond shark, festive Apollo shark) at 20 cm (8 in), and *Osteochilus hasselti* at 30 cm (12 in). Although these are large fishes, they are peaceful. Many people often keep juvenile specimens in their community tanks, acquiring larger accommodation for them as they grow. Given plenty of space, growth is steady. They like clean, clear water with a reasonable flow, such as that from a power filter. Feeding is no problem: they are omnivores but do have a liking for green foods and will graze on algae or nibble at plants. *Osteochilus hasselti* is particularly fond of Java moss and will keep the rampant growth of this in check. If you do not have many plants in the tank or if the fishes are grazing too heavily on them, lettuce leaves make a good alternative. The fishes tend to ignore them if they are left to float but, if planted they are classed as fair game and eaten. Do ensure that you have a good cover on the aquarium as these fishes will jump, especially if frightened.

Members of the genus *Labeo* are generally referred to in the trade as sharks. For those of you who like big fishes, *Labeo chrysophekadeon* (black shark) may be worth considering keeping. Growing to 60 cm (24 in), this deep-bodied shark is a very powerful, active creature that can be quarrelsome, so is best kept

Balantiocheilus melanopterus (silver or Bala shark) is a fish that is prone to leaping from the water so ensure that you have a tight-fitting cover glass to keep them in. Floating plants will help discourage jumping.

Epalzeorhynchus frenatus (red-finned shark) is less of a nuisance than *E. bicolor* (red-tailed black shark), but should nevertheless be housed with similar-sized fishes, and given a varied diet.

Captive breeding has produced an albino strain of *Epalzeorhynchus frenatus* (albino red-finned shark) but unfortunately has done nothing to improve its disposition towards other fishes.

Cyprin*iformes*

Consider keeping *Labeo chryso-phekadeon* (black shark) only if you are willing to provide a very large aquarium. The growth rate of these creatures is phenomenal.

Very active fishes, *Epalzeorhynchus kallopterus* (flying fox) need space. Give them a well-planted aquarium in which each individual fish can establish a territory.

The Algae Eater

Gyrinocheilus aymonieri is sold under various names: Indian algae eater, Chinese algae eater, and sucking loach. To the newcomer it seems to be the answer to all his problems – a fish that will eat algae. Small specimens are fine in the community aquarium, but it is potentially a large fish (25 cm/10 in plus) and it grows quickly, becoming more and more boisterous, digging out depressions in the gravel, and even sticking itself on to the sides of larger fishes much to their annoyance. Damage to the victim's protective mucus (some sucking loaches even develop a taste for this "food") may result, creating a potential site for infection. Youngsters hang from the sides of the aquarium using their sucker mouths, looking like rows of little thermometers. To permit them to breathe while holding station, there is a small spiracle on the head that allows water to pass into the mouth and out over the gills yet still allows enough suction for the fish to hold on. As well as eating algae. *G. aymonieri* will eat small invertebrates, flake, and frozen foods.

alone. Even at half this size it requires a 100 x 50 x 50 cm (36 x 18 x 18 in) aquarium and a filtration system to match. Unless you feel you can cope with this, it is best left to public aquaria to maintain. It is omnivorous but likes a predominance of vegetable matter in its diet. In southeast Asia the flesh is considered to be very good eating, and it is an important food fish.

There is a small African *Labeo* that is highly prized among aquarists, *L. variegatus* (harlequin shark, variegated shark). Growing to only 30 cm (12 in) at most, it is much more manageable and much more attractive as a juvenile. Youngsters are mottled dark brown over a light cream to beige background and there are traces of orange/red in their fins, but as the fishes mature they lose this colouring and turn grey. Small specimens tolerate other fishes but they can become aggressive when mature. It is one of those fishes that are best grown up along with their tankmates rather than trying to introduce medium- to large-sized fishes into the adult shark's territory. An omnivore, it is no trouble to keep or feed.

Epalzeorhynchos kallopterus (flying fox) is an ideal fish for the larger, well-planted community aquarium. Although loners, several specimens can be kept in the same aquarium without fights breaking out, provided they can define their territories. Flying foxes are almost too good to be true: they are tolerant of other fishes, graze algae but do not chew at the plants, and are tolerant of most water conditions as long as extremes are avoided. Their occasional tendency to dash around may, however, be unsettling for some timid species.

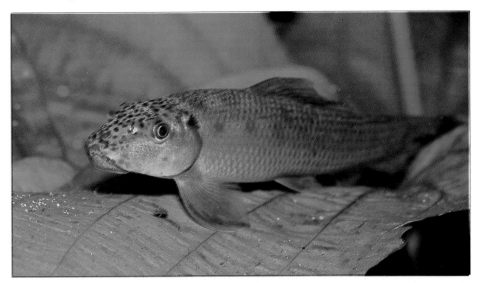

Young specimens of *Gyrinocheilus aymonieri* (algae eater, sucking loach) are often kept to rid a tank of algae. Unfortunately as they grow they become far too large and boisterous and harrass other fishes.

Loaches

Being bottom-dwelling species, the loaches are either eel-like or have a triangular body cross-section, their flat bellies being in contact with the substrate. Loaches may have very small scales covering all the body; be partially scaled, in which case the scales are missing from the underside; or naked. When you think about it, the absence of some or all of the scales is a very sensible arrangement, because if scales were present on the belly of the fish, they would be dislodged as the fish moved over rocks and sharp gravel, leaving it open to infection.

Their distribution ranges across Europe and Asia down to, and including, the Malay archipelago, and also includes the extreme north of Africa (Morocco). The main genera encountered by aquarists are: *Acanthopsis*, *Acanthophthalmus*, *Botia*, *Cobitis*, *Lepidocephalus*, *Misgurnus*, and *Nemacheilus*. With such a wide range, from the temperate zones down to the tropics, some genera, for example *Misgurnus*, contain species that are suited to tropical aquaria (for example *M. anguillicaudatus* – Chinese weatherloach) and others (*M. fossilis* – European weatherloach) which should be kept in a coldwater aquarium.

With the exception of some

B. macracantha (clown loach) is a firm favourite among hobbyists. Aquarists often fail with this fish because of poor water conditions and low temperatures, and are rarely aware of its potential size.

Nemacheilus species, loaches have a bifid (two-pronged) spine beneath the eye, which they can erect and lower at will. These spines are quite sharp and can inflict damage on other fishes as well as becoming entangled in nets. Loaches will often erect the spines when frightened and many a transportation bag has been punctured in this way. To reduce the chances of the fishes being able to puncture the bags make sure that the corners are taped up. A loach will also use its spines to defend its territory: in the aquarium they like to hide away in caves which they defend against other fishes.

The mouth is surrounded by three or four (depending on species) pairs of barbels which are covered with taste receptors, which aid the fishes when they are searching through the substrate for food. In the wild, their

The colour patterning on *Botia lohachata* (Pakistani loach) can vary considerably. In captivity these creatures can be quite argumentative, and if keeping several provide plenty of hiding places.

diet consists primarily of small worms and insect larvae, but in captivity they will take flake and tablet foods as well as small frozen and live foods and algae. They are also very fond of fish eggs and will try and steal these even if the parents are guarding the eggs.

Many loaches are able to use their intestine to take oxygen from the atmosphere, and so can survive in waters that are low in oxygen. They are also very sensitive to barometric pressure and this may cause them to dash about the aquarium at times. *Misgurnus* (weatherloaches) are probably best known for this (hence their common name).

In the aquarium, provide your loaches with a soft substrate. Some, such as *Acanthopsis choiorhynchus* (horse-faced or long-nosed loach) like to burrow under the sand until only their eyes are visible. Caves among rocks and plant roots are also desirable, so that each fish can have a small territory. Most loaches will live in harmony with other fishes, but some, notably *Botia berdmorei* and *B. lohachata* (Pakistani loach), quarrel amongst themselves and, just to be different, *B. modesta* (orange-finned loach) picks fights with other fishes, preferring to

Acanthopsis choiorhynchus (horse-faced loach) likes to bury itself in the substrate, which therefore needs to be fine-grained.

Botia modesta (orange-finned loach) is a nocturnal fish. Feed after "lights out" while the room light is still on.

shoal with its own kind. During these disputes, clicking noises can be heard. It is thought that these may be caused by rapid jerking of the bifid spine in its socket.

The *Botia* genus is well represented in the aquarium by species ranging in size from the small *B. sidthimunki* (dwarf loach, pygmy chain loach) which grows to only about 5 cm (2 in), up to the very impressive 30 cm (12 in) long *B. macracantha* (clown or tiger loach). These two species are popular among aquarists, *B. sidthimunki* because its size and gentle manner makes it ideal for the community aquarium, even with very small species, and *B. macracantha* because of its outstanding coloration.

Botia sidthimunki (pygmy chain loach) is relatively easy to keep and feed in a mature aquarium. They are shoaling fishes and several should be kept together. Unlike the other members of the genus, *B. sidthimunki* will spend time resting on plant leaves or twigs just above the substrate, or swimming in a shoal in the mid-waters of the tank during the day. At feeding time they will greedily take small live foods such as *Daphnia* and bloodworm as well as flake and tablet foods. A variety of foods and maintenance of good water conditions seem to be the key to

Acanthophthalmus sp. (kuhli loaches) need a fine substrate in which to burrow, and may infiltrate filters – don't throw them away during maintenance!

keeping these fishes healthy.

Botia macrancantha (clown loach) is a much more difficult fish to maintain. Because of its gregarious nature, the keeping of several individuals, as opposed to one or two, is a good start. Their size makes them suited to the large aquarium, but if you can grow them to 15 cm (6 in) or 20 cm (8 in) in captivity you are doing well. If stressed they are susceptible to white spot and any treatments should be used with caution – do not, under any circumstances, exceed the manufacturer's dosage instructions or the "cure" may prove fatal to your clown loach. *B. macracantha* is happy with a temperature in the 25–28°C (77–82°F) range.

Of the slim-bodied species, *Acanthophthalmus* species (kuhli loaches) are very popular. The trouble is, once you put them into the aquarium they disappear into the gravel, under the under-gravel filter plates, even up the intake pipe of external power filters if you forget to replace the strainer. They are, however, ideal for the community aquarium as they cause no problems, but you do need to keep three or four of them if at all possible as single

specimens are not so bold. They do come out to forage for food or rest among the plants, but, because of their burrowing habits, are probably one of the worst fishes to catch. They take live, flake, and frozen foods and growth from a skinny boot-lace into a rounded worm-like fish is rapid – an 8–10 cm (3–4 in) fish is a good-sized specimen. These fishes have been bred in captivity: they produce bright green eggs which are stuck to plants near the water surface.

The weather loaches are more seasonal imports and are among the larger loaches. *Misgurnus anguillicaudatus* can attain 50 cm (20 in) although 20–25 cm (8–10 in) is more usual in the aquarium. It is found from the Amur region of Siberia down through China, Korea, Hainan, and even Japan, and seems to prefer colder conditions, although it will tolerate temperatures up to 25°C (77°F) for a short time in summer. Typical loaches, much of their time is spent buried in the substrate. Breeding occurs in late spring or early summer. The eggs are laid on plants or fibrous roots and left to fend for themselves.

No community aquarium should be without a small shoal of *Botia sidthimunki* (chain loach) swimming about or resting on wood and plants.

COLDWATER CYPRINIFORMES

Continuing with the loaches, *Nemacheilus barbatulus* (stone loach), *Misgurnus fossilis* (European weatherloach), and *Cobitis taenia* (spined loach, spotted weatherloach) are ideal for coldwater aquaria. Maintenance is the same as for their tropical cousins except that the temperature should be kept below 20°C (68°F).

Nemacheilus barbatulus (stone loach) is often fished for by children and, along with *Gasterosteus aculeatus* (stickleback), is one of the first fishes they are likely to try and keep.

Cobitis taenia (spined loach) is another "first fish". Both of these loaches require cool, clean, clear, well-oxygenated water to survive in captivity.

The Goldfish

Kept by man for many, many years, *Carassius auratus* (the goldfish) is probably the best known of all aquarium/pond fishes. The wild form of this fish is a dull green to brown animal with little to recommend it as a potential aquarium fish, but a mutation occurred which developed lovely gold patches on the body which eventually turned the whole fish gold. The goldfish had been born. Its first recorded breeding in Europe took place in Holland in 1728. In its native China it has been domesticated even longer (since around 800 AD), and many fancy strains have been developed. The standard goldfish is the ideal pond fish, developed from the wild green/grey specimens into the reds and golds we see today.

Man has developed a multitude of variants with both single and double tails and various colours. Generally speaking, the single-tailed types, including the common goldfish, comets, and shubunkins, are excellent pond fishes. Small specimens of these types also make good hardy aquarium fishes which may live in excess of twenty years. The double-tailed varieties are much more delicate and are best kept at warmer temperatures

(10–15°C/50–59°F; thus they will not overwinter in an outdoor pond) in an aquarium, where their fine body shapes and finnage forms can be better appreciated.

Goldfishes are tolerant of most water conditions but a large aquarium is required if you are to keep them well. The old-fashioned goldfish bowl is not suitable: it has limited surface area for the uptake of oxygen into the water, no room for a filtration system, and insufficient swimming space An aquarium is far better to keep a goldfish happy, and there are companies which produce a package which contains everything including the tank and filtration system – you just add fishes, plants, and water. Goldfishes are noted for being messy, greedy feeders that produce a lot of waste. Needless to say they require a very efficient filtration system to cope with this. There is a good range of goldfish foods available but don't forget to include some vegetable matter as well as live or frozen foods in their diet.

Do not try and overcrowd your fishes as this places a great deal of stress on them. If conditions become too warm and the dissolved oxygen level falls, the fishes will gasp at the surface, their fins will become clamped to their bodies, and signs of fin congestion (bloodshot bases to the finnage) will appear. A partial water change to lower the temperature, and a check on the filtration system, will usually counteract the problem, which could, however, also be indicative that your fishes are overcrowded.

Carassius auratus (the goldfish) comes in many man-made varieties such as this long-tailed form. Colour, shape, and fins many vary.

Breeding Goldfishes

Breeding goldfishes is relatively easy. In the garden pond it should occur naturally and some of the fry may survive to maturity. To breed under controlled conditions, condition your chosen pair well on live foods. When ready to spawn the male will develop tubercules on his head, operculum, and pectoral fins; the female will be noticeably rounder.

Use a 100 x 30 x 30 cm (36 x 12 x 12 in) tank with spawning mops suspended in it so that the pair can swim through them, depositing and fertilizing the eggs as they do so. Once spawning is complete the pair can be removed and the eggs left to hatch. Feed the fry copious amounts of small live foods. Allow plenty of space for growing on, and cull the numbers rather than crowding if only limited space is available.

Captive breeding has resulted in some, to our way of thinking, horrendous strains being produced. Some have enlarged, bulbous eyes (celestials and bubble-eyes) and these require special care, ensuring there are no sharp objects on which the fishes can damage themselves. Yet others have been bred to enhance cancerous growths on their heads (lionheads).

The choice is yours as to whether or not you wish to keep these types.

Koi Carp

Some of you may be tempted to keep *Cyprinus carpio* (koi carp) in an aquarium and we would like to advise against this. Koi are potentially large fishes best housed in large purpose-built ponds with powerful filtration systems.

Some *Carassius auratus* (goldfish) varieties are bred not only for body shape but also for colour as in this "black moor". These highly line-bred fishes are more delicate than the standard goldfish or comet and are best kept under more controlled conditions in an aquarium rather than in a garden pond.

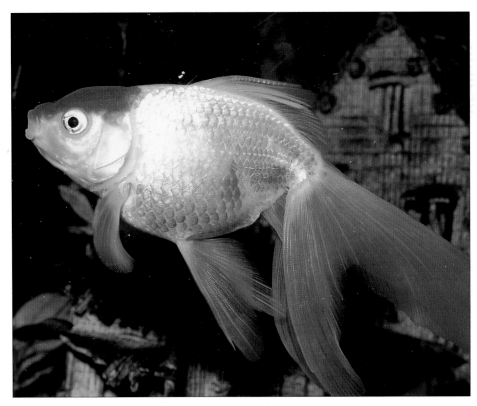

A twin-tailed goldfish is, again, a fish for the aquarium. Hobbyists, especially in the Far East, have selectively bred these fishes to such an extent that many can no longer swim properly because of the excess drag produced by their over-elongated finnage.

Bitterling

The various subspecies of *Rhodeus sericeus* (bitterling) are available during the summer months and are ideal for the aquarium as they are easy to keep, and feed on just about any small foods. They also have an unusual method of breeding, and need a swan mussel to spawn in. This alone makes them worth the effort.

When ready to breed, males are almost olive green along the top of the head and the back, with iridescent shades of blue, pink, and violet along the flanks. Females are yellower and show an ovipositor. Breeding is stimulated by a rise in water temperature to about 22°C (72°F).

Use a tank with a sand substrate and thickets of plants, and several live swan mussels (*Anodonta* sp.). The male keeps nudging the mussel with his mouth to stimulate it to remain open, while the female places her ovipositor in the mussel's outlet valve and deposits her eggs. The male follows, swiftly shedding his milt over the mussel and thereby fertilizing the eggs. Some 30 days later the fry leave the mussel and have to be raised on very fine live foods.

This Far Eastern bitterling, *Rhodeus ocellatus* (Hong Kong bitterling), is popular with coldwater fishkeepers. It requires similar conditions to its European counterpart.

Recent importations

Over the last couple of years some unusual fishes have been arriving from the Far East. One of these, *Myxocyprinus asiaticus,* is a large cyprinid (family Catostomidae) from China. Sold under the name Chinese sailfin, small specimens are highly coloured and very attractive; they are marbled with brown on a lighter cream or beige background, and the high dorsal fin makes them most appealing. The problem is that these small, endearing, 15–20 cm (6–8 in) fishes grow to more than 60 cm (24 in), so unless you can cope with this, leave them to public aquaria.

If you are going to try your hand, it is important to keep these fishes on the cool side and ensure that they have a very good filtration system to maintain water quality. Feeding does not seem to be fraught with any difficulties as the fishes accept flake, frozen, and live foods.

North America has also been the source of some unusual species such as *Notropis lutrensis* (shiner) and *Phoxinus erythrogaster* (southern red-bellied dace). Both are stream fishes that adapt well to aquarium conditions provided the tank is not overcrowded. They like high levels of oxygen and a good flow of water, so it is essential to maintain your filtration system well as any deterioration in water quality will lead to the demise of these fishes. The aquarium should have a sand or gravel substrate with pebbles and thickets of plants to provide cover. They are omnivorous, and flake, live, and frozen foods will all be taken, but ensure that you do not over-feed to the extent that uneaten food pollutes the water.

This North American fish, *Notropis lutrensis* (shiner), requires cooler temperatures in winter than in summer.

Phoxinus phoxinus (minnows) are common in unpolluted European streams. Given clean, cool, well-oxygenated water they can be a welcome addition to the aquarium.

The males of *N. lutrensis* are far more colourful than the silvery females. During the breeding season, the male develops tubercules around his snout. The fishes breed over sand, the pair depositing their eggs and then leaving them to fend for themselves.

Phoxinus erythrogaster is a very colourful fish that displays best if kept in a shoal. The males are much more highly coloured than the females, with their sides and bellies becoming deep red or sometimes yellow. These fishes spawn in the spring over open sand areas.

In order to encourage both these species to breed it is essential to keep them at cooler temperatures over the winter, say 10°C (50°F) for *P. erythrogaster* and 14-15°C (57–59°F) for *N. lutrensis*, as warming of the waters seems to be one of the triggers for spawning.

Cyprinodonts

Poecilia sp. (sailfin molly) such as this male are large fishes which can reach 10 cm (4 in). Needless to say they need a spacious aquarium.

The ever popular *Poecilia reticulata* (guppy) has become a nuisance in some areas as escapees have populated local waterways.

The cyprinodonts are a large group of relatively small fresh- and brackish water fishes. Because they have teeth in their jaws they are often referred to as toothcarps. Aquarists tend to divide them into two groups, those which produce live fry (livebearers) and those which lay eggs (killifishes).

Most of the livebearers in the aquarium trade belong to the family Poeciliidae, but other, not necessarily closely related, families are also livebearers, including the Anablepidae, Goodeidae, and Hemirhamphidae.

In this section we will be dealing with only those fishes which are Cyprinodonts, so half-beaks will be found in the Miscellaneous chapter. One other livebearer you will have to look for elsewhere is *Anableps anableps* (four-eyed fish); these require very specialized brackish conditions, so full details regarding their lifestyle and captive requirements may be found in the brackish chapter.

Although you will find killi-fishes in this chapter, you may find it a little more difficult to locate the real thing! Despite their often stunning beauty, their (largely undeserved) reputation for being "difficult", specialist fishes has led to few dealers stocking them. Do not be deterred – locating unusual fishes often adds to the fun of our hobby.

Gambusia holbrooki (mosquito fish) have been used in biological pest control, being introduced to eat mosquito larvae and hence curb the spread of Malaria.

LIVEBEARING TOOTHCARPS

These livebearers will probably be the first fishes encountered by the novice aquarist, although they are not necessarily the best fishes for the new fishkeeper. Yet some will survive and breed in a newly set up tank – "cultivated" platies are probably the best for this, followed by guppies and cultivated swordtails.

The Poeciliidae

Most of the livebearing fishes encountered by the hobbyist belong to this "American" family. We use the term "American" because representatives are native to the southern states of the USA, Central America, and South America as far south as Argentina. They are also native to many of the Caribbean islands. This is not, however, the limit of their distribution.

Originally, the guppy hails from northern South America, Barbados, and Trinidad. It is now bred commercially in many countries, from the fish farms of the USA to those of the Far East, Israel, and Europe. Accidental escapes from these fish farms have allowed the guppy to extend its range in recent times, but in the days of the British Empire guppies were introduced all over the tropics to eat mosquito larvae and help reduce the risk of Malaria. Later *Gambusia holbrooki* were found to be more efficient for this purpose and were introduced to many parts of the world. Indeed the common name of *Gambusia holbrooki* is mosquito fish because of this connection. In recent times the resulting damage to native species of fish has become apparent, with dozens in decline or close to extinction because of these introduced fishes. Nowadays the mosquito fish is also dubbed "fish killer" and sometimes even referred to as "biological pollution" because of the damage it is doing to native faunas.

Since all livebearers use internal fertilization of the eggs as part of their reproductive strategy, they have had to evolve a method of transferring sperm from the male to the female. In Poeciliids the anal fin of the male is developed into a gonopodium, a sexual organ formed by the fusion of the third, fourth, and fifth rays of the fin. At its tip there are various spines and hooks which are often called "holdfasts", and which are used by the male to hold on to the female during mating. At this time the gonopodium is directed forwards and a groove formed down which the sperm is channelled to the cloaca of the female.

In all livebearers, the young fishes develop in the body cavity of the female and are born fully formed and able to fend for themselves. Since they are so well advanced at birth it is not necessary for them to produce hundreds of young at a time; broods vary but 20 to 40 seems to be the average. Large female swordtails, however, have been known to produce over 250 fry at one time. Interestingly enough, females of most, if not all, species of the Poeciliidae are capable of storing sperm, so

Xiphophorus maculatus (platy) is an accommodating fish suited to the community aquarium. Several varieties are available.

The tiny *Heterandria formosa* (mosquito fish), on the other hand, is best kept in a planted species aquarium with alkaline water.

Xiphophorus helleri (swordtail) will breed without any assistance from the aquarist. Ensure your aquarium does not become over-populated.

Xiphophorus variatus (platy) is quite prolific. They like a varied diet that includes some green foods.

many successive broods can be produced from a single mating. In this family the best known genera are *Poecilia*, which includes the guppy, and *Xiphophorus*, which includes the platies and swordtails.

Xiphophorus variatus has been bred to produce not only different colour forms but also different finnage shapes. This fish is a pin-tail form. *Xiphophorus* varieties will readily interbreed, but careful line-breeding is required to maintain these fancy strains.

Guppies

Wild guppies are small fishes; the males have splashes of colour on their bodies and the females are a dull grey/brown with a dark triangular "gravid spot" near their vent. These wild forms bear little resemblance to the man-made guppies with which we are familiar today. Indeed, one could be forgiven for thinking that the latter are an entirely different fish. Their fecundity and swift maturation has made them ideal candidates for the breeder, especially the commercial breeder, and many colour forms have been produced. Not content with line breeding for colour, the males have also been bred to enhance body size and finnage shape and size. More recently attention has been paid to the females, and these formerly somewhat drab creatures are now available with colourful tails, and even with colour starting to spread onto the body. Unfortunately, a problem which is encountered from time to time with some of these highly coloured females is that the colour has been artificially induced by the use of hormones.

A side effect of this is to make them sterile.

In the aquarium, the commercially bred guppy requires a well-planted aquarium with companions that will not bully it or nip at its flowing fins. Several males kept together may tear at each others' fins, so try to keep both sexes – it gives them something else to think about! They are not too fussy about water conditions provided it is not too soft, and as for their dietary requirements, anything they can fit in their mouths will do. Guppies are true omnivores which are capable of eating anything which comes their way. They have a long gut and no discernible stomach which means they can eat only small amounts at one sitting, but will be looking for their next meal within the next half hour. To appease this almost continuous hunger they are often seen "nipping" at plants but, although this can be annoying, they rarely do any real damage, preferring to take algae off the leaves rather than tear the actual leaves. Even so, tender new shoots sometimes disappear. Feeding some lettuce or peas will

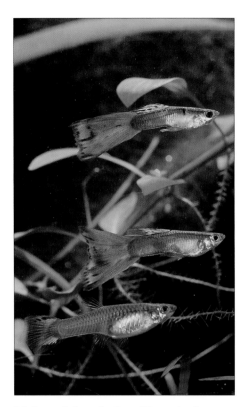

Male and female *Poecilia reticulata* (guppy) are easy to tell apart. Males have a gonopodium and more flamboyant finnage (top two fishes); the females are dull in comparison.

often help solve the problem, as will a multitude of small feeds throughout the day. Various live foods are also avidly consumed, including their own young.

In the aquarium females will drop their young at monthly intervals and provided there is shelter in the form of plenty of fine-leaved plants that reach up to the surface, or a layer of *Riccia*, some of the fry will survive. Alternatively, females can be moved into special breeding traps or tanks to give birth.

If you want to maintain the colour strains or finnage forms you will need to set up special breeding aquaria where you can monitor the fishes and check which ones you wish to breed with which. If all forms are kept together you will end up with a horrible mish-mash of fin shape and colour, because they will readily interbreed.

To maintain colour and finnage forms of *P. reticulata* you must separate young males and females as soon as possible so as to control who breeds with whom.

Platies and Swordtails

Platies and swordtails are almost as fecund as guppies. As in the guppy, a female can produce several broods from a single impregnation, and again, like the guppy, they have been manipulated by commercial breeders to produce variations in colour and finnage.

Platies like harder water and they will cope with the conditions of a newly set up aquarium, so they can be one of the first fishes that are used to mature the system after the nitrite peak has been passed. They like plants, both as cover and as food, but prefer to graze on soft green algae. This fondness for algae can be used to our advantage as they will help overcome the algal bloom that often occurs in a new aquarium. Despite this fondness for plant matter, these fishes too are true omnivores and require regular feeds of a good quality flake food as the basis of their diet, plus live or frozen foods if they are to achieve their full potential.

There are a number of different wild species of platy but only two are generally found in retail outlets. These have been extensively hybridized together, and with the common swordtail, to produce a number of colour forms and fin types. Once a fish has been hybridized with another species, the scientific name ceases to apply to the descendants no matter what they look like. Aquarists, however, still use the scientific names of the fishes that these cultivated forms resemble. The most common types available are listed below.

In the *Xiphophorus maculatus* type we get such varieties as red, blue, comet, and wagtail (this last has to be a hybrid because it requires the combination of the

Being easy to breed and swift to mature, *Xiphophorus helleri* (swordtail) is cultivated by fish farmers to develop different colour forms such as these black individuals.

Green swordtails such as these are considered closest to the wild stock. Here we see the characteristic well-developed sword on the smaller male.

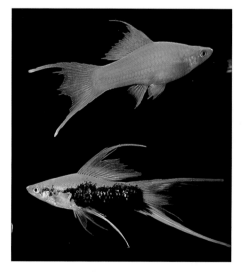

Fish breeders have also developed lyre-tailed forms of the swordtail, as seen here.

The red swordtail is still the most popular form but it is very hard to obtain quality stock.

comet gene from this species of platy with a swordtail gene from the common swordtail); and from *Xiphophorus variatus* come the sunset, marigold, tiger, and tuxedo varieties, among others. All these varieties cross easily so you often find that you have a colour that doesn't really conform to any named type, but if you like it, that's fine.

Xiphophorus helleri (cultivated swordtails) are like large versions of platies. The males may be identified by their gonopodia and also, as they mature, by their sword, an extension of the lower rays of the caudal fin. It is a common myth that swordtails undergo a sex reversal in later life, with females developing a gonopodium and sword. This myth stems from the fact that many swordtail males take much longer to "sex out" than others of the same size, and thus appear to be females – until the sword and gonopodium eventually develop. Occasionally old females will cease to breed and develop a gonopodium and sword just like a male. These fishes, however, are unable to father fry and still do not truly change sex.

Xiphophorus helleri has, like the platy and guppy, been exploited by the trade, and several fancy fin forms are commonly available. These include the lyretail (sometimes called double-sword) and the high-fin (also called Simpson and top-sail). These come in a multitude of colour varieties, including red, black, tuxedo, albino, and red-eyed red.

They need a fairly large aquarium as they are very active fishes, especially if several males are kept together, because they will be continually posturing to

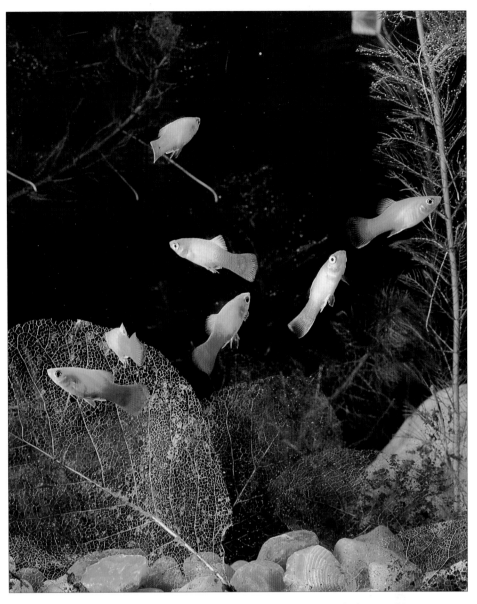

Check the dealer's tanks carefully when purchasing your fishes and ensure that they are healthy. They should show no signs of ill health such as clamped fins, rapid breathing, or scratching.

each other and displaying to females. Thickets of plants are useful, not only to provide sanctuary for the female who wishes to give birth or retreat from the attention of a male, but also for the other fishes in the aquarium to get out of the way if they want to. During these bouts of frantic activity the fishes may jump, so do ensure that you have a tight cover on the aquarium.

Hard water is a must to maintain these creatures for any length of time, but do not add salt to it (this also applies to guppies and platies). In soft water the fishes often seem not to develop properly. Other than that, they are very easy to keep and breed. One word of warning on the breeding side: a fully grown female can be 10 cm (4 in) or more in length and is much too large for the plastic breeding traps sold for livebearing fishes. If confined to one of these contraptions she may become so stressed that she damages herself trying to jump out, or may fret and even die. Far better to use a specially converted aquarium using the same principle.

Mollies

Now to one of the more spectacular members of this family, the sailfin molly. There are three species of sailfin molly of which two are common in the hobby, *Poecilia latipinna* and *Poecilia velifera*. As with the cultivated platies and swordtails, they have been hybridized over the years to develop more colour varieties.

They like hard, alkaline water: but failing this a little salt can be added. About a level 5 ml spoonful (1 level tsp) per 4.5 litres (1 gallon) is sufficient, though they will tolerate a lot more. Indeed, sailfins are at their best in brackish to marine conditions, and marine aquarists often use mollies to mature new systems. Before adding salt to your community it is vital to ensure that the other fishes and plants will tolerate it. If not, then set up a special tank for your mollies.

Poecilia latipinna is native to the southern USA and down into Mexico, and tolerates lower temperatures than are considered normal for "tropical" fishes (20–24°C/ 68–77°F). It is best to keep the cultivated forms at the upper end of this range. There are several colour varieties, for example, gold, black, and albino. The wild form is greenish with iridescent spangles on its flanks, but specimens with black speckling are also found, and it was from these that the black molly forms were developed.

Males are clearly distinguishable by their gonopodium and majestic dorsal fin. When courting a female, the male flashes his fin up and down to attract her attention. Fry are produced every four to five weeks. Move the female to a special aquarium, with thickets of fine-leaved and floating plants, to give birth, after which she can be removed.

Poecilia salvatoris (liberty molly) (for many years thought to be a form of *Poecilia sphenops*), occurs in Guatemala and Belize. Not often seen, it is a beautiful fish with red, black, and white dorsal and caudal fins. It is hardier than the sailfin types and will tolerate soft water without the addition of salt.

The black molly is the result of crossing a black form of *P. latipinna* with *P. sphenops*. This popular hybrid comes in several varieties including the lyretail and the balloon.

Maintaining Mollies

Mollies are easy to keep provided you maintain good conditions. If water quality deteriorates, the temperature is too low, or there is a combination of these factors, mollies are often the first to show signs of distress, for example fins clamped to their bodies while they move listlessly or even rest on the bottom or "shimmy" on the spot. If the temperature turns out to be correct, then a partial water change will usually rectify the problem.

Like other Poeciliids, mollies are true omnivores, eating just about anything which comes along. It is often recommended to add plenty of green food to their diet, and some people even suggest that it is difficult to maintain them in really good health without it. This, however, is simply not the case. Many specialist molly breeders feed no additional vegetable matter but nevertheless successfully breed and raise thousands to adult size. Mollies *will* browse on lettuce, peas, algae, and soft-leaved aquarium plants when nothing better is available, but this is because they are hungry all the time. Live foods such as *Daphnia*, bloodworm, and mosquito larvae are consumed with relish, as are minced fish and frozen foods. Feed as often as possible to obtain the best growth rates.

A hybrid fish, the outcome of a cross between *P. latipinnia* and *P. sphenops*, the black molly is easy to keep provided you keep it warm and pay careful attention to maintaining good quality water.

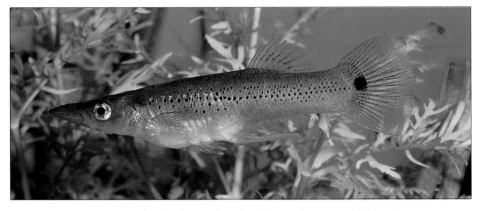

Belonesox belizanus (pike livebearer) is highly predatory and best kept in a species aquarium. It prefers live foods.

Other Poeciliids

Amongst the Poeciliids there are four other species which bear special mention: *Alfaro cultratus* (knife livebearer), *Belonesox belizanus* (pike livebearer), *Heterandria formosa* (mosquito fish), and *Limia melanogaster* (black-bellied or blue limia).

The Knife Livebearer

The knife livebearer has two rows of scales along the lower edge of the caudal peduncle which look like the blade of a knife. Pale in colour, the iridescent sheen on the bodies of healthy fishes makes them well worth keeping. Males grow to about 5 cm (2 in) and females 7.5 cm (3 in). They can be successfully kept in a community tank with peaceful fishes of similar size.

Females produce up to 100 young every month or so. The parents are cannibalistic but floating plants will help cut down on fry losses. Remove the fry to a rearing tank as soon as you see them. Because of their nervous disposition, it is unwise to move a heavily pregnant female.

These fishes do best when fed live foods but will also take flake foods. Feed the fry on newly hatched brine shrimp.

The Pike Livebearer

The pike livebearer is a different fish altogether. Males grow to about 10 cm (4 in) and females to about 18 cm (7 in). They are out-and-out carnivores, taking anything that moves, from insect larvae to small fishes and even their own kind. The jaws literally bristle with very fine teeth. It is possible to wean them on to dead foods but this takes time and patience.

Their very nature dictates that they should be kept in a species aquarium. Typical ambush predators, they like to lurk in the seclusion of plants and lunge out to take their prey. Their potential size dictates a roomy aquarium. The water should be warm (26–28°C/79–82°F) and kept clean by means of good filtration and regular partial water changes.

Females should be allowed to give birth in a nursery tank and then returned to the main aquarium. As many as 250 fry may be produced by a large female. Getting sufficient small live foods for the youngsters can be a problem as they will eat day-old guppies as well as *Daphnia* right from the start, and if they do not get enough, they will eat each other. To minimize cannibalism, plant the rearing tank heavily.

The Mosquito Fish

Heterandria formosa is one of the smallest of livebearers: males reach only 2 cm (³/₄ in), and females 3.5 cm (1³/₈ in). It is native to North America from Florida to North Carolina.

Provide a well planted species aquarium and hard alkaline water at a temperature of 20–24°C (68–77°F). They can be kept outside during the summer and this enhances their brown colouring, perhaps due to the constant supply of live food.

Fry are produced on a "conveyer belt system", with embryos at every stage of development at any given time, so that fry are born one or two at a time on a continuous basis. They are very large in relation to the mother and able to take small live foods. This method of reproduction (superfoetation) gives them a much better chance of survival.

The Black-bellied Limia

Mature females of *Limia melanogaster* have a blue-black patch covering half the belly near the anal fin, and numerous black vertical bars on the flanks. The dorsal has several black crescent markings. In males the lower half of the body, from the gonopodium to the tail, is deep bluish black. His flanks and dorsal fin markings are as in females and the dorsal and caudal fins are yellow to orange.

Black-bellied limias like a well-planted aquarium with efficient filtration and regular partial water changes. The temperature should be between 22–26°C (72–79°F), and the diet varied.

From 10 to 50 fry are produced monthly, and they will feed on small commercial foods and newly hatched brine shrimp within an hour of being born.

KILLIFISHES

The egglaying cyprinodonts have always been regarded as difficult because they are believed to require special conditions, namely soft acid water, but while this is true for some species it certainly isn't the rule for all of them. Many are exceptionally colourful and this alone makes them good aquarium fishes, but to see them at their best requires dedication on the part of the aquarist. It takes a lot of time and patience to maintain banks of small species aquaria, remove eggs from spawning mops, or dry out peat and then raise the fry. For those of us who have kept killifishes the work involved is worth it. If you haven't very much space, then try with a single species tank.

In nature, killifishes are found throughout the tropics with one exception, Australia, and some have even entered the temperate zones. Most are small fishes, but a larger one that is becoming a fairly regular import is *Lamprichthys tanganicanus*, from Lake Tanganyika, which can grow to 13 cm (5½ in). This is a really beautiful fish, with a pale yellowish body overlaid by brilliant blue spots in the male, or silver spots in the female. This is a hardwater killifish which will fit in well with other fishes of a similar size, although it is best kept in a school of 6 to 10 individuals.

Killifishes are predominantly insectivores, and a supply of live foods is very important as some will refuse to take anything that doesn't move. *Daphnia*, *Cyclops*, and mosquito larvae are the usual standbys, but you can also hatch brine shrimp eggs, or culture whiteworm and microworms, to feed to your

fishes. Feeding is very important if you are to achieve any success in breeding them, and this applies not only to getting the adults into condition but also to growing on the fry. It is frequently a lack of attention to correct diet rather than water quality that brings about the demise of many killifishes (and so deters the amateur aquarist from continuing with these fishes). Another factor in their demise can be a poor choice of companion fishes. For example, the trailing finnage of the males is far too great a temptation for some of the barbs which will harass the killifishes, damaging their fins. This can lead to a fatal infection or to the killifishes being bullied to the point where they are prevented from feeding. Needless to say, most species are best kept in a single-species aquarium.

Substrate Spawners

Sometimes referred to as "annual fishes", these killies inhabit ponds that evaporate during the dry season so that the adult fishes perish. To ensure the survival of the species, the fishes spawn in the substrate and the developing eggs remain in the dried-out mud until the next rains. Not all the eggs hatch at the first wetting. This is because if the first downpour turned out to be a freak shower and the pond then dried up again, the fishes would die out. Some of the eggs, therefore, need a second or even third wetting before they will hatch, thus securing the survival of the species.

Aphyosemion oeseri deposits its eggs on fine-leaved plants. Alternatively use mops and pick off the eggs, ready for hatching in another tank, which should be filled with water from the breeding aquarium.

Cynolebias nigripinnis (Argentine pearl fish) should be kept in a species aquarium. Males are more highly coloured than females.

Pterolebias sp. are South American substrate spawners. Males are larger and have longer finnage than females.

Aphyosemion sjoestedti (blue gularis) should be kept in soft, slightly acid water. They spawn in the substrate.

Aphyosemion deltaense can be aggressive. Ensure the female is ready to breed before putting a pair together.

In the aquarium, some substrate spawners ("annual" fishes) can live for longer than a year because their water source does not dry out.

Examples of this method of reproduction are the South American genera *Cynolebias* and *Pterolebias*, and the African genus *Nothobranchius*. Each species has its individual requirements, for example water temperatures and exact storage time for the eggs, so you will need to check up on these, but we will give you some general guidelines for breeding these fishes.

Breeding Substrate Spawners

The males are larger than the females with intense coloration and extended finnage; in total contrast, the females are normally a pale grey/brown and much smaller, so it is easy to tell whether or not you have a pair. It is normal to have to buy them in pairs, but if you are trying to breed from them, it is best to have one male and two females. This is because the male will drive the females very hard when spawning, and by introducing two females into the aquarium he has to divide his attentions between them.

Prepare the breeding aquarium with a peat substrate 4–5 cm (1½–2 in) deep and add a couple of clumps of fine-leaved plants such as *Elodea* or *Myriophyllum* as cover for the females. The water should be mature, soft, slightly acid (the peat will do this), and about 25 cm (10 in) deep. Sometimes it is necessary to boil the peat before putting it in the aquarium so that it will sink. Boiling also sterilizes the peat, so the eggs are less likely to suffer from any bacterial or fungal infections.

Condition the parents well with plenty of live foods such as *Daphnia* and insect larvae. When the females are full of roe place them in the breeding tank and allow them to settle before adding the male. His courtship display to the female consists of displaying his fins and posturing. If she is ready to spawn, the pair will dive into the substrate, the male clasping the female with his fins. In some species the pair disappear beneath the surface of the substrate, but in others the fishes seem just to push the eggs down into the peat. Once spawning is complete, the female will appear very thin and rest on the bottom. Remove her to another tank to recover and feed her well. The male should be placed in another aquarium until the female is ready to mate again.

Now you can drain the water and peat from the spawning aquarium through a net. An old pair of tights is useful for this but make sure there are no holes or ladders in the bit you are using, and don't forget to check with the owner first to make sure you can have them! Squeeze the water out of the peat so that it is damp and crumbly, then check it for eggs. Depending on the species, these will be small brown or white spheres about 1 mm (¹/₃₂ in) in diameter. Assuming that you find some, you can then store the peat and eggs in a plastic bag for the recommended time for that species. This is usually 3–4 months. LABEL THE BAG WITH THE SPECIES NAME, AND DATE IT. There is nothing more annoying than taking a guess at what's in the bag and how long it has been in the bottom of the airing cupboard. Eggs should be stored at

Nothobranchius rachovi (Rachow's *Nothobranchius*) is an African annual. Feed them plenty of live foods.

a temperature of about 22–24°C (72–75°F); the bottom of the airing cupboard is usually ideal but make sure by leaving a maximum/minimum thermometer in there for a while, and checking it each day to see what the average is.

After the requisite period of storage the eggs can be hatched. But before you start hatching them, prepare your fry food by setting up a brine shrimp culture so that the eggs hatch to coincide with fry needing to be fed – many fry have been lost because fry foods were not ready at the right time.

Place the peat/egg mix in an aquarium and add rain water which has been warmed to about 22°C (72°F). With any luck, within 24 hours you will see fry emerging. If you don't, then add some live food, e.g. *Daphnia*, to the aquarium; these will decrease the oxygen content of the water and this should trigger hatching. The fry of most species are large enough to take newly hatched brine shrimp as their first food. Don't forget to dry the peat out again and store it for another month before re-wetting as there may still be some dormant eggs in it.

Popular species of this type of killifish include *Nothobranchius guentheri*, *Nothobranchius rachovi*, *Cynolebias bellotti*, *Cynolebias whitei*, and *Cynolebias nigripinnis*.

Breeding Plant Spawners

The killifishes which lay (or, more correctly, hang) their eggs from plants are considered easier to breed. Again set up a breeding aquarium, but this time use a gravel substrate and either fine-leaved plants or spawning mops. Most people use spawning mops as they are more convenient than plants and can be removed every couple of days to harvest the eggs.

Spawning mops are made of yarn attached to a cork or polystyrene float so that the yarn hangs down into the water. Alternatively, they can be attached to a stone so that the yarn floats upwards. You will need to check where the fishes spawn – up in the plants or near the substrate – so that you can position your mops accordingly. If you don't know, provide both types.

Again, condition the parents well on live foods before placing them in the breeding tank. The male will chase the female through the plants/mops and some eggs will be deposited at each pass. Check the mops every couple of days and pick off the eggs. Some species lay them close to the knot at the densest part of the mop, others lower down the strands. Place the eggs in shallow containers (small ice cream containers or margarine

Procatopus similis (Nigerian lampeye) is a shoaling fish which must be kept in well-maintained water. They are not easy to keep and a diet of live foods is beneficial.

tubs are ideal) with water from the breeding tank to hatch. The containers can be kept on top of the aquarium or floated in it – either way they should not get too hot or too cold. On hatching, feed the fry on newly hatched brine shrimp, but be sure to keep the fish-hatching containers clean and free from debris by regular, small, partial water changes. Once large enough the fry can be moved to an aquarium to grow on.

This method of reproduction is practised by many members of the genus *Aphyosemion* and these highly coloured fishes are much prized amongst hobbyists. Popular species which are sometimes found in retail outlets include *Aphyosemion australe*, *A. gardneri*, and *A. striatum*. Other recommended species include *Epiplatys dageti*, *Epiplatys sexfasciatus*, and *Rivulus cylindraceus*. All require soft slightly acid water

A timid fish, *Epiplatys singa* (spotted *Epiplatys*) needs a quiet planted aquarium. Use aged water for water changes as they are sensitive to too much new water.

for breeding. Hard water species which breed in the same way include *Cyprinodon macularius*, *Cubanichthys pengellei*, *Fundulus chrysotus*, and *Profundulus labialis*.

Other Spawning Methods

As with all groups of fishes there are exceptions to the rule. This is certainly true of killifish reproduction, and there are many species which do not fit into the two neat groups described above. *Xenopoecilus* species, for example, use internal fertilization of the eggs which are then expelled by the female and hang from her vent like a bunch of grapes. They remain attached for the full 15 to 20 days it takes the embryos to develop before they hatch. Fishes that reproduce in this way are sometimes known as "egglaying livebearers".

Another species which bucks the trend is *Jordanella floridae* (American flagfish). In this species the pair lay their eggs at the base of a clump of plants or in a fanned-out depression in the substrate (sand is the best substrate for this). Spawning continues for several days after which the female should be removed. The male continues to look after the eggs and young until they are large enough to fend for themselves.

The beautiful *Aphyosemion australe* (Cape Lopez lyretail) is available in two different colour forms. This is the orange form.

Unlike *Epiplatys annulatus* (clown killifish), *E. dageti* (above) are ideal killifishes for beginners as they are easy to keep and breed.

Cyprinodonts

Killifishes for the Community Aquarium

Despite their reputation for being difficult, it is possible to keep some killifishes in a community aquarium, and here three species spring readily to mind: *Aplocheilus lineatus* (sparkling panchax) *Pachypanchax playfairi* (Playfair's panchax), and *Oryzias latipes* (rice fish or medaka). These are surface-dwelling species, so they make a useful addition to the aquarium in that they occupy an area of the tank that is usually ignored when buying fishes.

Aplocheilus lineatus (sparkling panchax) really live up to their name: the iridescent yellow spots on the scales shimmer in sunlight. These are true surface dwellers; they have long, straight backs with the dorsal fin set well back. Males are larger and more colourful than females, but the chief distinction between them is the six to eight vertical bars on the posterior half of the female's body. Predatory by nature, they feed almost exclusively on insect larvae and insects that fall on the water's surface. Whenever possible, and especially if trying to

Rivulus milesi (yellowtail panchax) will proliferate in a well-planted species aquarium. This fish is a male; females are plainer.

breed them, feed live foods, especially mosquito larvae which they love. Fortunately for the aquarist, if you do not have a good supply of live foods, they will also take flake and frozen foods which they catch as the food sinks. They don't, however, like to feed from the substrate. Being predatory, they will eat small fry so don't expect to find many young guppies or swordtails surviving in your aquarium if you choose to keep sparkling panchax.

A layer of floating plants will help discourage the sparkling panchax from jumping and will

Cyprinodon variegatus (sheepshead minnow) is found along the eastern seaboard of the USA in brackish water.

provide a spawning site. They tend to leap when feeding or if chased by other fishes, but the plants give them a retreat where they can hide instead of leaping about.

Although they will spawn on plants in the community aquarium, you can also put spawning mops in the tank and the fishes will usually lay some of their eggs on these. The mops can then be transferred to shallow containers for the eggs to hatch. If you are using Indian fern (*Ceratopteris thalictroides*) or water lettuce (*Pistia stratiotes*) as floating cover, the fishes will spawn amongst the dangling plant roots. In this case, the plant can be removed but do replace it with another one. If you have the time, you can pick the eggs off the mops or plant roots. Hatching takes about two weeks, and when the fry hatch they are quite large and will accept such foods as newly hatched brine shrimp and powdered flake. A more natural alternative is to float rafts of mosquito eggs in the hatching containers; as the tiny mosquitoes hatch, the young fishes feed on them.

Do not keep the fry in their hatching containers too long or

Aplocheilus lineatus (sparkling panchax) is an easy to keep surface dweller. They thrive on a diet of mosquito larvae. Be sure to keep the aquarium tightly covered – these fishes jump when frightened.

they will become stunted. Prepare a growing-on tank with water from the main aquarium and use a filtration system that will give a gentle flow. The water should be shallow but can be deepened as the fishes grow. You should see the young fishes in a small shoal, swimming in the water flow, and if you add some small floating plants such as *Riccia* these will give them somewhere to hide.

Pachypanchax playfairi (Playfair's panchax) is found in the islands of Madagascar, Zanzibar, and the Seychelles. It is a pretty fish, whose dark body has bright iridescent spots. They are territorial and can be aggressive but, provided they are kept with similar-sized fishes (say 5–7.5 cm/2–3 in) in a well-planted aquarium they usually do no harm. They occupy the upper levels of the tank and like to lurk amongst the plants. Keep the aquarium tightly covered because they do jump.

If happy in the aquarium, they will breed. The eggs are laid on plants and the adults are cannibalistic towards both their eggs and the resulting fry (they will eat smaller fishes of any kind), but with plenty of plant cover a few fry will survive. Alternatively, the fishes can be maintained in the community aquarium but then transferred to a specially set up tank, containing plenty of plants for breeding, should you wish to raise a lot more fry. When spawning is complete (5–7 days), remove the parents and leave the eggs to hatch. A good pair may produce up to 200 eggs which hatch in about 12–14 days. The fry will feed avidly on live foods so ensure you have the brine shrimp ready.

Oryzias latipes (rice fishes) are lively shoaling fishes that need to be kept as a small shoal otherwise they will pine away. Small, 4 cm (1¹/₂ in) at most, they make ideal community fishes as long as there are no larger fishes to bully them. Ensure that the tank is well planted and that you have a tight-fitting cover glass as rice fishes may jump. Feeding them is no problem as they take commercially prepared flake and frozen foods, although they do seem to benefit from live foods, developing a really bright sheen all over the body.

Males are larger than females, with a metallic blue sheen on the body and larger dorsal and anal fins. Their anal fin may have slightly extended rays giving the edge a ragged appearance. There is a gold form of this species as well as the normal wild form. Other species include *Oryzias melanostigma* and *Oryzias celebensis*.

These creatures have an interesting way of reproducing. First of all they internally fertilize the eggs a few hours before the latter are expelled by the mother (another "livebearing egglayer").

When the female finally produces a bunch of eggs, they remain attached to her by a thin thread until such time as she brushes against a plant, to which they then adhere. She actually looks as if she has a cluster of eggs stuck to her vent, and may carry them for a couple of days before finally attaching them to a plant. The fishes spawn regularly, with a bunch of eggs being produced on a weekly basis, but if the opportunity arises, they will eat them. So if you wish to raise them in any number they should be spawned in a separate aquarium and the eggs carefully removed from the female's vent as soon as you see them. They are then placed in one of the small containers mentioned above. Once the eggs hatch the fry can be reared in the same way as other killifishes.

Sometimes the eggs fail to hatch or the fry stop feeding. There is no obvious reason why this should be, as other aquarists have great success with them in a wide range of conditions from soft acid to hard alkaline water.

Pachypanchax playfairi (Playfair's panchax) is a large killifish which can grow to 10 cm (4 in). Females are slightly smaller than males and are more uniformly coloured. They spawn on plants, producing large numbers of eggs, so ensure you have sufficient space for the resulting fry.

Cyprinodonts

Characins

The characins are a large group of freshwater fishes found in South and Central America and Africa. They are characterized by the Weberian Apparatus (the linkage of bones between the swim-bladder and the inner ear) that allows them to hear high frequency sounds. Although most characins have an adipose fin (a small fin on the back between the dorsal and caudal fins, the function of which is unknown) there are a few genera in which it is lacking, and just to confuse the issue even more, in one or two species, for example, some pencilfishes, some individuals have an adipose fin and others do not.

Characins are divided into 11 families, according to Eschmeyer (1990). Other authors recognize 14 to 15, but for our purposes it makes little difference, and there is no doubt that ichthyologists will go on debating the numbers of families for years to come. There are at present about 30 genera with some 200 or so species in Africa, and 250 genera with over 1000 species in Central and South America.

Their methods of feeding and diet vary greatly; there are the out-and-out predators such as *Hydrocynus goliath* (African tiger fish, wolf tetra), and *Phago* sp. (fin- or tail-biters); herbivores such as *Prochilodus* and *Distichodus*; and insectivores, which include the majority of the species. Most of the characins we keep in our tanks are insectivores, which will feed quite readily on live, frozen, and flake foods. The predators,

Larger, shoaling species require plenty of open water in the aquarium. Always check on their dietary requirements: some are herbivores and require supplementary feeds of lettuce, spinach, or prepared vegetable diets to deter them from eating plants.

Not often available, *Hemigrammus ulreyi* (Ulrey's tetra) is simple to keep provided you have soft, slightly acid water. If fed live or frozen mosquito larvae, they will develop an intense golden yellow line along the flanks and a sheen on the body.

Ever popular, *Nematobrycon palmeri* (emperor tetra) is well suited to the densely planted aquarium. Being an insectivore it does not harm plants and provided you have some *Vesicularia dubayana* (Java moss) or fine-leaved plants they may spawn.

however, can cause a bit of a moral dilemma as some of them will accept only live fishes. So, do you feed them live fishes or do you starve the predator? The decision has to be yours. The rule is, if you can't feed it, don't try and keep it. Probably the most difficult characins to keep in captivity are members of the genus *Phago*. These are usually referred to as fin-biters or

tail-biters, and this is precisely how they feed, by taking chunks out of the fins of other fishes.

Generally, characins are shoaling fishes (with a few exceptions) that live in clean, clear, running waters. In the aquarium they are sensitive to any deterioration in water quality. They also require water that has a high oxygen content and, again, will suffer if this requirement is not met.

African Tetras

Some of the genera we are concerned with here are *Alestes*, *Brycinus*, *Micralestes*, *Phenacogrammus*, *Arnoldichthys*, *Ladigesia*, and *Lepidarchus*. All require similar conditions in captivity and most make excellent community fishes for the larger aquarium. Always on the move, they need space to swim, so a long, well-planted aquarium is ideal. Create a current with a power filter to give the fishes something to swim against, but don't make it so strong that they are flattened against the opposite side of the aquarium.

Arnoldichthys spilopterus (African red-eyed tetra) grows to about 8 cm (3¼ in). A shoal should include both males and females. Males have more colour and are slimmer fishes; their anal fin is convex and has red, yellow, and black stripes. Females are deeper-bodied and their anal fin is virtually straight with a black tip. They require a large aquarium with plenty of open swimming space. Regular partial water changes, along with plenty of meaty foods such as mosquito larvae and bloodworm (live or frozen), will help to bring mature specimens into breeding condition . A good pair of these tropical egg-scatterers can produce in excess of a thousand eggs. The fry grow rapidly if well fed and can be 5 cm (2 in) long at about two months old.

Young *Phenacogrammus interruptus* (Congo tetra) should be well fed on frozen and live insect larvae.

Another popular species is *Phenacogrammus interruptus* (Congo tetra). Fully grown males are a truly magnificent sight with their extended finnage and delicate hues; by contrast females have short fins. When young they cannot be sexed as all have similar coloration and similarly-shaped fins. It is best to purchase a shoal of youngsters and grow them on, providing copious amounts of live foods, especially mosquito larvae and bloodworm. If you cannot get live foods then frozen are a good substitute. This way you get good quality fishes at a more reasonable price than by buying adults that may be too old to breed anyway. Congo tetras are egg-scatterers, so if they spawn in the community aquarium most of the eggs will be eaten. They can, however, be spawned successfully using mesh and Java moss.

Other fishes you may like to consider, and which require the same sort of conditions are *Brycinus longipinnis* (long-finned characin), *Alestes nurse* (nurse tetra), and *Micralestes acutidens*.

Two delicate fishes that are also suitable for a community aquarium, provided the other inmates are small and the water is soft and slightly acid, are *Ladigesia roloffi* (Sierra Leone dwarf characin or jelly bean tetra) and *Lepidarchus adonis* (Adonis characin or jelly bean tetra – common names can be confusing). Both are small fishes, *L. roloffi* attaining 4 cm (1½ in) at most and *L. adonis* only 2 cm (¾ in). The main criterion for keeping these fishes is water quality: the water must be mature but without nitrates. A plentiful supply of small live foods is also beneficial, but not essential. Make sure the aquarium is well covered as *L. roloffi* jumps, especially when frightened. Some floating plants are beneficial as they seem to give the fishes a sense of security, making them less likely to jump.

Both species can be bred given the soft acid conditions required for spawning. *Lepidarchus adonis* (Adonis characin) places its eggs amongst fine-leaved plants and they hatch in about 36 hours. *Lepidarchus roloffi* (Sierra Leone dwarf characin) spawns just above a peat substrate. Neither fish is prolific, and the fry of both are very small and therefore require extremely fine, almost powder-fine, foods. Infusoria are good as a first food, followed by newly hatched brine shrimp.

Brycinus longipinnis (long-finned characin) looks its best in sunlight. Be warned – they may jump!

Adult Congo tetras require soft acid conditions and some vegetable matter in their diet.

Arnoldichthys spilopterus (African red-eye) is a must for the larger community aquarium.

The Distichodus

Distichodus species are well known as plant eaters, but this should not deter you from trying to keep them at one time or another. All seem happy in water conditions of about 10–20 dH, neutral to slightly acid, and a temperature of 23–27°C (73–81°F) is suitable.

Feed them heavily with plant material, such as lettuce, peas, chickpeas, spinach, watercress, and courgette, and also flake and tablet foods. It is not unheard of for them to take live foods such as bloodworm, put in the tank to feed other occupants.

Several species are available to the hobbyist, two of them small. *Distichodus decemmaculatus* (dwarf *Distichodus*) from the Central Zaïre basin grows only to 6 cm (2¼ in) at most, but, unfortunately, is rarely imported. This is a great pity as it makes an excellent fish for a community aquarium, being small, peaceful, and quite attractive with its moss-green body and vertical black stripes. The other species available is *D. affinis*, which grows to 12 cm (4½ in) and is found in the lower Zaïre basin. It is ideally suited as a companion fish for catfishes and some of the peaceful cichlids.

There are three species which are very similar, all with red fins with spots at the base of the dorsal: *D. affinis* (12 cm/4½ in), *D. noboli* (8 cm/3¼ in), and *D. notospilus* (15 cm/6 in). *D. affinis* has rounded lobes to the caudal fin and the base of the anal fin is longer than the base of the dorsal fin. *D. noboli* also has rounded lobes to the caudal fin, but the anal fin has a shorter base than the dorsal. *D. notospilus* is very similar to *D. noboli*, but the tips of the caudal fin are

You may be tempted to buy a young, highly coloured specimen of *Distichodus sexfasciatus*, but think ahead. Although it will retain much of its colour, this fish can grow to 25 cm (10 in) and at that size it is a powerful creature that needs a spacious aquarium and good filtration. It can also take fright very easily, so make sure you have a tight-fitting hood or cover glass or you may find your fish on the floor.

Distichodus affinis attains only 7.5 cm (3 in), and may be kept with other medium-sized robust fishes such as *Thorichthys meeki* (firemouth cichlid). Feed plenty of vegetable matter otherwise any plants in the aquarium will be decimated.

Young *Distichodus lusosso* are attractively coloured. As they grow these herbivores require larger accommodation and may be housed with some of the larger peaceful catfishes such as *Pseudodoras niger*, with whom they will not compete for food.

pointed. Their ranges also differ: *D. affinis* is found in the lower Zaïre basin, *D. noboli* in the upper Zaïre, and *D. notospilus* from Camerun to Angola.

The larger members of the genus include *D. lusosso* (40 cm/ 16 in), *D. sexfasciatus* (25 cm/ 10 in), and *D. fasciolatus* (30cm/ 12 in). These three require a

large aquarium: 150cm (60 in) or more long and wide enough for the fishes to turn round with ease. They also require very efficient filtration. These fishes make excellent companions for the larger peaceful catfishes such as *Auchenoglanis occidentalis* (giraffe catfish), large barbs, and/ or other large, peaceful characins.

South American Tetras

This is the largest group of characins encountered by aquarists, and includes all the well-known species such as *Paracheirodon innesi* (neon tetra), *Hasemania nana* (silver-tip tetra), *Hemigrammus erythrozonus* (glow-light tetra), *Paracheirodon axelrodi* (cardinal tetra), *Hemigrammus bleheri* (rummy-nose tetra, red-nose tetra), *Hemigrammus rhodostomus* (also known as the red-nose, or worm-nosed, tetra), *Hyphessobrycon erythrostigma* (bleeding heart tetra), *Nematobrycon palmeri* (emperor tetra), *Moenkhausia pittieri* (diamond tetra, Pittier's tetra); and so the list goes on.

The South American tetras are, in the main, small fishes which are well suited to life in the community aquarium. They require soft, slightly acid conditions such as usually prevail in a mature furnished aquarium. Many people fail with them because they are too eager to add

them to a new set-up. The tank needs to have been in operation for several months before adding even the more hardy species such as *H. erythrozona*. Six months to a year's maturation is best for the more delicate species such as cardinals. They are shoaling fishes, which like the company of their own kind, so rather than buying one or two of this species, one of that, and two or three each of several others, purchase eight or ten of your favourite and maybe six or eight of another. By doing this you will see more of the fishes, as given company they will not hide away in the plants.

Feeding is very simple. They will take commercial flake foods as a basic diet, but, in order to maintain some of the hues on the body, it is essential to feed either live or frozen foods. By varying the diet you will also be able to get the fishes into breeding condition should you wish to attempt to spawn them.

Breeding Tetras

Of the small tetras, neons have the reputation of being horrendously difficult to breed, and yet the truth is they can be spawned with almost the same ease as many of the barbs. The key to success lies in your choice of potential breeding stock and in how you set up the breeding aquarium.

In healthy well-fed fishes sexing is quite easy. Females tend to be larger and generally more rounded than males. As they fill up with roe this will become even more noticeable. The blue longitudinal stripe will also appear curved on the female, but straighter in the male. It may be a little difficult to see this difference, but body shape should be enough to separate the sexes without too many problems.

Take care in selecting the correct sizes of neon tetras to try to spawn. Big is not beautiful in this case. You need to look for fishes which are just over half grown. The 2–3 cm ($^3/_4$–1$^1/_4$ in) range seems best. If you only have a choice between extra large or very small fishes then take a group of small ones and grow them up. It is better to wait a few months than to try to breed fishes which are too old and will never spawn for you.

In preparation for the spawning attempt you need to condition your potential breeders with plenty of live foods, such as *Daphnia* and newly hatched brine shrimp. It is also important to lower the pH and hardness of the water in which your fishes are living, to prevent them from going into shock when they are transferred to the breeding tank; over the few weeks it will take to condition your breeders with live

Paracheirodon innesi (neon tetra) is commercially produced by the thousand for the aquatic trade so there is little fear of decimating wild stocks.

Hemigrammus erythrozonus (glow-light) is also mass-produced. Before buying check for any resulting abnormalities such as deformed gill covers.

Excellent water quality is essential for *Hemigrammus bleheri* (rummy-nosed tetra) as they are sensitive to any build up of nitrates.

Male *Hyphessobrycon erythrostigma* (bleeding heart tetra) are recognised by their elongated finnage. Keep in soft, slightly acid water.

food you should therefore slowly add rain water or demineralized water to the tank to soften the water and lower the pH.

Your breeding tank does not need to be particularly large (about 50 x 25 x 25 cm (18 x 10 x 10 in) will do), but it does need to be clean, so make sure it is thoroughly cleaned out, before use, with either a chemical disinfectant or very strong salt solution. Whichever you use, make sure all traces are thoroughly washed away.

The aquarium can then be filled with demineralized water or pure rain water. Depending on how you collect the rain water, the hardness reading will be zero or maybe slightly above. If it is above 10 ppm then it has probably been collected from a roof which is made of something which has dissolved in the rain water running off it. In this case, collect again, making sure only pure rain water is collected.

Once the aquarium is filled with rain or demineralized water, add a few handfuls of peat. At first this will float on the surface, but after a few days it will sink to the bottom and in the process stain the water brown. Now check the pH. Ideally it should read between 5.5 and 6.5. If it is too high, then you will need to boil some more peat in a pan of rain water or demineralized water for half an hour and then, once cooled, add this to the aquarium. Alternatively, you can add one of the chemicals available from your local aquarium shop to lower the pH, following the manufacturer's instructions to the letter.

Once the water chemistry has been dealt with, set the temperature at between 24–26°C (75–79°F) and add several artificial spawning mops made of nylon wool. Ideally these should be new ones or have been carefully cleaned before use.

The breeding tank is now ready for its intended occupants, which are best introduced in the evening, just before "lights out". Hopefully the next morning you should see your pair embracing off and on for a couple of hours. During these embraces the female turns to an almost vertical position with the male wrapped around her. Each time a few eggs are expelled and since they are only semi-adhesive some of them may fall through the nylon mops and drop to the bottom of the aquarium. During a good spawning up to 150 eggs may be laid. As soon as the pair have finished mating they should be removed to another aquarium (with matching water chemistry).

Sometimes a pair will not be ready to spawn as soon as you place them in the breeding tank. In this case leave them for a few days to see if they will spawn. If, after this time, they have still not bred, then remove them and try another pair, or wait for a week and try with the originals again. Under no circumstances should you risk pollution by feeding the adults in the breeding aquarium.

Once the adults have been removed cover the tank with dark brown paper to exclude some of the light. The next day the eggs should hatch; and on the fourth day after spawning the fry will become free-swimming and will need to be fed the very smallest of foods such as infusoria or a liquid fry food, followed after a week or so by newly hatched brine shrimp. Once feeding on brine shrimp, the fry grow quickly and will be sexable after about 12 weeks.

Young *Moenkhausia pittieri* (diamond tetra) look nothing like this beautiful male, but given good conditions, they will mature into quality fishes.

This is the original form of *Gymnocorymbus ternetzi* (black widow): fish breeders have developed albino and long-finned varieties.

Thayeria boehlkei (penguin) are usually seen "hovering" at an angle in mid-water. A shoaling fish, they like the company of their own kind.

A mature aquarium is essential for *Paracheirodon axelrodi* (cardinal tetra). Most failures are caused by unsuitable water.

Here we see the pigmented epigean version of *Asyanax mexicanus* (blind cave fish).

Pencilfishes

These fishes belong to the family Lebiasinidae and several species are available in the trade at one time or another. They may be kept in a community aquarium, but if the water conditions are less than ideal, or they are prevented from feeding by more boisterous fishes, it is better to house them in species tanks.

Pencilfishes are small and timid surface dwellers, and much of the day is spent motionless just below the surface so that they look like pieces of twig. Only at dusk do they come to life, when they start to feed on insects that have fallen on the surface or on small aquatic invertebrates. Some species will also search the substrate for food, sifting the mud and silt in search of small worms and so on. In the aquarium, they accept flake, brine shrimp, and small frozen foods but prefer live *Daphnia* and other pond foods. As they are most active in the evening, this is the time to feed them.

Ideally the water in the aquarium should be soft, slightly acid, and free from nitrates. Maintenance of good quality water is essential if you wish to succeed with these fishes. The pH may vary between 5.5 and 7.0 provided any changes are gradual. Use a dark substrate, and plant with clumps of *Cryptocoryne* with some floating plants such as Indian fern (*Ceratopteris*

Nannobrycon eques (hockey-stick or three-striped pencilfish) requires soft acid conditions and peaceful companions, and has a preference for live foods.

thalictroides) to keep down the light and also provide hiding places among its trailing roots. The temperature should be in the range 23–28°C (73–82°F).

The colour patterns on their bodies change from day to night; what appear as faint vertical black patches during the day become predominantly black markings at night, while those which were prominent during the day fade away.

Breeding these fishes is difficult but not impossible. The main requirements are a breeding tank with mesh that the eggs can fall through, a clump or two of Java moss or synthetic substitute on top of the mesh, very soft (2 dH or less) slightly acid water (about pH 6.0), dim light, a dark bottom (black paper beneath the tank works well), and a pair of willing fishes. If everything goes to plan, the eggs will be released and fall through the mesh before the parents can devour them, but sometimes the fishes will not spawn. This is usually because they have not been fed the right foods so that the diet has been lacking in amino acids. Feeding mosquito larvae and *Drosophila* (fruit flies) will usually rectify this. Of the two genera, *Nannobrycon* and *Nannostomus*, the latter is the easier to breed.

We suggest you try *Nannobrycon eques* (hockey stick or three-striped pencilfish), *Nannobrycon unifasciatus* (one-striped pencilfish), *Nannostomus beckfordi* (golden pencilfish), *Nannostomus harrisoni* (Harrison's pencilfish), *Nannostomus marginatus* (dwarf pencilfish), and/or *Nannostomus trifasciatus* (three-lined pencilfish).

The anal fin of male *Nannostomus harrisoni* (Harrison's pencilfish) is more colourful than the female's.

There are several colour forms of *Nannostomus beckfordi* (golden pencilfish), one of the easiest "pencils".

The body colour of *Nannostomus trifasciatus* (three-striped pencilfish) will intensify once they have settled in.

Splash Tetras

The splash tetras belong to the same family as the pencilfishes. Unfortunately the majority are rarely deliberately imported for the aquarium trade but do turn up occasionally in shipments of other fishes. The only one seen on a fairly regular basis is *Copella arnoldi* (splash tetra, jumping characin), the fish that gives the group its common name. A fairly unassuming fish to look at, males are larger, growing to 8 cm (3^1/$_4$ in), and have more colour in their finnage than females, 6 cm (2^1/$_4$ in).

Copella arnoldi (splash tetra) is a good community fish which inhabits the mid- to upper layers of the aquarium. If possible, keep a group, or if not, a pair, as their main attraction is their unusual method of reproduction. Water conditions are not critical: keep the hardness below 12 dH and the pH around neutral (so most community aquaria with plenty of plants will suit this fish). Regular partial water changes are essential to keep them healthy. If they become listless or hide all the time this usually indicates a slight deterioration in water quality. A partial water change will rectify the situation.

C. arnoldi (splash tetras) will jump to catch food and also when breeding. The addition of floating plants such as Indian fern (*Ceratopteris thalictroides*), and the provision of a good cover glass, will ensure that they do not leap to their deaths.

Feeding is not a problem as they accept flake, frozen, and live foods, but to condition them for spawning, offer plenty of live and frozen invertebrates such as *Daphnia*, bloodworm, and mosquito larvae; preferably live.

Breeding Splash Tetras

Place a pair in a small breeding tank (this need be only about 50 cm (18 in) long), using water from the main aquarium, and make sure that you have some broad-leaved plants such as *Echinodorus* sp. (Amazon sword plants) whose leaves reach just above the water surface. Place a tight cover glass over the aquarium and make sure the water level allows a small gap between the water surface and the cover glass.

When ready, the pair will swim together and then jump. Pressing their bodies close together and turning belly-up, they deposit a few eggs on the underside of a leaf or on the cover glass. This all happens in a split second and is repeated many times, with eight to ten eggs being deposited on the chosen site at each jump. By the end of spawning there will be a clutch of up to 200 eggs. As these are above the water, the male tends them, splashing water over them every 30 seconds or so, hence the common name. If unfertilized eggs fall off the leaf/cover glass the male ignores them. The eggs hatch after about 60 hours and the fry drop into the water. It takes another 36–48 hours for the fry

Copella arnoldi (splash tetra, jumping characin) is famed for its method of reproduction, in which the pair jump, turn, and press their eggs onto the underside of a leaf. As they like to jump, be sure to cover the aquarium tightly and use some floating plants to discourage this activity.

to absorb their yolk sacs, after which they require small foods such as newly hatched brine shrimp.

Other members of the genus may also be kept in the community aquarium, but their method of breeding is "normal". After conditioning, the pair spawn on a pre-cleaned leaf and the male tends the eggs, which hatch in about 30–36 hours. The fry require fine foods such as infusoria followed by newly hatched brine shrimp.

Copella guttata (red-spotted characin), a much larger fish (growing to 15 cm (6 in)), places its eggs in a depression in the substrate. Again, the male guards the eggs. On hatching, they should be raised in the same way as the other species.

Usually found near the surface, *Pyrrhulina brevis* (short-lined *Pyrrhulina*) make ideal companions for *Corydoras* catfishes and some dwarf cichlids. They can be quarrelsome when breeding – and they jump!

Hatchetfishes

When you think about surface-dwelling fishes for the community aquarium, usually the first ones that spring to mind are the hatchetfishes of the family Gasteropelecidae. The two genera usually encountered by the aquarist are *Gasteropelecus* and *Carnegiella*. These are easily differentiated as *Gasteropelecus* is larger (up to 9 cm (3½ in) in the case of *G. maculatus*) and has an adipose fin, whereas *Carnegiella* is smaller (4 cm (1½ in) in the case of *C. strigata*) and lacks an adipose fin.

These fishes are characterized by their straight dorsal profile, deeply keeled bodies, and pectoral fins set high on the body, looking like wings. "Hatchets" jump, not only to catch insects but also to escape predators. They also "fly": a strong set of muscles attached to the hypocoracoid bones (the deep "breastbone") enables them to flap their pectorals at great speed when they leave the water.

The two species most commonly available are *G. maculatus* (spotted hatchetfish) and *C. strigata* (marbled hatchetfish).

There are two sub-species of *C. strigata*, from different localities; *C. strigata strigata* is found around Iquitos in Peru, and *C. strigata fasciata* in Guyana. Of the two, the Guyanan fishes are the easier to keep.

Hatchets like a very good flow of highly oxygenated water and will hold station in a current strong enough to start breaking up the softer plants, so try to achieve a happy medium that satisfies the fishes but does not damage the plants. Always keep them in a shoal of at least five fishes: their reputation for being difficult to acclimatize to aquarium conditions is largely due to people trying to to keep single or at most two specimens – a recipe for disaster. *Carnegiella strigata* (marbled hatchetfish), in particular, is prone to white spot. If at all possible, quarantine the fishes for a minimum of two weeks before putting them in the community aquarium. Check the fishes in your dealer's tank; a reputable trader will have quarantined his or her fishes and offer you only healthy stock.

Unfortunately flake foods are not enough for hatchetfishes,

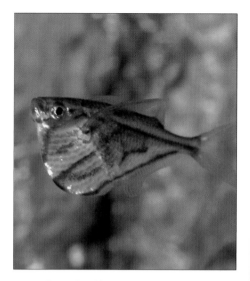

A surface dweller that likes a powerful flow from an external power filter, *Carnegiella strigata* (marbled hatchetfish) is regarded as "difficult", not only because of the need to provide it with a very varied diet but also because it is prone to white spot.

and it is necessary to take a little time and effort to provide them with live and frozen alternatives. They love fruit flies and mosquitoes, including mosquito larvae, so try and offer a varied diet of this type. Their mouths are upturned, indicating that they are surface feeders; although they will take food as it sinks, they will not forage on the bottom.

C. strigata (marbled hatchetfish) has been bred in captivity. This requires very soft, acid water. The eggs are deposited on the roots of floating plants but some will fall to the bottom. They hatch in 24–36 hours and the fry require very small live foods. Just keeping the parents healthy can be a challenge, so breeding them is even more so.

Two other species are occasionally available, but these are far more delicate than *C. strigata* and *G. maculatus*. They are *C. marthae* (black-winged hatchetfish), from Venezuela, where it is found in small woodland streams, and *C. myersi*, from the Peruvian Amazon and Bolivia.

Gasteropelecus sternicla (common hatchetfish) is more suited to a community aquarium although it too requires a very varied diet. Floating plants will provide security, but leave adequate feeding space.

Anostomids

You could be forgiven for thinking that these fishes are surface dwellers, because they have long, streamlined bodies and small upturned mouths. But nothing could be further from the truth. The anostomids, sometimes referred to as "headstanders", inhabit very fast-flowing waters in rocky stretches of rivers. They are found, head down, in narrow, vertical, rocky fissures. In the aquarium provide vertical crevices, which can be constructed from either actual rocks or plastic substitutes to lessen the weight.

Keep anostomids either as a single individual in the community aquarium, or in a group of seven or more. For reasons best known to themselves, they become very aggressive if kept in small groups – a similar situation to that encountered with *Barbus tetrazona* (tiger barbs) (see Cypriniformes chapter). They are predominantly herbivores and will graze on algae and plants. In the furnished aquarium offer lettuce leaves "planted" in the substrate and the fishes will take these in preference to the aquarium plants. Peas are another suitable substitute food. Small aquatic invertebrates such as mosquito larvae and blood-worms are also relished, and young fishes will take flake foods, especially vegetable flake.

Anostomus anostomus (striped headstander) is the species most often offered for sale. They are stunningly coloured, with dark gold and black stripes running the length of the body and bright scarlet patches at the base of the caudal fin. They adapt readily to aquarium life and will mark out territories in the tank. Provide them with strong filtration – ideally the water should be turned over twice an hour. They are reported to have been bred, but no details are as yet available.

Two other species are occasionally obtainable. *Anostomus ternetzi* is similarly coloured to *A. anostomus*, but is slightly smaller and lacks the red coloration in the caudal fin. It is a more peaceable species than *A. anostomus* and can be kept under similar conditions. *Anostomus taeniatus* also appears now and again, and is likewise a peaceful shoaling fish requiring the same aquarium conditions. It has a single black stripe along the body, with gold above and cream below. At night it changes its colouring to brown with faint cream markings.

Leporinus fasciatus (black-banded *Leporinus*) may quarrel among themselves, but are peaceful towards other fishes. Largely herbivorous, they may nibble plants.

Often mistaken for an anostomid because of its "head-down" method of swimming, *Chilodus punctatus* (spotted headstander) actually belongs to the family Curimatidae.

Anostomus anostomus (striped headstander) needs to be fed copious amounts of lettuce or peas to discourage it from decimating the aquarium plants.

Abramites hypselonotus (high-backed headstander) is a deeper bodied anostomid. Youngsters will tolerate one another, but when they get to about 10 cm (4 in) plus they can't stand the sight of each other.

Big Beasts

No piece about the characoids would be complete without mentioning some of the larger, more specialized fishes. Of these, the piranhas have a world-wide reputation. They belong to the family Serrasalmidae, which includes not only the carnivorous piranhas but also some large, peaceful herbivores.

Serrasalmus nattereri (red piranha) is a fine example of these fishes. It is the dream of many hobbyists to keep one or more, but few achieve this. Indeed, in some countries, for example the USA, they cannot be imported for fear of escapes, and/or release by irresponsible aquarists, into the wild, because of the danger of feral populations becoming established. This would decimate indigenous fish populations.

They are a fish that needs to be handled confidently but with extreme care – this cannot be over-stressed. If alarmed, their first reaction is to attack and bite, and as they are armed with a fearful set of teeth they can inflict serious wounds. Many a native fisherman has lost a toe to a piranha, but not when swimming in the water; more usually when he has caught the fish and it is flapping about in the bottom of the canoe. Even small specimens will bite.

When transporting them home they should be double-bagged, with a thick layer of newspaper between each of the polythene bags, so that if the fish bites through the inner bag, its teeth will not go through the soggy newspaper and puncture the outer one. Pack them one fish to a bag. Alternatively, transport them in rigid containers such as buckets with lids, and

The villain of the aquarium, *Serrasalmus nattereri* (red piranha) has a reputation to live up to. Whatever you do, do not take chances with these fishes; they have a sturdy set of teeth, and if cornered will not hesitate to lunge at your hand, the net, or anything else that they consider a threat.

again, one fish per container. Another word of warning: do not put your hands in the aquarium if you have any open wounds on them – it is not worth the risk.

In captivity they require a large aquarium with very efficient filtration and a good flow of water. Water chemistry is not critical: soft to medium hard water with a neutral or slightly acid pH is fine. As they are carnivores they produce a lot of high protein waste, so the efficiency of the filtration system is critical. Any deterioration in water quality will stress the fishes. Plant the aquarium with *Echinodorus* sp. (Amazon sword plants) and decorate with large pieces of wood that look like tree roots, to give the fishes some shelter.

Feeding piranhas is simple – they eat anything meaty, alive or dead – pieces of meat or fish are best. For young specimens use small pieces of food, and keep up a steady supply without over-feeding. Remember a hungry piranha is dangerous and will reduce a prey item to shreds. In the wild, piranhas are thought to feed on the fins of other fishes as well as whole ones.

Juvenile *S. nattereri* are silver-bodied with numerous black spots, while the pectoral and anal fins are reddish. As the fishes mature they lose their spots, becoming silvery with a more golden back, and with red on the throat and belly. If you wish to keep a group, it is best to purchase a shoal of youngsters and grow them up together; you will find that a hierarchy develops within the shoal. Provided you don't upset the *status quo* by adding more later, the shoal will flourish.

Serrasalmus nattereri has been bred in large aquaria. They spawn at first light and produce up to 1000 eggs. The male and female guard the nest for the first 24 hours, but the female is then chased away and only the male remains on guard. The young are relatively easy to rear on brine shrimp, but ensure that you have sufficient space to raise them. After about four weeks, they need to be graded by size otherwise the larger fishes will eat the smaller ones. Copious amounts of live foods, in ever-increasing sizes, are needed to raise them successfully.

In the same family, the Serrasalmidae, we also find some harmless herbivores, one of the largest being *Piaractus brachypomus* (Pacu). Large fishes that grow to well over a metre (40 in), they are suited to public aquaria rather than the home aquarium. Small specimens are sometimes available, but do give due consideration to their potential size before purchasing one. If you can provide an aquarium of 200 x 60 x 60 cm (84 x 24 x 24 in), with a filtration system to match, you are partway there, but be prepared to move the fishes on to larger accommodation.

Pacu are vegetarians. In the wild their diet consists of fruit and seeds, while in captivity they will eat just about anything "vegetable": bananas, figs, cherry tomatoes, courgette, lettuce, pond weed; their philosophy seems to be, "If it's vegetable we'll give it a try!" They have very inefficient disgestive systems and produce waste that forms food for other fishes. The large doradid catfish *Pseudodoras niger* makes an ideal companion for a pacu and will sift through the detritus when feeding.

On a more manageable level, there are other peaceful herbivores in this family, such as *Metynnis argenteus* (silver dollar), *M. hypsauchen*, and *Myleus rubripinnis*. Under aquarium conditions all reach a reasonable size (10–15 cm/4–6 in). Being shoaling fishes, they make ideal companions for catfishes and loaches. They require plenty of space: an aquarium of a metre (36 in) or longer is required for youngsters, and 120 cm (48 in) or more for a shoal of six to eight semi-adult fishes. Water conditions are not too critical as long as they are soft and slightly acid

A very large fish (1 metre/40 in) best suited to a public aquaria, *Piaractus brachypomus* (Pacu) is related to the piranha but is a harmless herbivore.

Another herbivore, *Metynnis argenteus* (silver dollar), should be kept in a shoal in a large aquarium with subdued lighting. Buy youngsters to grow on, offering vegetable foods.

A peaceful characin that rarely exceeds 10 cm (4 in) in captivity but may reach 35 cm (10 in) in the wild, *Myleus rubripinnis rubripinnis* requires highly oxygenated, clear water.

and warm, up to 28°C (82°F). Make sure the filtration system is efficient and, especially for *M. rubripinnis*, that the water is well oxygenated.

Provide a planted aquarium but use artificial plants or very robust species of live plants such

as *Microsorium pteropus* (Java fern) attached to wood and rocks, and large *Echinodorus* sp. (Amazon sword plants) and *Cryptocoryne* sp. planted in the substrate. Ensure that the plants are well established and growing vigorously before introducing the fishes to the aquarium. Provided you feed them well on a variety of vegetable foods (they are particularly fond of lettuce) the plants will not be harmed to any great extent.

Metynnis can be sexed by the anal fin, which in males is longer and more highly coloured than in females. They are shoal spawners and relatively simple to breed. The water needs to be soft, (less than 6 dH), acid (pH 6.0–7.0) and warm (26–28°C/79–82°F). These fishes like to spawn among floating plants, and a single female may produce up to 2000 eggs which fall to the bottom and are ignored. The fry are easily raised on small live foods, but many are lost because the average aquarist has insufficient space to cope with such large numbers of fry, both in terms of space and the quantities of food required.

Myleus rubripinnis is another matter entirely. These fishes are not readily sexable and so far have not been bred. They are more difficult to maintain than *Metynnis* because they do not tolerate any build-up of nitrates in the water, and they require higher levels of oxygenation.

Sometimes *M. rubripinnis* is seen with small spots on its body, looking like little tiny blisters about the size of a pinhead. At first they give the impression that the fish is covered with air bubbles but this is not so, they are the sign of a so far unidentified disease.

Anabantids

The anabantids are a large group of fishes found in the tropical waters of Africa and Asia. They are best known for their ability to breathe atmospheric air. The organ that they use for this is known as the labyrinth (hence the common name labyrinth fishes) and is situated on either side of the head in the gill cavity directly above the gills. The fish takes in air from above the water surface and passes it into two chambers, each of which has a rosette-like structure which looks not unlike a sponge. This has a very good supply of blood vessels close to the surface of the structure, and therefore the fish is able to absorb oxygen from the air.

Not only does this air breathing capability allow labyrinths to survive in waters that are oxygen deficient, it allows some of them to travel across land. The most notable of these is *Anabas testudineus* (climbing perch).

Labyrinth fish breeding strategies also reflect the low oxygen content of the water in which some species live. Some construct bubblenests to keep the eggs at the surface, others have floating eggs, and yet others hold their eggs in their mouths in a similar fashion to the mouthbrooding cichlids. Each method seeks to give the eggs the optimum conditions for development by keeping them in areas which are higher in oxygen or which will give them the greatest possible degree of protection.

The labyrinths are generally divided into two groups by the hobby: gouramis and climbing perches. The only problem with this arbitrary division is that gouramis can range in size from the 2.5 cm (1 in) *Trichopsis pumilus* (dwarf croaking gourami) to the huge *Osphronemus goramy* (giant gourami) which can attain lengths greater than 70 cm (28 in). This division also fails to take account of the various *Macropodus* (paradise fishes) and *Betta* (fighting fishes) species of which there are a growing number in the hobby.

Trichopsis pumilus (dwarf croaking gourami) is one of the smallest gouramis. Quite delicate, it is best kept in a species aquarium.

Pseudosphronemus cupanus (spike-tailed paradise fish) prefers a well-planted tank and small live foods.

Scientists, however, divide, labyrinths into four families: Anabantidae, containing the genera *Anabas*, *Ctenopoma*, and *Sandelia*; Belontiidae, containing *Belontia*, *Betta*, *Colisa*, *Ctenops*, *Trichogaster*, *Malpulluta*, *Parosphronemus*, *Pseudosphronemus*, *Sphaerichthys*, *Trichopterus*, and *Trichopsis*; Helostomatidae, with the single genus *Helostoma*; and Osphronemidae, also containing a single genus, *Osphronemus*.

One of the least demanding anabantids is *Macropodus opercularis* (paradise fish); it is suitable for the novice aquarist.

Ever popular, *Betta splendens* (Siamese fighter) has been line-bred to enhance both the finnage and coloration of the males. Wild males are less splendid.

Gouramis

By far and away the most popular group of fishes among the anabantids are the gouramis belonging to the family Belontiidae. Of these, members of the genus *Trichogaster*, such as *T. trichopterus sumatranus* (blue gourami), *T. microlepis* (moonlight gourami), and *T. leeri* (pearl gourami), are probably the easiest fishes to keep because they are tolerant of most water conditions. They are medium-sized fishes (10–15 cm/4–6 in) and are well suited to a community aquarium as long as their companions are not too small. Occasionally, however, large adults will bully other fishes and may have to be moved to an aquarium in which they are the smallest fishes. The only other problem which may occur is the gouramis having their ventral fins nipped by their tankmates.

When purchasing them from an aquarium shop, try to buy them in pairs. Some species are virtually impossible to sex as juveniles, but as adults it should be obvious. The easiest way to sex them is to look at the dorsal fin; in males this is slightly longer than in females and may culminate in a point. In *Trichogaster leeri* (pearl gourami) males, not only is the dorsal fin longer and pointed, but the anal fin has extensions to the fin rays, and the throat is a beautiful blood red when the fish is in good condition.

The larger gouramis do not need any special conditions, although they do prefer the water to be on the warm side. Anywhere between 25–28°C (77–82°F) seems to suit them. The aquarium should be heavily planted towards the back and sides, and a few caves can be created out of rocks or bogwood.

Colisa lalia (dwarf gourami). is another very popular gourami. They are ideal for the smaller community aquarium since they grow to a maximum of about 5 cm (2 in). They are normally sold only in pairs, mainly because the female is an uninteresting silvery colour with pale vertical bars, whereas the male's bars are a brilliant red alternating with blue. The temptation for the novice aquarist is to purchase the highly coloured fish: indeed, he or she may not even realize that the silvery creature is the female.

Other members of the genus *Colisa* are also suited to the smaller aquarium. The one you are most likely to come across is *Colisa sota* (honey gourami). Again females are rather drab, being a pale brown on the back and silver on the belly with a dark stripe running from the eye to the caudal peduncle. Males exhibit a similar coloration when they feel insecure, which they do in a shop tank, but once settled in your aquarium they will soon show their full colour. This consists of a lemon yellow dorsal fin and dark blue-black head, throat, and front portion of the anal fin. The rest of the body and fins is a lovely copper colour. These fishes are delicate, so be patient, and wait until you have more experience and your aquarium is mature before you try to keep them.

We suggest you try *Trichogaster trichopterus* (three spot or blue gourami), *T. leeri* (pearl gourami), *T. microlepis* (moonlight gourami), *T. pectoralis* (snakeskin gourami), *Colisa lalia* (dwarf gourami), *Colisa fasciata* (giant gourami), and *Colisa labiosa* (thick-lipped gourami).

Trichogaster trichopterus sumatranus (blue gourami) may sometimes bully other, smaller fishes. Make sure their companions are large enough to look after themselves.

Trichogaster microlepis (moonlight gourami) can be very timid. This can be overcome by providing thickets of plants and some floating plants for privacy and security.

Male *Trichogaster leeri* (pearl gourami), such as the one shown here, are even more colourful when in breeding dress. Keep these fishes as pairs and, provided there are no boisterous tankmates, they may spawn.

You may wish to keep the west African *Ctenopoma kingsleyae* (Kingsley's *Ctenopoma*) in your community aquarium. Beware: *C. kingsleyae* is far more predatory than the other fishes shown here, and small tankmates may disappear.

Despite being a large fish (it can grow to more than 20 cm/8 in), *Trichogaster pectoralis* (snakeskin gourami) is very peaceful and thus a popular aquarium inmate.

Male *Colisa lalia* (dwarf gourami) are far more colourful than the plain silver females. They will sometimes breed in the aquarium but don't expect many fry to survive, especially if there are other fishes around.

Colisa sota (honey gourami) is easy to keep in a quiet community aquarium, or a species aquarium if you wish to breed them. Condition them on small live and frozen foods and, when ready, they will build a bubblenest.

Breeding Gouramis

To breed these bubblenest builders, you will need an aquarium at least 100 cm (36 in) long for the larger species and 60 cm (24 in) for the smaller ones. Provide some thickets of plants which reach to the surface, and use only minimal filtration to create a very gentle water movement. The plants have a dual purpose: firstly they provide shelter for the female when the male becomes a little too pushy, and secondly, some species add plant matter to the bubblenest to help bind the bubbles together. It is also important to have a tight-fitting cover glass over the aquarium so that the air space just above the water surface is warm and humid at all times.

Colisa sota builds its nest tucked away in a quiet area and usually near some plants. During construction the male will interrupt his work to display to the female.

The distance between the water and the cover glass should be about 5–10 cm (2–4 in).

Condition the prospective parents well on live or frozen foods. When they are ready to breed, the male will show interest in the female, seeming to be stimulated by the more rounded appearance of her belly. At this time, he will pick a quiet area of the aquarium, usually in a corner or very close to a clump of plants, and start to build a bubblenest, taking air into his mouth from the water surface and expelling it through his gills. The mucus-covered bubbles float upwards and are kept in a small area by the floating plant leaves. If there is a strong current in the aquarium, the delicate nest will be swept away.

Every so often the male will break off from building his bubblenest and court the female. This will usually take the form of much fin-spreading and wagging his body to and fro. This shows what a splendid male he is and helps excite the female. By the time the nest is complete she will be so worked up that she will spawn straight away. If she is not ready to spawn, however, they will fight, and the male may tear her fins. In this case you will have to move her out of the

breeding set up and try again with another female, or return the original one a week later when she may have reached spawning condition.

Once spawning is under way you are in for a real treat. The pair embrace, with the male wrapping himself around the female and then turning her over on to her back as the eggs and milt are expelled. The eggs are lighter than water and float up to the surface. Once the male has recovered from the embrace he collects the eggs together towards the centre of the nest and carefully encases each one in a bubble of mucus-coated air. When the female has recovered from the embrace she helps collect the eggs. Once this task is complete the pair embrace again. During spawning up to 1000 eggs may be laid by the larger gouramis, but a more average spawning will contain about 250 eggs.

When spawning is complete, the male chases the female away and sets about tidying up the nest. First of all he searches round for any missed eggs and places them in the nest, then he blows more bubbles and builds up the nest even more. Once satisfied all is well, he settles down to wait for the fry to hatch. This takes about 48 hours after which the fry can be seen with their tails hanging down from the nest. The male now has his work cut out making sure that any which fall out of the nest are caught up and pushed back in.

On the fifth day the fry become free-swimming and capable of looking after themselves. Soon afterwards the male starts to think of them as food rather than family, eating any he finds. Obviously he must be removed before this happens.

The fry of the larger species are easy to raise so long as you have a good supply of small live foods. Infusoria are necessary as a first food, and can be cultured in a separate container using banana skins or other vegetable matter. Alternatively use commercially produced liquid fry food which can be fed directly to the fry and will also create an infusorial bloom in the aquarium. These foods are needed only for the first week, after which they can be phased out and newly hatched brine shrimp used instead. A wide variety of small live foods, such as microworm and sifted *Daphnia*, need to be included in the diet to produce good, healthy youngsters. Fine-powdered fry food can be fed as a supplement but if fed to the exclusion of live foods will produce poorer results. The fry will grow fairly swiftly and, as broods can be large, ensure you have enough space to grow them on.

Colisa lalia (dwarf gourami) spawn in a similar manner to the larger species, but the courtship and nest of *C. sota* (honey gourami) are slightly different. Whereas the other species use quite a lot of vegetable matter in

Male *Colisa sota* (honey gourami) are more colourful than females, but youngsters rarely show any colour, so buy a group to grow on.

the nest, honey gouramis tend to use little or none at all. The nest is also much more untidy, but the eggs are kept in a single very tight clump right at the centre of the construction. Courtship is also a little different, with the male standing on his tail, so to speak, with his nose pointing towards the surface. His colours are heightened even more at this time, and he spreads all his fins to their utmost and wags his body to and fro.

In these small species the fry are also smaller, looking like little slivers of glass when they first hatch. Really small fry foods are needed and regular, small feeds throughout the day are better than one or two large meals. Be sure to keep the aquarium clean when feeding heavily, as uneaten food will cause a deterioration in water quality.

A word of warning: one of us, when breeding *Trichogaster*

trichopterus (three spot or blue gourami) for the first time, used an aquarium with very gentle undergravel filtration. Everything was fine while the eggs and fry were in the bubblenest, and even for the first few days when they were free swimming there did not seem to be anything amiss. Then, one morning, a glance into the aquarium revealed a lot of fry trapped in the gravel. They had been resting on the bottom and, even with what appeared to be a very gentle water flow, had been sucked into the substrate with disastrous results – their spines had been damaged. The best part of the brood was lost and a hard lesson was learned. For future spawnings an air-operated sponge filter was used and proved extremely successful. Not only did it filter the tank, but the young fishes were often to be found pecking away at the micro-organisms on the sponge.

Combtails

Belontia signata (combtails) are not usually recommended for community tanks because as they get older they become somewhat belligerent, especially if they attempt to breed. At this time quarrels may break out between males as they tussle for the dominant female. In a species aquarium, the shoal develops a pecking order. Smaller fishes may be harassed to such an extent that they remain hidden all day. These medium- to large-sized fishes may be kept with others that are able to stand up for themselves.

Combtails will breed in the community aquarium. If several are kept together and they are well cared for, they will pair naturally, find themselves a prospective breeding site, and herd the other fishes out of the way. The eggs are laid in clumps under a plant leaf, usually in a single layer of bubbles. Once free swimming, the fry are very easy to raise as they will take flake and newly hatched brine shrimp. The problems arise as they grow, because the larger ones tend to bully their smaller siblings and it is not unusual to get a large number of runts in the brood.

Belontia signata (combtail) can be belligerent; keep them either with fishes of a similar size and disposition or in a species aquarium. When raising fry remove the larger, more aggressive fishes to allow the smaller ones to grow on.

Paradise Fishes

The first exotic aquarium fish to arrive in Europe was *Carassius auratus* (the goldfish), followed in the 1860s by *Macropodus opercularis* (paradise fish). One of the main reasons this fish survived the journey so far from its native haunts of southeast China and Korea was that it is so hardy. They can comfortably tolerate temperatures down to 15°C (59°F) and have even been known to survive temperatures as low as 5°C (41°F). Unfortunately they are somewhat aggressive towards smaller fishes and adult males will fight as aggressively as Siamese fighting fishes. At one time they were considered "king" of the aquarium world, but that was long ago before the more beautiful, but more delicate, truly tropical species were available. Today you can still find the "original" species in shops, but there are also a number of different species of paradise fish which are seen from time to time. Most of these are smaller and more peaceful, but lack the lovely blue and red vertical stripes of the original. This coloration makes it even now a worthy addition to the larger community aquarium where the smallest inmate is about 10 cm (4 in) long. As adults your paradise fishes will achieve a maximum size of 12.5 cm (5 in).

Spawning usually takes place under a large leaf at the water's surface. It follows the typical gourami procedure, with the male building a bubblenest, but the female is often badly mauled by the male if she is not ready to spawn, so provide plenty of cover for her to hide in.

Macropodus opercularis (paradise fish) has been available to the hobby since the late 19th century. Its tolerance of poor water quality and low temperatures meant that it could be transported to Europe by ship from its native southeastern China and Korea.

The Delicate Bunch

Several of the smaller species are surrounded by myths and noted for being "difficult". That may be so, but with a little careful planning and preparation it is possible to keep and breed them – homework again! You will, however, need a little more experience before you attempt to keep and breed any of these. They are included here as a challenge for the future!

Sphaerichthys osphronemoides (chocolate gourami) is a fish that one of us cannot resist. They require soft, acid conditions and excellent water quality. It is the maintenance of good water quality that seems to be the key to success with these fishes and with the other small species such as *Trichopsis vittatus* (croaking gourami), so pay attention to the filtration system and remember to carry out regular partial water changes.

It is best to prepare an aquarium specifically for these creatures, ensuring that it is both well planted and that the water is matured before attempting to introduce the fishes. Wood is good for decor as the tannins leaching from it are beneficial to the fishes. In real terms, an aquarium that has been up-and-running for six to nine months is ideal. One of us tends to use a tank previously used for growing on small tetras and once they have been moved on to other accommodation, a shoal of young gouramis can be housed in the mature aquarium thus vacated.

The only adjustment made to the tank is the water temperature, which should be a little higher for the gouramis, around 26–28°C (79–82°F). The size of the shoal will depend on the size of the aquarium, for example a 50 x 25 x 25 cm (18 x 10 x 10 in) will accommodate 6 to 8 *Trichopsis vittatus* (croaking gourami), and a 60 x 30 x 30 cm (24 x 12 x 12 in) a shoal of 10 to 12 *Sphaerichthys osphronemoides* (chocolate gourami). Although this may seem very few fishes for tanks of this size, it is easy to maintain water quality, and should the fishes become picky towards each other, they have enough space to get out of each other's way. It is preferable to purchase young fishes and allow them to grow on and pair themselves, rather than trying to determine pairs of older fishes.

One of the keys to success with these creatures is in the feeding: they prefer small live foods such as *Daphnia*, *Cyclops*, mosquito larvae, whiteworm, and so on. If you cannot provide these then frozen foods are excellent substitutes. Most of the fishes will accept flake foods which can be used as well as the frozen/live foods.

Some controversy surrounds just how *S. osphronemoides* (chocolate gourami) breeds. This may have something to do with the fact that there are possibly four different types of chocolate gourami, and that each may have a different spawning procedure. Of the two forms which have been observed, *Sphaerichthys osphromenoides selatanensis* is a mouthbrooder in which the male carries the eggs, while the other, *Sphaerichthys osphromenoides osphromenoides*, has been noted as being both a mouthbrooder, in which the female carries the eggs, and a bubblenest builder.

The chocolate gouramis we worked with were mouthbrooders, in which the female took the

Make sure you keep a careful check on water quality when keeping *Sphaerichthys osphronemoides* (chocolate gourami), because any deterioration can leave these fishes open to bacterial and fungal infections and to skin parasites.

Trichopsis vittatus (croaking gourami) derives its common name from its ability to produce croaking sounds. They can be difficult to acclimatize and should be housed in an understocked aquarium and fed with live or frozen foods at first.

large yellow eggs into her mouth and incubated them and the resulting fry for about 18 days. When released, the fry were brown and yellow and took newly hatched brine shrimp.

The male *Trichopsis vittatus* (croaking gourami) constructs a nest close to the substrate in a cave or hollow beneath a large leaf or in a tangle of plant roots. He collects the eggs after spawning and spits them into the nest. He alone cares for the nest and fry. Up to 300 fry may result and they are quite tiny, so prepare plenty of infusoria and, later, newly hatched brine shrimp.

Fighting Fishes

Everyone tries their hand at keeping *Betta splendens* (Siamese fighter) at some time in their aquatic career. Although they are often kept in community aquaria, this is not the right place for them, particularly not for the males. The trailing finnage is a great temptation to other fishes who will often harass the slower-moving fighter and nip or tear his fins. This puts him under stress; often he will refuse to feed and may even develop bacterial or fungal infections on the damaged fins. In the worst eventuality he may hide away and eventually die. Females, on the other hand, seem to be able to fend for themselves in the average community aquarium of non-aggressive fishes.

In retail outlets male fighters are displayed individually, usually in small compartments within a larger tank. Although at first glance this system may seem cruel, it is designed specifically for their safety and well-being, allowing the fishes to display to each other while preventing them from causing actual bodily harm to either party. If kept together they will actually fight to the death. The water in the system is warm and clean, the fishes are properly fed and, even though they have no aeration system, being air

The male *Betta splendens* (Siamese fighter) diligently guards his bubblenest, adding bubbles as required and retrieving any eggs that fall out.

breathers they are able to cope with the situation.

For anyone who is serious about keeping and breeding fighters, special tanks should be used. These are divided into compartments using sheets of perforated mesh or glass dividers which leave a slight gap at the top and bottom, large enough to allow a flow of water through the whole aquarium yet small enough for the fishes not to be able to get into the next compartment. Using such a set-up, it is possible to provide well filtered water to maintain the creatures in the optimum conditions.

When breeding *Betta splendens*, set up a special tank, which need not be too deep but should contain thickets of plants to give the female cover and also to provide anchorage for the bubblenest. Make sure that the female is well fed and full of roe before attempting to put her with the male. Initially it is best to isolate the female in a jar

floating in the breeding tank. The male will start to construct the bubblenest and from time to time display to the female, spreading his fins and shaking. After a hour or so the nest will be quite large and the female will be excited enough to try to follow the male under it. This is the time to try to introduce her to him. If all goes well, the pair will go back to the nest where the male will wrap himself around the female, so that his vent is in close proximity to hers and then, as the fishes roll slowly in the water, the eggs and sperm will be released. The eggs are heavier than water and will sink towards the bottom. The male will now break off the embrace and catch the falling eggs in his mouth, gently blowing them into the nest; once the female recovers she will join in this task.

The spawning takes several hours to complete, during which time up to 250 eggs will be laid. Once the pair have finished

A large bubblenest builder, *Betta bellica* (slender *Betta*) grows to about 10 cm (4 in). Keep them in pairs.

spawning remove the female as quickly as possible, taking care not to disturb the nest. If she is left in the tank, the male may kill her while protecting the nest. For the next couple of days he will dedicate his life to looking after the eggs. Since they are heavier than water every so often one or more will fall out of the nest. The male will carefully catch these in his mouth and push them back into the nest.

On the third day the eggs will hatch but the fry will not become free swimming until late on the fifth or even sixth day after spawning. The fry are quite small and require newly hatched brine shrimp as their first food. Once they are free swimming, the male must be removed before he eats his offspring.

Recently several other species of *Betta* have been available to the hobbyist. Not all are suited to the community aquarium, and not all build the well-known bubblenest when breeding, but instead mouthbrood the eggs: so ensure you do your homework before you purchase them.

One of those more likely to be encountered is *Betta pugnax*, a mouthbrooder. A pair will live quite happily in a soft water community aquarium provided the other occupants are peaceable. Although relatively drab, they have an interesting method of reproduction. The female produces a batch of 10 to 20 eggs which are held in a "cup" formed by the male's anal fin. She then picks up these eggs in her mouth and spits them into the male's. The sequence is repeated until the clutch of up to 100 eggs is complete, and they are then brooded by the male. The fry are easily raised on infusoria and brine shrimp nauplii.

The Kissing Gourami

Helostoma temminckii (kissing gourami) are usually kept because of their novel way of testing each other's strength. The kissing action is not, as we might suppose, a sign of affection between male and female, but a trial of strength between two males, and forms part of the courtship ritual as they try to impress a suitable female. These creatures are very useful in the aquarium because they will pick away at algae, taking it off plant leaves without damaging them. Their preferred food is plankton but it is impossible to provide sufficient of this in the aquarium; they will accept small live foods as well as flake instead.

There are two colour forms of the kissing gourami, the green and the pink. The green fish is considered the wild form and the pink the aquarium form, the latter being the most commonly available to the aquarist. They grow quite large, some 10–15 cm (4–6 in), in captivity, so be prepared to give them space.

They are very adaptable, tolerating most water conditions, but they do like to be warm, in the 26–28°C (79–82°F) range. As they are not quarrelsome they may be kept safely with other similarly-sized fishes.

Although they can be bred in the aquarium, do this only if you have plenty of space – a pair will produce up to 10,000 eggs! In their native lands they are bred commercially as food fishes.

The wild form of *Helostoma temminckii* (green kissing gourami) (*above*) and the pink form shown below are plankton feeders, but fortunately for aquarists they will accept small prepared foods. They will also clean algae from plant leaves.

A courtship ritual or just a harmless trial of strength? *H. temminckii* are difficult to sex. Females are generally more round in the body and their anal fin is also rounded.

The Giant Gourami

Osphronemus goramy (giant gourami) is another fish that is predominantly a food fish as it grows to a large size – 40 cm (16 in) being a good-sized aquarium fish. The largest specimen recorded, however, measured 1 metre (36 in). They are long-lived and you can expect a well-cared-for aquarium specimen to be around for 10–15 years or even longer. Taking this into account, it is important to be prepared to make this sort of commitment before you purchase one of the "dear little things" in the dealer's tank. Those "little things" grow into "big things", and quickly.

If it wasn't for their size, they would make ideal fishes for beginners since they are tolerant of most water conditions, eat just about anything in the vegetable line (peas, banana, mango, cooked rice, and so on, as well as commercial foods) and don't fight. This is probably why we see them in large community tanks in public aquaria. Couple that with the fact that many people try to give the fish away when it has outgrown its home aquarium, and you find that public aquaria are inundated with offers of these creatures. So, the message is: "think before you buy". If you won't be able to house it when it grows bigger, leave it in the dealer's tank.

Climbing Perch

Anabas testudineus is probably the best-known species of this group, but is probably the least frequently kept.

There is a legend in the East that *Anabas* climbs palm trees and drinks the sap. This was first recorded in 1787 by a Lieutenant Daldorf of the Danish East India Company based at Tranquebar. He had found a climbing perch lodged in a crack in the bark of a palm tree growing beside a pond. It took an Indian naturalist to dispel this notion. Dr Das put forward the alternative explanation that these fishes are often found in trees, having been placed there by predatory birds who had captured them while they were migrating across land. So *Anabas* has acquired a common name which has nothing to do with how it gets up into trees!

When migrating from pond to pond, it not only uses its fins to help propel itself across the ground but also spreads each gill cover in turn so that the sharp spines on the latter anchor it to the ground while the fins push the fish forward, allowing it to move in a jerky side to side motion. This solves the problem of surviving when the pools dry up, and should the fish be unable to find another water source, it can bury itself in damp mud to survive. This remarkable creature can live for up to 48 hours out of water provided the conditions are damp. Being so hardy, they were able to withstand transportation by sailing ship and in around 1870 were put on display at the London Zoo Aquarium.

In the aquarium, they are very easy to keep, being tolerant of most water conditions. The one thing they do need is warmth, so a temperature averaging 26°C (79°F) is beneficial. Provide plenty of plant cover and some pieces of wood for shelter. This also helps create territories in the aquarium and should reduce the amount of squabbling.

Feeding the climbing perch couldn't be easier – if it's edible, they eat it. True omnivores, they consume pellets, rice, vegetable matter, live foods, flake, and so on. They are best kept with their own kind, in a fairly large aquarium, and under such conditions they will pair and may even breed. The floating eggs hatch in some 24 to 36 hours, but the fry are small, so be prepared to provide large quantities of infusoria in the first instance.

A true omnivore, *Osphronemus goramy* (giant gourami) feasts on just about anything you care to offer in the way of nourishment from peas and banana to flakes and pelleted foods.

The African Connection

The African anabantids belong to the genus *Ctenopoma* and although they are usually referred to by their generic name, they are also known as bush fishes or even climbing perch. To avoid such confusion here, we'll stick to *Ctenopoma* (bush fish).

At first glance, you might be forgiven for thinking that these chunky fishes with protrusile mouths look more like cichlids than anabantids. In their natural habitat they may be found in weedy areas of forest streams, as well as quiet stretches of rivers, ponds, lakes, swamps, and irrigation ditches. Being carnivores, they hunt for live foods and will take anything from insect larvae to other fishes as the opportunity arises. This makes a normal community tank a no-go area as far as keeping them is concerned, but some may be housed with other fishes of similar size and temperament.

Take care when handling bush fishes, they have serrated edges to their gill covers and when intimidated may flare the latter. If this takes place when the fishes are sparring with each other there are no problems, the trouble starts if you are trying to catch them, as the serrations easily entangle in the net. If this happens, do not try to pull the fish from the net; put net and fish in the aquarium and the fish will usually release itself. If it doesn't then cut the net rather than risking injury to the fish.

Most of the smaller species we come across in the hobby, such as *Ctenopoma ansorgii* (ornate *Ctenopoma*), *Ctenopoma fasciolatum* (banded *Ctenopoma*), and *Ctenopoma oxyrhynchus* (mottled *Ctenopoma*), may be kept with

Ctenopoma acutirostre is one of the more accommodating members of the genus. It can be kept with smaller fishes provided they are not small enough to be regarded as food. Feed meaty foods, and especially small live shrimps such as *Mysis*. It prefers a quiet tank with plenty of privacy.

other fishes too large to be eaten. They like a well-planted aquarium with soft, slightly acid water which must be warm: anything less than 24°C (75°F) is considered cold! Their method of feeding is to drift close to the prey and then lunge at it, so if you are keeping them with other fishes, it is important to make sure they are getting a chance to feed. If they are being kept away from the food, try feeding at both ends of the aquarium at the same time so that the more voracious feeders don't know which way to turn and the bush fishes have a chance. If the problem persists, then remove the bullies or set up a new tank for the bush fishes.

The most common species in the trade is *Ctenopoma kingsleyae*. Some scientists now consider this to be a colour morph of *Ctenopoma petherici* so you may see it for sale under this name as well. Whatever its scientific name it is a beautiful grey fish. Each scale on the body is clearly defined and the fins are almost clear with white edges. These fishes grow quite large (to about 20 cm/8 in) so they are not suited to the average community aquarium, which is a pity, as they are easy to keep.

If you wish to try and breed bush fishes you will need to check on the individual species' breeding strategy. Some, for example *Ctenopoma fasciolatum*, build bubblenests while others are termed non-brooders, producing large numbers of eggs that float to the surface. This is the reproductive method practised by *Ctenopoma kingsleyae*. The eggs of such species may be scooped out and hatched elsewhere. If hatching fry separately, use water from the main aquarium and keep the hatching aquarium clean. The fry are quite large and will take brine shrimp nauplii from day one.

199

Miscellaneous Freshwater Fishes

Telmatherina ladigesi (Celebes rainbowfish) need hard, alkaline water and regular partial water changes.

This chapter includes popular aquarium fishes that do not fit into any of the preceding fresh water groups.

Rainbowfishes

Rainbowfishes have been known in the aquarium trade for many years but until recently only a few species have been commonly available. Of these only *Telmatherina ladigesi* (Celebes rainbowfish), *Bedotia geayi* (Madagascar rainbowfish), and *Melanotaenia splendida* (eastern rainbowfish) have made any real impression. The last species is often referred to as *Melanotaenia nigrans* but the latter was probably not in the hobby until the end of the 1970s.

Recently this neglected group has aroused much more interest, with more species available in the shops and still more through the specialist societies which are springing up worldwide. The reasons for their popularity are obvious when you consider the type of fishes we are dealing with here. Most species measure between 3–15 cm (1¼–6 in) as adults and are peaceful, lively fishes which fit in well in most communities. They also have very attractive colours and a hardy disposition, which all adds up to the perfect aquarium fish.

From the scientific point of view the group of fishes we aquarists call rainbowfishes are split into three families:- Atherinidae (silversides), Melanotaeniidae (rainbowfishes), and Pseudomugilidae (blue-eyes). They are found in all sorts of habitats, from mountain streams to lowland rivers as well as lakes, ponds, ditches, and swampy regions. We recommend that the new aquarist starts with members of the Melanotaeniidae, such as *Melanotaenia*, *Glossolepis*, and *Chilatherina*, which tend to be the easiest to maintain.

Provide them with a well-planted aquarium of 100 cm (36 in) or more in length: rainbows are very active fishes and some of these species can grow to in excess of 10 cm (4 in). They do well in soft to medium-hard water (up to say 10–15° dH) but are sensitive to poor water quality and will remain near the bottom with their fins clamped to their bodies if water conditions are not to their liking. Regular partial water changes and a good filtration system will avoid this. Many like alkaline conditions: we suggest *C. bleheri* (Bleher's rainbowfish), *C. campsi* (highlands rainbowfish), *G. wanamensis* (Lake Wanam rainbowfish), *M. boesemani* (Boeseman's rainbowfish), *M. herbertaxelrodi* (Lake Tebera rainbowfish), and *M. trifasciata* (banded rainbowfish).

Another species worth mentioning is *Iriatherina werneri* (filament or threadfin rainbowfish). The males are eye-catching because of their long trailing fin filaments and their flag-like dorsal fins. Females are less gaudy. These small "rainbows" grow to at most 3.5 cm (1½ in) and the females are usually smaller at 3 cm (1¼ in). When first available in the trade only males were sold, but females are now available. They should be kept in a planted aquarium with soft, slightly acid water and a temperature of 24–28°C (75–82°F). They have been bred using either groups or pairs of fishes. The eggs are deposited in clumps of Java moss and hatch in 12 days. The fry require tiny foods such as rotifers and will even take

There are several subspecies of *Melanotaenia splendida* (eastern rainbowfish).

Bedotia geayi (Madagascan rainbowfish) requires plenty of live foods to maintain its colour and condition.

Melanotaenia splendida fluviatilis (crimson-spotted rainbowfish) is found in clear, slow-moving streams.

To help maintain the red colour of *Chilatherina bleheri* (Bleher's rainbowfish) it is important to vary the diet.

some fine commercially prepared foods or powdered egg yolk. If using powdered foods of any kind take extra care not to overfeed and pollute the water.

One member of the family Atherinidae commonly found in aquarium shops is *Bedotia geayi* (Madagascan rainbowfish). This is a hard water species which needs to be kept in a school of six or more to feel really secure. Regular partial water changes and a clean environment are a must to keep this species in tip-top condition. This is a larger species which can attain 15 cm (6 in) in the aquarium.

The other most commonly encountered member of this family is *Telmatherina ladigesi* (Celebes rainbowfish). Once again it is a schooling species which prefers to be in a group of six or more and can be sensitive to water quality. Both are hard water species, but will adapt to most water conditions provided the change is made slowly and acid conditions are avoided.

The family Pseudomugilidae includes a group of smaller rainbowfishes which are only just beginning to make an impact in the aquarium trade. There are about ten species in the family but only two have been seen with any regularity in aquarium shops. *Pseudomugil signifer* (Pacific blue-eye), comes from hard, slightly alkaline biotopes and is also found in brackish habitats. They adapt well to most aquarium conditions but do not like acid water. Females are rather drab, having a plain brownish body and clear fins, but males have bright yellow to orange fins with black leading edges. In some strains the anal and dorsal fins are elongated. Maximum size is about 5 cm (2 in) and they will fit in well in a community aquarium with similar-sized fishes.

The other species which can sometimes be found is one of the most beautiful of all the small rainbows, *Pseudomugil furcatus*. Females are rather plain

with just a hint of yellow in the fins, but males have the most spectacular golden yellow coloration which suffuses much of the body and fins. The base of the posterior dorsal fin and the anal fin are black, edged with yellow, and the tail has about six black central rays bounded by six yellow rays above and below. The top and bottom lobes are edged in black.

This is a peaceful hardy species which does well in the aquarium. It grows to only about 4 cm (1½ in) and makes an ideal inmate for a community of small species. It likes hard alkaline water, and regular partial water changes are a must to keep it in good condition.

To get both colour and size on your rainbows you will need to feed them on plenty of live or frozen foods. They are particularly fond of mosquito larvae, *Mysis* shrimp, bloodworm, and *Daphnia*. These foods will also help to bring them into breeding condition.

Melanotaenia boesemani (Boeseman's rainbowfish) loses some colour with each captive-bred generation.

A truly beautiful fish, there are several colour forms of *Melanotaenia trifasciata* (banded rainbowfish).

Iriatherina werneri (threadfin or filament rainbowfish) is quite easy to keep in soft, slightly acid conditions.

Breeding Rainbowfishes

Rainbows spawn by placing their eggs among fine-leaved plants. Most spawn over a period of several days and partial water changes, coupled with early morning sunlight falling on the aquarium, will often act as a trigger. Maybe 20 or so eggs are produced daily over a period of several days (egg numbers vary from species to species and on the size of the parents), and are hung by threads from the plants. The problem arises when the fry hatch as they do so at the same intervals as the eggs were laid, thus you find you have very tiny, newly hatched fry mixed with those that are a week old. Many hobbyists overcome this by spawning rainbows on mops such as those used for killifishes. It is then easy to pick off the eggs and raise the fry separately in batches. If you have only a community tank in which to keep your rainbows, a mop can be provided for the fishes to spawn on and removed every day or two to pick off eggs.

Raising the fry can be very hard work. In some species they are minute and require infusoria (*Paramecium* is very useful if you can get a culture going) and very fine brine shrimp nauplii, but once you have found the right foods and managed to get the hatching times of fishes and foods to coincide, growth of the fry is steady – under no circumstances can it be termed fast. Regular small feeds four to six times a day work best, and during this time the rearing tank needs to be kept scrupulously clean. Sponge filters are very useful but it is also necessary to siphon out any dead brine shrimp before it decays. Partial water changes also help to maintain water quality.

Although many people like to mix rainbow species in the community aquarium, this is not a wise practice if you are intending to breed these fishes, as one female can look very like another and they may interbreed, producing unsaleable hybrids.

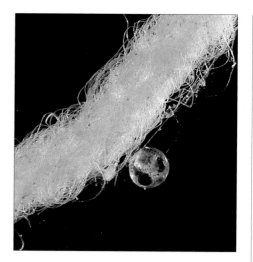

Rainbowfishes will spawn on mops in a similar manner to killifishes. Here we can see an "eyed-up" egg of *Chilatherina bleheri* (Bleher's rainbowfish). The eggs are quite tough and can be picked from the mop with your fingers and transferred to hatching trays.

A shoal of adult rainbows such as *Melanotaenia trifasciata* and *M. boesemani* is ideal for larger furnished aquaria.

Chilatherina sentaniensis (Lake Sentani rainbowfish) benefits from regular partial water changes and a varied diet which includes aquatic insect larvae.

The males of *Glossolepis incisus* (red rainbowfish) live up to their common name; females are plain silver coloured fishes.

Male *Melanotaenia lacustris* (Lake Kutubu rainbowfish) have a gold stripe down the centre of their heads when in breeding dress.

Electric Fishes

If you have read through the cat-fishes chapter you will already be aware of *Malapterurus electricus* (electric catfish). There are, how-ever, several other fishes that are able to produce electricity. Some use it to find their way around and others for defence and stun-ning prey, and all are aided by the fact that water is a good con-ductor. The electric organs are modified muscle cells; those fishes that stun their prey have large, powerful electric organs (*Electrophorus electricus* (electric eel) is a good example of this), whereas those which use elec-tricity for navigation have much smaller and less powerful organs. Interestingly electric fishes have very small eyes   and inhabit silty waters with poor visibility where electro- navigation is an asset.

A word of caution: THESE FISHES ARE NOT FOR BEGIN-NERS. Electric eels can deliver a shock of more than 500 volts and that is powerful enough to stun a horse. Even though you may fancy keeping one for its novelty value, please give the matter very careful consideration before proceeding. They are powerful creatures that require specialist handling, and if you have young children who may put their hands in the aquarium, do not even think about it.

Members of the African genus *Mormyridae* (elephant noses) use electric pulses to find their way around, communicate with each other, and passively defend terri-tory. The electric organ is small, weak, and situated near the cau-dal peduncle. These fishes are so sensitive to water quality that in Germany they have been intro-duced into a water supply to monitor drinking water purity; if

Electrophorus electricus (electric eel) is a very large and potentially dangerous fish. Think hard before buying – it can deliver a shock that can stun a horse.

their electrical pulses increase from the normal 800 per minute this indicates a deterioration in the water purity.

In the aquarium the most commonly kept species is *Gnathonemus petersi* (Peter's elephant nose). If your aquarium has been established for a year or more, everything is going well, and it is not overstocked, you could try to keep one or two elephant noses. They are quite peaceful but if you are intending to keep more than one, make sure they are of similar size, as large specimens will sometimes bully smaller, weaker ones.

Elephant noses are nocturnal so ensure that there are caves or other suitable places for them to hide in during the day. If you are keeping more than one specimen it is important that the fishes can hide away in separate areas of the aquarium so that their elec-tric fields are not permanently interacting with each other.

Feed them in the evening,

Gnathonemus petersi (Peter's ele-phant nose) requires a fine substrate so that its delicate snout is not dam-aged when searching for food.

offering flake, frozen, and live foods. They are particularly fond of frozen bloodworm. They use their soft "snout" to detect food in the substrate, and this organ can easily be damaged by sharp gravel, so fine sand is more suitable.

As we have already stated, they are sensitive to poor water conditions. In the aquarium regular partial water changes (with aged or conditioned water) are advantageous.

Another species of weakly electric fish, this time from South America, is *Apteronotus albifrons* (ghost knife fish) whose common name stems from tribespeople in Guyana who believe it to be inhabited by a ghost or evil spirit.

This fish grows large, up to 50 cm (20 in), much too big for a community aquarium. It is mentioned here because it too has a weak electric organ near the caudal peduncle which it uses to locate food. Should you wish to keep it, do remember they can sometimes be aggres-sive. They need a furnished aquarium with plenty of hiding places and will even tolerate larger peaceful companions once they have become used to aquarium life. Feeding these fishes poses little difficulty as they are omnivores, taking every-thing from pieces of meat to tablet foods.

Sun Bass and Darters

There are some wonderful alternatives to goldfishes for the cold-water aquarium, such as the sun bass and darters. Both groups could be kept in a garden pool in the summer months, but because of their colour and/or lifestyle you would not see them very often.

Sun bass, or sunfishes as they are sometimes called, are North American fishes of the family Centrarchidae. Some very large members of this family are held in high regard by anglers. Aquarists, however, are mostly interested in the smaller species which can easily be accommodated in an aquarium. Sunfishes are very attractive, with numerous coloured spots and spangles on their flanks, and, when seen in sunlight, it is not surprising that they are sought after for the cool water aquarium.

One of the smaller species, *Elassoma evergladei* (pygmy sunfish, Everglades pygmy sunfish, Florida pygmy sunfish), is found in the eastern USA from North Carolina to Florida. As may be expected from its distribution, this fish has a wide temperature range (10–30°C /50–86°F) and is often kept in the tropical aquarium. It is small, reaching only 3.5 cm (1¹/₂ in).

The three species of *Enneacanthus* are slightly larger fishes ranging from 8–10 cm (3¹/₄–4 in) in length and are not recommended for inclusion in the tropical tank: they like the water temperature to rise to about 22°C (71-72°F) in the summer and cool to 10°C (50°F) or so during the winter months. *Enneacanthus chaetodon* (the black-banded sunfish) is found in the states of New York, New Jersey, and Maryland; *E. gloriosus*

Enneacanthus chaetodon (black-banded sunfish) is often overlooked in dealer's tanks. Although suitable for garden pools provided their companions are of a similar size and disposition, they are best kept in a cool water aquarium.

Enneacanthus gloriosus (blue-spotted sunfish) can be kept and bred in an aquarium, but pay special attention to their temperature requirements if you are attempting to breed them.

(the blue-spotted sunfish) is more wide-ranging, occurring from New York State down the eastern seaboard to Florida; and *E. obesus* (diamond sunfish, little sunfish) from New England to Florida.

All prefer a planted aquarium with a sand or fine gravel substrate, and all are sensitive to poor water conditions and rapid, frequent temperature fluctuations. Care is needed when making water changes to ensure that the pH is not raised – *E. obesus* in particular will suffer – and even healthy fishes will become susceptible to fungal infections if, for example, they are suddenly switched from slightly acid water to anything more than slightly alkaline conditions (above 7.5 is likely to prove harmful). At worst the fishes will die.

Feeding is simple as they readily take frozen foods such as bloodworm and mosquito larvae. Live foods are preferred, but they will accept flake. To condition them for breeding it is essential to give them as varied a diet as possible.

Breeding Sunfishes

Sunfishes are more likely to breed if they have been kept in cooler water during the winter. We have found that keeping *E. chaetodon* in an unheated greenhouse in a 50–70 litre (10–15 gallon) vat with external power filtration, sand substrate, a few plants, and a diet of frozen and live foods (much of which fell in

A stream fish, *Etheostoma caeruleum* (rainbow darter) adapts well to the aquarium provided it has cool conditions and well-oxygenated, clear water, as rising temperatures in spring and summer are a natural "trigger" for breeding.

naturally) provided ideal conditions for the fishes to breed.

In *Enneacanthus* it is hard to differentiate the sexes: females are heavier-bodied and their colours may be slightly more intense. One way to tell takes a little practice; observation of their behaviour. The males stake out territories and defend them; this is more obvious when they are about to breed but can also be detected at other times. Spawning is preceded by courtship and nest building. The male digs a pit in a sheltered area of the tank and defends it vigorously. He courts his chosen female and eventually the sticky eggs are deposited in the nest. After spawning the female can be removed, leaving the male to guard the nest and fry. Once these are free swimming, the male can also be removed. The fry are raised on small live foods.

Recently, one of the North American darters, *Etheostoma caeruleum* (rainbow darter), a native of central North America but with some population pockets in New York State, has been made available to hobbyists. A small bottom-dwelling fish, it needs cool conditions (4–18°C/ 39–64°F), and suffers considerably if the temperature rises above this. Some aquarists even use cooling systems to keep the water temperature down during the summer months. It inhabits fast-flowing streams with very clean, highly oxygenated water and something approaching these conditions should be aimed for in the aquarium. It is very sensitive to silty and polluted conditions. Reaching 7.5 cm (3 in), it is an ideal aquarium fish and may breed. In the wild it spawns in gravel beds during spring and early summer.

Gobies

Many gobies are brackish water fishes but there are some that are at home in fresh water. Most are bottom-dwellers, lurking among stones and roots, and scuttling from place to place in search of food. They are carnivores and require live foods and/or dead meaty foods (frozen bloodworm for small species and pieces of fish or meat for larger ones). Aquarists use the term "goby" to cover two families of fishes, the Gobiidae, or true gobies, and the Eleotridae, or sleeper gobies.

The Eleotridae have long slender bodies and their ventral fins are separate whereas the Gobiidae have a similar body shape but the ventral fins are fused to form a sucker that helps the fish to maintain position in fast-flowing waters. Members of both families adapt well to aquarium life, but do check to see how big they grow before putting them into a community aquarium. *Oxyeleotris marmoratus,* for example, can grow to 50 cm (20 in) and has a voracious

Hypseleotris cyprinoides **is quite at home in a community aquarium. It will eat flake, but prefers live foods such as** *Daphnia,* **failing which use frozen foods.**

appetite, consuming the equivalent of its own body weight in a day – your neons wouldn't stand a chance.

Of the sleeper gobies, *Hypseleotris cyprinoides* is a peaceful addition to the general community aquarium, where it will coexist with other fishes without any problems. Far more colourful is *Tateurndina ocellicauda* (peacock or eye-spot sleeper)

native to New Guinea, where it is found in lowland rivers and pools. Their colour alone makes them an instant success among aquarists, and that you can breed them is a bonus.

Peacock gobies need a well-furnished, softwater aquarium. If kept with other fishes, these should be equally peaceful otherwise you will not see an awful lot of your gobies – they will retire to the quieter, darker regions. Males, although slightly larger, are slimmer than females. The females have more yellow on the belly region and brighter yellow on the outer edges of the dorsal and anal fins. These small fishes, 7.5 cm (3 in) at most, breed in small cracks and crevices or caves. Half a coconut shell makes an acceptable spawning site. The male courts the female by shaking and shimmering his body and fins in front of her. The pair then retire to the spawning site where the eggs are deposited on a flat surface; the female is then chased away by the male, who remains on guard to tend the eggs and brood. The fry are easy to raise because they will

A native of New Guinea, *Tateurndina ocellicauda* **(peacock or eye-spot goby) has been bred in captivity. Fortunately the new generation retains the wonderful coloration of the parents.**

Gobiodes broussonnetii (dragon or eel goby) is a predator and definitely not for the community aquarium!

Mogurnda mogurnda is attractive when young, but grows to 17cm (7 in) and likes eating fish!

accept brine shrimp nauplii as a first food.

Of the true gobies, *Stigmatogobius sadanundio* is a very popular, if infrequently imported, goby. In complete contrast to the peacock goby, this fish requires hard alkaline water and under no circumstances should you try to acclimatize it to acid conditions. Although these little gobies are territorial bottom-dwellers, they do not bother mid-water fishes, so they may safely be kept with swordtails or sailfin mollies in a planted aquarium that has rocks and caves to provide seclusion and help territorial boundaries to be defined.

These fishes benefit from a fluctuation in water temperature over each 24-hour period (with a lower temperature at night). They will tolerate temperatures between 20–26°C (68–79°F). You can also add 1–2 level teaspoons of aquarium salt per 11 litres (2.5 gallons) – if your plants and other fishes will tolerate it – but this is not essential.

If, however, you wish to try and breed them, a species tank is best. At this time the water temperature needs to be at the upper end of their range (about 24–28°C/75–82°F), and the addition of salt as detailed above certainly helps to induce spawning. A sand or fine gravel substrate with rocks and caves is required. Flowerpots laid on their sides, or completely inverted with a small triangular piece cut out as an entrance, are ideal. The gobies lay their eggs on the ceilings of caves so an inverted pot makes a good substitute. A pair may produce 1000 or so eggs each of which is attached to the cave ceiling by a fine thread. Both parents tend the brood and the fry are relatively easily reared on newly hatched brine shrimp.

One of the most beautiful of all the gobies, which turns up from time to time in retail outlets, is *Chlamydogobius eremius* (desert goby). It is very a small species which will grow to about 6 cm (2¼ in) in the aquarium, although the female tends to remain a little smaller. She is a rather plain silvery-grey fish with a black spot in the second dorsal fin. The male, however, is a lovely lemon-yellow colour on the body, which contrasts spectacularly with the blue fins edged in yellow or white.

This is another hardwater species which prefers a pH above 7.5 and a hardness in excess of 12 dH. The temperature should be maintained at 24–26°C (75–79°F). The tank should have a white (or other pale colour) sand substrate and plenty of rocks and caves. The males are very quarrelsome towards each other but peaceful towards other species.

It is supposedly a cave spawner which lays its eggs on the ceiling of a cave, but it will also spawn in the open on a rock. Whichever method is used, the male will guard the eggs and young until they are free swimming. Up to 50 eggs are laid in a clutch. These take up to seven days to hatch and the fry will require newly hatched brine shrimp as their first food. The fry grow quickly and are sexable after only three months, and are sexually mature at about six months of age.

Spiny Eels

At some time or other you may wish to try your hand at keeping spiny eels, members of the family Mastacembelidae. Despite their common name they are not related to the true eels, but just have a similar long thin shape. They are found in brackish and fresh waters in Africa and southeast Asia. These long, sinuous fishes are excellent burrowers and will undermine rocks and plants in the aquarium. They have long, prehensile noses which they use to sift through mud and sand in search of worms and other buried food. As these fishes grow they become more predatory. Captive specimens are not very fond of flake and tablet foods, so be prepared to feed them on frozen foods with the occasional meal of aquatic invertebrates such as *Tubifex* for small specimens. Larger fishes are particularly fond of earthworms.

Mastacembelus erythrotaenia (fire eel) is an aquarium favourite, probably because they look so sweet in dealers' tanks. Young specimens bury themselves beneath wood or rocks with only their heads sticking out. Large numbers are available in the trade and many people buy them without realizing just how big they can grow: 50 cm (20 in) is not unusual in captivity and their potential is 1 metre (36 in). At these sizes they are predatory and will eat small fishes when they come out to feed at night.

Although youngsters are gregarious, as they grow they become intolerant of their own kind but may be kept with other large, mid-water fishes or some of the larger armoured catfishes. Water with a hardness of up to 15 degrees and a pH on the acid side of neutral seems to suit these fishes. Ensure that the substrate is soft and has no sharp pieces of sand or gravel that may cut the fishes as they burrow.

The fire eel is one of the most delicate species of the genus and very particular attention should be paid to maintaining the water quality. They are also excellent jumpers and escape artists, which will wriggle through the smallest of openings, so ensure you cover the tank tightly.

Two other species that are sometimes available are *M. circumcinctus*, a small fish growing to only 16 cm (6¼ in) and *M. armatus* (spiny eel) which grows to 75 cm (30 in). Both require very similar conditions to the fire eel.

Bichirs and Reedfishes

In the tropical waters of Africa we find a very interesting family of fishes, the Polypteridae (bichirs, reedfishes, or lobe-finned pike). They have elongated, snake-like bodies which are covered with enamelled, diamond-shaped (ganoid) scales. Their swim-bladder is modified to allow them to breath from the atmosphere and thus survive in oxygen-deficient waters. In the aquarium they will surface at regular intervals to take in gulps of air, regardless of whether the water is well oxygenated or not. If they are prevented from reaching the surface they will die.

They are carnivores and prey on anything that will fit into their mouths, from fishes to worms, insect larvae, and frogs. In the aquarium they will take dead foods such as pieces of fish or meat. Shrimps or prawns can be broken up and fed with some of the shell on.

There are two genera: *Erpetoichthys* (reedfishes or snakefishes), which has a single species *E. calabaricus*, and *Polypterus* (bichirs) with several species. Both may be kept with other fishes provided their companions are large enough not to be considered prey. They are excellent escape artists, especially the reedfish, which will wriggle out of the smallest gaps, even those where external filter pipes enter the tank. They can be deterred by trapping a piece of net curtain between the cover glass and the tank so that it covers this small gap and the pipe. If necessary, tape the net to the outside of the aquarium to hold it in place. Should your fish be found on the carpet in a semi-desiccated condition, do not give up hope. One of us found her

Mastacembelus erythrotaenia (fire eel) requires a diet of meaty foods such as worms, shrimps, and chopped mussels.

reedfish covered with dog hairs and rather stiff on the floor one morning. With nothing to lose she returned it to the aquarium. Four hours later the fish was swimming about – still covered in dog hairs and its finnage looking somewhat ragged – but it was alive. What's more important, it recovered completely from its little outing.

Erpetoichthys calabaricus (reedfish) is a peaceful fish, even with its own kind, but it should not be kept with anything small enough to be considered food. It grows quite long and slim, reaching a maximum of 40 cm (16 in). These fishes prefer their water to be soft and slightly acid and a normal community aquarium of appropriate-sized fishes is ideal for them.

The bichirs can be quarrelsome when kept together, especially if there are not enough hiding places in the aquarium, but their aggression is not usually directed towards other species. They are tolerant of most water conditions provided extremes of pH and hardness are avoided. Some species seen regularly in the hobby are *Polypterus ornatipinnis* (ornate bichir) which can grow to 45 cm (18 in), *P. delhezi* (armoured

Polypterus senegalensis (Senegal or Cuvier's bichir), like the other species, are great escape artists. Be sure to cover the aquarium tightly.

When *Polypterus palmas* (marbled bichir) breed, the eggs are left to fall to the bottom of the aquarium.

bichir) 35 cm (14 in), and *P. senegalensis* (Senegal or Cuvier's bichir) and *P. palmas* (marbled bichir) both 30 cm (12 in).

Some species have been bred in captivity. During spawning the male spreads out his anal fin so that it is slightly cupped and places it beneath the vent of the female. The eggs and sperm are

expelled into the cupped fin. Some species, for example *P. ornatipinnis*, lay their eggs among plants, while others, such as *P. palmas*, let them fall to the bottom. Hatching takes four to five days but the fry are not free swimming until a few days later. They will take newly hatched brine shrimp.

This contrasts with the breeding strategy of *Polypterus ornatipinnis* (ornate bichir) which deposits its eggs amongst plants.

The Butterfly Fishes

For anyone looking for something a little out of the ordinary, nothing could be better than the butterfly fish. Known scientifically as *Pantodon buchholzi*, it is a surface-dwelling predator. The mouth is like a drawbridge and they will take any insect or even fish that fits into it. Apart from this, they make excellent companions for medium-sized (over 8 cm (3 in)) mid- or bottom-dwelling peaceful fishes.

The aquarium need not be deep, 15–20 cm (6–8 in) is acceptable, but you can, of course, house them in deeper aquaria when they are kept with other fishes. For preference the water should be soft, acid, and well filtered. Any deterioration in water quality may lead to fin degeneration and loss of appetite.

They like to lurk beneath rafts of floating plants; cork bark floating on the surface provides a natural looking alternative and a place to put a dish of maggots to hatch into flies for the fishes to eat. "Butterflies" love to jump for flies – butterflies love to jump, period! The floating cork/plant layer helps to discourage this, but, better safe than sorry, make sure the aquarium is tightly covered. Other foods relished are any surface-dwelling insects, be they larvae or adults; meal worms, spiders, woodlice, maggots (buy uncoloured maggots from a fishing tackle shop and store them in a plastic box, with ventilation holes, in a cool place), large flakes, and sometimes floating pellets. Frozen foods are eaten as they fall through the water but anything that reaches the bottom is usually ignored.

There has been some success breeding these creatures. Males have a convex anal fin with the central rays forming a tube, while that of females is straight. Correct feeding is crucial to bring them into spawning condition: they need a varied diet including plenty of live food.

The fishes spawn over a long period each day, and the eggs, which are lighter than water, float to the surface. They can be easily scooped out to be hatched in another tank using water from the parents' aquarium. The eggs are transparent at first but over the next nine hours or so turn dark brown, almost black; they hatch in about 36 hours. Raising the fry is exceedingly difficult. Try *Artemia* nauplii as a first food and make regular, small, partial water changes, and you may have some success.

Pantodon buchholzi (butterfly fish) will jump to catch insects – keep the aquarium tightly covered.

Glassfishes

As suggested by the common name, the Chandidae (glassfishes) have transparent bodies which allow you to see the skeleton and many of their internal organs. Two species crop up every now and again in the trade: *Chanda ranga* (Indian glassfish) and *Chanda wolffii*. The larger of the two is *C. wolffii* at 20 cm (8 in) although it is most unusual for them to reach this size in captivity even if they are fed correctly.

Although a great talking point in public aquaria, glassfishes are shrouded in mystery when it comes to keeping them in the aquarium. They are regarded as "difficult" and to a degree this is true. Although they are peaceful enough, they do not benefit from being kept in the teeming metropolis of the average community, preferring the quiet of a species aquarium.

Use a 75 cm (30 in) aquarium with a dark substrate of lava chips or very dark gravel; not peat, as this will acidify the water; glassfishes like medium-hard and slightly alkaline water. Before they are introduced the system needs to be mature with the plants growing well; use those that will tolerate salt in the water as these fishes benefit from 1–2 level teaspoons of aquarium salt per 11 litres (2.5 gallons) of water. Being somewhat timid, when first introduced they may hide, but once they feel secure you will see them more and more often. They are territorial and take a little time to sort out their own space, but once they have established this there are no further problems.

Both species will accept flake foods, but flake alone is not enough for the fishes to survive.

The diet needs to include small invertebrates as well as frozen foods. Sometimes it can be difficult to find the right dietary combination to succeed with these creatures. One of us based her feeding regime on live *Daphnia* and bloodworm every day, with frozen and flake foods used to supplement this, and achieved reasonable success in keeping these fishes.

Indian glassfishes spawn quite readily provided they have been well conditioned on a wide variety of foods. Rather than using a single pair, use several pairs in the same aquarium. Spawning can be triggered by sunlight falling on the aquarium, raising the temperature slightly, the addition of some fresh water and, if all this fails, separate the males and females for a few days. The former have a blue edge to the dorsal and anal fins. The female is more yellowish and, if we look closely at their (conveniently visible) internal organs, the front of her swim-bladder is rounded (pointed in the male).

Each spawning pass produces about half a dozen sticky eggs that adhere to the plants (Java moss is very good for this purpose); spawning continues until the pair have laid 200 or so eggs. Although the parents ignore both eggs and fry, it is wise to remove them just in case they feel peckish. The eggs hatch in 24 hours and the larvae are tiny.

The larvae festoon the plants until they become free swimming some three days later. Now the problems really start. Although they will take brine shrimp nauplii, they do not actively hunt for it but merely snap at it as it passes by. The addition of an air-operated sponge filter, which will keep the food moving

Chanda ranga (Indian glassfish) is difficult to feed because it requires live foods and will not survive on flake foods alone.

Although larger than *C. ranga*, *Chanda wolffii* is a shy fish, which benefits from being kept in a species aquarium rather than the hurly-burly of the community tank.

about, helps, but feeding them on a single food is not adequate; just as the adults need variety, so do the fry. It is a case of try anything small enough, feed little and often, and then just hope you have got it right.

A word of warning. Glassfishes have been imported with arcs of fluorescent colour in their bodies, and sold to unsuspecting hobbyists as "disco fishes". These fishes have been injected with a coloured dye. This action causes distress and damage to the fishes and is a potential cause of infection. This practice is frowned upon by most hobbyists and reputable traders and should be discouraged by not buying such specimens. Not only species of *Chanda* have been treated this way, but the glass catfish, *Kryptopterus bicirrhus,* has also suffered.

Leaf Fishes

If you are looking for something a little out of the ordinary you may like to consider the leaf fishes. These members of the family Nandidae occur in South America, Africa, and Asia. *Monocirrhus polyacanthus* (South American leaf fish) and *Polycentrus schomburgki* (South American leaf fish or Schomburgk's leaf fish) are found in north-eastern South America; *Polycentropsis abbreviata* (African leaf fish) occurs in west Africa; and *Nandus nandus* (nandus) in Asia, from India to Thailand. Breeding strategies vary: *M. polyacanthus* lays its eggs on a leaf, *P. schomburgki* spawns in a cave, *P. abbreviata* uses a bubblenest, and virtually nothing is known about what *Nandus nandus* does. All are rarely seen in the trade but we have chosen one to illustrate some of their needs.

Monocirrhus polyacanthus inhabits still and slow-moving waters in the Peruvian Amazon. We include it here so that you don't inadvertently buy one and place it in your community aquarium with disastrous results. These fishes are out-and-out predators and will not accept

As can be seen here, *Monocirrhus polyacanthus* (South American leaf fish) can vary greatly in colour. A single specimen can be brown but half an hour later have changed to cream.

You must be prepared to feed live fish to *M. polyacanthus*; otherwise do not attempt to keep them. Remember they will regard small tankmates as snacks.

dead foods at all, so if you are contemplating keeping them, think hard before buying.

Primarily brown in colour, they look just like dead leaves. They can vary their body colour: one day they may be dark brown, another golden, and a third "cloudy". At night they take on what can only be described as a cloud pattern – brown patches on a lighter beige/brown background.

Monocirrhus polyacanthus needs to be kept in a species aquarium. The tank should include bogwood, be well planted with large *Echinodorus* sp. (Amazon sword plants), and have very gentle filtration so there is little water movement. The fishes are timid and difficult to acclimatize, so once they have settled in do not add any other fishes. The set-up needs to be mature with slightly acid soft water. If the water is not right – perhaps too high in nitrates – the fishes will stop feeding and rest with their fins clamped.

For much of the day they will float motionless, head down in the water, looking to all intents and purposes like floating leaves. To make the illusion complete, they have a small fleshy barbel on the tip of the lower lip which looks just like a leaf stalk. Put some live food (fishes) in and the leaves come to life, fluttering their fins so that they drift towards the prey; when close enough, the jaws open and the prey is engulfed. They should be kept only if a continuous supply of small live fishes can be provided as their food.

They breed in a similar manner to some of the cichlids. The pair clean a leaf and the female deposits the eggs thereon. These and the resulting fry are guarded by the male. Rearing the fry is easy if, and only if, you can provide enough live foods. The fry will consume their own body weight in food each day, and when you have 300 hungry mouths to feed, this is an awful lot of live food.

The Halfbeaks

The halfbeaks occur in southeast Asia and are found in both fresh and brackish environments. Most of those available in aquatic outlets have been acclimatized to freshwater conditions (with maybe a level teaspoonful of salt per 4.5 litres/1 gallon), so you should have no problems with them. They are shoaling fishes which live at the water surface, and if you look at the position of the dorsal fin you will see that it is set well back on the body so that it does not break-up the dorsal profile and stick out of the water, betraying the presence of the fish to any predator.

The lower jaw of these fishes is extended and fixed, and as they cruise just beneath the surface this allows them to feed on surface-dwelling insects or any that fall onto it. In captivity these insectivores require live foods: they will take *Tubifex* (from a feeder), fruit flies, indeed, any small flies will be avidly consumed. The problem for the aquarist is to get enough of the right foods. In summer the garden provides plenty of insects such as aphids – but don't use any that have been sprayed with insecticide; mosquito larvae, pupae, and adults are also relished. Alternatively you can use a hand net (for example an aquarium net) to sweep long grass and you will be amazed at the number of bugs that you catch. To feed the fishes, first of all ensure that you have a tight-fitting cover glass or all your insects will escape. (This also helps to keep the fishes in the aquarium as they are very good jumpers.) Release the bugs into the space between the water and the cover glass. If using some creepy-crawlies such as small spiders, float a small piece of cork bark on the water and set the bugs adrift on this "raft". As they near the edge, the fishes see them and leap to catch them. Alternatively, use floating plants.

Being surface dwellers, they can be accommodated in a shallow aquarium. The water should be hard with a little salt added if the tap water in your area is soft. If necessary use buffers to maintain the pH at about 7.0.

Three genera are regularly imported via the trade: *Dermogenys*, *Nomorhamphus*, and *Hemirhamphodon*. All three produce live young.

The halfbeaks most often imported nowadays are members of the *Nomorhamphus* genus. They tend to have much thicker bodies than the other genera and the lower jaw is shorter, barely protruding beyond the upper. Often the lower lip is black-pigmented. Any one of several different species may be offered for sale under the name of Celebes halfbeak; all grow to about 10 cm (4 in) and will eat anything small enough to fit into their mouths, even a small neon tetra, so make sure you keep them only with fishes of a similar size.

The males of this genus have the front rays of the anal fin shortened to form the copulatory organ. Mating usually takes place just after sunrise when the male will be seen courting the female. About six weeks later up to 20 young will be born. Although these are very large at birth (up to 2 cm (3/4 in)), the parents will still eat them if given the chance, so remove them to another aquarium for rearing. They will eat newly hatched brine shrimp as their first food, but grow quickly and soon require the same foods as their parents.

Members of the *Dermogenys* genus turn up from time to time.

Dermogenys pusillus sumatranus (wrestling halfbeak) is the easiest of the halfbeaks to breed. They produce a brood about once a month. As with other halfbeaks, the lower jaw is vulnerable to damage during shipment, so check carefully before buying.

Hemirhamphodon pogonognathus (thread-jawed or long-snout halfbeak) is very difficult to maintain in captivity. Firstly you must ensure that the fishes have suffered no damage to their snouts in transit, and secondly you must provide an almost constant supply of live foods.

These are often called "wrestling halfbeaks", the common name is derived from the males' habit of wrestling with each other to determine which is strongest and establish a pecking order. The most commonly available species is *Dermogenys pusillus*. They have a much longer beak than the Celebes halfbeak and this is vulnerable to damage during shipment. Such damage is often followed by infection and death, so make sure you purchase only specimens with a complete lower jaw. These are the easiest of the group to breed in captivity, with broods of up to 30 being born every month or so.

The other genus of halfbeaks to regularly appear in retail outlets is *Hemirhamphodon*. *H. pogonognathus* (thread-jawed or long-snout halfbeak) is somewhat different from the other members of this group in having the front part of the anal fin extended instead of shortened. Again this fin is used as a copulatory organ during mating.

This species is by far and away the most difficult of the group to establish in captivity. They have a very long and thin lower jaw which is often broken when the fish is being shipped, and such an injury will almost always lead to death.

They are also more choosy about their diet. All halfbeaks are insectivores but most can be weaned on to floating flake foods. While this will not be enough to keep them in tip-top shape, it will tide them over lean times when live foods are unavailable. The thread-jawed halfbeak, however, is very reluctant to take this alternative regardless of how hungry it is, so do not buy one unless you are confident of maintaining a year round supply of live foods. It will take live foods such as *Daphnia* and bloodworms from the upper part of the aquarium but, unlike the other halfbeaks, will not follow these foods down to the lower strata.

The fry are produced over a period of several weeks with a couple being born every day. Eventually a brood will number 30 to 40. If well fed the adults should not eat them but it is wise to remove them for rearing in another aquarium, just to be on the safe side. The fry will eat all small live foods offered provided these are near or on the surface of the water. Newly hatched brine shrimp can be offered, but position a strong light above the aquarium to draw the shrimps to the surface where the halfbeaks will eat them. Any dead shrimps must be siphoned out before they decay.

Snakeheads

If you like large predators then these are the fishes for you. Depending on species they range in size from about 15 cm (6 in) to well over 1 metre (36 in) when full grown. All are predators which feed on live fishes and other live foods, but in the aquarium they can be weaned on to dead fishes such as whitebait, and pieces of fish and meat as well as large earthworms. As with all large predators, feed them only when they are hungry. In young fishes this tends to be almost every day but in adults it may be only once a week – when they will gorge themselves.

Snakeheads have an accessory breathing organ which allows them to live in water with a low oxygen content, and, like some of the labyrinths, they often go "walkabout" in the wild, moving from pond to pond in search of food. Obviously a tight-fitting cover glass is important, held in place by a heavy weight if your fish is big.

In general snakeheads are tolerant of poor water conditions, but this does not mean you can neglect the filtration. They are large predators which produce high protein waste, necessitating a filtration system capable of preventing any build-up of toxins such as ammonia, and regular water changes to minimize nitrates. Snakeheads make long-lived hardy pets which will feed from your fingers once they become accustomed to you. The only limiting factor is size, but this is not as much of a problem as you might think. If well fed, they tend to sit around doing nothing, so a large aquarium is wasted on them. Provided the tank is at least twice the length of the adult snakehead and the

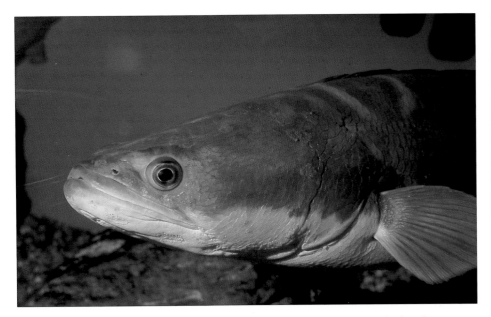

Channa micropeltes (red snakehead) is bought from unscrupulous dealers by unsuspecting aquarists, not realizing just how big these fishes grow.

width at least equal to its adult length, then it will be happy.

They are not fussy when it comes to decor, and although bogwood and plants can be included to create a more natural effect, they adapt well to a bare tank with a gravel substrate. Filtration can be by internal power filter, and while not light-sensitive they do seem to prefer subdued lighting. Temperature can be anywhere between 22-26°C (72–79°F).

Of those species generally available, the one most often offered for sale is also one of the most unsuitable. *Channa micropeltes* has the common name of red snakehead because of its coloration when young. Babies (and we do mean *babies*) of about 15 cm (6 in) body length have two black stripes running the full length of their reddish body. The red is strongest below the first stripe and is very striking. Unfortunately it fades as the fish grows – as do the black stripes – until you are left with a not particularly attractive, metre-long (36 in), grey and black mottled fish. A much

better species to try is *Channa orientalis*, which grows to only 30 cm (12 in) and, while a drab fish as a youngster, develops a lovely blue sheen to the body and fins as it matures. The fins are edged with bands of black and yellow.

Snakeheads tend to be loners and are usually maintained one to an aquarium. If you have the space you might like to try breeding them. In all species the male cares for the eggs, but some are mouthbrooders, while others guard the eggs which float at the surface under thick plant cover. In the larger species the eggs may number up to 3000, but in the smaller mouthbrooders only about 40 are produced.

C. micropeltes is no small fish; at 1m (40 in) it has lost not only its charm but also its colour. This will make finding it a new home difficult if you can no longer cope.

Sticklebacks

Remarkably few European native fishes are kept by aquarists and yet some meet all the criteria of a good aquarium fish, that is, small size, pretty colours, and interesting behaviour. The sticklebacks meet all these criteria in full and yet are very rarely even thought of when choosing aquarium fishes.

The sticklebacks are a small family of fishes which live in fresh, brackish, and marine waters of the northern temperate zones. Two species make good inhabitants of the cool water aquarium. These are *Pungitius pungitius* (ten-spined stickleback) and *Gasterosteus aculeatus* (three-spined stickleback). In general it is best to house these species separately from each other in a single species aquarium about 60 cm (24 in) in length. Although they are schooling species, males become territorial during the breeding season and will fight and badly injure each other if the aquarium is too small. It is wise, therefore, to keep only one male and a group of females.

The tank should have a fine gravel substrate, plenty of plants, and lots of caves and pots to provide hiding places. The water will need to be soft unless you can find a wild population which is living in hard water conditions. Aeration is needed to maintain the oxygen level during warm weather, and ideally the aquarium should be sited where the temperature will fall as low as possible (without freezing) during winter. This helps stimulate the fishes to spawn in the spring.

Once settled in they will spend much of their time out in the open looking for food. For fishes caught in the wild this will

When in breeding condition the male *Gasterosteus aculeatus* (three-spined stickleback) developes a vibrant red coloration. At this time he is ready to entice a willing female into his nest.

G. aculeatus is often overlooked as an aquarium fish by hobbyists but is a firm favourite with school children, who like to catch them.

Pungitius pungitius (ten-spined stickleback) is similarly overlooked, yet both are very interesting and breedable aquarium fishes.

need to be live foods such as bloodworms, *Daphnia*, and whiteworms. It is a rare wild fish which can be weaned on to flake foods, but most will eventually accept frozen foods and small pieces of fish or meat.

During spring and summer the male will come into breeding condition and it is then that you see the real beauty of these species. Ten-spined stickleback males turn a velvety black and have bright orange pectoral fins. Three-spined stickleback males develop the most beautiful red coloration over much of the body, particularly on the throat.

The male will select a suitable site and build a nest. This will be on the bottom of the aquarium in the case of the three-spined stickleback and a few inches above the bottom in the other species. It is made of pieces of plants stuck together with a "glue" produced by the male. Once it is complete the male will entice a ripe female into the nest and spawning will take place. As other females become ready to spawn they too will be invited into the nest to spawn. In between the male will look after the eggs and later guard the fry. The fry will eat newly hatched brine shrimp, and as soon as they are large enough to handle should be removed to another aquarium for rearing.

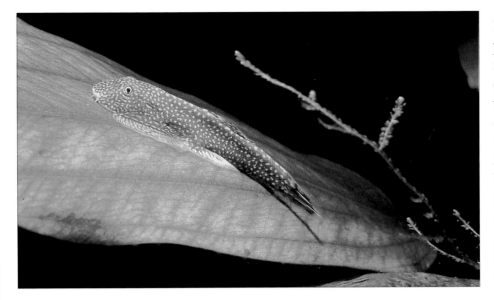

In this chapter we have introduced you to some of the more unusual fishes available in the hobby but it doesn't end there. On this page we will give you just a taste of what else in the way of "oddballs" is out there if you are prepared to look. Some of these unusual species have bizarre habits and very specific environmental and dietary requirements, so don't forget: NEVER purchase them on impulse, but always check on their size, behaviour, and needs first.

Above: *Gastromyzon punctulatus* inhabits fast-flowing streams. Cool, well-oxygenated water is essential, so do not keep this fish in an over-populated community aquarium as the oxygen levels will be too low for it to survive.

Right: *Xenomystus nigri* (African knifefish) grows to 30 cm (12 in). It can be quarrelsome. Do not keep with small fishes as it has a large mouth and will eat anything that fits in it! It prefers calm water, and, because it is nocturnal in the wild, muted lighting, or at least shady areas to which to retire.

Scleropages formosus (Asian arawana, dragonfish) is a protected species, but it is now being bred on fish farms in the Far East and limited numbers of youngsters are being made available to the hobby. The maintenance of these large mouthbrooding fishes should not be undertaken lightly.

There are two subspecies of this fish: *Badis badis badis* and *Badis badis burmanicus*. The former is blue and the latter predominantly red. Both are small, carnivorous fishes that look rather like some South American dwarf cichlids. Sometimes known as chameleonfishes, they come from still waters in India, and are more peaceful than other members of the Nandiae.

Brackish Water Fishes

Retail outlets tend to stock only a few brackish water fishes because people usually want either marines because of their flamboyant colours or freshwater as they are easiest. The main brackish water fishes available are scats, monos, archers, *Arius* catfishes, mudskippers, *Anableps*, and *Brachygobius*, plus, if you want to see them at their best, sailfin mollies (*Poecilia* sp.). This last group has been dealt with in the Cyprinodonts chapter.

Just because these fishes all come from slightly saline waters doesn't mean that they can be kept in the same aquarium, so we will look at each type separately and, where appropriate, make some suggestions as to which may be kept together.

Four-eyed Fishes

There are three species of *Anableps* (four-eyed fish) found in fresh and brackish waters of Central and South America. On the Pacific coast of Mexico, Guatemala, El Salvador, and Costa Rica *Anableps dowi* (the Pacific four-eyes) can be found. This species is only rarely imported, which is a pity since it is the most attractive member of the genus. It has a greenish brown body with a bright yellow stripe running along its full length. It is usually found in brackish water but one population in Mexico lives in fresh water.

Anableps microlepis (fine-scale four-eyes) occurs on the Atlantic shoreline of South America from the Orinoco to the Amazon. This

The eye of *Anableps anableps* is divided to allow the fish to see both above and below water.

fish is usually found in marine habitats and only rarely enters brackish water. It has two or three rather poorly defined brown stripes along the sides.

Anableps anableps (striped four-eyes) has the same range as the fine-scale four-eyes but lives primarily in brackish water and rarely enters fresh or marine habitats. It has five horizontal stripes along the body which can be more or less distinct depending upon the fish's mood. This is the species most commonly imported by the trade, but some consignments contain a few fine-scale four-eyes as well.

Anableps anableps (striped four-eyes) is a real oddity. A predator, it will take insects from the surface as well as small fishes that stray into its vicinity. Make sure you do not use any sharp-edged decor on which this fish could damage its eyes. This warning applies equally to equipment, such as filter pipes.

All four-eyes are large (25 cm (10 in)), surface-dwelling live-bearers which get their common name from their eyes, which are divided into two segments, enabling them to see both above and below the water's surface at the same time. This is a very useful ability which helps them to spot food or danger as they cruise around the shallow lagoons and river mouths which are their usual habitats.

Anableps have very specific requirements. The aquarium should have shallow, warm (25–28°C (77–82°F)), brackish water and the air space above it should be kept very humid. This can be achieved by a tight-fitting cover glass which also serves to keep the fishes in the aquarium – they are excellent jumpers and frequently leap when catching flies. A sand or gravel "beach" is also welcome, and the fishes will come partly out of the water to rest on this.

A good filtration system is essential. *Anableps* are large fishes which feed on high protein foods so the system must be able to cope with their waste products. External power filters are ideal, and their return pipes can be positioned so that they create a feature in the aquarium, for example a waterfall over rocks on a beach.

Avoid any sharp objects in the tank, to prevent damage to the fishes' eyes. If you want rocks, use rounded pebbles, and if using wood, again select rounded pieces (or do it yourself with sandpaper). Salt-tolerant plants may be used to decorate the aquarium, but ensure that there is plenty of open swimming space at the surface.

Although they are principally insectivores in the wild, feeding in captivity is relatively simple, as they will take frozen bloodworm as well as small pieces of mussel, shrimp, meat, and fish. If they turn up their noses at one of these, try something else, but do vary the diet, and if you can offer live foods, do so. Most specimens will also feed on flake and sometimes tablet foods.

Breeding Four-eyed Fishes
Breeding these fishes is problematical from the outset in that more females than males occur in the trade, and it is often just luck that you find a male among the females in a dealer's tank. But this is only half the problem: the copulatory organ (modified anal fin) of the male is left- or right-handed, that is, it curves either to the left or the right, and the genital opening in females is also biased to the left or right. This means that a right-handed male can mate only with a left-handed female and vice versa. To overcome this, it is necessary to keep groups of four-eyed fishes and let them pair themselves. Indeed, these fishes seem far happier if kept as a small shoal of six to eight individuals.

Four-eyed fishes are by no means prolific. Under good conditions they produce four broods a year, and each time the female gives birth to only about eight fry. These are large, up to 5 cm (2 in) but more usually 2.5 cm (1 in) and this gives them a better chance of survival than smaller fry. From the outset they can take insect larvae, and growth is steady provided they are well fed and regular partial water changes are carried out. It is a good idea to raise the fry apart from the parents so that you can make sure they are getting sufficient food.

Mudskippers
Mudskippers are notoriously difficult to maintain in captivity because of the demands they place on the aquarist. Species imported include *Periophthalmus barbarus*, *P. catonensis*, and *P. kaelreukeri*, but these names are often confused and identification is uncertain. All have similar habits and can be found along the east African coast from the Red Sea to Madagascar and on into southeast Asia and Australia. In nature they are found in estuarine conditions such as those in mangrove swamps, a favourite habitat. Here, in the tidal zone, they dart about on the mud and clamber up onto the mangrove roots using the pectoral fins as "legs" and sinuous movements of the rear part of the body to push themselves forward. They often go undetected until they begin flicking their colourful dorsal fins up and down to signal to each other. If danger threatens, each fish will leap from its basking site back to the safety of the water with one flick of its tail end. As the waters recede the fishes dig pits in the mud. Bearing all this in mind, we have to try and create something similar to a mangrove swamp in the aquarium if we are going to stand even a remote chance of keeping these creatures alive and healthy for any length of time.

Periophthalmus papilio (mudskipper) requires rocks and roots so it can climb out of the water.

Public aquaria have managed this quite well, using large enclosures and employing wave machines so that water gently laps the shore. Tree roots are bedded into a soft sand substrate that slopes down into and continues below the water. A few pebbles scattered around help to give everything a natural appearance. Some salt-tolerant plants may be grown in the substrate, and mosses and Java fern attached to the tree roots. Or they may even cheat and use plastic plants, both terrestrial and aquatic. For most of us wave machines occur only in our dreams. So we will ignore this little luxury and see what else we can do.

The aquarium needs to be wide, and long, because it is easier to create a long shallow slope along the length of the tank rather than from front to back (this can be achieved but your substrate will have a much steeper gradient). The sand can be held in place by a series of terraces made from rounded pebbles. If you don't use these, the sand will just even itself out and defeat the object. Add some vine roots sited below the water but projecting out of it so you can attach terrestrial plants and the fishes can clamber out. Some people like to float a small piece of cork bark on the water so the fishes can clamber out onto this as well. If there are no places for them to crawl out of the water, they will, in desperation, stick on to the glass.

Partially fill the aquarium with brackish water to a depth of about 15 cm (6 in) and use an external power filter to help maintain good quality water. As with the aquarium for *Anableps*, the filter return pipe can be used

Periophthalmus papilio (mudskipper) is a predator with a fearsome set of teeth. The eyes, set well on top of the head, give it excellent vision when hunting. They can sometimes be seen resting in shallow water with just their eyes above the surface.

The colourful dorsal fin of *Periophthalmus* species is used for signalling. When basking on mud flats or defending territories they flick the fin up and down in order to communicate with each other.

If there is no other resting place out of the water, *Periophthalmus* species will try to attach themselves to the aquarium glass.

to create a feature in the above-water part of the tank, for example water cascading over roots or rocks.

One of the most important points when keeping mudskippers is to maintain humidity and warmth in the section of the aquarium above the water. The air temperature here should equal the water temperature 25-30°C (77-86°F) otherwise the fishes may become chilled, so the cover glass must fit very well. The one drawback with this is that if the room is cold, condensation tends to form on the glass and it becomes difficult to view the interior of the tank.

When buying your mudskippers take the time to find good, healthy stock and make sure that they are feeding. As these fishes are territorial, they sometimes quarrel in the dealer's tanks, so check your purchases for damage. The stress of being caught, transported, and perhaps chilled slightly is enough for them to have to cope with, without the possible infections that may occur on nipped fins. Because of their territoriality, it is better to keep just three or four well rather than a lot that are constantly fighting. Also bear in mind that the little juveniles of 5–6 cm (2–2¼ in) grow into large adults of 12.5–15 cm (5–6 in).

These fishes can become very tame and will even feed from your hand – but beware of the teeth. It is better, if you value your fingers, to use a pair tweezers if you wish to "hand" feed. They will take just about anything meaty, but, especially when first imported, prefer live foods. Worms of all kinds are preferred, and crickets make mealtimes fun because you can watch the fishes stalk them. Flake and frozen foods can also be given. Take care not to overfeed as decaying flake and frozen foods can quickly pollute the substrate, especially in the above-water section. Likewise, do not overdo live worms or you may find yourself with a worm colony in the aquarium.

Monos and Scats

Monodactylus argenteus (monos) and *Scatophagus argus* (scats) have been grouped together as they are both shoaling fishes which will live in harmony in a large brackish-water aquarium. Although they are usually sold as small specimens, the potential for *Scatophagus argus* is 30 cm (12 in) and for *Monodactylus argenteus* 25 cm (10 in). Both fishes have been recorded from fresh, brackish, and marine waters, so it is important to see what conditions your stock are being kept in at the time of purchase. Monos are found along the African coast and into Indonesia. Scats are found along the coasts of the Indian and Pacific Oceans, with Tahiti the easternmost limit of their range.

In captivity, these fishes need to be kept in groups and do very well in brackish aquaria provided they are given plenty of space. They love to swim so do not try to keep them in cramped conditions. Water quality is very important so ensure that your filtration system is working efficiently and, to supplement it, add a protein skimmer. It is important to keep nitrate levels to a minimum otherwise the scats in particular will suffer. Regular water changes, not just topping up to compensate for evaporation, are essential.

Scats love to eat plants, which rules out real greenery. Tank decor may consist of wood and rocks with some artificial plants for added colour. Bear in mind their love of plants when feeding the fishes. Monos are not as fond of plants but do benefit from some vegetable matter in their diet. Both species are omnivorous so provide a varied diet that includes items such as live

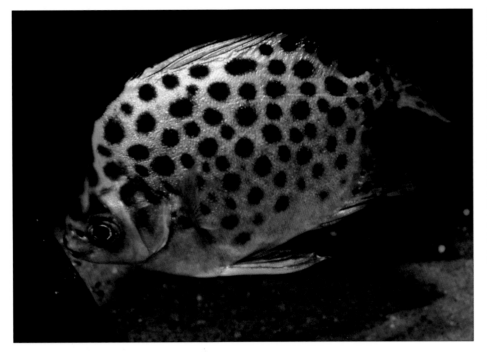

Young *Scatophagus argus* (scats) are attractively marked. We suggest plastic plants and/or wood for decor as these omnivores have a great liking for plants. Remember to include vegetable matter in their diet.

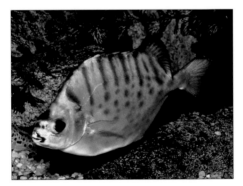

Adult *S. argus* have different markings on the body. To grow your fishes to adulthood ensure that you maintain good quality water and avoid any build up of nitrate.

foods, flake, lettuce, peas, oatmeal, frozen shrimps, bloodworm, and so on. The more varied the diet, the better the colour of the fishes. A word of caution here: in his book *Aquarium Fishes* (Volume 1), Hans Baensch notes that scats feeding on Java fern (often used for herbivores to feed on) died after eating it, whereas fishes that did not survived.

Young fishes are quite highly coloured. Monos show a lot of yellow in the dorsal, and distinct

Monodactylus argenteus (monos) are large shoaling fishes that may be kept with scats. Feed a varied diet to ensure good coloration, although this will fade as they grow.

black bars on the silvery body, but unfortunately this intense colouring fades as the fishes mature and they become a rather dull greyish/silver with only a few traces of the yellow and black. Scats also vary in coloration from juvenile to adult. The juveniles have a yellow background colour with distinct black spots. As they mature, the body becomes silvery-bronze, still with some black spots, and traces of red appear along the dorsal surface.

Archer Fishes

No one can fail to be intrigued by a fish that shoots down its prey, and in public aquaria there is almost always a small crowd of people around the archer fish tank, all hoping that the fishes will perform.

The "archer" usually offered for sale is *Toxotes jaculator*, a widespread species found from the Gulf of Aden, all around the Indian coast, into southeast Asia and even in northern Australia. It is yet another fish that will tolerate fresh, brackish, and marine conditions. The one thing they won't tolerate is cold: they like a water temperature of 25–28°C (77-82°F), and many captive specimens are lost because they are kept too cool.

Archers are ideally suited to a paludarium (an aquarium that has both underwater life and above-water plants). The tank should be large enough to accommodate four to six fishes (they can reach 20 cm/8 in or so) and can be planted with *Sagittaria* and Java fern and decorated with wood, which can extend above the water's surface. Out of the water, above and to the back of the tank, grow some terrestrial plants which overhang the water, because it is on their foliage that insects will land and from which the fishes will attempt to shoot them down.

Keep fishes of approximately the same size together as it is quite common for larger specimens to intimidate smaller ones, preventing them from feeding or nipping at their fins. Injured fishes are vulnerable to fungal or bacterial infections and this situation needs to be avoided. Some people like to keep young scats and monos with their archers, but the problems start when the scats and monos grow too large and become too active for the archers' liking.

In order to observe the feeding habits of *Toxotes jaculator* (archer fish) it is necessary to house them in a palludarium so that terrestrial plants may be grown overhanging the water, and to provide insects as prey.

Feeding Archer Fishes

Feeding archers is simple. They like to take their food from the surface and will consume flake as well as live insects. Once acclimatized to aquarium life they will also accept frozen blood-worm and the like. However, the purpose of keeping these fishes is usually to observe their novel method of catching their prey.

First you need a supply of prey items. Small crickets can be purchased at shops that deal in reptiles. Alternatively, you can use flies: purchase some uncoloured maggots from your local fishing tackle shop and

In such an environment it is possible to witness *T. jaculator* "shooting" down prey items such as flies or spiders with jets of water, or leaping to snatch them from the plant leaves.

place a few in a small straight-sided dish (use a jar lid or similar) and place it among the plants. The maggots will pupate and subsequently hatch into flies, ready for your archer fishes to shoot down. (Store maggots in a bait box in the fridge to keep them for any length of time.) Add more maggots to the dish as the old ones hatch, to maintain a good supply of flies. The trouble is that the archer's aim is not that good, so it can take several attempts before it gets its fly. Remember to ensure that your paludarium is properly covered otherwise you will have a house full of bluebottles!

The furthest an archer can spit is about 150 cm (60 in), which means that the fishes can easily hit a fly anywhere in the paludarium. It also means that they could just as easily hit the lights – cold water on hot lights can mean that the lights "blow", so ensure that you protect them behind a sheet of glass.

There is another species of archer fish sometimes seen in the trade, *Toxotes chatareus*. It requires similar conditions and foods to *T. jaculator*, but doesn't spit at its prey, instead taking it from the water surface. It differs too in body depth and colour: *T. jaculator* is silvery-white with dark blotches and the body is fairly deep, whereas *T. chatareus* is more coppery-coloured with black bars and a black blotch, and has a slimmer body.

The fishes shown here are *Arius see-mani* (shark catfish), a juvenile (*above*) and a semi-adult (*below*). Small speci-mens grow rapidly but fortunately they do not fight so it is possible to keep more than one in the aquarium. They are likewise peaceful towards other fishes – unless they are small enough to eat!

Shark Catfishes

Most people regard catfishes as purely freshwater fishes but there are marine and brackish water species as well. Imported under the names *Arius seemani* and *Arius jordani*, they are collectively known in the trade as the shark catfishes, and have been a regular, if somewhat seasonal, import over the last twelve years or so. Their common name probably derives from their vague resemblance to sharks when they are swimming.

When they originally appeared on the market it was believed that they, like all the other catfishes in the trade – with exception of *Plotosus lineatus* (marine catfish) – were freshwater fishes. Many were lost, but it was noted that those kept in harder water showed a better survival rate. Then research by aquarists revealed that they were probably brackish, if not marine, and that they were also migratory. They proved to be no trouble when kept in brackish water other than that their growth rate was rapid and they required large aquaria.

Shark "cats" are found along the western seaboard of the Americas, from California down to Colombia. Young specimens are imported at about 5–10 cm (2–4 in) in length, and these will live for a while in fresh water, but as they grow they require more saline conditions so in this respect they are ideal for a brackish aquarium. They are gregarious and very active. Don't be tempted to keep young shark catfishes in your community aquarium, even on a temporary basis, while you prepare a suitable tank for them. Although they will love it, you will find that your other fish stocks become seriously depleted and the shark "cats" will have a smile from whisker to whisker.

They can be kept with other fishes such as *Scatophagus argus* (scats) and *Monodactylus argenteus* (monos), but we have found that it is best to keep them from the outset as a group of four to six in brackish conditions in a species aquarium. The colour on the fishes becomes more intense if they are in a group and they are more active. Indeed, they are one of the few catfishes that are not nocturnal. Provide a sandy substrate and some rounded pieces of bogwood to decorate the aquarium, rather than rocks on which these "naked" catfishes (they have thick skin and no scales) may damage themselves. They are active and sometimes take fright, so they might dash themselves against sharp rocks and any scratches or grazes would show up clearly on their bodies. Lighting can be quite dim as plants are unnecessary in this aquarium. The fishes like to spend some time resting in the shelter of the wood or cruising just above the substrate. Provide external power filtration to create not only good quality water, but also a good current against which the fishes can swim. They become very listless if water quality deteriorates or water flow diminishes, and, if conditions become too bad, their barbels will start to degenerate as will their fin membranes. Regular partial water changes and maintenance of the filtration system will prevent this.

Feeding is not a problem. They like a varied diet and will

Female *Arius seemani* (shark catfish) develop fleshy pads on the ventral fins when they come into breeding condition. Unfortunately few home aquaria are large enough for a pair of breeding-sized specimens.

consume large quantities of pelleted foods, flake (for small specimens), pieces of meat, fish, and prawn, in fact just about anything. The temptation is to overfeed them and you must resist this. Feed on alternate days and only then if the fish does not still have a bloated appearance after gorging itself on its previous meal.

As the fishes grow, the colour changes slightly. Youngsters are silvery with velvety black fins, but as they begin to mature they become silvery grey, and if well maintained, develop a delightful coppery sheen. The black in the finnage diminishes until only a trace remains at the base.

A word of warning: shark cats grow very large. In the aquarium they quickly reach 30 cm (12 in), but at this size they are only one-third grown. The likelihood of breeding them in captivity in home aquaria is remote. From field observations and captured specimens we know that they practice oral incubation, with the male brooding both the eggs and fry. We also know that in some species the female grows a fleshy pad on her ventral fins, and it

has been suggested that the eggs are held by this pad so that the male can then take them into his mouth. This pad has also been observed on aquarium specimens but, so far, that's as far as captive breeding has got.

Take care when handling these fishes. They have stout spines on the dorsal and pectoral fins and these spines can easily become entangled in nets. The sharp points of the spines can also inflict a nasty wound to the hand of the unwary aquarist who is cleaning out an aquarium, and although at first it doesn't hurt, it usually swells and becomes rather painful. Bathing in hot water has been found to relieve the pain.

As a total aside, ariids are also known as crucifix fishes. This came about because native fishermen found that they could decorate the catfish's skull. The underside is usually painted with a scene of Christ on the cross while the dorsal surface (top) is decorated so that it looks like a monk in flowing robes. These artefacts are then sold to tourists – a great way to earn a living from old fish skulls.

Bumblebee Gobies

Now for something a lot smaller. *Brachygobius* (bumblebee gobies) are suitable for those of you who cannot keep a large brackish water aquarium, because they will be quite happy in a 60 x 30 x 30 cm (24 x 12 x 12 in) tank. Although these fishes are small, we do not recommend using anything smaller than this because it is more difficult to maintain good water conditions in a small body of water.

There are two species available, *Brachygobius xanthozona* (bumblebee goby) and *Brachygobius nunus* (golden-banded goby), but because they look very similar, both are usually labelled "bumblebee gobies" in dealers' tanks. Both are small, 4–4.5 cm (1 1/2–1 3/4 in) in length at most, and both have broad yellow and black vertical bands on the body, but in *B. xanthozona* these bands are more clearly defined. Both are found in fresh and brackish waters in Asia, but *B. xanthozona* has the more restricted range.

Like all gobies, these fishes spend much of their time darting about among rocks and pebbles, or resting on wood or leaves in the mid to lower regions of the aquarium, so design your decor with this in mind. Fine gravel makes a good base for a scattering of pebbles and rocks together with a piece of bogwood. Attach some Java fern to the wood, and plant other salt-tolerant plants in thickets to the rear and sides of the aquarium. If possible

People often fail to keep *Brachygobius xanthozona* (bumblebee goby) because they do not realize that these fishes require a diet of predominantly live foods. Although they can be weaned onto frozen substitutes it is rare for them to accept flake.

provide a cave or two, which can be half flowerpots either left just as they are or camouflaged with stones – the choice is yours, but make sure there are plenty of other hiding places because bumblebees are territorial, so it is important to have sufficient rocks, wood, and so on, so that each fish can stake a claim to its own patch. Then, provided you don't add more gobies or move the rocks around, there will be no real battles, just the fishes shaping up to each other if one inadvertently enters the territory of another.

Feeding bumblebees can be quite a problem, as only rarely will they accept flake foods. If you are lucky, they will take frozen bloodworm and *Daphnia*, if not, then you must be prepared to provide live foods of all kinds. They are particularly fond of whiteworm and *Tubifex*, and will also take most other aquatic invertebrates. If you have limited supplies of these available, it is suggested that you also culture brine shrimps and let these grow on a little before feeding them to your fishes.

Although they will live in hard (above 15° dH) fresh water, they really seem to prefer warm, brackish conditions. Make sure that you have an efficient filtration system as any deterioration in water conditions can cause stress and they may suffer from bacterial or fungal infections. This doesn't mean that there has to be a torrent of water flowing through the tank – flow rate does not equate with efficiency – just a gentle turnover of the water is fine; the fishes won't enjoy being washed away.

Breeding Bumblebee Gobies

A water change with fresh water (that is, a reduction in salinity) will often provide the trigger for the fishes to spawn. Males are more colourful than females but at spawning time the females are easy to spot because they are much fuller in the body and, about 48 hours prior to spawning, will show an ovipositor. The pair will spawn either beneath a rock or in a cave, laying up to 200 eggs. At about 28°C (82°F), the eggs will hatch in four days and the male guards the fry. At this time he will defend his brood against all comers, including the female, so she must have a hideaway to retreat to. For the first few days after the fry become free swimming, the shoal moves about the lower levels of the aquarium, but it isn't long before they, like their parents, adopt a bottom-dwelling lifestyle. One of the problems is providing sufficient live foods. It is critical that the timing of brine shrimp hatching coincides with the fry needing it.

Growth is steady provided you can supply enough live foods and plenty of space, so you will probably need to set up another tank in which to grow on the fry. Most losses seem to occur because the fry starve.

Keeping these little gobies in a species aquarium is all very well and good, but it does seem an awful waste of the top layers of the aquarium. A pair of sailfin mollies (*Poecilia* sp.) make excellent companions for the gobies and in brackish waters they really show their true colours and tend not to suffer from the bacterial or fungal infections that sometimes break out on those kept in fresh water. Being opportunists, they will take the live foods put in for the gobies, but you will soon learn how much will keep both species happy.

A word of warning here: don't let the aquarium become over-populated with young mollies or they may overload the filtration and the resulting deterioration in water quality will lead to the demise of your gobies. It will be far better to grow the young mollies on in another tank.

Non-breeding Etroplus maculatus (orange chromides) are difficult to sex, so grow on half a dozen youngsters and allow them to pair naturally.

The Asian Chromides

Two species of cichlid are found almost exclusively in brackish water: *Etroplus suratensis* (green chromide, 45 cm (18 in)) and *E. maculatus* (orange chromide, 10 cm (4 in)). Both occur in coastal regions of southern India and Sri Lanka, chiefly in brackish estuaries and lagoons. The salinity of both types of habitat is variable, depending on the state of the tide and the fresh water input, which varies with the seasons.

Both species are found in close association with each other and with beds of *Halophila* (seagrass), which provides them with shelter and spawning sites. *E. maculatus* lays its eggs on the narrow leaves of the plants, no easy task when the latter are waving to and fro in the current, so to ensure accuracy it uses its pelvic fins as guides, one each side of the leaf. The larger *E. suratensis* prefers to dig pits, exposing the roots of the seagrass and sometimes using them as a spawning substrate.

The green chromide is a peaceful herbivore which breeds seasonally; the orange, on the other hand, is an opportunistic feeder, eating, *inter alia,* parasites and necrotic skin which it cleans from its larger relative, and the latter's spawn! The relationship is, nevertheless, symbiotic as both benefit from it. *E. maculatus* will also cannibalize the eggs and fry of its own kind, but only those of other pairs – they are excellent parents, guarding their fry for weeks, even months.

The orange chromide will breed continuously if its food supply is adequate. In nature it lives colonially; it requires a territory of at least 180 cm² (24 sq in) per pair if this is to be tried in captivity.

E. suratensis must have highly oxygenated brackish water and be housed in a large aquarium (120 x 45 x 45 cm (48 x 18 x 18 in) is the minimum for a pair). Far too many of these lovely fishes die in captivity as a result of ignorance of these basic requirements, and the reason this species is rarely bred is probably because few individuals survive to adult size. Plastic plants are ideal shelter – real

Etroplus maculatus (orange chromides) are excellent parents, protecting their fry for some time. The fry feed initially on the parents' body mucus.

ones are likely to be eaten, and few of those available will withstand the salinity necessary for the fishes.

E. *maculatus* can be kept in similar conditions, but will also thrive in hard alkaline fresh water; do remember that individuals that have been accustomed to brackish water must be acclimated slowly to different conditions. Like many cichlids they will utilize flowerpots for shelter, but plants (real or plastic), ideally those with long, straight narrow leaves (such as *Vallisneria*), should be provided as spawning substrates. A temperature of 27-28°C (80-82°F) will suit both species.

The green chromide must be offered predominantly vegetable foods, such as scalded lettuce and spinach, as well as vegetarian flake and pellets. Like most nominally vegetarian cichlids, it also enjoys live fare such as pond foods and earthworms.

E. *maculatus* is, by contrast, an out-and-out carnivore, and should be given suitably sized live foods, cod roe, chopped shrimp/prawn, and suitable dried foods.

Although adult female E. *maculatus* develop white markings on the upper and lower edges of the tail when breeding (or thinking about it), juveniles and unpaired adults exhibit no visible sexual dimorphism. No reliable way of sexing green chromides is known. It is thus best to purchase half a dozen juveniles, growing them on together and letting them pair naturally.

Orange chromides are easy to breed, either in a species aquarium or in a community of small to medium hard or brackish water fishes. Although "scrappy" among themselves, and territorial towards other similarly-sized cichlids, they will not normally harass non-competitors such as

mollies, though it must be said that livebearer fry are relished as snacks! If the aquarium is sufficiently spacious, both chromides can be kept together, and the green can be housed with other brackish species such as scats and monos, but preferably in a deep (60 cm (24 in)) aquarium so as to allow vertical habitat segregation. Personally, however, we would prefer to "coddle" the greens a little, and allow them the privacy of their own tank. A "seasonal" increase in temperature and salinity may trigger breeding, as they spawn in the dry season in nature.

As in some South American cichlids (*Symphysodon* sp. and *Uaru* sp.), the fry of both species feed on parental body mucus as well as micro-organisms. Failure of the first few broods in young adults may be due to failure to synchronize mucus production with hatching.

Marines

In this chapter we will look at most of the families which contain species suitable for the marine aquarium. Some include many such species and others only one or two. We provide a general description of the family and its members' requirements in captivity, together with details of any species which deviate from the "norm". Please treat this section as a basic guide to marines and not a marine aquarist's bible – that would take at least a volume, not just part of one. You will find a reading list at the back of the book, should you wish to investigate further.

Clowns and Damsels

The single family Pomacentridae is generally divided into two groups by aquarists: the clown-, or anemone-fishes; and the damselfishes. Both groups include a number of genera, some of which are detailed below.

The damsels are usually considered hardy because they will tolerate the high nitrite and ammonia levels present in a new marine system. They are therefore often introduced to a new system at too early a stage by the impatient aquarist. This is unfair to the fishes as when placed under such unnecessary stress they become susceptible to white spot and velvet. You must be patient unless you want to fail with your marine aquarium before you've really started.

Damsels are very active little fishes that add colour to the aquarium. Several may be kept together provided you have a

Chromis caerulea (green chromis), from the Red Sea and the Indian and Pacific Oceans, are active shoaling fishes which are peaceful and easy to keep. They accept most foods, from live brine shrimp to frozen, and flake, and are compatible with marine invertebrates.

Pomacentrus melanochir (blue-finned damsel) can be quite aggressive so choose tankmates with care. A small fish, it grows to about 7 cm (3 in). This rather uncommon species is easy to feed, and will take dried foods.

Like the other damsels, *Abudefduf assimilis* should not be introduced to the marine aquarium too soon as the stress of new conditions can leave them open to white spot and velvet infections.

An aggressive and territorial fish, *Dascyllus melanurus* (black-tailed humbug) should be kept in a shoal and with other fishes that can take care of themselves. *D. aruanus* (humbug) is similar in appearance and habits.

Amphiprion frenatus (tomato or fire clown) in a *Radianthus* sp. anemone. These fishes require a varied diet that includes some vegetable matter.

Adult *Amphiprion clarkii* (Clark's or yellow-tailed anemonefish) live as pairs in an anemone. They are bred commercially.

Amphiprion ocellaris (percula clown or clown anemonefish) is a wide-ranging species whose colour can vary depending on the origin of the population.

large enough aquarium for them to define their own territories, otherwise they may pick on each other. Much time is spent swimming about, but put a net in the aquarium and they will all disappear into nooks and crevices, making it virtually impossible for you to catch them without destroying the entire decor. Telling the sexes apart is difficult, although they sometimes show a genital papilla which is broad and blunt in females and narrow and pointed in males. When you are more familiar with these fishes, their behaviour will indicate the dominant males.

There are several species of bright blue damsels that are easily confused, so it is fortunate for us that they all have similar requirements. Feeding is simple as they accept anything from flake to live and frozen foods and even algae.

Members of two genera of damsels, *Abudefduf* and *Dascyllus* have been spawned in the aquarium and they both deposit their eggs on rocks.

Some species you may like to try are: *Abudefduf cyaneus* (blue damsel), *Abudefduf saxatilis* (sergeant major), *Chromis xanthurus* (yellow-tailed damsel), *Dascyllus aruanus* (humbug or white-tailed damsel), and *Dascyllus trimaculatus* (domino or three-spot damsel).

Clownfishes or anemonefishes are well known for their symbiotic relationship with anemones, especially those of the genera *Heteractis* and *Stoichactis*. The fishes are immune to the stinging cells of the anemones and it is thought that it is their body mucus that protects them. Although these fishes can be kept in the aquarium without an anemone, you

Pairs of *Amphiprion ocellaris* (percula clown or clown anemonefish) will take up residence in an anemone. If they are happy in the aquarium they may breed, laying their eggs on a flat suface close to the host anemone. This species is probably the best known anemone fish.

A. ocellaris requires a varied diet to bring it into breeding condition. Include live food such as adult brine shrimp.

would then miss out on seeing them behave as they would on the reef, and it must be regarded as cruel to deprive them of their natural partners. In captivity an anemone will normally become the home of a single pair (in the wild, large anemones will house groups of fishes) and they will keep all the others at bay. In an average aquarium keep just one pair of "clowns" as otherwise the dominant pair may harass any others or even kill them.

There are several species readily available in the trade: *Amphiprion akallopisos* (skunk clown), *Amphiprion clarkii* (Clark's or yellow-tailed anemonefish, banded clown), *Amphiprion ephippium* (tomato, red saddleback, or fire clown), *Amphiprion frenatus* (tomato, fire or bridled clown), and *Amphiprion ocellaris* (percula clown or clown anemonefish) are some of these.

Clowns are easy to keep and will feed on all the commercially available marine fish foods including flake, frozen, and live.

Several species are also bred commercially so, if possible, purchase captive-bred specimens to help conserve wild stocks. Captive-bred species available to the hobbyist are: *A. akallopisos*, *A. bicinctus* (two-banded anemonefish), *A. clarkii*, *A. ephippium*, *A. frenatus*, *A. melanopus* (red and black anemonefish), *A. ocellaris*, *A. polymnus* (saddleback anemonefish or saddleback clownfish), and *Premnas biaculeatus* (maroon clown or spine-cheeked anemonefish).

Clowns will also breed readily in the aquarium. The pair prepare a spawning site close to the host anemone – so close that the anemone's tentacles may brush over it. The male cleans the rock but the female remains at a distance until she is almost ready to deposit her eggs, before joining him in this task. Some 200–300 eggs are deposited on the rock and the male guards them. As the yellowish eggs mature they darken and eventually you can see the eyes of the fry. Hatching takes 7–10 days. Raise the fry in

a separate aquarium on very fine foods such as rotifers in the first instance, and later on brine shrimp nauplii. Be prepared for initial losses to other fishes in the parents' aquarium, and later in the rearing tank, especially if you have not prepared enough live foods or do not take sufficient care over cleanliness. Most people prefer to raise a few fry (for instance, about two dozen) successfully, rather than fail because they were unable to cope with a couple of hundred.

Amphiprion bicinctus (two-banded anemonefish or banded clown) is a peaceful, small species reaching 7 cm (3 in) at most. They are easy to feed, taking live, frozen and prepared foods. Like all of their genus they should be kept with an anemone in captivity.

Angels

At first glance, the novice marine keeper could be forgiven for confusing the marine angelfishes (family Pomacanthidae) with the butterflyfishes (family Chaetodontidae). An easy way to tell them apart is by the spine on the gill cover of angelfishes. These colourful fishes are much sought after by marine aquarists and some command high prices.

Unfortunately very few species are suitable for the beginner as they are very sensitive to poor water conditions and many are extremely difficult to feed. Despite being offered a wide variety of live and frozen foods, sponge-based foods, and algae, some will still be very reluctant to feed. When purchasing your fishes ask to see them feed – reputable dealers will not offer fishes for sale unless they are acclimatized to captive conditions and feeding well. It is better to gain some experience with other species before trying your hand with angels. Your dealer will be more than pleased to advise you about the suitability of your aquarium and which species would be best for you.

In the aquarium these fishes can be very territorial so only single specimens should be kept. Juveniles are much easier to acclimatize to aquarium conditions than adults. Several species have very similar forms, the youngsters having a very dark navy blue background colour with white and/or blue vertical lines or a black background with yellow lines; for example *Pomacanthus semicirculatus* (Korean or semi-circle angelfish) and *P. imperator* (emperor angelfish). Just to confuse us even further, a single species will change its markings

This juvenile *Pomacanthus semicirculatus* (Korean angelfish) will change colour dramatically when it becomes adult, losing the stripes seen here.

Holocanthus tricolor (rock beauty) is aggressive and requires a spacious aquarium. Its natural diet is sponges and in consequence it can be difficult to feed in captivity.

Provide plenty of hiding places to keep *Centropyge bicolor* (bicolor cherub or oriole angel) happy. A peaceful fish, it may be kept with marine invertebrates.

several times as it passes through the juvenile, semi-adult, and adult stages, and even as adults the male and female may be differently marked or coloured.

There is one genus, *Centropyge* (dwarf angelfishes), that is much more suitable for the home aquarium. These fishes are small, growing to around 10 cm (4 in) or so, with some species smaller (for example *C. acanthops* (African pygmy or fireball angelfish) at 7.5 cm (3 in), in the wild), and others larger (for example *C. eibli* (Eibl's angel-fish), 11.5 cm (4¹/₂ in), in the wild).

Dwarf angels are highly coloured, peaceful, and, once settled, feed readily on most live, frozen, and commercially prepared foods. They also like to graze on algae, which form a large part of their diet. Unlike their larger cousins, the dwarf angels can be kept with invertebrates. They are often found in pairs and, if you can get a pair, it may be possible to breed them; indeed *C. argi* (pygmy angelfish, purple fireball or cherubfish) have been known to surprise their owners by producing a clutch of eggs in the aquarium.

Some species you may wish to try are: *C. argi, C. bispinosus* (coral beauty), and *C. flavissimus* (lemonpeel angelfish).

Butterflyfishes

"Butterflies" are coral reef fishes that feed by poking their long snouts into crevices in the reef to graze on algae, corals, and sponges. They have very laterally compressed (flattened from side to side) bodies which allow them to slip easily between the coral branches in search of food.

This is another group of fishes that are not really suitable for the novice, but it is quite likely that you will be tempted by their unusual body form and bright colours sooner or later. They need a mature set-up and very stable water conditions. Any variations can result in a fish that was feeding well and apparently happy becoming lethargic and going off its food virtually overnight.

Getting them to feed can be a major problem. Some are grazers, while others include plankton and other small live foods in their diet. You must be prepared to offer a wide range of foods until you find out precisely what they prefer. Young specimens may sometimes be settled in by feeding live brine shrimp. As with the angelfishes, try and see them feeding before purchase

Chaetodon melanotus (black-banded butterflyfish) is peaceful but check that the fish is feeding properly before purchase.

A Caribbean species, Chaetodon capistratus (four-eyed butterflyfish) is not for beginners as newly imported specimens are difficult to feed.

and ask what they are being fed so that you can continue with the same foods.

Juvenile butterflies have a different colour pattern to adults. Some species, for example C. trifascialis (chevroned butterflyfish) can also change their colour pattern when frightened or during the night. Unfortunately the chevroned butterfly does not easily adapt to captivity and these observations are from divers' reports.

Of all the butterflies, Chaetodon kleini (sunburst or Klein's butterflyfish) and C. lunula (racoon butterflyfish) are both peaceful and relatively simple to keep; indeed, once acclimatized, C. kleini is probably the easiest. Not a large fish, it

grows to barely 10 cm (4 in) in captivity, although it can attain 12.5 cm (5 in) in its native waters of the Indo-Pacific.

If you would prefer a fish that is a little different to look at, then Forcipiger flavissimus (long-nosed butterflyfish) might be your choice. This is a very striking fish, yellow-bodied with a black head and a false eye-spot on the rear edge of the anal fin. It feeds by thrusting its long snout into nooks and crannies and, should a predator attack while it is feeding head down, it will strike at the butterfly's eye-spot, hopefully doing little damage other than taking a mouthful of fin, which will grow back, allowing the fish to live to fight another day.

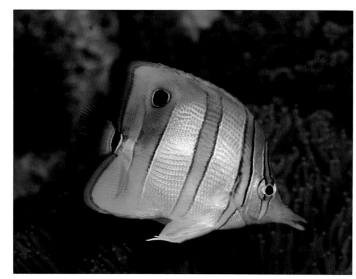

Keep Chelmon rostratus (copper-band butterflyfish) in a mature aquarium as it is sensitive to poor water quality.

Heniochus acuminatus (wimplefish or pennant coralfish) like plenty of swimming space and some green food.

Surgeons and Tangs

These fishes have a very distinctive ovoid shape and very sharp spines on the caudal peduncle that can be erected at will by some species and are fixed in others. It is these scalpel-like blades that have given rise to the common name of surgeon fishes. They are found swimming in large shoals over the reefs, but in captivity they squabble amongst themselves unless the aquarium is very large. If you are keeping more than one, try and introduce them at the same time, as a dominant, established fish will often attack any newcomers, especially if the new fishes are of a similar size, slashing at them with its spines. Care is needed when handling surgeons and tangs as the spines may not only slice through nets and bags, but can also cut the hand of the unwary handler.

Surgeons and tangs belong to the family Acanthuridae. They require a large amount of algae in their diet, and in the aquarium they will graze almost continuously on any algae present. If there is insufficient algae it is most important that you feed a suitable substitute such as lettuce or spinach. Most surgeons will also take frozen and small live foods. Juveniles are voracious feeders so ensure that you feed little and often otherwise they will starve.

One of the favourite species is *Acanthurus leucosternon* (powder blue surgeon), because of its delicate blue coloration. Keep only a single specimen as they will fight with their own kind. Even dealers keep only one to a tank to avoid quarrels breaking out. Ensure that your surgeon has plenty of space: they are large, active fishes that can grow to 20 cm (8 in) in the aquarium, and up to 25 cm (10 in) in the wild, and need a very well established aquarium with stable water conditions and a good growth of algae. Supplement the diet with lettuce if necessary.

Zebrasoma flavescens (yellow tang) is a very bold and territorial fish. If you have a small aquarium then only a single specimen is advisable, but if you have a large tank (over 1.5 m (60 in)), then you can consider more. A shoal of at least six is advisable so that they spend their time checking on each other but never get round to doing any real damage. Yellow tangs feed on algae and will strip a tank clean in next to no time. You can culture algae on stones in a separate aquarium, swopping pebbles as the fishes clean them, but even this may not be enough, in which case use lettuce, spinach, peas, and/or frozen and flake "green" foods.

Less troublesome than the yellow tang is *Paracanthurus hepatus* (regal tang), a beautiful fish with a royal blue body with black markings and a bright yellow caudal fin. It is usually possible to keep more than one together in the aquarium. Again ensure you can provide this herbivore with enough green foods.

Keep a single specimen of *Acanthurus leucosternon* (powder blue surgeon) as it can be very quarrelsome with its own kind.

Zebrasoma veliferum (striped sailfin tang) is peaceful when young; juveniles like these adapt to aquarium life more easily than adults. All sizes may harm marine invertebrates.

If you have a large enough aquarium, *Zebrasoma flavescens* (yellow tang) can be kept in a shoal if the aquarium is large enough. They like to graze on algae.

Wrasses

The Labridae form a large, widely distributed, and very speciose group. Tiny species are only a few centimetres (1–2 in) in length while the big boys of the family can be up to two metres (6½ ft) long. Colour and body shape can vary so much that it is a surprise to find that they all belong to the same family. They swim using their pectoral fins, the powerful caudal being utilized to give extra thrust initially – a sort of first gear if you like. Their mouths are small, with strong lips and protruding teeth.

In all the tropical wrasses we are likely to encounter, the males have developed from functional females; to use the technical term, each wrasse is a protogynous hermaphrodite. Wrasses breed in two ways. In the first method, a group leaves the reef and swims towards the surface, expelling eggs and milt as they go, the fertilized eggs being swept away by the current. The fishes then return to the reef. In the second method a male courts a female in an elaborate courtship display. The pair then leave the reef for the water's surface. Swimming in parallel as they reach the surface, they spiral, the eggs and milt are expelled, and the fishes complete the loop back down to the safety of the reef. Wrasse eggs hatch in about 24 hours and the larvae spend the first month of their life in the plankton swarms.

Juvenile wrasses are very suitable for the aquarium, as they are colourful, active, and easy to feed. Most of the species kept will take a wide variety of frozen foods including shrimps, mussels, *Mysis*, and so on.

Wrasses change colour from juvenile to adult. *Bodianus rufus*

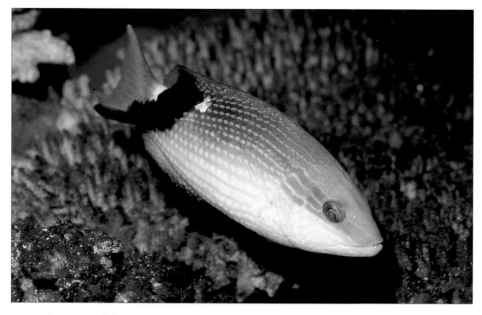

As with many of the wrasses, juvenile specimens of *Bodianus hirsutus* are more suited to aquarium life than adults.

Even in the home aquarium *Labroides dimidiatus* (cleaner wrasse) will go about its business. Here it is cleaning *Centropyge loriculus* (flame angel).

(Spanish hogfish) is a classic example. Juveniles are yellow with blue over the front upper half of the body and dorsal fin, while adults are yellow and red. Many juveniles wrasses act as cleaners to large fishes. These "client" fishes go to "cleaning stations" on the reef so that cleaner fishes can pick the parasites from them.

At night, wrasses seek out a safe place to rest. Some hide away in crevices in the reef, others bury themselves in the sand either completely or with just their eyes showing. In the aquarium it is not unusual to find them in the sand and in the undergravel system. This is annoying when you are trying to catch them, as they dive into the sand.

Of all the wrasses, the most useful in the aquarium is *Labroides dimidiatus* (cleaner wrasse). When being cleaned, client fishes will remain stationary. Sometimes dark fishes will allow their colours to fade so that the cleaner can see the parasites and remove them with its terminally positioned mouth. This diet alone is not enough for the cleaner in captivity, and it must be fed additional small foods such as live brine shrimp and finely chopped shrimp or meat. A word of warning: there is a blenny, *Aspidontus taeniatus* (the predatory false cleanerfish), which is a cleaner wrasse look-alike. The colouring is virtually the same in both fishes and the easiest way to tell the two apart is by the mouth, which in the true cleaner wrasse is terminal, that is, at the end of the snout, while on the false cleaner it is sub-terminal – below the snout.

Other wrasses that you might try are: *Halichoeres chrysus* (banana wrasse or golden rainbow-fish), *H. trispilus* (four-spot or banana wrasse), *Novaculichthys taeniorus* (dragon wrasse), and some members of the genus *Coris*, such as *C. gaimardi* (clown wrasse or red labrid) and *C. angulata* (twin-spot wrasse), although these are safe for the aquarium only when young; when mature they can be quite destructive.

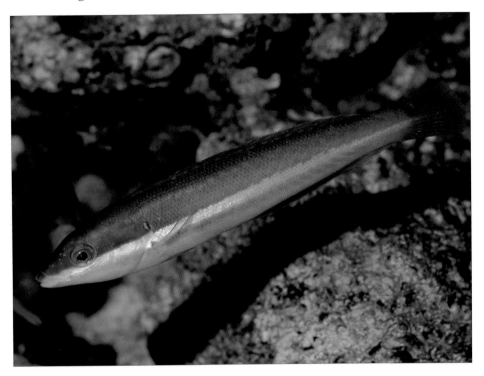

Coris julis (rainbow wrasse) is a candidate for the cold water marine aquarium. Native to the Mediterranean and eastern Atlantic, it thrives on a diet of small live foods. At night it may bury itself in the substrate.

The juveniles of *Coris gaimardi* (clown wrasse or red labrid), such as that shown here, change colour dramatically during their life; adults are dark bodied with numerous blue spots and a yellow tail.

Grammas

Found in the Caribbean and western Pacific, *Gramma* species (family Grammidae) are sometimes referred to as fairy basslets and pygmy basslets.

Gramma loreta (royal gramma) is surely one of the most popular aquarium fishes because of its striking coloration: the front half of the fish is a brilliant purple while the rear is yellow-orange, and where the two colours meet the scales appear dotted with orange on a purple background.

The royal gramma spends a lot of time hiding in caves and crevices, and it takes some time for it to feel secure enough in the aquarium to venture out into bright light. Inoffensive towards most fishes, apart from those that inhabit the same sort of nooks and crannies, it can be aggressive towards its own kind. Even so, several can be kept together in a sufficiently large aquarium. One male and several females may coexist peacefully and perhaps breed. They have been spawned quite frequently in captivity. A pair make a pit and nest similar to that constructed by sticklebacks, and the larger fish, presumed to be the

Provide *Gramma loreto* (royal gramma) with plenty of hiding places. They feed readily on frozen and flake foods but be sure to also include some vegetable matter in their diet.

male, guards the nest. Fry have not yet been raised successfully.

Feeding these fishes poses little difficulty as they will take most fine frozen and live foods such as brine shrimp, as well as marine flake.

A second species of *Gramma*,

G. melacara (black-cap gramma) a bright purple fish with a black stripe along the top of its head and into the dorsal fin, is sometimes available in the hobby. It is far more territorial than *G. loreto* and only a single specimen should be kept in the aquarium.

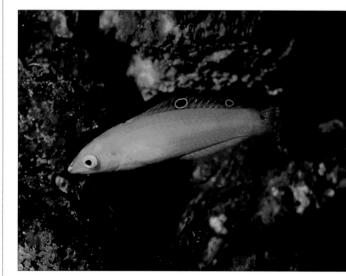

Thalassoma lutescens is peaceable, so avoid keeping it with boisterous species.

At 35 cm (14 in) *Lienardella fasciata* (harlequin tuskfish) needs a large aquarium and similar-sized companions.

Marines

Dottybacks

Dottybacks are closely related to the fairy basslets (and like them are sometimes known as pygmy basslets), and in behaviour patterns the two are virtually indistinguishable. The main difference is in their geographic range: dottybacks (Pseudochromidae) are found in the Red Sea and parts of the Indo-Pacific whereas the fairy basslets (Grammidae) are confined to the Caribbean and the western Pacific.

Generally small, they live in crevices in the reefs so the aquarium should have plenty of rocky hiding places. They are quite peaceful towards other fishes although individuals of the same species will fight. They are easy to feed on small live foods such as *Mysis* and will also take small frozen foods and marine flake.

One species, *Pseudochromis paccagnellae* (false gramma, dottyback, royal or Paccagnella's dottyback), is very similar to the royal gramma but there is a very fine, almost invisible, white line along the boundary between the bright pink/purple and yellow. Unfortunately this fish is not quite as accommodating as the royal gramma and may nip the fins of other fishes or quarrel with those of similar appearance.

Two other species you may wish to keep are *Pseudochromis diadema* (flash-back gramma) and *P. porphyreus* (strawberry gramma); the latter can be antisocial especially if there are not enough hiding places.

Catfishes

Many people are drawn to *Plotosus lineatus* (marine catfish) because of its coloration and the behaviour of very young specimens, which are gregarious and shoal together in a tight ball as a form of protection if danger threatens. This behaviour has been witnessed many times in the wild by divers but rarely are they kept in sufficient numbers for it to occur in the aquarium. The writhing, wriggling mass looks not unlike the waving tentacles of an anemone and usually successfully confuses a would-be predator. As the fishes mature they lose this shoaling habit and become loners. Another drawback for the aquarist is that they also lose the bright longitudinal white stripes of the juveniles and become dull brown.

Plotosus are elongate, almost eel-like, catfishes. Around their mouths there are four pairs of barbels which are covered in taste buds and aid the fishes in their search for food. The second dorsal, caudal, and anal fins are united, that is they are all joined together so that the fish has one continuous fin around the rear part of the body. The body is naked. The dorsal and pectoral fins all have a sharp, serrated spine, and great care should be taken when handling this species as the spines are also venomous and can inflict a nasty, painful wound which may become swollen and inflamed. If stung by your catfish, bathe the wound in very hot water as this will ease the pain, and if pain persists seek medical advice and say which fish has stung you. The spines are also likely to become entangled in nets.

Not all species are marine; in Australia there are several freshwater representatives of the Plotosidae, for example *Tandanus tandanus* (catfish or dewfish).

Keep young fishes as a group of six or more as single specimens will pine away. They feed from the substrate on anything meaty, be it alive or dead. Chop pieces of fish or meat to a suitable size. They are greedy feeders, and if overfed will look as though they have swallowed a golf ball. Should this happen, do not feed them again until their bellies have returned to more or less their normal shape. Even though they are quite peaceful, it is best not to trust large specimens with any fishes they might be able to swallow.

P. lineatus has been bred, albeit mostly by accident, in the aquarium. They spawn in a depression in the substrate and the male guards the eggs. The young fishes can be raised on small live foods such as brine shrimp nauplii.

Left: *Pseudochromis diadema* (flash-back gramma) looks like *Gramma loreto* (royal gramma) but has two fine white lines between the yellow and purple on the body.

Right: Young *Plotosus lineatus* (marine catfish) form tight shoals to confuse would-be predators.

Lionfishes

Another popular family of fishes that also has venomous members is the Scorpaenidae. Commonly referred to as lion-, dragon-, scorpion-, or turkey-fishes, they are some of the most majestic creatures to be kept in the marine aquarium. The finnage is flamboyant:, for example in *Dendrochirus brachypterus* (turkey-fish, short-finned lionfish), the pectoral fins are expanded and spread like large paddles, while in *Pterois radiata* (white-fin or tail-bar lionfish) the white pectoral fin spines are elongated and give the fish a very spiky appearance. The dorsal may also be flamboyant, composed of individual spines which may or may not have a trailing edge of fleshy membrane. BE WARNED: just as caterpillars have warning colours to deter predatory birds, so lionfishes have flamboyant fins and bright colours to warn predators. They have poison glands in the fins which can inflict extremely painful wounds, and ought to come with a warning label: HANDLE WITH CARE. As with injuries from the plotosids, wounds should be bathed in hot water, as hot as you can stand, to help coagulate the poison and alleviate the pain. Failing this, see your doctor.

Lionfishes require plenty of space in the aquarium so that they can display and manoeuvre without damaging their finnage. They hunt by drifting towards their prey and, when close enough, gulping it in. In the wild they have been seen hunting in packs at the edges of reefs. Needless to say we are unlikely to see such behaviour in the home aquarium. Newly imported fishes will often take only live food such as guppies or mollies

Take extra care when handling any of the lionfishes such as this *Pterois radiata* (white-fin or tail-bar lionfish), as the fins can inflict painful wounds.

but it is very rare indeed that these fishes cannot be weaned off live foods and onto dead ones. Many dealers will already have got the lionfish feeding on dead foods before offering it for sale, but check before buying, especially if it is against your principles to use live fishes as food. Aquarists often find that their lionfish becomes hand-tame – perhaps this is not the right phrase; "tongs-tame" is closer to the truth, as morsels of food such as prawns or pieces of fish are best offered in aquarium tongs to avoid getting the hands stung.

They are peaceful and can be kept together or with other peaceful species, but do not tempt fate by keeping them with fishes small enough to be eaten.

The breeding behaviour of this fish has been witnessed in the aquarium. A pair glide up to the surface and release a gelatinous ball of eggs. After hatching, when they are about 1 cm (3/8 in) in length, the fry return to the substrate. One report states that under artificial conditions, *P. lunulata* produced pelagic eggs

0.8 mm (5/16 in) in diameter in a gelatinous secretion, and at 27–30°C (81–86°F) these hatched in 24 hours.

Several species are available: *D. brachypterus* (dwarf lionfish) is the smallest reaching perhaps 10 cm (4 in) in captivity. They look a lot larger because of the extended fins – the sizes given here are body lengths. Both *Pterois radiata* and *P. antennata* (scorpionfish or spotfin lionfish) can grow to about 15 cm (6 in) in the aquarium, and the largest species, *P. volitans* (lionfish or turkeyfish) may be 20 cm (8 in) or more.

The mouths of all the predatory lionfish are large. This is the business end of *Pterois volitans* (lionfish or turkeyfish), used to engulf smaller fishes (tankmates included!) at a single gulp.

Seahorses and Pipefishes

The Syngnathidae (seahorses and pipefishes) are not the easiest of creatures to maintain in the aquarium. They place great demands on the aquarist, in terms of maintaining a well-balanced, mature set-up with the best quality water conditions and of providing a constant supply of live foods.

Members of the Syngnathidae have very small mouths and it is therefore important to supply small foods, which can be anything from brine shrimps to newly born guppies. Seahorses and pipefishes need frequent feeding – at least five times a day – and you need constant supplies of suitable foods on hand. To achieve this it is necessary to culture your own, and brine shrimps are probably the easiest; the fishes do, however, like variety in their diet, and it is now possible to obtain starter cultures of rotifers which the

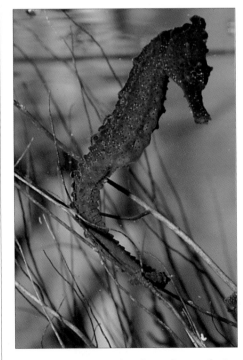

Hippocampus sp. (seahorse) use their tails to anchor themselves to coral branches. Be sure to provide them with suitable anchorage points in your aquarium.

sygnathids will also consume. These cultures come complete with instructions for propagating. Occasional feeds of *Daphnia* are also accepted if you are unable to provide anything else. Always check with your dealer that the seahorses or pipefishes are feeding before you purchase them and, if necessary, watch them feed. When settled, both pipefishes and seahorses can usually be persuaded to take some of the smaller frozen foods but they should not be expected to survive on these alone.

Pipefishes are generally better swimmers than seahorses, and spend much of their time sculling in and out of crevices in the reef. *Doryhamphus excisus* (bluestripe pipefish) is often available, but before buying it, do ensure that you can supply enough small food items. Small specimens acclimatize to aquarium conditions far better than adults.

Seahorses are very poor swimmers and spend most of their time anchored to coral branches by their prehensile tails. You must be sure to provide such anchor points in the aquarium. Seahorses like a quiet tank, and do not appreciate a swift flow of water, nor do they like the company of larger, very active fishes. Bottom-dwelling fishes such as *Synchiropus* sp. (mandarins) make excellent tank mates.

Seahorses have an interesting method of reproduction. The male carries the eggs in a brood pouch on his belly. After courtship, the pair come close together in a nuptial embrace so that the female's oviduct is close to, if not resting on, the brood pouch of the male, and she instantly expels some eggs into the pouch. This happens several

Male *Hippocampus* sp (seahorses) brood the eggs in a pouch on their belly. This "pregnant" male will soon "give birth".

times until spawning is complete. The male then wriggles about as if to rearrange the eggs in his pouch. The exact point at which fertilization takes place is not known, but many assume that it is when the eggs are in the pouch.

The incubation period varies from species to species and can be anything from two to eight weeks; for *Hippocampus kuda* (yellow or Pacific seahorse) incubation is four or five weeks. To expel the young, the male bends forwards and then backwards, thrusting his pouch forward so that one or two youngsters are pushed out with what can only be described as explosive force. Raising the fry is very hard work as the amount of fine live foods required is great, but when you succeed with them, it is worth all the effort.

Both *H. kuda* and *H. erectus* (Florida or northern seahorse) are regularly available.

Puffers and Porcupinefishes

The puffers' claim to fame is their ability to inflate themselves when danger threatens. They belong to the family Tetraodontidae and are easily differentiated from the Diodontidae (porcupinefishes) by their smooth scales and their teeth: puffers have four teeth, two at the top and two at the bottom.

Not all species inflate themselves completely: *Tetraodon* species (there are some freshwater members of this genus) can fully inflate their bodies whereas *Canthigaster* species only partially inflate themselves. Inflation is achieved by the fish taking in either water or air. You may be tempted to encourage your puffer to perform this feat as a party piece, but don't, as it is very stressful for the fish.

Puffers require a spacious aquarium with good filtration that can cope with the amount of mess they make when feeding. They are greedy feeders and will take finely chopped meat and fish, which goes everywhere; some may remain uneaten so be sure to check for left-over food and remove it before it pollutes the tank.

Species frequently seen are *Arothron hispidus* (stars and stripes puffer or white-spotted blowfish), *A. meleagris* (golden, spotted, or Guinea fowl puffer), and *Canthigaster valentini* (valentine or black-saddled puffer).

Porcupinefishes have a single pair of teeth, one tooth at the top and one at the bottom. These are very strong and are used to crush molluscs and crustaceans. They require very similar conditions to the puffers and will also feed on chopped meaty foods. These fishes may become hand-tame, but watch your

Arothron nigropunctatus (black-spotted puffer) is normally deflated, inflating itself only when frightened.

Resist the temptation to poke your puffer until it inflates. This is unnecessarily stressful for the fish.

fingers as they can give a nasty nip with their powerful teeth.

Needless to say neither the puffers nor the porcupinefishes should ever be kept with invertebrates as they will only try to eat them.

Two species of the porcupinefish family Diodontidae, *Diodon holacanthus* (longspined porcupinefish or balloonfish) and *Diodon hystrix* (common porcupinefish or porcupine puffer) are widely distributed in all warm seas. A third, *Chilomycterus schoepfi* (spiny boxfish, striped burrfish) has a more restricted range, occurring in the tropical Atlantic and the Caribbean.

In the aquarium they grow to about 15–17.5 cm (6–7 in) depending on the species, but they grow much larger in the

wild. Their behaviour varies: *D. holacanthus* should not be kept with other fishes; *D. hystrix* is more sociable and generally peaceful with other fishes, but *C. shoepfi* is quarrelsome with its own kind, never mind any other companions.

Care is needed when handling and transporting puffers and porcupinefishes. When caught they usually inflate, and when bagged will often try to bite their way out through the corners. An inflated porcupinefish can also puncture bags with its spines. Double or even triple bagging, in strong bags with the corners well taped, is recommended. Alternatively, transport them in rigid containers such as buckets or ice-cream containers with tight-fitting lids.

Arothron hispidus has a formidable set of teeth, so watch your fingers!

Triggerfishes

This is another group of fishes that you should not keep with invertebrates. "Triggers" have a very strong set of teeth which they use to eat invertebrates such as sea urchins – your fingers may also come under attack so take care. Even so some specimens become hand-tame, and will feed delicately from your fingers. It's up to you whether you take the risk; we take no responsibility for injured or lost fingers!

This family, the Balistidae, gets its common name from the way in which the fishes can lock their dorsal fin, which is normally held down in a groove flush with the body, but can be raised at will, and if necessary, locked into the upright position by the third dorsal ray. This defensive mechanism allows the fish to wedge itself in a cave, or in a predator's mouth so it cannot be swallowed and is eventually spat out!

Triggers in general have compressed ovoid bodies. They swim by undulating their dorsal and anal fins; the initial propulsion sometimes comes from the caudal fin, although this is more often used to get the fish rapidly out of trouble. During the day, they cruise about the aquarium. They are loners, which even in the wild come together only to breed, so one per aquarium is the rule.

The chances of breeding in the aquarium are remote (especially if you are keeping only one specimen!) and details of breeding behaviour are limited to observations by divers. On the reef males patrol a territory which may include the territories and nests of several females. These nests are just depressions in the substrate.

Despite the single specimen

Rhinecanthus aculeatus (Picasso trigger) grows to 23 cm (9 in) in the aquarium. It is a bold and sometimes aggressive fish, but immensely popular because of its coloration.

A fish that will eat just about any foods, *Odonus niger* (black triggerfish), is popular among aquarists. "Any foods" does of course mean corals and other marine invertebrates.

Balistoides conspicillum (clown trigger, big-spotted triggerfish) should not be kept with smaller fishes. Triggers appreciate crevices as nocturnal refuges, and may also use these to elude capture.

Like all triggerfishes, *Balistes vetula* (queen triggerfish) has a formidable set of teeth which are used to eat molluscs and crustaceans. It may become tame enough to be fed by – or, if you are careless, on – hand.

limit, these fishes are much sought after by aquarists. Two of the most popular are *Rhinecanthus aculeatus* (Picasso trigger) and *Odonus niger* (black trigger). The former is very colourful, its lighter body being splashed with colours reminiscent of the work of Pablo Picasso, hence its common name. In contrast, *O. niger* is a dark, plain-coloured fish. The body colour is not, as the name suggests, black, but can vary with the mood of the fish from dark green to dark blue; the red teeth are very conspicuous. Another highly colourful species is *Balistoides conspicillum* (clown trigger). All three will grow to about 22–23cm (8$\frac{1}{2}$–9 in) in captivity, so consider them only if you have a large aquarium.

Some bottom-feeding triggers have a very unusual feeding method. They eat the starfish *Acanthaster planci* (crown-of-thorns), and in order to avoid the creature's spines they blow jets of water at it so that it flips over onto its back, exposing the soft underparts. They deal with spiny sea urchins in much the same way. Mid-water swimming species will take plankton and green foods. Most aquarium species are bold feeders and will take frozen foods as well as grazing on algae.

At night, triggers rest in caves and crevices so be sure to provide such sites in the aquarium decor. These will also act as refuges, into which they will wedge themselves at any glimpse of a net.

Filefishes

Filefishes, like triggerfishes, belong to the family Balistidae. They have a double dorsal fin, the first (anterior) of which has a spine that can be locked in an upright position. Filefishes make welcome additions to the community aquarium, being quite small (at least when compared to triggerfishes) and for the most part peaceful.

Chaetodermis pencilligerus (the tassel filefish), is unusual and makes a good talking point for an aquarium. They have various fleshy appendages on their body and a dorsal fin which looks like small tassels, hence the common name.

During their initial acclimatization period it may be necessary to offer them live foods, but they quickly adapt to frozen foods, especially if the other inmates of the aquarium are feeding well.

Mandarins

The Callionymidae contains one of the most favoured genera of marine fishes, *Synchiropus*. Two species are regularly available, *S. splendidus* (mandarinfish) and *S. picturatus* (psychedelic fish). Of the two, *S. splendidus* is the more gaudily coloured. Small fishes, they behave in a similar way to gobies, flitting about on the substrate, resting on rocks just above the bottom, or hiding in caves with just their heads poking out. If frightened they will often burrow into the sand.

Males can be identified by the longer extensions on their dorsal and anal fins. Mandarins have produced eggs in the aquarium but so far no fry have been raised. They swim to the surface to release their eggs and milt, and the fertilized eggs then drift with the currents.

Keep either a single fish or a sexed pair in a quiet, well-established aquarium with plenty of rocks to provide hiding places and growths of algae for the fishes to browse through in search of small foods. Two males may fight to the death. Their companions should be calm, peaceful species.

They will avidly consume brine shrimp nauplii, *Tubifex*, and rotifers, but will not survive on these alone. They are thus best kept in a mature aquarium containing abundant marine invertebrates, where they will be able to supplement their diet with the micro-organisms on which they feed in nature. These shy, retiring fishes can sometimes be very difficult to get to feed initially.

Below: Synchiropus splendidus **(mandarinfish) are small, shy fishes. Males develop a long extension to the dorsal fin.**

Oxymonacanthus longirostris **(long-nosed filefish) grow to 10 cm (4 in) at most. They need to be kept with quiet, peaceful species.**

Synchiropus picturatus **(psychedelic fish) is a bottom-dwelling fish.**

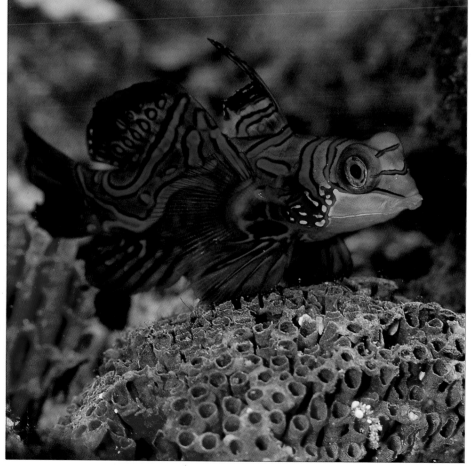

Cardinalfishes

These hardy little fishes of the family Apogonidae are ideal for beginners. As they are nocturnal, it takes them a little while to become accustomed to the brightly lit home aquarium. The two species normally encountered are *Sphaeramia nematopterus* (spotted or pyjama cardinalfish) from the Indo-Pacific region and *Apogon maculatus* (flamefish) which is found in the western Atlantic. Both are peaceful fishes and need to be kept with equally quiet companions.

Acclimatizing cardinalfishes to captive conditions can be fraught as they are finicky feeders. At first they will often take only small live foods such as *Artemia*, but eventually they will take frozen substitutes. Don't even bother trying to get them to accept flake food, they will starve rather than take it.

As far as is known, all are mouthbrooders, with either the male or female, or sometimes both, performing the parental duties.

Below left: Apogon maculatus (flamefish) is a nocturnal feeder.

Below right: Sphaeramia nematopterus (pyjama cardinalfish or spotted cardinalfish) should be fed live foods in the first instance.

Blennies

Blennies (family Bleniidae) are for the most part very active bottom-dwelling fishes that are a delight to keep in the home aquarium. In the wild many species have mimetic associations with other fishes.

The most famous example of this mimicry is exhibited by *Aspidontus taeniatus* (false cleaner wrasse, a most misleading common name as it is certainly not a wrasse) whose main claim to fame is that it uses its resemblance to the real cleaner wrasse to fool larger fishes into believing that it is a cleanerfish and will clean them of parasites. Instead, it takes scales off them and small bites out of them. It certainly doesn't spend its time skulking around the substrate.

Keep blennies in a reef-like set-up that provides plenty of hiding places. Some are very shy and aquarists prefer to keep these in a species aquarium or with other very placid fishes. They are fairly elongate fishes that like to rest on rocks, with their heads held high so that they can survey their surroundings and maintain their territories. They have two small hair-like growths above their eyes.

Most feed readily on algae and small invertebrates and will even

Ecsenius bicolor (bicolour blenny) needs a quiet aquarium with other small, peaceful fishes. Its natural timidity will usually diminish, given time.

take frozen and flake foods. Ideal for the beginner are *Ecsenius midas* (Midas blenny), a golden yellow fish which poses few problems once settled, and *E. bicolor* (bicolour blenny).

Blennies may breed in the aquarium. Males are generally larger than females and, when breeding, may go through several colour phases. For example, the male bicolour blenny becomes red with white bars when spawning, a complete contrast to his normal brown and orange coloration. When spawning is complete he assumes a dark blue hue with light patches on his flanks. The adhesive eggs are laid in the shelter of caves or under stones.

The false cleaner wrasse lays its eggs in empty shells or in the shelter of rocks, where the male can easily guard the eggs.

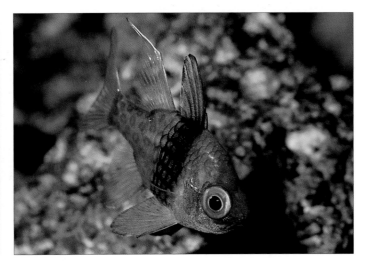

Hawkfishes

Hawkfishes deserve their common name. They have a habit of "sitting" amongst coral branches until they see a possible meal, then swooping down on it and returning swiftly to their perch. Most members of this family, the Cirrhitidae, encountered by aquarists are small, inoffensive creatures, growing to no more than 15 cm (6 in). They are quite distinctive, with robust bodies and large heads. The dorsal fin spines all have a tuft of filaments at their tips.

It is assumed that they live in harems, with a male having a large territory containing up to seven females. During the day the male ignores the females but at twilight his passion is aroused and he visits each member of his harem. If he finds one that is ready to spawn, the pair will swim upwards in an arc and release eggs and milt at the apex of the curve. The female then returns to the reef while the male moves on to find another partner. All this takes place before the light goes completely.

Oxycirrhites typus (longnosed hawkfish) are believed to be harem breeders with males holding a large territory which encompasses the smaller territories of several females.

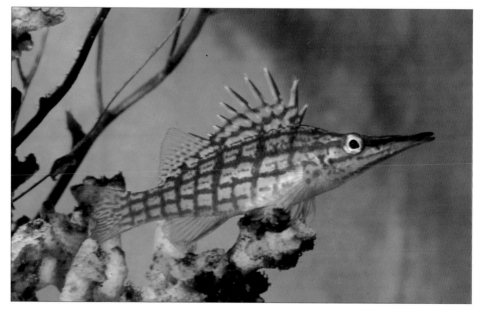

A fish that may be kept in a small group, *Oxycirrhites typus* (longnosed hawkfish) spends much time "perching" on coral branches.

Neocirrhites armatus (scarlet hawkfish) is much sought after because of its dramatic coloration and peaceful nature. It is also easy to feed, taking both frozen and flake foods. Like other hawkfishes it will appreciate "perches" such as branched corals.

In the aquarium, hawkfishes should be supplied with suitable perches so that they can hunt for prey. The best known species in aquarium circles is *Oxycirrhites typus* (long-nosed hawkfish), whose long snout makes it quite distinctive. The aquarium needs to be well-established with very clear, well-oxygenated water. Feeding this fish is not difficult, it will take brine shrimp and *Mysis* shrimp as well as frozen foods such as plankton. They may be kept as a pair. Females are larger than males, and the latter have darker red lower jaws and black edges to the ventral and caudal fins.

Another desirable species of hawkfish suitable for the community aquarium is *Neocirrhites armatus* (scarlet hawkfish). Once settled into the aquarium it will accept all foods of a suitable size, including flake.

Gobies

The family Gobiidae is the largest family of marine fishes with over 2000 species, and provides us with some of the most colourful little fishes for the community aquarium. The ventral fins of gobies are fused together to form a sucker-like disc which enables them to hold station in rough waters. They have two dorsal fins and can thus easily be distinguished from the blennies, which have only one. They are found throughout the world's seas, from the cold polar zones to the equator, and some are found in freshwater habitats.

In the aquarium these benthic fishes need plenty of hiding places. If they are frightened they need to retreat to these bolt-holes until the threat has passed.

They are very easy to feed provided you remember that they are small fishes and therefore require small foods. They will take all the normal marine fish foods but ensure that you chop meat and fish to a suitable size. For variety, offer live foods such as *Mysis* occasionally.

Gobies spawn in burrows and caves, under rocks, in empty shells, or similar sheltered places, hanging their eggs from the ceiling. The male guards the brood. Several species have been bred regularly in captivity by both aquarists and commercial fish breeders, but rearing the fry is exceedingly difficult.

For the beginner there are several species to choose from: *Gobiodon citrinus* (lemon goby), *G. okinawae* (yellow goby), and *Elecatinus oceanops* (neon goby) are but a few of those that will settle well into aquarium life.

Elecatinus oceanops (neon goby) is widely available and is

Gobiodon citrinus (lemon goby) is well suited to beginners as it is easy to feed and keep. It rests among coral branches or on rocks. The body mucus is poisonous to deter predators.

commercially bred. It is easy to maintain in a well-balanced aquarium and feeds well on small foods, from plankton to small brine shrimps. This goby may be kept with larger fishes as it will clean them of parasites.

They will frequently breed in the home aquarium. Provide the fishes with a short length of plastic pipe (a substitute for a cave) partly buried in the substrate. The male courts the female by making very exaggerated swimming motions and becomes much darker in colour. The eggs are laid in the pipe and will hatch about a week later. By providing the fishes with a pipe to spawn in, the eggs and the male guarding them can easily be transferred to another tank for hatching and rearing. On hatching, the fry require the smallest of planktonic foods such as rotifers and are not large enough to take newly hatched brine shrimp until they are about two weeks old.

Another goby suitable for aquaria, *Lythrypnus dalli* (Catalina or blue-banded goby) is a

Lythrypnus dalli (blue-banded or Catalina goby) is best kept in a species aquarium, especially if you want to breed them.

Californian species that is frequently bred. It requires cooler conditions than most tropical species, being happiest if the water remains below 22°C (71.6°F). They are best maintained in a species aquarium. Keep several specimens, and, if they are well fed on small live foods and provided you have males and females, they will establish a breeding colony.

Some of the gobies have a very short life span of about 18 months to two years, so don't expect them to survive for very much longer.

Marines

Squirrelfishes

Squirrelfishes (family Holo-centridae) are large, active nocturnal fishes which are usually red in colour. By day they hide away on the reef, but those imported for the aquarium trade soon adjust to swimming about during the day.

Being active, they need a large, spacious aquarium. They are also shoaling fishes and benefit from being kept in the company of their own kind. Any small fishes in the aquarium may be intimidated by the boisterousness of the squirrelfishes so keep them only with other similarly sized fishes.

Squirrelfishes have large eyes, indicative of a nocturnal fish, so that they can make the best use of any available light. Their dorsal fin has a spiny anterior part and a soft-rayed posterior part. Take care when netting these fishes as their scales and gill covers are very rough, and, along with the dorsal spines, may become entangled in the net. Should this happen, rest the net and fish in the aquarium and it will usually free itself. If this still doesn't work and you do need to release it, take great care not to dislodge scales, damage the gill covers, or tear the fins; if necessary, cut the net away.

Offer a variety of meaty foods. They will also take small fishes so choose their companions with care!

Two species often encountered are *Holocentrus diadema* (common squirrelfish) and *Myripristis murdjan* (big-eye squirrelfish or blotcheye). You can tell the difference between the two genera by the large spine at the rear of the gill cover, which is present in *Holocentrus* but lacking in *Myripristis*.

A nocturnal fish, *Myripristis murdjan* (big-eye squirrelfish or blotcheye) needs its large eyes to seek out food at night. Although in the aquarium they rapidly adopt a diurnal lifestyle – especially at mealtimes!

Wormfishes

These delightful little fishes belong to the family Microdesmidae, and are also referred to as firefishes. In the aquarium they should be kept as single individuals or as a pair – not that you can tell the sexes by any external characteristics, so it would be more accurate to say two fishes – provided you have a reasonable-sized aquarium. In the wild they are seen hovering above the substrate in groups, which at the first sign of danger retreat to their bolt-holes. In the aquarium, however, they are not so tolerant of each other, and if you try to keep more than two, the weaker fishes will be chased, harassed, and even bitten so badly that they may die.

Four species are seen in the hobby: *Nemateleotris magnificus* (firefish), *N. decora* (purple firefish), *N. helfrichi*, and *Ptereleotris evides* (spot-tailed gudgeon). Of these, *N. helfrichi* is the least often seen.

Nemateleotris have very long extensions to their dorsal fins, and use these not only to signal to each other but also to lock themselves into their bolt-holes in the same way that catfishes lock themselves in crevices.

The most commonly available species is *N. magnificus*. They are easy to feed on small foods and will benefit from being fed live brine shrimp two or three times a week. They are not too fussy about water conditions but do appreciate a good flow of water through the tank. Once established in the aquarium they become less nervous and cease to dive into their bolt-holes every time someone passes by the aquarium. Avoid keeping them with boisterous species or you will never see them, as they will retreat to their hiding places and stay there.

Ptereleotris evides are larger fishes which can attain 12 cm (4³/₄ in). Several specimens can be kept together provided the aquarium is large enough. Juveniles usually live in groups but adults are found in pairs. They adapt well to aquarium life, posing no great problems in terms of maintenance or feeding. As long as they receive a varied diet, they will take anything including flake, frozen, and live foods. Unlike *Nemateleotris*, when frightened *P. evides* flees from its territory rather than hiding in a cave. This species may be kept with medium-sized peaceful fishes.

Ptereleotris tricolor **are trouble-free fishes as far as maintenance in the aquarium is concerned. Ensure you feed them a varied diet. Although they are small, do not try to keep more than two, or weaker ones will be bullied.**

Like other wormfishes, *Nemateleotris magnificus* **(firefish) needs to be able to construct a burrow. Make sure the substrate material is suitable for this.**

Jawfishes

This is another group of small, bottom-dwelling fishes, this time from the family Opistognathidae. They are ideal both for the community of small fishes and for the mixed aquarium containing some invertebrates.

They are typically seen hovering almost upright above their burrows, and will lunge at any passing prey be it alive or dead. They construct their burrows in the substrate so ensure that you have a good covering of sand in which they can do this. At night they retreat into their burrows, tail first, and cover the entrance with a small shell or pebble. Several may be kept in the same tank, provided there is room for each to have its own burrow. They are most tolerant of their own kind as well as of other species. The only problems that may arise are if too many cave/burrow-dwelling species are kept and there are insufficient hiding places for all of them.

They feed on most meaty foods such as crustaceans, and will also take very small fishes if the opportunity arises.

The species usually seen in aquaria is *Opistognathus aurifrons*

Groups of *Opistognathus aurifrons* **(yellow-headed jawfish) may be kept in a community tank with other small, peaceful species. Males and females look alike.**

(yellow-headed jawfish). Typical of the group, they quickly retreat to their burrows if danger threatens; needless to say this makes them extremely difficult to catch. If frightened they will also jump, so ensure that the aquarium is tightly covered. They show no sexual dimorphism so you may never know if you have a pair. However, if you come across a fish incubating eggs in its mouth, that one is the male.

When *Opistognathus aurifrons* **retreats to its burrow it covers the entrance with a small stone or shell.**

Boxfishes

These fishes of the family Ostraciidae are undoubtedly oddities. Their bodies are rigid, having a framework of bony plates which are fused together. The only moveable parts of the fish are the fins and the caudal peduncle. You should avoid keeping these creatures with cleanerfishes, which may damage their very sensitive skin.

Because their bodies are rigid, it is very difficult to tell whether or not these fishes are getting enough to eat. When buying them, avoid any specimens that appear to have concave sides, as these are probably starving and may have passed the point of no return. Unfortunately when the fishes get to this point it is virtually impossible to get them to feed again. It is annoying when you see fishes in this condition because they are much easier to feed than some other marines; you need only to feed regularly and watch to see if the boxfishes are getting their fair share. They move deliberately and fairly slowly so other fishes often get to the food first; if this is happening feed a little more food after the greedier fishes are sated, and watch to make sure the boxfishes feed.

Members of the Ostraciidae are able to release a poison into the water when threatened. This can be very dangerous, especially in the confines of an aquarium or when transporting them. The toxins can be so concentrated that they can be fatal not only to other fishes but also to the boxfish. To avoid fatalities, some aquarists advise settling the boxfish into the aquarium ahead of the other fishes to lessen the chances of the boxfish becoming frightened and releasing toxins.

Easily recognized by its distinctive shape which makes it popular as an aquarium "oddity", *Lactoria cornuta* (long-horned cowfish) is a large fish; 40 cm (16 in) is a very good size for aquarium specimens.

One of the largest members of the family is *Lactoria cornuta* (long-horned cowfish) which can grow to 40 cm (16 in) in captivity. This species is easy to recognize by the two bony projections ("horns") on the head and two more on the rear of the body. They will browse on algae and pick at invertebrates. Keep them singly as they are intolerant of their own kind.

At the other end of the size range is *Ostracion meleagris* (spotted or Pacific boxfish) at 20 cm (8 in). This is a fish for the experienced aquarist only, as it can be very difficult to acclimatize to aquarium conditions and may also suffer from bacterial infections of the skin and eyes. The maintenance of exceptionally good quality water is essential for this species; otherwise it makes a good, peaceful fish for the aquarium. Males are far more colourful than females, having a dark background colour with white spots on the upper part of the body while the flanks are bluish-violet with dark spots. Females have the same colour pattern all over their bodies: dark brown or black with white spots.

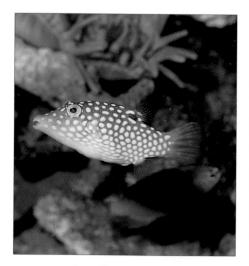

Ostracion lentiginosus (blue-spotted boxfish) require excellent water conditions in the aquarium. They are peaceful and need similar companions. Feed them small, meaty foods. Smaller than their cousin the cowfish, they are likewise interesting – but quite difficult – aquarium "curiosities".

Rabbitfishes

The Siganidae (rabbitfishes) are widely caught as food fishes in the tropics. They are related to the surgeonfish and may be found with them.

Rabbitfishes are predominantly vegetarian and spend much of their time grazing on algae. Fortunately for us, they will also accept flake and live foods once they have settled into the aquarium. Handle these fishes with care as the dorsal and anal fin spines are venomous. Indeed, anyone wading through their native waters and inadvertently stepping on one of these fishes will receive a nasty wound. They are active fishes that require a spacious aquarium.

Lo vulpinus (fox-face, badger-fish or fox-fish) is well known in the hobby, being very popular because of its bright yellow coloration and striking black-and-white face. It is easy to maintain provided you remember to include plenty of vegetable matter in its diet.

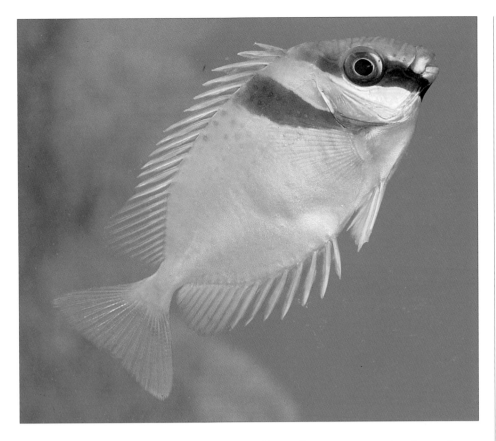

Siganus virgatus (silver badger fish or double-barred spinefoot) also appears in dealers' tanks now and again. Like *L. vulpinus* it settles well to aquarium life, though it can be somewhat intolerant of its own kind.

Above: Siganus sp. are, in the main, vegetarians which graze on algae. Be sure to provide suitable foods.

Below: Lo vulpinus (fox-fish) is a popular aquarium fish. Take care when handling rabbitfishes or when working in the aquarium as the dorsal spines are poisonous.

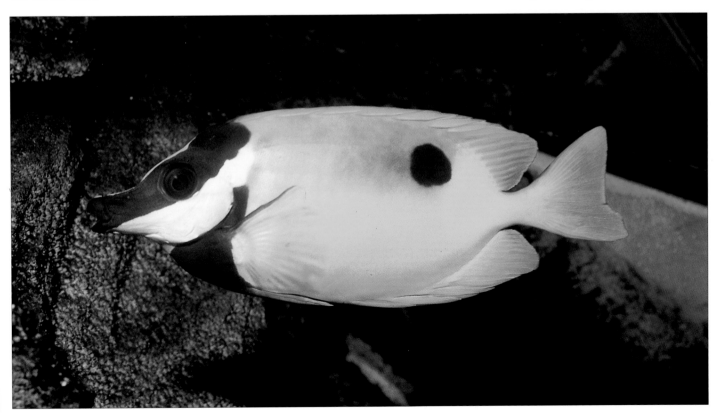

Sea Bass and Groupers

The sea bass (family Serranidae) are a large family of predatory fishes, some of which have found great favour among aquarists. The Serranidae contains over 370 species which are found in both tropical and temperate waters around the world. Because they form such a large group it is difficult to generalize, so we will look at just a few species that you might like to contemplate keeping.

Starting with some of the smaller species: *Anthias squamipinnis* (Anthias, orange sea-perch, lyre-tail coralfish or wreckfish), may reach 12.5 cm (5 in) in the wild, but in the aquarium it is usually smaller. These very attractive fishes are bright orange-yellow with deeply forked lyre-tails and long ventral fins. Shoaling fishes, they need to be kept in a group. Males are more brightly coloured than females and their third dorsal spine is longer. The dominant male will take charge of a group of fishes. They prefer live foods but can be trained to take dead meaty foods. Even so, it may be necessary to put food into the aquarium near the return pipe from the filter so that it appears to be moving when the fishes lunge at it.

Chromileptes altivelis (panther or polka-dot grouper) is another popular fish, because of all the groupers it probably has the smallest mouth! It may be kept with other larger or similarly sized fishes but never put it with anything it could consider food. Young specimens are white with large brown or black blotches all over, including the fins. As the fishes mature, they retain the white background but the number of dark spots increases. In

Chromileptes altivelis (panther or polka-dot grouper) is a piscivore so it should not be kept with fishes small enough to be eaten. The spotted pattern acts as camouflage on the reef.

Another predator is Calloplesiops altivelis (marine betta or comet grouper), a very attractive fish. The false eye-spot confuses predators as to which end is which.

Unless you have a very large aquarium do not even consider keeping a fish such as Promicrops lanceolatus (Australian Jewfish). It can grow to 3.7 metres (12 ft)!

the home aquarium they stand out, but when seen against the reef the spots and blotches allow the fishes to blend into the background. If you have enough space and can supply plenty of live foods then several can be kept together. With a great deal of patience, panther groupers can be persuaded to take dead

meaty foods. In captive conditions they are likely to grow to 30 cm (12 in) at most.

Two of the most beautiful members of the family Plesiopidae are *Calloplesiops altivelis* (marine betta, comet grouper) and *C. argus* (marine betta). These avid hunters should not be kept with fishes small enough to be considered food. Their appearance is designed to deceive: their eyes are well camouflaged by the white spotted patterning which covers the body and fins, while the false eye spot at the base of the dorsal fin is extremely conspicuous. Should a predatory fish attack the marine betta it will aim for this eye, as most predators like to swallow their prey head first. It will get a shock, getting only a mouthful of fin and a few scales while the betta swims away to heal its wounds and re-grow its fin. Bettas take some time to settle and may need to be fed live fish in the first instance, but will later take other meaty foods.

Calloplesiops altivelis has been bred in the aquarium by a Dutch aquarist. In brief, a ball of eggs were stuck to the wall of a cave. The larvae hatched after dark some five to six days later. The fry were well pigmented and fed almost immediately. Several changes of colour and body form occurred before the young looked like miniature adults at three months old, and they would forage for food *en masse*. The sexes of the parents could not be determined and both suffered damage to their fins while spawning. The eggs were guarded by one parent, presumably the male, who did not eat during the five to six days that he guarded the spawn.

Glossary

Acidity/Alkalinity: the measure of the number of hydrogen ions in water, expressed in terms of pH. Neutral is pH 7, above pH7 is alkaline and below pH 7 is acid (see also pH).

Aeration: the movement of water created by a supply of compressed air into the aquarium.

Algae: simple aquatic plants, from tiny, single-celled, types to large seaweeds.

Biotope: any area that supports its own distinct community.

Bottom-sifter: a fish that eats by sifting through the substrate.

Brackish water fishes: fishes from water containing a measure of salt, but not as saline as seawater, such as river estuaries.

Brood: all the offspring of one family.

Brood pouch: a pouch or cavity in certain fishes where the eggs develop and hatch.

Bubblenest: a nest of bubbles which harbours the eggs of some fishes.

Carnivore: meat-eater.

Cloaca: a cavity in the pelvic region into which the alimentary canal and the genital and urinary ducts open.

Cold water fishes: fishes needing no heating of their water.

Congeneric: belonging to the same group.

Conspecific: belonging to the same species.

dH (of water): measurement of the amount of dissolved salts in water.

Diurnal (of feeding): feeding during the day (see also nocturnal).

Dimorphism: the occurrence of two distinct individual types within an animal species.

Egg-layer: fishes that lay eggs which are then fertilized and hatched outside the female's body.

Epigean: living on or close to the surface of the water.

Filtration: the system for keeping the aquarium water clean.

Fimbriated: having a fringed margin around a part of the body.

Fresh water fishes: fishes from water containing no salt.

Fry: the young of a fish.

Genus: a group of closely related species.

Gonopodium: the male livebearing fish's copulatory organ.

Habitat: the physical environment of any individual species.

Hardness (of water): (see dh of water).

Herbivore: plant-eater.

Ichthyologist: person who studies fish.

Infusoria: tiny organisms which can be used as food for fry.

Insectivore: insect-eater.

Labyrinth organ (air breathing): an additional breathing organ to enable some fishes to breath directly from the atmosphere.

Lacustrine: living close to the shore of a lake.

Livebearer: fishes whose fertile eggs develop inside the female's body.

Marine fishes: fishes that live in seawater.

Maxillary: upper jaw.

Milt: fertilizing fluid of a male fish.

Mineral salts (in water): inorganic substances found naturally in water.

Mouthbrooder: fishes who hold their eggs and young in the oral cavity, during incubation, and also after the young are able to swim if danger approaches.

Mulm: accumulated fish waste, debris, unprocessed food, etc.

Nocturnal (of feeding): feeding at night (see also diurnal).

Operculum: external gill cover.

Osmosis: the passage of water through a membrane from a weaker to a more concentrated solution.

Ovipositor: a thin tube on the female's body used for planting eggs on surfaces, ready for fertilization by the male.

Parasite: a plant or animal that lives in or on another, gaining nourishment.

pH (of water): a logarithmic scale which describes acidity/alkalinity in water (see also acidity/alkalinity).

Piscivore: fish-eater.

Plankton: tiny organisms living on the surface of the water.

Salinity (of water): the amount of mineral salts present in seawater.

Species: any taxonomic group into which a genus is divided, the members of which are capable of interbreeding.

Specific gravity: the ratio of the density of a substance to that of water.

Sympatrically: taking place or existing in the same or overlapping geographical areas.

Bibliography

Note: Some of the publications listed below are now out of print but we have included them because they are still available through public libraries.

Allen, G.R., *Butterfly and Angelfishes of the World. Vol. II. Atlantic Ocean, Caribbean Sea, Red Sea, Indo-Pacific.* Mergus Verlag GmbH, Melle, Germany. 1979.

Amlacher, E., *A Textbook of Fish Diseases.* T.F.H. Publications, Neptune City, New Jersey, U.S.A. 1970.

Andrews, C., *Fish Breeding.* Salamander Books Limited, London, U.K.. 1986.

Andrews, C., Excell, A. and N. Carrington, *The Manual of Fish Health.* Salamander Books Limited, London, U.K.. 1988.

Axelrod, A. assisted by S.R. Shaw, *Breeding Aquarium Fishes.* T.F.H. Publications, Neptune City, New Jersey, U.S.A. 1967.

Bailey, M.C., *A Beginner's Guide to the Mbuna of Lake Malawi.* British Cichlid Association Information Pamphlet No. 117, 1992.

Boyd, K.W., *The Complete Aquarium Problem Solver!* Tetra Press, Melle, Germany. 1990.

Breder, C.M and D.E Rosen, *Modes of Reproduction in Fishes.* T.F.H. Publications, Neptune City, New Jersey, U.S.A. 1966.

Brichard, P., *Cichlids and all other Fishes of Lake Tanganyika.* T.F.H. Publications, Neptune City, New Jersey, U.S.A. 1989.

Burgess, W.E., *An Atlas of Freshwater and Marine Catfishes.* T.F.H. Publications, Neptune City, New Jersey, U.S.A. 1989.

Conkel, D., *Cichlids of North and Central America.* T.F.H. Publications, Neptune City, New Jersey, U.S.A. 1993.

Dakin, N., *The Book of the Marine Aquarium.* Salamander Books Limited, London, U.K.. 1992.

Debelius, H. and H.A. Baensch, *Marine Atlas.* Mergus Verlag GmbH, Melle, Germany. 1994.

Eschmeyer, W.N. *Catalogue of the Genera of Recent Fishes.* California Academy of Sciences, San Francisco, U.S.A. 1990.

Ferraris, C., *Catfish in the Aquarium.* Tetra Press, Melle, Germany. 1991.

Fryer, G. and T.D. Iles, *The Cichlid Fishes of the Great Lakes of Africa.* Oliver and Boyd, London and Edinburgh, U.K.. 1972.

Géry, J., *Characoids of the World.* T.F.H. Publications, Neptune City, New Jersey, U.S.A. 1977.

Greenwood, P.H., *A History of Fishes.* Ernest Benn Limited, London, U.K.. 1975.

Jocher, W., *Food for the Aquarium and Vivarium.*

Studio Vista Limited, London, U.K.. 1966.

Kabata, K., *Diseases of Fishes. Book 1: Crustacea as Enemies of Fishes.* T.F.H. Publications, Neptune City, New Jersey, U.S.A. 1970.

Konings, A., (Ed.) *Enjoying Cichlids.* Cichlid Press, St Leon-Rot, Germany. 1993.

Konings, A., *Cichlids and all Other Fishes of Lake Malawi.* T.F.H. Publications, Neptune City, New Jersey, U.S.A. 1990

Konings, A., *Malawi Cichlids in Their Natural Habitat.* Cichlid Press, St Leon-Rot, Germany. 1995.

Konings, A. *Tanganyika Cichlids.* Verduijn Cichlids and Lake Fish Movies, Holland and Germany. 1988.

Linke, H. and W. Staeck, *African Cichlids I: Cichlids from West Africa.* Tetra Press, Germany. 1995.

Linke, H. and W. Staeck, *American Cichlids I: Dwarf Cichlids.* Tetra Press, Germany. 1995.

Loiselle, P.V., *The Cichlid Aquarium.* Tetra Press, Germany. 1995.

Merrick, J.R. and G.E. Schmida, *Australian Freshwater Fishes.* J.R. Merrick, Macquarie University, Australia. 1987.

Mills, D., *The Practical Encyclopedia of the Marine Aquarium.* Salamander Books Limited, London, U.K.. 1987.

Mühlberg, H., *The Complete Guide to Water Plants.* E.P. Publishing Limited. 1980.

Rataj, K. and T.J. Horeman, *Aquarium Plants.* T.F.H. Publications, Neptune City, New Jersey, U.S.A. 1977.

Riehl, R. and H.A. Baensch, *Aquarium Atlas Vol. I.* Mergus Verlag GmbH, Melle, *Germany. 1987.*

Riehl, R. and H.A. Baensch, *Aquarium Atlas. Vol. II.* Mergus Verlag GmbH, Melle, Germany. 1993.

Riehl, R. and H.A. Baensch, *Aquarien Atlas Voll. III.* Mergus Verlag GmbH, Melle, Germany. 1994.

Sandford, G. and R. Crow, *The Manual of Tank Busters.* Salamander Books Limited, London, U.K.. 1991.

Barbus callipterus (clipper barb) is a West African barb. Growing to 9 cm (3 ½ in) it is an undemanding species recommended for beginners. Ensure the tank is tightly covered as these fishes like to jump.

Seuss,W., *Corydoras.* Dähne Verlag GmbH, Ettlingen, Germany. 1993.

Spotte, S., *Fish and Invertebrate Culture.* John Wiley and Sons, New York, U.S.A. 1979.

Stawikowski, R. and U. Werner. *Die Buntbarsche der Neuen Welt: Mittelamerika.* Reimar Hobbing GmbH, Essen, Germany. 1985.

Stawikowski, R. and U. Werner., *Die Buntbarsche der Neuen Welt: Südamerika.* Reimar Hobbing GmbH, Essen, Germany. 1988.

Steene, R.C., *Butterfly and Angelfishes of the World. Vol. I. Australia.* Mergus Verlag GmbH, Melle, Germany. 1977.

Sterba, G., *Freshwater Fishes of the World.* Studio Vista, London, U.K.. 1967.

van Duijn Jnr., C. *Diseases of Fishes.* Iliffe Books Limited, London, U.K.. 1967.

Watson, I.G. and R. Sznober, *A Beginner's Guide to South American Dwarf Cichlids.* British Cichlid Association Information Pamphlet No. 118. 1992.

Wickler, W., *Breeding Behaviour of Aquarium Fishes.* T.F.H Publications, Neptune City, New Jersey, U.S.A. 1973.

Zupanc, G.K.H., *Fish and Their Behaviour.* Tetra Press, Melle, Germany. 1985.

Table of Weights and Measures

1000 cubic centimetres = 1 litre
1 litre of water weighs 1 kilogram
1 cubic foot of water = 6.23 imperial gallons
1 imperial gallon of water weighs 10 lb
1 US gallon = .8 imperial gallon (approx)
1 imperial gallon = 4.55 litres

There are many fishes, such as this *Brachyplatystoma juruense*, that are just too large for the average home aquarium.

Acknowledgements

Picture Acknowledgements

The Publishers gratefully acknowledge the following photographers for permission to reproduce their work in this book.

Key: A: Above, B: Bottom, C: Centre, L: Left, R: Right, T: Top.

David Allison: 215, 237 (L), 243 (T), 244 (BL, BR), 245 (T), 246, 247 (TR, BR), 249 (B).

Mary Bailey: 3, 12 (2nd from T), 12 (T), 13 (B), 21, 39 (B), 43 (B), 63, 75 (B), 83 (T), 107 (B), 113 (B), 115, 118, 126 (T), 128, 130 (AR, BR), 131, 132 (2nd from T, 3rd from T, B), 133, 134 (TL), 135, 136, 137, 138, 139, 140 (B).

Bruce Coleman: Jon and Des Bartlett: 239 (R). **Jane Burton**: 1, 2, 4, 7, 9, 10 (T, C), 11, 14, (T, L), 15, 16, 17, 18, 20, 25, 26, 34, 37, 38 (T), 39 (T), 45, 49 (T), 51, 53, 55, 56 (T), 57, 59 (B), 65, 69, 71, 72, 73, 75 (C), 76, 77, 81 (B), 85 (L), 86 (L), 88, 89, 90, 97, 100, 102, 103, 105, 109, 112, 114 (TR), 119, 120, 121, 122, 124 (BL, BR), 130 (T), 134 (TR), 163 (T), 169 (T), 170, 171, 174 (2nd from T), 179 (T), 187 (L), 216 (T), 231 (T), 233 (T), 234 (B), 236 (T), 242 (R), 249 (T). **Alain Compost**: 220 (C). **Jeff Foott**: 167 (B). **Udo Hirsch**: 132 (T). **Charles and Sandra Hood**: 237 (R), 244 (T). **Allan Power**: 235 (B). **Andrew J. Purcell**: 216 (AL, AR). **Hans Reinhard**: 44, 50, 67, 78, 116 (B), 140 (T), 162 (B), 164 (T, C), 169 (B), 172, 184 (T), 190 (BL), 193, 203 (T), 210. **Hector Rivarola**: 174 (T). **Carl Roessler**: 238 (T). **Kim Taylor**: 166 (B), 222 (B). **John Visser**: 220 (B).

Mike Sandford: 8, 10 (B), 12 (2nd from B, B), 13 (T),14 (R), 16, 19 (R), 22 (T), 23, 35, 36, 38 (B), 40, 42 (TL, BL), 46 (B), 54, 58 (B), 61 (T, L, R), 64, 66, 68 (B), 70 (B), 83 (B), 87, 96, 99, 100, 113 (T, C), 114 (TL), 117, 124 (T), 125, 126 (B), 127, 129, 141, 142, 143, 144, 145, 146, 147, 148, 149, 150, 151, 152, 153, 154, 155, 156, 157, 158, 159, 160, 161, 162 (TL, TR, BL), 163 (B), 164 (B), 165, 166, 167 (T, C), 168, 173, 174 (C, 2nd from B, B), 175, 176, 177, 178, 179 (BL, R), 180, 181, 182, 183, 184 (BL, C, R), 185, 186, 187 (TR, CR, BR), 188, 189, 190 (T, C, BR), 191, 192, 194, 195, 196, 197, 198, 199, 200, 201, 202, 203 (B), 204, 205, 206, 207, 208, 209, 211, 212, 213, 214, 217, 218, 219, 220 (T), 221, 222 (T), 223, 224, 225, 226, 227, 228, 229, 230, 231 (BL, BR), 232, 233 (BL, BR), 234 (T), 235 T), 236 (BL, BR), 238 (B), 239 (L), 240, 241, 242 (TL, BL), 243 (BL, BR), 245 (B), 247 (TL, BL), 248, 250, 252.

Publisher's Acknowledgements

For supplying aquatic equipment :
Morden Waterworld
Morden Hall Garden Centre
Morden Hall Road
Morden, Surrey SM4 5JG
Tel: 0181 646 1066

Author Acknowledgements

The authors would like to thank the following for advice and assistance: Mike Sandford and Nick Fletcher, who cast a critical eye over both content and grammar; Dr Keith Banister for scientific and taxonomic advice: Jeff Challands who used his computer and expert knowledge to allow our otherwise incompatible computers to communicate by floppy disc, thus avoiding the need for much re-typing; and Ad Konings for educating two insular Brits on the subject of metric tank sizes.

Also both our households for their tolerance and understanding during the disruption to domestic bliss occasioned by the writing of this book; and Dorothy and John Baker for their help in looking after MB's horse.

Finally, our particular thanks to British Telecom for taking only a week to restore viable communication between us at a critical stage of the enterprise....

The Anatomy of the Fish

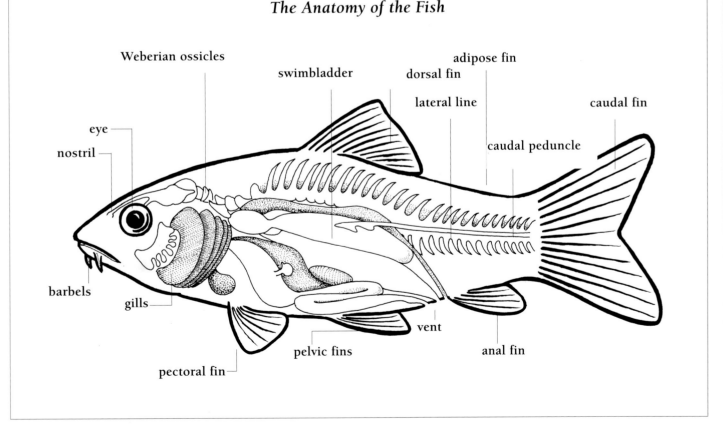

Weberian ossicles · swimbladder · adipose fin · dorsal fin · lateral line · caudal fin · eye · nostril · caudal peduncle · barbels · gills · vent · anal fin · pelvic fins · pectoral fin

Index

Abramites hypselonotus (high-backed headstander), 187
Abudefduf assimilis, 228
Abudefduf cyaneus (blue damsel), 229
Abudefduf saxatilis (sergeant major), 229
Acanthopsis choiorhynchus (horse-faced loach), 162
Acanthopthalmus (kuhli loach), 57, 162, 163
Acanthurus leucosternon (powder blue surgeon), 233
Acarichthys, 133
Aequidens sp. cl. rivulatus (Green terror), 133
Agamyxis pectinifrons, 151, 152
Air pump, 48, 92, 93
Alestes nurse, 180
Alfaro cultratus (knife livebearer),173
Algae, 75-76
Altolamprologus compressiceps, 137
Amblydoras hancocki (Hancock's talking catfish), 151
Ammonia, 27, 28
Amphilophus, 132
Amphilophus citrinellus (Midas cichlid), 59, 130
Amphiprion akallopisos (skunk clown), 230
Amphiprion bicinctus (two-banded anemonefish or banded
    clown), 230
Amphiprion clarkii (Clark's/yellow-tail anemonefish), 229, 230
Amphiprion ephippium (tomato, red saddle-back or fire
    clown), 230
Amphiprion frenatus (tomato/fire/bridled clown), 229, 230
Amphiprion melanopus (red and black anemonefish), 230
Amphiprion ocellaris (percula clown or clownfish), 229, 230
Amphiprion rubricinctus (Fijian clown), 4
Amphiprion polymnus (saddleback clown or anemonefish), 230
Anabantids, 23
Anabas testudineus, 190, 198
Anableps 218, 219, 220
Anableps anableps (striped four-eyes), 167, 218
Anableps dowi (Pacific four-eyes), 218
Anableps microlepis (fine-scale four-eyes), 218
Anchor worm, 114, 115
Ancistrus, 146, 148, 149
Ancistrus temminckii (bristlenose), 148
Anemone fishes, 13, 229, 230
Angels: freshwater, 134; marine, 231
Anomalochromis, 139
Anostomus anostomus (striped headstander), 187
Anostomus taeniatus, 187
Anostomus ternetzi, 187
Anthias squamipinnis (anthias, orange sea-perch, lyre-tailed
    coralfish, wreckfish), 250
Aphyosemion australe (Cape Lopez lyretail), 176
Aphyosemion deltaense, 174
Aphyosemion gardneri, 174
Aphyosemion oeseri, 174
Aphyosemion sjoestedti (blue gularis), 56, 174
Aphyosemion striatum, 174
Apistogramma 131, 135
Apistogramma nijsseni (panda dwarf cichlid), 135
Apistogramma norberti, 135
Apistogrammoides, 135
Aplocheilus lineatus (sparkling panchax), 177
Apogon maculatus (flamefish), 243
Apteronotus albifrons (ghost knife fish), 203
Aquarium (see also tanks),
        general maintenance, 108, 110
        setting up, 76-103
        stocking density, 10
        weight of, 78
Archer fishes, 38, 222, 223
Archocentrus centrarchus, 132,
Archocentrus nigrofasciatus (convict cichlid), 132
Argulus, 114
Arius, 218
Arius jordani, 224
Arius seemani (shark catfish), 223, 224
Arnoldichthys spilopterus (African red-eyed tetra), 180
Arothron hispidus (stars and stripes puffer, white-spotted
    blow-fish), 240
Arothron meleagris (golden, spotted), 240
Arothron nigropunctatus (black-spotted puffer), 240
Artemia (brine shrimp), 43
Aspidontus taeniatus (false cleanerfish), 235, 243
Aspidoras, 143, 145
Aspidoras pauciradiatus, 145
Astatoreochromis, 138
Astatotilapia burtoni, 140
Astrodoras asterifrons (stargazing dorad), 141, 151
Astronotus ocellatus (oscar), 2, 15, 107, 134
Astyanax mexicanus (blind cave characin), 61, 183
Auchenoglanis occidentalis (giraffe catfish), 181

Aulonocara,136, 137
Badis badis, 217
Balantiocheilus melanopterus (silver or Bala shark), 160
Balistes vetula (queen triggerfish), 241
Balistoides conspicillum (clown or big-spotted trigger), 241
Banjo catfish, 150
Barbs, 36, 155-157
Barbus arulius (arulius barb), 156
Barbus barilioides, 156
Barbus callipterus (clipper barb), 253
Barbus conchonius (rosy barb), 156, 157
Barbus cumingi (Cuming's barb), 156
Barbus eugrammus (striped barb), 157
Barbus everetti (clown barb), 156
Barbus fasciatus (striped barb), 156
Barbus filamentosus (black-spot or filament barb), 156,157
Barbus gelius (golden dwarf barb), 157
Barbus nigrofasciatus (ruby barb), 157
Barbus "odessa" (Odessa barb), 156
Barbus oligolepis (checker barb), 156, 157
Barbus orphoides, 156
Barbus schuberti (golden barb), 156, 157
Barbus schwanenfeldi (tinfoil barb), 156,157
Barbus tetrazona (tiger barb), 121, 156
Barbus ticto stoliczkae, 156
Barbus titteya (cherry barb), 155, 156
Bedotia geayi (Madagascar rainbowfish), 200, 201
Belonesox belizanus (pike livebearer), 173
Belontia, 190
Belontia signata (combtail), 194
Betta, 190, 197
Betta bellica (slender Betta), 196
Betta pugnax, 197
Betta splendens (Siamese fighter), 44, 120, 190, 196
Biotodoma, 133
Bitterling, 166
Blennies, 243
Bloodworm, 42
Bodianus hirsutus, 234
Bodianus rufus (Spanish hogfish), 234
Bogwood, 58, 62, 63, 85
Bosmina, 42
Botia berdmorei, 162
Botia lohachata (Pakistani loach), 162
Botia macracantha (clown loach), 5, 14, 162, 163
Botia modesta (orange-finned loach), 162
Botia sidthimunki (chain loach), 163
Boxfishes, 248
Brachydanio albolineatus (pearl danio), 158
Brachydanio rerio (zebra danio), 158
Brachydanio rerio var. frankei (leopard danio), 155, 158
Brachygobius (bumblebee gobies), 218, 225, 226
Brachygobius nunus, 225
Brachygobius xanthozona, 225
Brachyplatystoma juruense, 252
Brine shrimp, 43
Brochis, 143
Brochis britskii (Britski's Brochis), 145
Brochis splendens (emerald catfish), 145
Bujurquina, 133
Butterflyfishes; freshwater, 210; marine, 232

Calloplesiops altivelis (marine betta or comet
    grouper), 250
Calloplesiops argus, 250
Canthigaster valentini (valentine or black-saddled puffer), 240
Carassius auratus (goldfish), 10, 26, 164, 165, 195
Cardinalfishes, 243
Carnegiella marthae (black-winged hatchetfish), 186
Carnegiella myersi, 186
Carnegiella strigata (marbled hatchetfish), 72, 186
Catfishes, 141-154
Centropyge acanthops (African pygmy or fireball angel), 231
Centropyge argi (pygmy angel, purple fireball, cherub), 231
Centropyge bicolor (bicolor cherub or oriole angel), 231
Centropyge bispinosus (coral beauty), 231
Centropyge eibli (Eibl's angelfish), 231
Centropyge flavissimus (lemonpeel angelfish), 231
Centropyge loriculus (flame angel), 234
Chaca bankanensis (frogmouthed catfish), 142
Chaetodermis pencilligerus (tassel filefish), 242
Chaetodon capistratus (four-eyed butterflyfish), 232
Chaetodon kleini (sunburst or Klein's butterflyfish), 232
Chaetodon lunula (racoon butterflyfish), 232
Chaetodon melanotus (black-banded butterflyfish), 232
Chaetodon trifascialis (chevroned butterflyfish), 232
Chalinochromis, 138
Chanda ranga (Indian glassfish), 211
Chanda wolfii, 211
Channa micropeltes (red snakehead), 215
Channa orientalis, 215

Characins, 179-189
Chelmon rostratus (copper-band butterflyfish), 232
Chilatherina bleheri (Bleher's rainbowfish), 201, 202
Chilatherina campsi (highlands rainbowfish), 200
Chilatherina sentaniensis (Lake Sentani rainbowfish), 202
Chilodonella, 115
Chilodus punctatus (spotted headstander), 187
Chilomycterus schoepfi (spiny boxfish, striped
    burrfish), 240
Chlamydogobius eremius (desert goby), 207
Chloramine, 27
Chlorine gas, 27
Chromidotilapia, 139
Chromileptes altivelis (panther or polka-dot
    grouper), 250
Chromis caerulea (green chromis), 228
Chromis xanthurus (yellow-tailed damsel), 229
Chuco, 132
Cichlasoma, 132, 133
Cichlids, 21, 52, 59, 128-140, 226-227
Cleithracara, 135
Climbing perch anabantids, 198
Cobitis, 162
Cobitis taenia (spined loach), 164
Colisa, 190, 191
Colisa fasciata (giant gourami), 191
Colisa labiosa (thick-lipped gourami), 191
Colisa lalia (dwarf gourami), 191-193
Colisa sota (honey gourami), 113, 191, 192, 193
Combtails, 194
Constipation, 113
Copadichromis, 137
Copella arnoldi (splash tetra, jumping characin), 185
Copella guttata (red-spotted characin), 185
Corals, 58, 100, 101
Coral sand, 28, 54, 56, 99, 101
Coris gaimardi (clown wrasse or red labrid), 235
Coris julis (rainbow wrasse), 235
Cork bark, 62, 63
Copora nicaraguensis, 132
Corydoras, 8, 10, 108, 143, 144, 145, 185
Corydoras adolphoi, 38
Corydoras baderi, 144
Corydoras barbatus, 143
Corydoras loxozonus, 143
Corydoras paleatus (peppered catfish), 144
Corydoras panda, 144
Corydoras sterbai (Sterba's Corydoras), 143
Costia, 115
Crenicara, 135
Crenicichla (pike cichlids), 134
Ctenops, 190
Ctenopoma (bush fish), 190, 199
Ctenopoma acutirostre, 199
Ctenopoma ansorgii (ornate Ctenopoma), 199
Ctenopoma fasciolatum (banded Ctenopoma), 199
Ctenopoma kingsleyae (Kingsley's Ctenopoma), 191, 199
Ctenopoma oxyrhynchus (mottled Ctenopoma), 199
Ctenopoma petherici, 199
Cubanichthys pengellei, 176
Cunningtonia, 138
Cyathopharynx, 138
Cyclochaeta, 115
Cyclops, 42
Cynolebias bellotti, 175
Cynolebias nigripinnis (Argentine pearl fish), 174, 175
Cynolebias whitei, 175
Cynotilapia, 136
Cyphotilapia frontosa, 138
Cypriniformes, 155-166
Cyprinodon macularius, 176
Cyprinodon variegatus (sheepshead minnow), 177
Cyprinodonts, 167-178
Cyrtocara moorii (blue dolphin), 137
Dactylogyrus, 113
Danio aequipinnatus (giant danio), 158
Daphnia, 42
Dascyllus aruanus (humbug or white-tailed damsel), 228-229
Dascyllus melanurus (black-tailedhumbug), 228
Dascyllus trimaculatus (domino or three-spot damsel), 229
Decor, 50-75, 79, 81, 85-86, 99-101
Dendrochirus brachypterus (turkeyfish, short-fin lionfish), 238
Dermogenys pusillus, 214
Dermogenys pusillus sumatranus (wrestling half beak), 213
Dianema longibarbis (porthole catfish), 143
Dianema urostriata (flagtailed catfish), 143
Dicrossus, 135
Dimidiochromis compressiceps (Malawian eyebiter), 19, 137
Diodon holacanthus (longspined porcupine, balloonfish), 240
Diodon hystrix (porcupine puffer), 240

Discus – see *Symphysodon*
Distichodus, 179, 181
Distichodus affinis, 181
Distichodus decemmaculatus (dwarf *Distichodus*), 181
Distichodus lusosso, 181
Distichodus noboli, 181
Distichodus notospilus, 181
Distichodus sexfasciatus, 181
Doradids, 151, 152
Doryhamphus excisus (bluestripe pipefish), 239
Dottybacks, 237
Dropsy, 113
Dysichthys, 150
Dysichthys marginalis, 42

Ecsenius bicolor (bicolour blenny), 243
Ecsenius midas (Midas blenny), 243
Elassoma everglladei (pygmy sunfish), 204
Elecatinus oceanops (neon goby), 245
Electric fishes, 203
Electrics, 87-93
Electrophorus electricus (electric eel), 203
Enneacanthus chaetodon (black-banded sunfish), 204
Enneacanthus gloriosus (blue-spotted sunfish), 204
Enneacanthus obesus (diamond or little sunfish), 205
Epalzeorhynchus kallopterus (flying fox), 161
Epalzeorhynchus bicolor (red-tailed black shark), 160
Epalzeorhynchus frenatus (red-finnedshark), 160
Epiplatys annulatus, 176
Epiplatys dageti, 176
Epiplatys sexfasciatus, 176
Epiplatys singa (spotted *Epiplatys*), 176
Equipment, 44-49
Equipment failure, 117
Eretmodus, 138
Erpetoichthys (reedfishes or snakefishes), 208, 209
Erpetoichthys calabaricus (reedfish), 209
Etheostoma caeruleum (rainbow darter), 205
Etroplus maculatus (orange chromide), 226, 227
Etroplus suratensis (green chromide), 226, 227
Euthanasia, 117
Eutropiellus buffei (African debauwi cat), 154

Farlowella (twig catfishes), 141, 146, 147, 148
Feeding, 36-43, 124-125
Fighting fishes, 196
Filefishes, 242
Filters, 28-32, 47-48, 90-93, 111
Filtration, 28-30
Fin-rot, 113
Fish leech, 115
Fish louse, 114
Flukes, 113
Flying foxes, 161
Foods, 36-43
Forcipiger flavissimus (long-nosed butterflyfish), 232
Four-eyed fishes, 218, 219
Fundulus chrysotus, 176
Fungus, 113

Gambusia holbrooki (mosquito fish), 167, 168
Gasteropelecus maculatus (spotted hatchetfish), 186
Gasteropelecus sternicla (common hatchetfish), 186
Gasterosteus aculeatus (three-spined stickleback),
    114, 122, 216
Gastomyzon punctulatus, 217
Geophagus, 133
Geophagus surinamensis complex, 133
Gill parasites, 113
Glossolepis incisus (red rainbowfish), 202
Glossolepis wanamensis (Lake Wanam rainbowfish), 200
Gnathonemus petersi (Peter's elephant nose), 203
Gobies: freshwater, 206-7, marine, 245
Gobiodes broussonnetii (dragon or eel goby), 207
Gobiodon citrinus (lemon goby), 245
Gobiodon okinawae (yellow goby), 245
Gramma, 236
Gouramis, 191-193
Gramma loreto (royal gramma), 236,
Gramma melacara (black-cap gramma), 236
Gravel, 28, 56, 57, 80, 81
Guinacara, 133
Guppy see *Poecilia reticulata*
Gymnocorymbus ternetzi (black widow), 8, 183
Gymnogeophagus, 133
Gyrinocheilus aymonieri (sucking loach or Chinese
    algae eater), 36, 146, 161
Halfbeaks, 213, 214
Halichoeres chrysus (banana wrasse), 235
Haplochromis, 138
Haplochromis sauvagei, 126

Hardness - see Water
Hasemania nana (silver-tip tetra), 182
Hatchetfishes, 186
Hawkfishes, 244
Heating, 47, 89
Helostoma temminckii (kissing gourami), 85, 197
Hemichromis guttatus (jewel cichlid), 118, 140
Hemigrammus bleheri (rummy- or red-nose tetra), 182
Hemigrammus erythrozonus (glow-light tetra), 182
Hemigrammus rhodostomus (red-nose tetra), 182
Hemigrammus ulreyi (Ulrey's tetra), 179
Hemirhamphodon, 213, 214
Hemirhamphodon pogonognathus (thread-jawed or
    long-snout halfbeak), 214
Hemisynodontis membranaceous (moustache cat), 153
Heniochus acuminatus (wimplefish, pennant fish), 232
Herichthys, 132
Heros, 133, 134
Herotilapia, 132
Heterandria formosa (mosquito fish), 168, 173
Hexamita, 113
Hippocampus erectus (Florida or northern seahorse), 239
Hippocampus kuda (yellow or Pacific seahorse), 239
Hole-in-head, 112, 113
Holiday, going on, 117
Holocanthus tricolor (rock beauty), 231
Holocentrus diadema (common squirrelfish), 246
Hoplarchus, 133
Hydrocynus goliath (African tigerfish, wolf tetra), 179
Hydrometer, 21, 46, 49, 98
Hypancistrus zebra, 149
Hyphessobrycon erythrostigma (bleeding heart tetra), 182
Hyphessobrycon pulchripinnis (lemon tetra), 8
Hypostomus (plecs), 146
Hypselecara, 133
Hypseleotris cyprinoides, 206

Ichthyophthirius multifiliis, 116
Illness, diagnosis and treatment of, 110-112
Intestinal parasites, 114
Iodotropheus, 136
Iriatherina werneri (filament or threadfin rainbow), 200, 201

Jawfishes, 247
Jordanella floridae (American flagfish), 176
Julidochromis regani "kipili", 63
Julidochromis transcriptus, 137

Killifishes, 13, 21, 123, 174-178
Koi carp, 165
Krobia, 133
Kryptopterus bicirrhus (Asian glass catfish), 153, 211

Labeo chrysophekadeon (black shark), 160, 161
Labeo variegatus (harlequin variegated shark), 161
Labeobarbus festivus (diamond or festive Apollo shark), 160
Labeotropheus, 136
Labeotropheus fuelleborni, 34, 129
Labidochromis caeruleus, 136
Labroides dimidiatus (cleaner wrasse), 100, 234, 235
Labyrinths, 190
Lactoria cornuta (long-horned cowfish), 248
Ladigesia roloffi (jelly bean or Sierra Leone characin), 180
Laetacara, 135
Lamprichthys tanganicanus, 174
Lamprologus, 137, 138, 139
Lamprologus ocellatus, 128
Lamprologus signatus, 138
Lepidarchus adonis (Adonis characin or jelly bean tetra), 180
Lepidiolamprologus, 137
Lepidocephalus, 162
Leporinus fasciatus (black-banded *Leporinus*), 187
Lernaea, 114
Lienardella fasciata (harlequin tuskfish), 236
Lighting, 48, 49, 73, 89, 99
Limbochromis, 139
Limia melanogaster (black-bellied or blue limia) 173
Livebearers, 123-4, 167-73, 213-4, 218-9
Living rock, 97, 99
Lo vulpinus (fox-face, badgerfish, fox-fish), 249
Loaches, 162, 163
Loricaria (whiptail catfish), 124
Loricariichthys, 148
Loricariids, (suckermouth catfishes), 146-149
Lythrypnus dalli (blue-banded or Catalina goby), 245

Macropodus opercularis (paradise fish), 190, 194
Malapterurus electricus (electric catfish), 61, 154, 203
Malawi bloat, 113, 136
Malpulluta, 190
Mandarins, 242

Marine and brackish water set-up, 97-101
Mastacembelus armatus (spiny eel), 208
Mastacembelus circumcinctus, 208
Mastacembelus erythrotaenia (fire eel), 208
Mbuna 136
Megalodoras irwini, 151, 152
Melanochromis, 136
Melanochromis chipokae, 12
Melanotaenia (rainbowfishes), 117, 123, 200-202
Melanotaenia boesemani (Boeseman's rainbowfish), 200, 201
Melanotaenia herbertaxelrodi (Lake Tebera rainbowfish), 200
Melanotaenia lacustris (Lake Kutubu rainbowfish), 202
Melanotaenia nigrans, 200
Melanotaenia splendida (Australian rainbowfish), 200, 201
Melanotaenia trifasciata (banded rainbowfish), 200, 201, 202
Mesonauta (festive cichlids), 133-4
Metynnis argenteus (silver dollar), 189
Metynnis hypsauchen, 189
Micralestes acutidens, 180
Microgeophagus, 135
Microgeophagus altispinosa, 113
Microgeophagus ramirezi (ram/butterfly), 5, 8, 19, 73
Microworm, 125
Misgurnus, 162
Misgurnus anguillicaudatus (Chinese weatherloach), 162, 163
Misgurnus fossilis (European weatherloach), 162, 164
Moenkhausia pittieri (diamond tetra, Pittier's tetra), 182, 183
Mollies, 102, 172, 218, 226
Monocirrhus polyacanthus (South American leaf fish) 212
Monodactylus argenteus (mono), 10, 221, 224
Mormyrids (elephant noses), 203
Mosquito larvae, 42
Mudskippers, 76, 219-20
Myleus rubripinnis, 189
Myriypristis murdjan (big-eye squirrelfish, blotch eye), 246
Myxobolus, 117
Myxocyprinus asiaticus (Chinese sailfin), 166, 256

Nandids (leaffishes), 212
Nandopsis, 132
Nandopsis octofasciatus (Jack Dempsey), 130
Nandopsis dovii, 128
Nandus nandus (nandus), 212
Nannacara anomala, 135
Nannobrycon eques (hockey-stick or 3-striped pencilfish), 184
Nannobrycon unifasciatus (one-striped pencilfish), 184
Nannostomus, 184
Nannostomus beckfordi (golden pencilfish), 184
Nannostomus harrisoni (Harrison's pencilfish), 184
Nannostomus marginatus (dwarf pencilfish), 184
Nannostomus trifasciatus (three-striped pencilfish), 184
Nanochromis nudiceps, 139
Nanochromis parilus, 139
Neetroplus, 132, 139
Nemacheilus, 162
Nemacheilus barbatulus (stone loach), 164
Nemateleotris decora (purple firefish), 246
Nemateleotris helfrichi, 246
Nemateleotris magnifica (firefish), 246, 247
Nematobrycon palmeri (emperor tetra), 179, 182
Neocirrhites armatus (scarlet hawkfish), 244
Neolamprologus, 137-8
Neolamprologus buescheri, 137
Nimbochromis livingstonii, 137
Nitrate 27, 28
Nitrite, 27, 28
Nitrogen cycle, 27-28, 122
Nomorhamphus, 213
Notestes robustus, 40
Nothobranchius, 175
Nothobranchius guentheri, 175
Nothobranchius rachovi (Rachow's *Nothobranchius*), 175
Nothobranchius furzeri, 21
Notropis lutrensis (shiner), 166

Odonus niger (black triggerfish), 241
Oodinium, 116
Opistognathus aurifrons (yellow-headed jawfish), 247
Ophthalmotilapia ventralis, 138
Opsodoras stubeli, 152
Oreochromis, 140
Oreochromis mossambicus (Mozambique mouthbrooder), 120
Oryzias celebensis, 178
Oryzias latipes (rice fish or medaka), 177, 178
Oryzias melanostigma, 178
Osphronemus goramy (giant gourami), 190, 198
Osteochilus hasselti, 160
Ostracion lentiginosus (blue-spotted boxfish), 248
Ostracion meleagris (spotted or Pacific boxfish), 248
Otocinclus, 146, 149
Otocinclus paulinus, 146

Index

255

Oxycirrhites typus (longnosed hawkfish), 244
Oxyeleotris marmoratus, 206
Oxygen, 10, 32, 34
Oxymonacanthus longirostris (long-nosed filefish), 242

pH – see Water
Pachypanchax playfairi (Playfair's panchax), 177, 178
Palludarium, 64, 218, 219-220, 222-223
Panaque, 146
Panaque maccus (clown plec), 149
Panaque nigrolineatus (royal plec), 58, 141
Pantodon buchholzi (butterfly fish), 210
Papiliochromis, 135
Paracanthurus hepatus (regal tang), 233
Paracheirodon axelrodi (cardinal tetra), 182, 183
Paracheirodon innesi (neon tetra), 105, 182
Paradise fishes, 194
Parananochromis, 139
Paraneetroplus, 132
Paratheraps fenestratus, 132
Paratheraps synspilum, 39
Paratilapia, 140
Parorotocinclus, 146, 149
Parotocinclus maculicauda, 146
Peckoltia, 149
Pelvicachromis pulcher (krib), 128
Pelvicachromis taeniatus "Nigeria", 139
Pencilfishes, 184
Periophthalmus barbarus, 219
Periophthalmus catonensis, 219
Periophthalmus kaelreukeri, 219
Periophthalmus papilio (mudskipper), 76, 219, 220
Petrotilapia, 136
Petrochromis, 138
Phago (fin or tailfishes), 179
Phenacogrammus interruptus (Congo tetra), 11, 180,
Phoxinus erythrogaster (southern red-bellied dace), 12, 166
Phoxinus phoxinus (minnow), 166
Phractocephalus hemioliopterus (red-tailed catfish), 4, 15
Piaractus brachypomus (pacu), 189
Pimelodus pictus (angelic pim), 154
Piranhas, 188
Plagioremus rhinorhynchus (blue striped blenny), 50
Plants, 64-76
  Amazon swordplant, 64, 69, 95
  Anubias, 71
  Aponogeton, 71, 72
  Bacopa, 74
  Cabomba, 64, 68
  Caulerpa, 66, 75, 97
  Ceratopteris thalictroides, 72, 74
  Cryptocoryne, 64, 69, 70, 73
  Duckweed, 72
  Echinodorus, 64, 69, 95
  Echinodorus paniculatus, 69
  Echinodorus tenellus, 95
  Elodea, 68
  Hygrophila, 64, 68
  Indian fern, 72, 74
  Java fern, 67, 68, 74
  Java moss, 67, 72
  Microsorium pteropus, 67, 68, 74
  Myriophyllum, 68
  Nymphaea (lilies), 71
  Pistia stratiotes, 72, 75
  plastic, 62, 63
  Riccia, 72
  Rotala, 68, 74
  Synnema, 68
  Vallisneria, 66, 74, 75
  Vesicularia dubayana, 67, 72
  Water lettuce, 72, 75
Platydoras costatus (humbug catfish), 151, 152
Platies, 113, 168, 171
Plotosus lineatus (marine or saltwater catfish), 223, 237
Poecilia, 102, 167, 168, 218, 226
Poecilia latipinna (sailfin molly), 102, 167, 172, 226
Poecilia reticulata (guppy), 2, 14, 120, 124, 167, 169
Poecilia salvatoris (liberty molly), 172
Poecilia sphenops, 172
Poecilia velifera (sailfin molly), 172, 226
Polycentropsis abbreviata (African leaf fish), 212
Polycentrus schomburgki (South American leaf fish), 212
Polypterus (bichirs), 208
Polypterus delhezi (armoured bichir), 209
Polypterus ornatipinnis (ornate bichir), 209
Polypterus palmas (marbled bichir), 209
Polypterus senegalensis (Senegal or Cuvier's bichir), 209
Pomacanthus imperator (emperor angelfish), 231
Pomacanthus semicirculatus (Koran angelfish), 231
Pomacentrus coeruleus (electric blue damsel), 54

Pomacentrus melanochir (blue-finned damsel), 228
Pop-eye (exophthalmus), 114, 115
Power cuts, 117
Premnas biaculeatus (maroon clown), 230
Procatopus similis (Nigerian lampeye), 176
Prochilodus, 179
Profundulus labialis, 176
Profundulus similis, 176
Protein skimmer, 31, 47, 98
Pseudochromis diadema (flash-back gramma), 237
Pseudochromis paccagnellae (false gramma), 237
Pseudochromis porphyreus (strawberry gramma), 237
Pseudodoras niger, 152, 189
Pseudohemiodon laticeps, 148
Pseudomugil furcatus, 201
Pseudomugil signifer (Pacific blue-eye), 201
Pseudosphronemus cupanus (spike-tailed paradise fish), 190
Pseudotropheus, 136
Pseudotropheus zebra, 136
Ptereleotris evides (spot-tailed gudgeon), 246, 247
Ptereleotris tricolor, 247
Pterois antennata (scorpionfish, spot-fin lionfish), 238
Pterois lunulata, 238
Pterois radiata (white-fin or tail-bar lionfish), 238
Pterois volitans (lion or dragon fish), 12, 238
Pterolebias, 174, 175
Pterophyllum scalare (angelfish), 122
Pungitius pungitius (ten-spined stickleback), 216
Pyrrhulina brevis (short-lined *Pyrrhulina*), 185

Quarantine 106-107, 112

Rabbitfishes, 249
Rainbowfishes, 117, 123, 200-202
Rasbora borapetensis (red-tailed rasbora), 159
Rasbora hengeli, 159
Rasbora heteromorpha (harlequin), 159
Rasbora maculata (pygmy or spotted rasbora), 159
Rasbora trilineata (scissortail), 159
Rasbora pauciperforata, 159
Rasbora reticulata (reticulated rasbora), 127
Rasbora vaterifloris (pearly rasbora), 159
Rhinecanthus aculeatus (Picasso trigger), 241
Rhodeus ocellatus (Hong Kong bitterling), 166
Rhodeus sericeus (bitterling), 166
Rineloricaria (whiptails), 146, 147, 148, 149
Rivulus cylindraceus, 176
Rivulus milesi (yellowtail panchax), 177
Rocks, 58, 59, 61, 81, 84,-86, 99-100
Rocky shoreline, 34, 50, 60, 126, 136-138

Salinity, 21, 98
Sandelia, 190
Sarotherodon melanotheron, 140
Scatophagus argus (scat), 221, 224
Scleropages formosus (Asian arawana, dragonfish), 217
Seahorses, 239
Serrasalmus nattereri (red piranha) 188
Sharks, 160, 161
Shock, 19, see also Stress
Siganus virgatus (silver badgerfish), 249
Skin slime disease, 115
Snakeheads, 215
Sorubim lima (shovel-nose catfish), 142, 154
Spathodus, 138
Spawning mops, 123, 138, 176
Specific gravity, 98
Sphaeramia nematopterus (spotted or pyjama cardinal), 243
Sphaerichthys, 190
Sphaerichthys osphronemoides (chocolate gourami), 23, 195
Spiny eels, 208
Splash tetras, 185
Squirrelfishes, 246
Sticklebacks, 216
Stigmatogobius sadanundio, 207
Stress, 102, 104
Sturisoma, 146, 147, 148, 149
Sturisoma panamense (regal whiptail), 147
Substrate, 54, 56, 57
Sun bass (sunfishes), 204, 205
Surgeons, 233
Swim bladder disease, 115
Swordtails, 6, 88, 124, 168, 170, 171
Symphysodon 134
Symphysodon aequifasciata (discus), 34, 112
Synchiropus, 239, 242
Synchiropus picturatus (psychedelic fish), 242
Synchiropus splendidus (mandarin fish), 242
Synodontis angelicus (angelic catfish), 153
Synodontis multipunctatus (cuckoo catfish), 153

Synodontis nigriventris (upside-down catfish), 142, 153

Taeniacara, 135
Tandanus tandanus (catfish or dewfish), 237
Tanganicodus irsacae, 138
Tangs, 233
Tanichthys albonubes (white cloud mountain minnow), 158
Tanks
  breeding, 121, 123
  hospital, 112
  quarantine, 106-7
Tateurndina ocellicauda (peacock or eye-spot goby), 206
Teleogramma, 139
Teleogramma brichardi, 128, 139
Telmatherina ladigesi (Celebes rainbowfish), 200, 201
Temperature, 32
Tetraodon (puffers), 16, 240 ·
Tetraodon palembangensis, 102
Tetras, 15, 179-180, 182-183, 185
Thalassoma lutescens, 236
Thayeria boehlkei (penguin), 183
Theraps, 132
Thermometers, 49, 94
Thermostats, 47, 48
Thorichthys, 132
Thorichthys meeki (firemouth), 12
Thorichthys pasionis, 132
Tilapia, 140
Tomocichla, 132
Toxotes chatareus, 223
Toxotes jaculator (archer fish), 38, 222, 223
Trichogaster, 190, 191
Trichogaster leeri (pearl gourami), 191
Trichogaster microlepis (moonlight gourami), 191
Trichogaster pectoralis (snakeskin gourami), 191, 192
Trichogaster trichopterus, 18, 64, 191, 193
Trichopsis pumilus (dwarf croaking gourami), 190
Trichopsis vittatus (croaking gourami), 195
Trichopterus, 190
Triggerfishes, 241
Tropheus, 138
Tropheus duboisi, 129, 153
Tubifex worms, 39, 42
Tufa rock, 99, 137

Uaru amphiacanthoides, 63, 134

Vieja, 132
Velvet, 116

Water
  chemistry, 19-25
  conditioners, 27
  effects of, (sudden) changes in, 18
  hardness, 19, 34, 22-24, 127
  management, 16-34
  marine and brackish water set-up, for, 21, 97, 98
  monitoring, 18, 31, 34
  movement, 10, 32, 33
  oxygen content, 10, 32, 34
  pH (acidity/alkalinity), 24, 25
  quality, 16, 18, 26-32, 122
  temperature, 32
  testing kits, 18, 34, 49
Water boatmen, 42
White clouds, 158
White spot, 116
Whiteworms, 42
Wormfishes, 246
Wrasses, 234, 235

Xenomystus nigri (African knifefish), 217
Xenopoecilus, 176
Xiphophorus (platy), 113, 168
Xiphophorus (swordtail), 6, 88, 124, 168
Xiphophorus helleri (swordtail), 168, 170, 171
Xiphophorus maculatus (platy), 168, 170
Xiphophorus variatus (platy), 168, 171

Zebrasoma flavescens (yellow tang), 233
Zebrasoma veliferum (striped sailfin tang), 233
Zeolite, 28, 122